ADVERTISING AND MARKETING LAW IN CANADA

Second Edition

Brenda Pritchard
Susan Vogt

LexisNexis™
Butterworths

ASSOCIATION OF CANADIAN ADVERTISERS
ASSOCIATION CANADIENNE DES ANNONCEURS

Advertising and Marketing Law in Canada, Second Edition
© LexisNexis Canada Inc. 2006
August 2006

Members of the LexisNexis Group worldwide

Canada	LexisNexis Canada Inc, 75 Clegg Road, MARKHAM, Ontario
Argentina	Abeledo Perrot, Jurisprudencia Argentina and Depalma, BUENOS AIRES
Australia	Butterworths, a Division of Reed International Books Australia Pty Ltd, CHATSWOOD, New South Wales
Austria	ARD Betriebsdienst and Verlag Orac, VIENNA
Chile	Publitecsa and Conosur Ltda, SANTIAGO DE CHILE
Czech Republic	Orac sro, PRAGUE
France	Éditions du Juris-Classeur SA, PARIS
Hong Kong	Butterworths Asia (Hong Kong), HONG KONG
Hungary	Hvg Orac, BUDAPEST
India	Butterworths India, NEW DELHI
Ireland	Butterworths (Ireland) Ltd, DUBLIN
Italy	Giuffré, MILAN
Malaysia	Malayan Law Journal Sdn Bhd, KUALA LUMPUR
New Zealand	Butterworths of New Zealand, WELLINGTON
Poland	Wydawnictwa Prawnicze PWN, WARSAW
Singapore	Butterworths Asia, SINGAPORE
South Africa	Butterworth Publishers (Pty) Ltd, DURBAN
Switzerland	Stämpfli Verlag AG, BERNE
United Kingdom	Butterworths Tolley, a Division of Reed Elsevier (UK), LONDON, WC2A
USA	LexisNexis, DAYTON, Ohio

National Library of Canada Cataloguing in Publication

Pritchard, Brenda L.
   Advertising and marketing law in Canada / Brenda Pritchard, Susan Vogt. — 2nd ed.

Includes index.
ISBN 0-433-45036-3

   1. Advertising laws—Canada. 2. Marketing—Law and legislation—Canada. I. Vogt, Susan, 1953- II. Title.

KE1610.P75 2006	343.71'082	C2006-903453-2
KF1614.P75 2006		

Printed and bound in Canada.

For my mother.

Susan

For my sons Jesse and Taylor — truly the "wind beneath my wings" and for my Mom and Dad who showed me that there is always room at the top. And for the newly revised chapters in this book, I would like to acknowledge Bob, the new chapter in my life.

Brenda

FOREWORD

Advertising and Marketing Law in Canada provides a valuable framework for marketers navigating the regulatory environment in Canada.

Since it was first published in 2004, the publication has gained growing recognition as required reading for any marketer doing business in Canada, offering a comprehensive overview of relevant federal and provincial laws, marketing best practices and self-governing codes of conduct which have been developed by leading organizations such as the Canadian Marketing Association.

We continue to recommend it to our members as an excellent guide to understanding the basics of marketing and advertising law and best self-regulatory practices. As with any legal issue, however, care must be taken to determine when you should consult with your own legal counsel.

In today's business environment, the adherence to laws governing marketing and advertising, together with the introduction of self-regulatory initiatives, are of paramount importance as consumers, government, special interest groups and the media are demanding of more ethical business practices. Moreover, consumer trust in an organization, its products and services is directly impacted by the ways in which an organization interacts with the marketplace and the observance of laws and best practices which oversee marketing conduct.

This second edition of *Advertising and Marketing Law in Canada* includes new, updated information on several marketing-related legal issues. These include privacy law, false and misleading claims, procedures for resolving competitors' disputes, guidelines for the use of comparative advertising, trademarks and amendments to food and drug regulations related to labelling requirements. Moreover, the publication features helpful instructions on uniquely Canadian issues, such as special rules for marketing in Quebec, dealing with talent, unauthorized use of celebrities, Internet and Web advertising and guidelines for marketing to children and teenagers.

My sincere congratulations to Brenda Pritchard and Susan Vogt — two of Canada's leading advertising and marketing lawyers — who co-authored the second edition of Advertising and Marketing Law in Canada, a comprehensive, no-nonsense legal guide which every advertising and marketing professional should have in their office.

John Gustavson
President and Chief Executive Officer
Canadian Marketing Association

ABOUT THE AUTHORS

Brenda Pritchard is the National Group Leader, Advertising Law, with the national law firm of Gowlings, with more than 22 years experience practising exclusively in advertising and marketing law. Brenda's practice includes: advertising copy review; coupon, premium and contest promotions; negotiation of music, talent and artistic rights for use in production; merchandising and publishing contracts and negotiation; performers' union arbitrations, Advertising Standards Canada hearings and defending against misleading advertising charges. Brenda is a frequent writer and speaker on Canadian advertising law in Canada and internationally, and is Past-Chair of the Media and Communications Law Section of the Canadian Bar Association and member of the IBA, ABA, CCTFA and AdLaw International. Consistently named one of Canada's 500 leading lawyers by L'expert, recognized by Martindale Hubbell, and listed in Chambers Global's "The World's Leading Lawyers for Business", she is the most frequently recommended advertising and marketing lawyer in Canada.

Susan Vogt is a Partner with Gowlings and has 18 years of experience in advertising and marketing law. She is listed in the Lexpert and Martindale-Hubbell directories as a leading lawyer in this field. Susan practises exclusively in the areas of advertising and marketing law and trademark prosecution with an emphasis on the automotive, packaged goods and pharmaceutical sectors. Fluently bilingual, she specializes in packaging, print and broadcast ads (in English and French), contests and promotions, food and drug regulatory issues, comparative advertising disputes, celebrity endorsement contracts, sponsorship agreements, trademark and copyright licences, adaptation of foreign-sourced advertising to Canadian requirements and trade disputes before Advertising Standards Canada. A frequent speaker at advertising industry conferences, Susan has written dozens of columns on marketing law as a regular contributor to *Strategy* magazine.

CONTRIBUTORS LIST

SARAH CHENOWETH

Sarah Chenoweth is an associate in the advertising and marketing law group at Gowlings in Toronto. Her practice includes advertising and packaging review in the food, cosmetics and automotive sectors. She also focuses on contests, privacy law, consumer protection and cost of credit disclosure issues, as well as promotional contracts and licence drafting. Sarah is the editor of Gowlings' advertising publication *Adbytes*. Sarah can be reached at sarah.chenoweth @gowlings.com.

ERIC GROSS

Eric is a senior corporate/IP law partner at Gowlings' Toronto office and has been working with advertising agencies and their clients for over 25 years. He has particular expertise in the business issues that affect advertisers and agencies. Eric's practice includes many aspects of advertising and intellectual property law. Eric has been peer-reviewed and named in the field of advertising in the inaugural edition of *The Best Lawyers in Canada* 2006 directory. Eric can be reached at eric.gross@gowlings.com.

JOHN LECKIE

John Leckie is a partner at the Vancouver office of Gowlings and practises exclusively in the areas of advertising law and trademarks. John's clients include major advertisers and Vancouver advertising agencies as well as several crown corporations. Prior to entering the legal profession, John spent several years in the advertising industry. He can be reached at john.leckie@gowlings.com.

STEPHEN PIKE

Stephen Pike is a partner and the head of Gowlings Business Law Group in Toronto. His practice is concentrated in the corporate and commercial area, providing business law advice and negotiating contracts on a wide range of matters involving Canadian and foreign corporations participating in all the facets of the consumer and commercial products and consumer and commercial services sectors, both on an ongoing basis and for specific transactions and initiatives, including marketing, advertising, licensing, manufacturing, product distribution, product liability, credit, regulatory and corporate law compliance matters. He advises American and international businesses establishing new operations in Canada and in respect of their ongoing Canadian operations. Stephen can be reached at stephen.pike@gowlings.com.

LEWIS RETIK

Lewis Retik is an associate at Gowlings who focuses much of his practice on advertising and packaging issues. He works with companies in the NHP, food, pharmaceutical and cosmetic industries to ensure products comply with regulatory requirements. Lewis received his law degree from the University of New Brunswick and was called to the Ontario bar in 2002. He can be reached at lewis.retik@gowlings.com.

ANDRÉ RIVEST

André is a litigation partner at Gowlings' Montreal office whose practice includes commercial law and advertising. Andre is fluently bilingual and deals with Quebec-specific advertising issues raised by the *Charter of the French Language*, the Quebec *Consumer Protection Act*, the Quebec *Lotteries Act* and other legislation. André has regular contact with the relevant Quebec regulators at the Office de la langue francaise, the Consumer Protection Office and the Regie des alcools, des courses et des jeux. He can be reached at andre.rivest@gowlings.com.

SHELLEY SAMEL

Shelley Samel is a senior associate at Gowlings' Toronto office. She practises exclusively in the area of advertising and marketing law and has particular expertise in cosmetics, food and drug advertising and packaging, as well as promotion and privacy law. Shelley is a frequent speaker on advertising law issues at conferences and is a member of the Promotion Law Association. She can be reached at shelley.samel@gowlings.com.

ARIANE SIEGEL

Ariane Siegel practises communications and technology law with Gowlings Toronto. A member of the firm's Technology Practice Group, she has a specialized background in commercial law, regulatory and policy matters pertaining to the communications industry, including issues relevant to broadcasters and telecommunication service providers. Ariane's legal practice is focused on advising Canadian and international clients on Canadian communications regulation and information technology law matters. She has a strong interest in the protection of personal information and regularly advises private sector organizations, including financial institutions, marketing agencies, retailers and the entertainment industry on compliance with Canada's new privacy legislation. Ariane can be reached at ariane.siegel@gowlings.com.

JOEL B. TALLER

Joel is a senior partner at Gowlings' Ottawa office and one of the few lawyers in Canada who also has a BSc in physiology and pharmacology. Joel advises a variety of national and international clients on regulatory matters involving foods, natural health products (*i.e.*, herbals, homeopathics, vitamins, minerals, amino acids, probiotics), nutritional health supplements, drugs, traditional herbal medicines, cosmetics and medical devices. Joel is a member of the Pharmaceutical Association of Canada, CCTFA, NDMAC, the Canadian Health Food Association and other industry associations. Joel can be reached at joel.taller@gowlings.com.

WILLIAM VANVEEN

William is a senior litigation partner at Gowlings' Ottawa office who practises principally in the areas of competition law, civil litigation and criminal law. Bill has particular expertise in dealing with federal and provincial regulatory offences. Bill is the co-author of the loose-leaf service entitled *Competiton Law Service*. Prior to joining Gowlings, he was a professor at the University of Windsor Law School. Bill can be reached at william.vanveen@gowlings.com.

About the Association of Canadian Advertisers

The Association of Canadian Advertisers (ACA) is the first call for marketers seeking authoritative and dependable leadership, guidance and support in all matters related to marketing communications. Founded in 1914 and incorporated in 1917, the ACA is Canada's only association exclusively representing client marketers. The association speaks on behalf of over 200 companies and divisions across all product and service sectors, which collectively account for estimated annual sales of $350 billion.

The ACA helps members maximize the value of their investments in marketing communications by:

- Leading initiatives that enhance knowledge and understanding of practices that build brands, business and shareholder equity
- Safeguarding the right of marketers to commercial free speech, while informing them of their attendant responsibilities
- Providing forums for learning, networking and professional development that enrich expertise and capabilities in the management of marketing communications
- Being a resource that members depend on for proprietary services and customized solutions

For further information about the ACA, please visit www.ACAweb.ca.

The publisher acknowledges the valuable input of the Association of Canadian Advertisers to the preparation of the first edition of this work and its continued support to the development of this subsequent edition.

ABOUT THE CANADIAN MARKETING ASSOCIATION

With more than 800 corporate members, the Canadian Marketing Association (CMA) is the largest marketing association embracing Canada's major business sectors and all marketing disciplines, channels and technologies. CMA is the marketing community's leading advocate on the key public policy issues affecting both consumer and business-to-business marketers. As well, the Association is the principal provider of knowledge, marketing intelligence and professional development opportunities for marketers; and a catalyst for networking and business opportunities within the marketing community.

www.the-cma.org

PREFACE

We are very pleased to present the second edition of our book. Two years have passed. Many things have changed in Canadian advertising law. However, the following preface from our first edition holds true.

It is said that "familiarity breeds contempt". What then, can we be thinking in writing a book to familiarize our clients, their competitors and their lawyers with the intricacies of advertising and marketing law?

There is nothing so frustrating as creating a brilliant advertising campaign only to discover that it was flattened by "Dr. No", your advertising lawyer — except maybe to receive your lawyer's rejection of the campaign without any plausible explanation of why it doesn't work, or more importantly, how you could change it to make it work.

Thus, our theory, developed over the 20 years we have been practising advertising law, is that enlightened clients make much better partners in the quest for creative legal solutions.

We have tried, therefore, wherever possible, to keep the legalese to a minimum and to pepper our book with lots of examples (and even "horror stories") to make Canadian advertising law both easier to understand and easier to explain to your clients and marketing partners.

ACKNOWLEDGEMENTS

The Authors would like to thank the following individuals in our Advertising National Practice Group for their research and creative input:

Evelyn Ackah
Shelagh Carnegie
Thierry Carrière

TABLE OF CONTENTS

Chapter 1

PRINCIPLES OF ADVERTISING AND MARKETING LAW

A.   INTRODUCTION

"So what exactly does an advertising lawyer do?", asked the cab driver, eager to take advantage of his ten minutes of free legal advice.

"We help people make their commercials".

"Oh, so you make sure they're not false and don't use other people's patents and stuff". His was a better explanation than many lawyers could give.

Advertising permeates contemporary society and can take many shapes and forms. Advertising can be defined as anything that directs public attention to the desirable qualities of a product or service.

Not surprisingly, advertising law is difficult to encapsulate, because it deals with the multitude of legal issues that confront an advertising agency or marketer. Canadian advertising is highly regulated, with specific federal and provincial legislation as well as scores of self-regulatory codes, policies and bodies.

Our purpose in writing this book is to provide the advertising/marketing executive with the basic tools necessary to recognize and understand the legal issues affecting your business. The book is not intended to replace advertising lawyers, but rather to enhance your working relationship with them.

B.   THE COMPETITION ACT

The most important piece of federal legislation to the advertising industry in Canada is the *Competition Act*.[1] In a nutshell, this Act prevents false or misleading advertising and sets out certain prohibitions over how

---

[1]   R.S.C. 1985, c. C-34.

competitors may deal with each other as well as how businesses treat their suppliers and customers.

The good news, for those who wish to make a living in this industry without going to jail, is that in March 1999, the vast majority of the *Competition Act* provisions relating to advertising were decriminalized. From that date, in all but the worst cases, you will stay away from jail for misleading advertising and the maximum civil penalty is $100,000 for a first offence and $200,000 for repeat offenders.

The bad news is that the standard of proof for false and misleading advertising has been lowered considerably, making it easier to commit an offence without a subjective intent to mislead.

While the *Competition Act* will be dealt with in later chapters of this book in greater detail, the following basic principles are important:

(1)   You can't make false claims in your ads.

> EXAMPLE:
>
> BUY THIS VACUUM AND GET A YEAR'S SUPPLY OF VACUUM BAGS ABSOLUTELY FREE!
>
> When there is a $12 administration fee for the vacuum bags.

(2)   Even if the claim is literally true, you can't use it if it gives a false or misleading general impression.

> EXAMPLE:
>
> DRIVE AWAY IN A CORVETTE FOR JUST $29,000!
>
> When the visual is a flashy convertible with sport package that sells for $40,000.

(3)   Double entendres should be avoided, *i.e.*, when a claim has two meanings and one of them is true and the other false.

> EXAMPLE:
>
> NUMBER ONE IN THE CATEGORY.*
>
> *Number one in sales but not number one in quality.

(4)   You must substantiate claims *before* you make them.

> EXAMPLE:
>
> WE ARE ALMOST POSITIVE THAT INDEPENDENT TESTS TO BE CONDUCTED

NEXT MONTH WILL PROVE WE LAST
LONGER!

(5) *You* have the burden to prove your claims — you can't rely on your competitors' inability to disprove them!

EXAMPLE:

WE CHALLENGE ANY OTHER LAUNDRY
DETERGENT TO PROVE THEY ARE BETTER
THAN XYZ POWDER.

(6) Miceprint disclaimers cannot be used to contradict false headlines or body copy, they can only clarify and modify.

EXAMPLE:

DON'T PAY A CENT UNTIL 2008!*

*Except for taxes and $750 freight.

(7) You can't have a continuous sale — eventually the sale price becomes the regular price of your goods.

EXAMPLE:

HELD OVER FOR THE FOURTH MONTH —
SAVE 50% ON ALL SKIS AND BOOTS!

(8) Generally, items should never be on sale more than half the time they are offered for sale *or* at least half your stock should be sold at the "regular price".

EXAMPLE:

SAVE $200*

*Compared to the price we charged two years ago.

(9) When you hold a contest, you must disclose the basic terms and conditions of the contest prior to forcing consumers to buy your goods. (*i.e.*, you can't hide them inside your cereal box).

EXAMPLE:

WIN A TRIP TO ORLANDO!

No purchase required. See details inside.

(10) As a manufacturer, you can't dictate the price at which a retailer sells your goods and in particular, you can't set a minimum price.

However, you can influence the price downwards (*e.g.*, "Dealer may sell for less.").

EXAMPLE:

ALL ABC PRINTERS ONLY $399!*

*Dealer may sell for less.

(11) If you use a testimonial in advertising, be sure:

(a)   the person actually used the product or service;
(b)   you have a signed testimonial release; and
(c)   the claim is true.

(False testimonials are not acceptable even if the person believes it!)

EXAMPLE:

THIS CONDITIONER HAS MORE VITAMINS AND MINERALS THAN ANY OTHER ON THE MARKET! I LOVE IT THE BEST!

1.   The Competition Bureau of Industry Canada

The Competition Bureau of Industry Canada, is headed by the Commissioner of Competition and is responsible for the administration and enforcement of the *Competition Act* (the "Act"). The Industry Canada website is located at http://www.strategis.gc.ca.

The Act is a federal statute which contains criminal and civil provisions. The general goal of the Competition Bureau is to maintain and encourage competition in Canada and compliance with the *Competition Act*. The "Conformity Continuum" is the Bureau's comprehensive and integrated approach to achieving its goals. The Continuum involves non-adversarial measures such as educational and compliance mechanisms, plus adversarial or enforcement measures. The Bureau takes a balanced approach and chooses which of the measures or combination of measures is most appropriate to the offending conduct.

The Act was amended in 1999 and those amendments significantly altered the way the Bureau enforces the Act in relation to advertisers and marketers. Although misleading advertising still remains a residual criminal offence, the criminal law will now deal only with the most serious cases where misrepresentations are made knowingly or recklessly and generally involve significant harm. The criminal provision is found in section 52.1(a) of the Act.

The requirement that misrepresentations be made knowingly or reck-lessly adds a higher standard of proof. This is the *mens rea* (or "guilty mind") requirement found in criminal law. However, it is not necessary to prove that anyone was actually deceived or misled.

In initiating criminal proceedings, the *Misleading Advertising and De-ceptive Marketing Practices'* Guidelines[2] state that two criteria must be satisfied:

(1)   There must be clear and compelling evidence that the accused knowingly or recklessly made a false or misleading representation to the public.
(2)   The Commissioner must also be satisfied that criminal prosecution would be in the public interest.

The Guidelines list several factors that may be regarded when consid-ering what is in the public interest and several mitigating factors as well. Factors that may be considered in deciding whether to prosecute are the nature of the false or misleading claim, the number of people affected by the claim, whether a vulnerable audience (such as children or senior citizens) was specifically targeted and the amount of money made by the advertiser. If, on balance, the Commissioner is satisfied that the circum-stances warrant criminal prosecution, a recommendation may be made to the Attorney General of Canada who will make the ultimate determina-tion of whether to proceed. Also, under section 34(1), in addition to any other penalty, an order can be made to prohibit the continuation of the offence.

More significantly, the amended *Competition Act* created a civil route for dealing with misleading advertising. Misleading advertising as a civil offence can be found in Part VII.1 of the Act, which covers deceptive marketing practices. The goal of the civil route is to promote compliance with the Act, not to punish. This route offers a wide range of enforce-ment mechanisms, including cease and desist orders, the publication of information notices directed to affected parties and/or monetary penal-ties. These remedies, require a lower standard of proof than criminal remedies, that is, the Bureau does not need to prove that the false or misleading advertising was deliberate.

Until recently, in most instances, the Bureau would pursue the civil route. This route is much faster and more effective in putting a stop to misleading advertising. Unlike other reviewable trade practices such as price fixing, which are solely within the jurisdiction of the Competition

---

2   It should be noted, that the Guidelines do not reflect legal certainty but may be relied upon as reflecting the Commissioner's interpretation of how the law is to be applied on a consistent basis by the Competition Bureau.

Tribunal, misleading advertising cases can now be heard by the Competition Tribunal, the Federal Court Trial Division or any Provincial Superior Court. These changes ensure fast access to the process and a quick halt to deceptive conduct.

Once proceedings have been commenced against a person under section 52, the criminal misleading advertising section, the Commissioner cannot apply for an order under Part VII.1 against the same person on the basis of the same or substantially the same facts. The reverse is also true.

There is one other matter of concern. The Act does not specify how much time the Commissioner has to decide which adjudication route to follow. The Guidelines offer only vague reassurance by stating that "every effort will be made to arrive at this decision as quickly as possible and to notify the parties concerned once a decision is taken".

C.   THE PROVINCIAL CONSUMER PROTECTION ACTS — THE JURISDICTIONAL TUG OF WAR

Those of you who took politics or law courses will know all about the *British North America Act* (*"BNA Act"*) and the division of powers which defines what matters fall within either federal or provincial jurisdiction. Many matters fall within both.

Under the *BNA Act*, the provincial governments, under their authority to regulate local undertakings/industries, have authority to legislate on claims that may be false or misleading to consumers. Most provinces have similar provisions dealing with consumer advertising, protection and transactions. Quebec's *Consumer Protection Act* ("CPA"), as you will see in Chapter 17, is somewhat unique and more protectionist of consumers than the laws of other provinces.

The following are the key provisions for advertisers under provincial consumer protection laws:

(1)   **Credit Disclosure**
      Credit disclosure is governed by provincial law, and all provinces require disclosure of credit terms offered. Claims such as "Don't pay' til 2008!" and "Finance this car for only $249 a month" trigger those long television and print disclaimers that cause eye strain. Currently, each province has its own spin on credit disclosure, and several different versions of ads may be required for national campaigns. See Chapter 4 for details on price and credit advertising.

(2) **Chill out Period — Cancellation of Door-to-Door/Direct Sales Contracts**

Most provinces provide that any contract signed by the buyer other than at the seller's ordinary place of business may be cancelled within ten days of the buyer's receipt of his or her copy of the contract. For example, if an Ontario consumer signs a contract for a $1,000 vacuum cleaner from a door-to-door salesperson, the consumer will have ten days to cancel the contract by notice in writing. On the other hand, if a consumer goes to a department store and buys the vacuum cleaner, pays for it and takes it home, this provision will not apply and the consumer will be left with the department store policy on returning goods. In most provinces, direct sellers, including door-to-door salespeople and people who sell at "home parties", need to be registered and have appropriate bonds posted. See Chapter 15 for further details on the rules applicable to direct sellers and direct sales contracts.

(3) **Unsolicited Goods**

Generally, a seller who sends unsolicited goods to a consumer cannot bring any action against that consumer for payment of the goods or for their loss or damage. (*i.e.*, SENDER BEWARE). Unsolicited goods are generally governed by the provincial "negative option" selling provisions. Sellers who enter into contracts with consumers for the continuous supply of goods must carefully and conspicuously disclosure the nature, amount and timing of delivery of the goods in order to avoid classification of the goods as "unsolicited". Even if the continuous supply of goods is initially agreed to, goods may become "unsolicited" partway through the term of the contract if there is a material change in the nature or quality of the goods being supplied. Consent to such "material" change must be expressly obtained from the consumer.

(4) **Referral Selling**

Referral selling is prohibited in one form or another in the provinces of B.C., Alberta, Manitoba, Quebec and Nova Scotia. It had previously been prohibited in Ontario but the *Consumer Protection Act, 2002*,[3] which came into force in July, 2005, has eliminated the prohibition, and referral selling is permitted. See Chapter 15 for more details.

---

[3] S.O. 2002, c. 30, Sched. A, as am. S.O. 2004, c. 19, s. 7.

(5) **Implied Warranties**

All goods sold to consumers under provincial Sale of Goods Acts are subject to implied warranties that the items will be "fit for the purpose intended" and "of merchantable quality". The Consumer Protection Acts in some provinces provide that any contract that purports to negate or vary these fundamental warranties is void. For example, if you sell an "industrial vacuum cleaner" that is not suitable for heavy vacuuming, the consumer would be entitled to void the sales contract if it didn't work under industrial conditions.

(6) **False Advertising**

If a seller or lender makes statements in advertising which the provincial regulators believe are false, misleading or deceptive, the province can bring an action to stop the advertising and fine the advertiser. Many provincial consumer protection agencies are understaffed and only act if a consumer or competitor complains.

Due to this overlapping jurisdiction of the federal and provincial governments, an advertiser who makes false and misleading statements may find itself faced with a challenge from one or more of the provinces and/or the Competition Bureau.

D.   THE CANADIAN CODE OF ADVERTISING STANDARDS

1.   Consumer Complaints

Those of you who take public transit or read *Marketing* or *Strategy* magazine will have seen the ads posted by Advertising Standards Canada ("ASC") urging consumers to complain about advertising that offends them. The ASC's website can be found at <http://www.adstandards.com>.

At first blush, this seems to be a bane to advertisers and their agencies. However, the industry's self-regulatory system is preferable to facing a possible prosecution every time an ad is considered false or misleading or otherwise unacceptable.

ASC's *Canadian Code of Advertising Standards* ("the Code"), which is widely endorsed by advertisers, agencies and the media, sets out the basic principles of acceptable advertising in Canada.

Currently, the Code applies to all forms of advertising except (a) election advertising; (b) foreign advertising (unless the advertiser is Canadian); and (c) packaging and labelling (which is monitored by Industry Canada under the *Consumer Packaging and Labelling Act* and set out at <http://www.strategis.gc.ca>).

If an ad appears to violate a section of the Code, other than sections 10 and 14, based on even one consumer complaint, it will be referred to the

ASC's Consumer Response Council ("CRC") for adjudication. The advertiser is shown the consumer complaint (although the identity of the consumer is kept confidential) and is invited to respond to the complaint in writing. The CRC then determines whether a violation of the Code has occurred.

On September 1, 2003, the ASC changed the procedure for handling consumer complaints made under sections 10 or 14 of the Code, the safety and unacceptable depictions or portrayal sections respectively. Today, if such a complaint is made, the advertiser is asked to respond directly to the complainant. Where consent to the disclosure of the complainant's information has not been given, the advertiser responds to the ASC, which redirects the response to the complainant. If the complainant is unsatisfied with the response, they may request a review by the CRC. If no such review is requested, the file will be closed.

In January 2006, section 14 of the Code, entitled "Unacceptable Depictions and Portrayals", was revised to add a prohibition against advertisements which condone or encourage bullying. The section now reads:

Advertisements shall not...

(b)   Appear in a realistic manner to exploit, condone or insight violence, *nor appear to condone or directly encourage, bullying*; nor directly encourage, or exhibit obvious indifference to, unlawful behaviour;...

[italics signify the amendments]

ASC also provides for a "Special Interest Group" Complaint Procedure. The "Special Interest Group" is a category of complainant that closely resembles the consumer complainant except that the Special Interest Group complaint originates from an organization such as an advocacy group, for example, Mothers Against Drunk Driving ("MADD"). A Special Interest Group differs from an "advertiser" in a Trade Dispute, although a Special Interest Group may qualify as an "advertiser" in a Trade Dispute Procedure. Typically, the primary focus of a Special Interest Group, unlike that of complainants in a Trade Dispute, is not primarily of a commercial or business nature.

The process for receiving and handling Special Interest Group complaints is very similar to the process used in the Consumer Complaint Procedure except that the complaint is carefully evaluated to ensure it is not a disguised trade complaint.

The Code is also the basis for competitors' disputes, which are adjudicated under the Trade Dispute Procedure. The Trade Dispute Procedure allows businesses that believe their competitors have breached the Code, to bring complaints against each other to ASC. The Procedure has some great advantages, including the fact that it is expeditious. There are typically 30 to 40 days from receipt of a complaint to a decision. Further, the

Procedure is often much less costly than court proceedings and is confidential, except if the advertiser refuses to comply with a ruling.

Revisions to the Trade Dispute Procedure came into force on January 1, 2006. Some highlights of the revisions include:

• The definition of "advertiser" now explicitly includes trade associations.
• Each party to a dispute will now be given at least 12 working days' notice (formerly ten days) in writing of a scheduled Trade Dispute Panel hearing.
• A request for leave to appeal a Trade Dispute Panel decision by either party must be received in writing within four working days (formerly three days) of the party's receipt of a decision.
• If an Appeal Panel determines that an error in interpretation of the evidence or the Code has occurred, the Trade Dispute Panel decision will be set aside and replaced with that of the Appeal Panel. Previously, the Trade Dispute Procedure provided for a re-hearing of a complaint by a new Trade Dispute Panel.
• Submissions of confidential information related to surveys and tests by either party is no longer permitted. Previously, the Procedure permitted such evidence to be submitted on a "confidential basis". Confidential claims would be assessed by ASC and the other party would be provided the results of any confidential evidence in written summary form only.
• ASC can reactivate the Trade Dispute Procedure where the identical ads, originally the subject of a complaint, are repeated. This right may also be exercised if one or more of the critical elements of the offensive principal claims or tag lines are repeated in other ads. This is a new right available to ASC.
• If an advertiser fails to voluntarily comply with a Panel decision, or fails to fully satisfy enforcement requirements, ASC may notify the public that the advertising in question has been found to violate the Code. ASC may also specifically identify the violating advertiser. Previously, the Procedure did not specifically allow an advertiser to be identified.

In May 2005, ASC revised its *Guidelines for the Use of Comparative Advertising and its Guidelines for the Use of Research and Survey Data.* Please see Chapter 3 on claim substantiation for details regarding the revised Guidelines.

2.   The Code

The Code is reproduced in its entirety at the end of this chapter. As indicated in the preamble, the provisions should be followed both in letter and in spirit. Technical loopholes are not tolerated. To follow is a summary of the Code sections along with some examples of ads that have violated the sections.

(a)   Accuracy and Clarity

* Consistent with the *Competition Act*, ads must be accurate and truthful and not contain inaccurate or deceptive claims, verbal statements or visual representations.
* Ads must not omit relevant information.
* Pertinent details of an offer must be clearly stated.
* Disclaimers must not contradict more prominent messages and must be clearly visible and/or audible.
* Advocacy advertisements must clearly identify the advertiser responsible.

> EXAMPLE:
>
> An ad for a fitness club claims, "SO LITTLE NEVER BOUGHT SO MUCH. ONLY $7.50 PER MONTH."
>
> The ad fails to state that the advertised fee only allows use of the club between certain hours, three days per week and that additional mandatory fees will be charged.

(b)   Disguised Advertising Techniques

Remember the controversy in the 70's and 80's over subliminal advertising messages? For example, allegations of SEX spelled out in the ice cubes of liquor advertisements. Frankly, most advertising lawyers put them in the same category as "PAUL IS DEAD" when you played your Beatles' "Revolution No. 9" backwards. However, for some time, the Code had a provision prohibiting such subliminal messages. Creative directors say that it is difficult enough to get the product shot lighting right without trying to manipulate shadows for subliminal messages. Today, section 2 of the Code simply states that an ad shall not be presented in a format or style which conceals its commercial intent.

> EXAMPLE:
>
> An advertisement in a particular newspaper consisted of several "news articles" with a humorous

twist. These articles were printed in black and white and in the same style and format as other news articles in the paper. Advertising copy that clearly identified the advertiser appeared in a coloured box below the "news articles", but there was nothing to indicate that these articles formed part of the advertisement. The advertising was disguised as news content.

For this reason, many magazines which accept "Advertorials" from advertisers which have both editorial content as well as a subtle advertising message, require that they are labelled "Advertorial" or "Advertisement".

(c)   Price Claims

As a result of the changes in the *Competition Act* sections dealing with savings claims and regular price claims, the Code has been amended to permit regular price comparisons that either comply with the volume test (a substantial volume of the product was actually sold at the "regular price" recently) or the time test (the product was offered in good faith for a substantial period of time at the "regular price" before or after the savings claim).

> EXAMPLE:
>
> | | |
> |---|---|
> | SAVE | $100 |
> | OUR REGULAR PRICE | $200 |
> | SALE PRICE | $100 |
>
> (Legitimate where either ½ of the stock actually sold at $200 or was offered in good faith at $200 for at least ½ of the selling season.)

Qualifications such as "up to" or "x off" must be easily readable and in close proximity to the prices quoted and where practical, regular prices should be included.

> EXAMPLE:
>
> SAVE up to $50
> Sweater sale $20
> Our regular $70

> EXAMPLE:
>
> A travel service advertised a 10% savings on the cost of travel to Western Canadian destinations.

> The offer didn't say it was limited to residents of
> the destinations who purchased return tickets. Not
> only does this violate section 1 of the Code but the
> ad also contains a deceptive price claim.

Prices quoted in foreign currency in Canadian media must be identified. (For those of you who have subscribed to those fabulous U.S. lingerie magazines, unless you read the fine print, you will be in for a rude awakening. Prices are quoted in U.S. dollars and will be subject to taxes, G.S.T. and duty!)

(d) Bait and Switch

If an electronics retailer has *one* 40" colour TV (slightly scratched) available at $199, he cannot spend $10,000 placing an ad in an attempt to lure customers into the store to buy something else that is *not* on sale or at least not as attractively priced. Loss leaders are acceptable but only if the seller clearly states that "limited quantities are available" in the ad.

(e) Guarantee

Ads cannot offer a guarantee or warranty without a full explanation of its conditions and limits and the name of the guarantor or the ad indicates where such information may be obtained.

> EXAMPLE:
>
> LIFETIME UNLIMITED GUARANTEE!
>
> (See package for details.)

(f) Comparative Advertising

- Ads must not discredit, disparage or attack unfairly other products, services, ads or companies.

It seems that most aggressive comparative ads would violate this section. However, while truthful and accurate comparisons are not considered "unfair", grimaces or other uncomplimentary gestures about the competitor's product, visual innuendoes, comparisons between "apples and oranges" and misleading comparative suggestions about the competitor's products will be attacked as "unfair".

> EXAMPLE:
>
> YUCK! DID YOU TASTE THOSE OTHER NO-
> NAME TOASTER TREATS MOM BOUGHT
> FOR US? — THEY ARE GROSS!

EXAMPLE:

WHY USE THIS CHEAP CAPPUCCINO
MACHINE WHEN YOU CAN HAVE OUR
DELUXE CAPPUCCINO MAKER WITH 6
ATTACHMENTS FOR ONLY $300 MORE?

Ads should not exaggerate the nature or importance of competitive differences.

EXAMPLE:

OUR SKIN CREAM HAS 100% MORE VITA-
MIN E THAN THE LEADING BRAND!
(Fact: One has .01% Vitamin E
Other has .02% Vitamin E)

(g) *Testimonials*

• Testimonials must reflect the genuine, current opinion of the person or organization giving them. They must be based upon adequate information or experience and must not be deceptive.

EXAMPLE:

I AM SURE THIS IS THE MOST EFFECTIVE
DEODORANT IN THE WORLD!

Even if the endorser genuinely believes this, he cannot make this statement if it is untrue.

EXAMPLE:

VISUAL OF MODEL WITH GORGEOUS HAIR
STATING — "I USE THIS HAIR COLOUR
BECAUSE I'M RICH!"

When in fact her high-priced hairdresser used something else.

EXAMPLE:

A firefighter was visible through a clear bottle of an alcoholic beverage on an outdoor ad. The ad was posted on the outside wall of a building adjacent to the fire station. It was found that this ad improperly implied the endorsement of the product by firefighters at the station.

(h) *Professional or Scientific Claims*

- Professional or scientific claims may not be distorted.
- Ad claims should not imply a scientific basis which does not exist.
- Claims must be applicable to the Canadian context unless clearly stated.

> EXAMPLE:
>
> MOISTURIZES SKIN 10 TIMES BETTER THAN THE LEADING U.S. BRAND.
>
> EXAMPLE:
>
> CHOSEN BY MORE DERMATOLOGISTS THAN ANY OTHER BRAND.
>
> This statement relates to U.S. dermatologists. Canadian dermatologists, in fact, have different brand preferences.

It is shocking, as a Canadian lawyer, to see how many advertisers assume that both their technical and consumer preference research conducted in the U.S. is transportable to Canada. In some cases, the advertised products (or at least those of their competitors) have different formulations. Further, for some products and services, you cannot assume that Canadians will react similarly to Americans. Differences in ethnicity, weather conditions and demographics can all affect technical or consumer testing.

(i) *Imitation*

Most advertisers are aware that there is no copyright in an idea, just in the way in which that idea is expressed in fixed form. However, the Code goes farther than Canadian copyright law. It prohibits the imitation of the copy, slogans or illustrations of another advertiser in such a manner as to mislead the consumer.

> EXAMPLE:
>
> AN AD FOR BRAND X RUNNING SHOES FEATURES A NIKE-STYLE VISUAL OF A WOMAN CLIMBING A MOUNTAIN AND THE SLOGAN "JUST CLIMB IT".

(j) *Safety*

Ads must not display a disregard for safety or depict situations that might encourage unsafe or dangerous practices or acts.

EXAMPLE:

VISUAL OF TEENS JUMPING OFF THE ROOF
OF THEIR HOUSE INTO THE NEIGHBOUR'S
SWIMMING POOL.

Audio: NEED A BURST OF ENERGY? TRY
XXTRA KOOL ENERGY DRINK!

This section has, in our experience, been one of the most frequently cited in consumer complaints. Most complaints come from parents of young children, since children do not understand many dangers and have a tendency to imitate dangerous, but exciting things they see on television.

While broadcasters continue to air television programming which depicts violent, reckless and dangerous behaviour, advertisers are held to a higher standard. Parents never know when a particular ad may pop up on their screen although they can carefully monitor their child's choice of programming. For the most part, advertisers have no desire to be associated with an activity that may cause harm or danger to children. However, provocative behaviour is always more shocking and intrusive than boring behaviour — so its prevalence in cutting edge advertising is understandable. In some cases, a balancing of the media buy is in order. Ads placed in programming after 9 p.m. or in adult-directed print media may be much more acceptable than if placed during primetime, after school or on Saturday morning cartoons.

(k)   Superstition and Fears

Ads must not exploit superstitions or play upon fears to mislead the consumer.

EXAMPLE:

DO YOU WANT TO DRINK THE SAME KIND
OF WATER WALKERTON EXPERIENCED?

DON'T TRUST YOUR LOCAL DRINKING
WATER — DRINK XYZ BOTTLED WATER.

In our decades of experience as advertising lawyers, we have never seen a "superstition" complaint but we had some fun thinking of examples.

EXAMPLE:

WORRIED ABOUT THE BLACK CATS IN
YOUR NEIGHBOURHOOD?

GET PET REPEL AND KEEP AWAY BAD LUCK.

EXAMPLE:

NEVER EXPERIENCE 7 YEARS BAD LUCK AGAIN WITH NEW UNBREAKABLE WONDER MIRROR!

(l) *Advertising to Children*

Child-directed advertising must not (a) exploit their credibility, lack of experience or their sense of loyalty; or (b) present information or illustration which might result in their physical, emotional or moral harm.

EXAMPLE:

HEY KIDS — YOU CAN BE THE COOLEST KID IN YOUR NEIGHBOURHOOD WITH THIS NEW XLAZER GUN. TERRORIZE THE WIMPS AND BULLIES WITH THIS LIFELIKE REPLICA.

Note that in addition to provisions in the Code, the *Broadcast Code for Advertising to Children* applies to all child-directed broadcast advertising and must be complied with in order to place child-directed ads in broadcast media. These ads are precleared by the Children's Section at Advertising Standards Canada. Advertising to children under 13 is almost entirely prohibited in Quebec. Chapter 6 discusses children's advertising issues in detail.

(m) *Advertising to Minors*

Adult products must not be advertised in a manner that appeals particularly to minors. People featured in such ads must not only be adults but appear to be adults.

EXAMPLE:

EMINEM ENDORSING BEER.

EXAMPLE:

CONDOM ADS SET AT A HIGH SCHOOL PARTY.

The CRTC *Code for Broadcast Advertising of Alcoholic Beverages*, located at <http://www.crtc.gc.ca/eng/general/codes/alcohol.htm>, similarly restricts the use of characters or personalities that appeal to minors. The CRTC Code prohibits endorsement of a product directly, or by implication, by any person, character or group who is likely a role model of minors. The Code also prohibits the association of the product with youth or youth symbols. For this reason, you often hear "old songs" in beer ads and see "old athletes" endorsing these products.

(n)   Unacceptable Depictions and Portrayals

Advertisements shall not:

(a)   condone any form of personal discrimination, including discrimination based upon race, national origin, religion, sex or age;

(b)   appear to exploit, condone or incite violence; *nor appear to condone or directly encourage, bullying*; nor directly encourage, or exhibit indifference to, unlawful or reprehensible behaviour (see above explanation of amendments to this section of the Code);

(c)   demean, denigrate or disparage any identifiable person, group of persons, firm, organization, industrial or commercial activity, profession, product or service or attempt to bring it or them into public contempt or ridicule;

(d)   undermine human dignity, or appear to encourage or be indifferent to conduct or attitudes that offend the standards of public decency prevailing among a significant segment of the population.

> EXAMPLE:
>
> DON'T BE A CHEAP SCOT, BUY YOUR VALENTINE BEAUTIFUL ROSES FROM XYZ.
>
> EXAMPLE:
>
> DON'T END UP IN A DEAD END JOB LIKE GARBAGE COLLECTION. APPLY NOW FOR ULTIMATE CORRESPONDENCE COLLEGE.
>
> EXAMPLE:
>
> JOIN JOE'S GYM AND LEARN TO KICK-BOX. YOU'LL SOON BE ABLE TO BEAT UP ANYONE IN THE NEIGHBOURHOOD.
>
> EXAMPLE:
>
> ENRAGED OFFICE WORKER WAS SHOWN SMASHING HIS COMPUTER TO PIECES.
>
> The ad exploited, condoned and incited violence.

Appendix A

CANADIAN CODE OF ADVERTISING STANDARDS

SELF-REGULATION OF ADVERTISING IN CANADA

OVERVIEW

The *Canadian Code of Advertising Standards* (*Code*), which has been developed to promote the professional practice of advertising, was first published in 1963. Since that time it has been reviewed and revised periodically to keep it contemporary. The *Code* is administered by Advertising Standards Canada. ASC is the industry body committed to creating and maintaining community confidence in advertising.

The *Code* sets the criteria for acceptable advertising and forms the basis upon which advertising is evaluated in response to consumer, trade, or special interest group complaints. It is widely endorsed by advertisers, advertising agencies, media that exhibit advertising, and suppliers to the advertising process.

Consumer complaints to ASC about advertising that allegedly does not comply with the *Code* are reviewed and adjudicated by the English national and regional Consumer Response Councils and by their counterpart in Montreal, le Conseil des normes (collectively referred to as Councils and individually as a Council). These autonomous bodies of senior industry and public representatives are supported and co-ordinated by, but altogether independent from, ASC.

Trade complaints about advertising, based on the *Code*, are separately administered under ASC's *Trade Dispute Procedure*. Complaints about advertising from special interest groups are separately administered under ASC's *Special Interest Group Complaint Procedure*.

INTERPRETATION GUIDELINES

The *Code* may be supplemented from time to time by Interpretation Guidelines that enhance industry and public understanding of the interpretation and application of the *Code*'s 14 clauses. The Interpretation Guidelines can be found on ASC's website <http://www.adstandards. com>.

DEFINITIONS

For the purposes of the *Code* and this document:

"**Advertising**" is defined as any message (the content of which is controlled directly or indirectly by the advertiser) expressed in any language and communicated in any medium (except those listed under Exclusions on page 21) to Canadians with the intent to influence their choice, opinion or behaviour.

"**Advertising**" also includes "**advocacy advertising**", "**political advertising**", and "**election advertising**", as defined below.

"**Advocacy advertising**" is defined as "advertising" which presents information or a point-of-view bearing on a publicly recognized controversial issue.

"**Political advertising**" is defined as "advertising" by any part of local, provincial or federal governments, or concerning policies, practices or programs of such governments, as distinct from election advertising.

"**Election advertising**" is defined as "advertising" regarding a political party, a political or government policy or issue, an electoral candidate, or any other matter before the electorate for a referendum that is communicated to the public within a time-frame that starts the day after a vote is called and ends the day after the vote is held. In this definition, a "vote" is deemed to have been called when the applicable writ is dropped.

"**Special Interest Group**" is defined as an identifiable group, representing more than one individual and/or organization, expressing a unified viewpoint that is critical of the content of an advertisement, and/or the production method or technique, and/or the medium, used to carry the advertisement and convey its perceived message.

APPLICATION

The *Code* applies to "advertising" by (or for):

* advertisers promoting the use of goods and services;
* corporations, organizations or institutions seeking to improve their public image or advance a point of view; and

- governments, government departments and crown corporations.

EXCLUSIONS

Election Advertising

Canadians are entitled to expect that election advertising will respect the standards articulated in the *Code*. However, it is not intended that the *Code* govern or restrict the free expression of public opinion or ideas through election advertising, which is excluded from the application of this *Code*.

EXCLUDED MEDIA

The following are excluded from the definition of "medium" and the application of the *Code*:

(i)   foreign media (namely media that originate outside Canada and contain the advertising in question) unless the advertiser is a Canadian person or entity; and

(ii) packaging, wrappers and labels.

SCOPE OF THE CODE

The authority of the *Code* applies only to the content of advertisements and does not prohibit the promotion of legal products or services or their portrayal in circumstances of normal use. The context and content of the advertisement and the audience actually, or likely to be, or intended to be, reached by the advertisement, and the medium/media used to deliver the advertisement, are relevant factors in assessing its conformity with the *Code*. In the matter of consumer complaints, Councils will be encouraged to refer, when in their judgment it would be helpful and appropriate to do so, to the principles expressed in the *Gender Portrayal Guidelines* respecting the representations of women and men in advertisements.

CODE PROVISIONS

The *Code* is broadly supported by industry, and is designed to help set and maintain standards of honesty, truth, accuracy, fairness and propriety in advertising.

The provisions of the *Code* should be adhered to both in letter and in spirit. Advertisers and their representatives must substantiate their advertised claims promptly when requested to do so by a Council.

1.   ACCURACY AND CLARITY

(a)   Advertisements must not contain inaccurate or deceptive claims, statements, illustrations or representations, either direct or implied, with regard to a product or service. In assessing the truthfulness and accuracy of a message, the concern is not with the intent of the sender or precise legality of the presentation. Rather, the focus is on the message as received or perceived, i.e. the general impression conveyed by the advertisement.

(b)   Advertisements must not omit relevant information in a manner that, in the result, is deceptive.

(c)   All pertinent details of an advertised offer must be clearly and understandably stated.

(d)   Disclaimers and asterisked or footnoted information must not contradict more prominent aspects of the message and should be located and presented in such a manner as to be clearly visible and/or audible.

(e)   Both in principle and practice, all advertising claims and representations must be supportable. If the support on which an advertised claim or representation depends is test or survey data, such data must be reasonably competent and reliable, reflecting accepted principles of research design and execution that characterize the current state of the art. At the same time, however, such research should be economically and technically feasible, with due recognition of the various costs of doing business.

(f)   The entity that is the advertiser in an advocacy advertisement must be clearly identified as the advertiser in either or both the audio or video portion of the advocacy advertisement.

2.   DISGUISED ADVERTISING TECHNIQUES

No advertisement shall be presented in a format or style which conceals its commercial intent.

3.   PRICE CLAIMS

(a)   No advertisement shall include deceptive price claims or discounts, unrealistic price comparisons or exaggerated claims as to worth or value. "Regular Price", "Suggested Retail Price", "Manufacturer's List Price" and "Fair Market Value" are deceptive terms when used by an advertiser to indicate a savings, unless they represent prices at which, in the market place where the advertisement appears, the advertiser actually sold a substantial volume of the advertised product or service within a reasonable period of time (such as six months) immediately before or after making the representation in the advertisement; or offered the product or service for sale in good faith for a substantial period of time (such as six months) immediately before or after making the representation in the advertisement.

(b) Where price discounts are offered, qualifying statements such as "up to", "XX off", etc., must be in easily readable type, in close proximity to the prices quoted and, where practical, legitimate regular prices must be included.

(c) Prices quoted in advertisements in Canadian media, other than in Canadian funds, must be so identified.

4.   BAIT AND SWITCH

Advertisements must not misrepresent the consumer's opportunity to purchase the goods and services at the terms presented. If supply of the sale item is limited, or the seller can fulfil only limited demand, this must be clearly stated in the advertisement.

5.   GUARANTEES

No advertisement shall offer a guarantee or warranty, unless the guarantee or warranty is fully explained as to conditions and limits and the name of the guarantor or warrantor is provided, or it is indicated where such information may be obtained.

6.   COMPARATIVE ADVERTISING

Advertisements must not, unfairly, discredit, disparage or attack other products, services, advertisements or companies, or exaggerate the nature or importance of competitive differences.

7.   TESTIMONIALS

Testimonials, endorsements or representations of opinion or preference, must reflect the genuine, reasonably current opinion of the individual(s), group or organization making such representations, and must be based upon adequate information about or experience with the product or service being advertised, and must not otherwise be deceptive.

8.   PROFESSIONAL OR SCIENTIFIC CLAIMS

Advertisements must not distort the true meaning of statements made by professionals or scientific authorities. Advertising claims must not imply that they have a scientific basis that they do not truly possess. Any scientific, professional or authoritative claims or statements must be applicable to the Canadian context, unless otherwise clearly stated.

9.   IMITATION

No advertiser shall imitate the copy, slogans or illustrations of another advertiser in such a manner as to mislead the consumer.

10. SAFETY

Advertisements must not without reason, justifiable on educational or social grounds, display a disregard for safety by depicting situations that might reasonably be interpreted as encouraging unsafe or dangerous practices or acts.

11. SUPERSTITIONS AND FEARS

Advertisements must not exploit superstitions or play upon fears to mislead the consumer.

12. ADVERTISING TO CHILDREN

Advertising that is directed to children must not exploit their credulity, lack of experience or their sense of loyalty, and must not present information or illustrations that might result in their physical, emotional or moral harm.

Child-directed advertising in the broadcast media is separately regulated by the *Broadcast Code for Advertising to Children*, also administered by ASC. Advertising to children in Quebec is prohibited by the Quebec *Consumer Protection Act*.

13. ADVERTISING TO MINORS

Products prohibited from sale to minors must not be advertised in such a way as to appeal particularly to persons under legal age, and people featured in advertisements for such products must be, and clearly seen to be, adults under the law.

14. UNACCEPTABLE DEPICTIONS AND PORTRAYALS

It is recognized that advertisements may be distasteful without necessarily conflicting with the provisions of this clause 14; and the fact that a particular product or service may be offensive to some people is not sufficient grounds for objecting to an advertisement for that product or service.

Advertisements shall not:

(a) condone any form of personal discrimination, including that based upon race, national origin, religion, sex or age;

(b) appear in a realistic manner to exploit, condone or incite violence; nor appear to condone, or directly encourage, bullying; nor directly encourage, or exhibit obvious indifference to, unlawful behaviour;

(c) demean, denigrate or disparage any identifiable person, group of persons, firm, organization, industrial or commercial activity, profession, product or service or attempt to bring it or them into public contempt or ridicule;

(d) undermine human dignity; or display obvious indifference to, or encourage, gratuitously and without merit, conduct or attitudes that offend the standards of public decency prevailing among a significant segment of the population.

THE PRECLEARANCE AND REGULATORY MOSAIC

The *Code* is not intended to replace the many laws and guidelines designed to regulate advertising in Canada. Nor are the *Code's* provisions intended to be senior to any other aspect of Canada's preclearance and regulatory apparatus – to which some require mandatory compliance; others voluntary. As its name implies, the *Code* has as its primary purpose the expression of Canadian standards in advertising that, when followed, should result in responsible yet effective advertising without unreasonably blunting the underlying fundamental right to advertise lawfully-sold products and services in a fair but competitive manner.

ASC also provides advisory and copy clearance services, upon request, to various groups within the advertising and marketing industry through ASC Clearance Services. Every approved copy submission includes a written inscription, prominently displayed, advising the advertiser that the copy was approved only within the context of (and for as long as the copy complies with) the provisions of the applicable (named) Act, Regulations and Guidelines (if any).

The inscription may also note that an advertisement produced from the approved submission could provoke a consumer complaint under the *Code*, and that if such complaint is upheld by a Council, the advertiser will be requested by ASC to withdraw the commercial or amend it to comply with the *Code*.

CONSUMER COMPLAINT PROCEDURE

How To Submit Consumer Complaints To ASC

The procedure for consumers wishing to complain to ASC that an "advertisement" (as defined in the *Code*) contravenes the *Code*, is as follows:

ASC accepts complaints submitted by mail, e-mail, or fax. Telephoned complaints cannot be accepted.

To submit a complaint by e-mail:

- Complete the e-mail complaint form and follow the instructions provided on ASC's Consumer Complaint Submission Form.

To submit a complaint by letter:

- Include your full name, telephone number, complete mailing address and (if available) fax number and e-mail address.
- Identify the product or service being advertised, and the medium in which the advertisement appears:
  - For **Print Advertisements:** identify the name and date of the publication(s) in which you saw the advertisement(s) and include a copy of the advertisement(s).
  - For **Out-of-home Advertisements:** such as outdoor, transit or similar advertisements: identify the date on and exact location at which you saw the advertisement.
  - For **Broadcast Advertisements:** identify the station, time and date on/at which you saw/heard the commercial and provide a brief description of the commercial.
  - For **Cinema Advertisements:** identify the date of viewing and the name and location of the movie theatre at which you saw the advertisement and provide a brief description of the advertisement.
  - For **Internet Advertisements:** identify the date of viewing, website, and include a print-out of the advertisement and other applicable web pages (if any).
- Explain the reason or basis for the complaint and, if known, the provision(s) of the *Code* that may apply.
- Submit the complaint to ASC at the address, or fax number listed on our contact page.

HOW CONSUMER COMPLAINTS ARE RECEIVED AND HANDLED BY ASC AND COUNCIL

In keeping with their mandate within today's self-regulatory environment, ASC and Council carefully consider and respond to all written consumer complaints received by them about advertising that allegedly does not comply with the *Code*.

The critical factor in determining whether an advertisement should be reviewed by Council is not the number of complaints received. The fundamental issue is only whether an advertisement, if the subject of any number of complaints, appears to contravene the *Code*. Ultimately, that question can only be answered by Council in response to one or more *bona fide* complaints that originate from the public.

NON-REVIEWABLE COMPLAINTS

If, upon review, it appears to ASC or Council that a complaint is not a disguised trade complaint or special interest group complaint, and that based on the provisions of the *Code* reasonable grounds for the complaint appear to exist, then the consumer complaint will be accepted for processing. If at any time thereafter during the complaint review process, but prior to the release of Council's decision on the complaint, either ASC or Council concludes that, in reality, the complaint is a trade complaint or a special interest group complaint, but not a consumer complaint, the process will be discontinued and the complainant notified accordingly. In these cases, the complainant will be reminded that alternative approaches should be considered by the complainant for registering an advertising-related complaint, such as under ASC's *Trade Dispute Procedure* or *Special Interest Group Complaint Procedure*.

Council shall decline to accept, or to proceed further with, a complaint, or any part thereof, where it is of the opinion that:

(a) the specific advertisement(s) about which the complainant alleges a *Code* violation has/have not been identified;
(b) based on the provisions of the *Code*, reasonable grounds for the complaint do not appear to exist;
(c) the advertising, or such part of the advertising to which the complaint refers is, substantially, also the subject of litigation or other legal action then actively undertaken and pursued in Canada; or is under review, or subject to an order, by a Canadian court, or an agent or agency (or some other comparable entity) of the Canadian Government; or has been, specifically, approved by an

agency (or some other comparable entity) of the Canadian Government; or that

(d)   such advertising is not within the purview of the *Code* or the complaint is beyond the resources of ASC to resolve under this *Procedure*; or that

(e)   the complainant is abusing this *Consumer Complaint Procedure* by having as one of the complainant's primary intentions to generate publicity for a cause or issue.

COMPLAINT REVIEW PROCESS

If, after a complaint is received, there is a preliminary determination that there may be a *Code* infraction by the advertisement (i.e. an accepted complaint), the advertiser will be notified in writing of the nature of the complaint and, if informed consent is freely granted by the complainant to ASC, the identity of the complainant.

COMPLAINTS INVOLVING CLAUSES 10 OR 14

When an accepted complaint relates to the provisions of Clause 10 (Safety) or Clause 14 (Unacceptable Depictions and Portrayals), the advertiser will be asked to promptly respond (copying ASC), within a stated timeframe, directly to the complainant if the complainant has agreed to be identified. If the complainant does not wish to be identified, the advertiser will respond directly to ASC, who will redirect the response to the complainant. Complaints about alleged offences under Clauses 10 or 14 that are handled in this way will go forward for deliberation by a Council if the complainant notifies ASC that the complainant remains dissatisfied after receiving the advertiser's response, and if, after reviewing the advertiser's response, ASC believes the advertising still raises an issue under the *Code*. Otherwise, the matter will not be forwarded to a Council and will not proceed further.

COMPLAINTS INVOLVING ALL OTHER CODE CLAUSES

Where a preliminary determination has been made that there may be an infraction of one or more of the other clauses of the *Code* (*i.e.*, other than Clauses 10 or 14), the advertiser will be asked to respond directly to ASC by providing, in writing and without unreasonable delay, information requested by Council in order that Council may deliberate and reach a fully-informed decision about whether the *Code* has, in fact, been violated.

COUNCIL HEARING AND DECISION

Complaints directed to ASC will be initially evaluated by ASC staff. If a complaint raises a potential *Code* issue and it concerns national advertising in the French-language, or advertising that appears only in Quebec, the complaint will be evaluated and decided by le Conseil des normes in Montreal. Complaints about an advertisement will be directed to one of the regional Councils identified in Appendix A to the *Code* if the advertisement relates to local or regional advertising in the vicinity of that Council. Complaints from outside Ontario about national English-language advertising will be evaluated and decided by Council members who have national experience and exposure at a Council Hearing that includes English-language representation from the Council in the region where the complaint(s) originated. Otherwise, complaints about national English-language advertisements will be directed to the national Council in Toronto.

At the initial deliberation by a Council, the materials available for Council's review include, at a minimum, the complaint letter, the advertiser's written response, if any, and a copy of the advertising in question.

Council's decisions are by majority vote. Any member of Council may abstain from voting on any matter.

If a Council concludes an advertisement violates the *Code*, the advertiser, with a copy to the complainant, will be notified of the decision in writing and requested to appropriately amend the advertising in question or withdraw it, in either case without unreasonable delay.

If, at the initial deliberation by a Council, the complaint is not upheld by Council, both the complainant and the advertiser will be notified in writing with an explanation for Council's decision.

APPEALING A COUNCIL DECISION

Both the complainant and the advertiser are entitled to request an appeal from a decision of Council by filing a Request for Appeal addressed to the Standards Division or, if in relation to a Quebec decision, to la Division des normes. The Request for Appeal must be in writing and received at ASC within seven working days after the decision is sent to the parties. It must provide the appellant's reasons for believing the decision was in error. A request by an advertiser for an appeal will be considered if that advertiser undertakes in writing to withdraw the advertising in question within 11 working days after the Request for Appeal is received at ASC. The withdrawn advertising may be reinstated, however, if at the appeal hearing the Appeal Panel decides not to uphold the complaint. Advertisers will be granted a reasonable extension of time in which to withdraw the advertising if Council is satisfied that the advertising medium used to convey the advertising is unable to facilitate the withdrawal in the designated time.

A five-person Appeal Panel will be selected from among a roster of persons who did not serve at the original deliberation by a Council. The Appeal Panel will comprise two public representatives with the balance coming from the advertiser, advertising agency and media sectors. Each party will be given at least five working days advance written notice of the date of the appeal hearing.

Both the advertiser and the complainant will be requested to make their submissions in writing to the Appeal Panel. The submissions must be brief, confined strictly to the matters under appeal and received by the Standards Division at least two full working days in advance of the appeal hearing.

Decisions of Appeal Panels will be by majority vote and will be sent to both parties within five working days of the appeal hearing. At the appeal hearing, the complaint will be treated as a new complaint and the matter reconsidered in its entirety.

Decisions by Appeal Panels will be binding and final.

ADVERTISING COMPLAINTS REPORT

Each year, ASC will publish one or more reports on consumers' complaints to ASC about advertising. The principal purpose of these reports is to serve, for the benefit of the advertising industry and the interested public, as a guide to the interpretation of the *Code* as applied to advertising issues that concerned the public.

The advertising complaints reports will be divided into two sections. One section will provide details, including advertiser and advertisement identification, of those consumer complaints upheld under the *Code*. In this section, advertisers will be entitled to state their position on their advertisements about which a Council has upheld one or more complaints. The other section will summarize, without naming the advertiser, consumer complaints upheld by Councils about advertisements dealt with appropriately by the advertiser. Appropriate action by the advertiser means action voluntarily undertaken by the advertiser, without delay, to amend the advertisement to correct the alleged infraction, after being advised by ASC that a complaint had been received and before the matter was brought forward to Council for review and decision. Alternatively, the advertiser, without delay, may withdraw the advertisement from any further exposure, distribution or circulation and, in the case of retail advertising, provide a correction advertisement that appears in consumer-oriented media addressed to the same consumers to whom the misleading or offending advertising was originally directed.

RE-OPENING A CASE

ASC will have the discretionary right to reactivate the Consumer Complaint Procedure, in whole or part, including the imposition of sanctions provided in the *Code*, if an advertiser fails to fulfil its undertaking to withdraw or amend an advertisement; or if the matter underlying the complaint is of a continuing or repetitive nature, suggesting an avoidance of the provision(s) of the *Code*.

ADVERTISER'S FAILURE TO RESPOND OR PARTICIPATE

If an advertiser fails to respond in a timely manner to ASC's request for a copy of the advertisement that is the subject of a consumer complaint, ASC may ask the carrying media to assist ASC by providing it with a copy of the advertisement in question. If an advertiser fails to respond to a complaint or participate in the *Consumer Complaint Procedure* the complaint may be decided in the advertiser's absence based on the information already in the possession of the applicable Council and on any further pertinent information submitted by the complainant for Council's review.

FAILURE TO FOLLOW PROCEDURE OR COMPLY WITH DECISION

The *Code* is a reflection of advertising standards by which industry wishes to be held accountable. Because self-regulation is more than self-restraint on the part of individual companies or entities, the *Code* would be incomplete without effective sanctions to enforce compliance.

IF AN ADVERTISER FAILS TO VOLUNTARILY COMPLY WITH THE DECISION OF A COUNCIL, ASC:

- will advise exhibiting media of the advertiser's failure to co-operate and request media's support in no longer exhibiting the advertising in question; and
- may publicly declare, in such manner as Council deems appropriate, that the advertising in question, and the advertiser who will be identified, have been found to violate the *Code*.

FOR MORE INFORMATION

Questions regarding the interpretation and application of the *Code* should be addressed to ASC.

Advertising Standards Canada
175 Bloor Street East
South Tower, Suite 1801
Toronto, ON M4W 3R8
Telephone: 416 961-6311
Fax: 416 961-7904
e-mail: info@adstandards.com

Les normes canadiennes de la publicité
4823 Sherbrooke Street West
Suite 130
Montreal, Quebec H3Z 1G7
Telephone: 514 931-8060
Fax: 514 931-2797
e-mail: info@normespub.com

APPENDIX A: REGIONAL CONSUMER RESPONSE COUNCILS

Alberta Consumer Response Council
albertacouncil@adstandards.com

British Columbia Consumer Response Council
bccouncil@adstandards.com

Atlantic Consumer Response Council
atlanticcouncil@adstandards.com/en/Standards/canCodeOfAd
Standards.asp – top

Chapter 2

FALSE OR MISLEADING ADVERTISING

A.   INTRODUCTION

In the advertising business, false and misleading advertising is the root of all evil. Virtually every law and regulation directed at advertising is intended to prevent deceptive advertising claims and marketing practices.

Unless consumers are given accurate and complete information, the marketplace is skewed in favour of the dishonest trader. When there are too many misleading ads, consumer trust is eroded. Competitors suffer when their products or businesses are misrepresented or when a competitor makes unwarranted superiority claims. In Canada, this area of commerce is regulated by the *Competition Act*. In the end, the sanctions against false or misleading advertising are intended to ensure a level playing field for competitors and a marketplace where consumers can make informed and intelligent choices.

There is still room, in this marketplace, for whimsy, hyperbole and — to a limited extent — "The Greatest Show on Earth" style puffery. There is some room for overstating your case with the expectation that competitors will do the same and that consumers will be able to separate fact from fiction. There is no room, however, for anything which borders on deceit.

In Canada, there are many safeguards and prohibitions against false or misleading advertising. On the federal level, the *Competition Act*[1] contains civil and criminal sanctions against false or misleading advertising in any medium and criminal sanctions against deceptive telemarketing. On the provincial level, similar sanctions are set out in various consumer protection laws. In this, as in all other cases, particular attention must be paid to Quebec's *Consumer Protection Act* which strictly regulates credit advertising, children's advertising and other matters.

---

[1]   R.S.C. 1985, c. C-34.

There are also many product-specific laws and policy statements, such as the *Food and Drugs Act*; the *Guide to Food Labelling and Advertising*, administered by the Canadian Food Inspection Agency; and the *Guidelines to Consumer Drug Labelling and Advertising*, administered by Health Canada which all contain prohibitions against deceptive advertising and labelling.

Truth in labelling is governed by the same principles and many of the same regulations as truth in advertising. However, all labelling-specific issues are covered in Chapter 7 of this book.

Finally, and most significantly on a practical level, are the many industry self-regulatory codes ranging from the Canadian Marketing Association's Code to the *Canadian Code of Advertising Standards* administered by Advertising Standards Canada to regional codes with a limited reach such as the Ontario Motor Vehicle Industry Council's ("OMVIC") *Marketing Standards* directed at automobile dealers in Ontario. Invariably, the focus of industry codes is twofold: to maintain the credibility of their sector and to prevent, through self-regulation, government intervention in their advertising practices.

There is one additional avenue of recourse for competitors who are faced with false or misleading comparative advertising. If threatening letters fail and a Trade Dispute before Advertising Standards Canada is not a viable option, there is always the option of legal proceedings. Every year, legal actions are brought to enjoin comparative advertising which crosses the line. The use of lawsuits is often a strategic as well as a legal decision and the receptiveness of the courts to misleading advertising complaints is unpredictable.

B.   THE BASIC PRINCIPLES

The boundaries which separate an aggressive ad from one that falls into the false or misleading category are difficult to define. Reasonable people can differ in their assessments. If these were black or white issues, there would be fewer competitive Trade Disputes and fewer legal proceedings. Nonetheless, certain things are clearly forbidden and the case law and legal guidelines point to certain basic principles.

The *Canadian Code of Advertising Standards* contains the clearest statement of these principles. The following sections are particularly important:

1.   Accuracy and Clarity

(a) Advertisements must not contain inaccurate or deceptive claims, statements, illustrations, or representations, either direct or implied, with regard to a product or service. In assessing the truthfulness and accuracy of a message, the concern is not with the intent of the sender or precise legality of the presentation.

Rather, the focus is on the message as received or perceived, i.e., the general impression conveyed by the advertisement.

(b) Advertisements must not omit relevant information in a manner which, in the result, is deceptive.

. . .

(c) Disclaimers and asterisked or footnoted information must not contradict more prominent aspects of the message and should be located and presented in such a manner as to be clearly visible and/or audible.

. . .

6.   Comparative Advertising

Advertisements must not unfairly discredit, disparage or attack other products, services, advertisements or companies, or exaggerate the nature or importance of competitive differences.

C.   MATERIAL MISREPRESENTATIONS

Certain advertising falsehoods are conventional and acceptable. The background of your commercial can be picture-perfect. Children can be immaculate and well-behaved. Families with school-age children can be shown sitting down to an unhurried breakfast.

What is critical from a legal point of view, is any *material* falsehood relating to your product or its performance. "Material" means a misrepresentation which is likely to influence a consumer's behaviour or purchasing decisions. A misrepresentation which motivates consumers to avoid a competitor's products is as material as one which leads consumers to purchase yours. Whether or not a misrepresentation is "material" is usually self-evident. If a car dealer depicts his salesmen as charming and good-looking, this is unlikely to matter to consumers. If, however, a dealer falsely warrants that his prices are the lowest in town, this is clearly material and unlawful.

D.   OUTRIGHT DECEIT

There are relatively few cases of blatant dishonesty in mainstream advertising. Competitors and consumer watchdog groups such as the Automobile Protection Association and Ad Busters, tend to keep aggressive advertisers in the grey area. When a well-known and reputable company engages in deceitful advertising, it is rightfully perceived as a breach of trust.

There is, for example, the notorious Volvo case. Although this case was decided in the U.S., the applicable principles are the same in Canada. Volvo has a reputation for building safe and well-engineered vehicles. Nonetheless, in 1992, this message was conveyed in a deceptive way in a U.S. television spot. At a stage-managed monster truck event, "Big Foot" crushed every car in the line-up — except the Volvo which had been specially reinforced to withstand this abuse. The result: when the networks discovered that Volvo's shoot had been "rigged", the spot was pulled and Volvo paid a heavy price to its reputation. The irony is that Volvo had the strongest vehicle in the line-up, and the reinforcement was used to ensure that a difficult and expensive shoot went as planned. If this ad had been broadcast in Canada, it would have been challenged under the *Competition Act* or the *Canadian Code of Advertising Standards*.

It is less surprising when lesser-known advertisers engage in deceit. An Ontario case from the early 70's is typical. Newspaper ads for a quit-smoking plan quoted a certain Mrs. "H" as saying "I definitely look and feel 10 years younger." The problem was that she had never used the plan and though a former smoker, she stated at trial that she "had never felt 10 years younger". The company was prosecuted under the *Competition Act* and fined $1,000 (the 1973 penalty) for the false testimonial.

1.   The General Impression

The *Competition Act*, the *Canadian Code of Advertising Standards* and common sense all dictate that an ad must be examined as a whole to determine whether the general impression it conveys is false or misleading. Each element of an ad can be literally true and the entire ad can be unlawfully misleading. This is a question of consumer takeaway. Many advertising disputes revolve around consumer perception: an expensive proposition if properly conducted consumer surveys are required to resolve the dispute. At the end of the day, there are few hard and fast rules because every ad and the context for every ad are different.

(a)   Examples

A few Canadian examples of the general impression rule may help.

A television spot for pantyhose depicted a nail file drawn across a pair of pantyhose in two demonstrations: on a flat surface and stretched between an actor's hands. Absolutely no damage occurred in either case. But the same nail file tore a newspaper to shreds. It turned out that the nail file was harmful only if (a) the hose was held at a certain tension or (b) the flat surface demo was performed on a piece of velvet. The commercial was therefore deemed misleading because the general impression conveyed was that the pantyhose was tear-resistant in all situations.

In 1995, a major food company introduced a frozen pie crust product combining a regular bottom crust with a fitted top crust. To illustrate their innovative product, they ran print ads comparing their perfect pie crusts to a hump-backed pie made with two bottom crusts and captioned "Their idea of a top crust". Their competitor, the leading pie crust maker, successfully sued by claiming that the ad conveyed the misleading impression that their directions called for misshapen two crust pies when, in fact, they explained how to convert a bottom crust into a fitted top crust.[2] This case was marginal. A judge with a different sense of humour might have seen the tongue-in-cheek nature of the ad and come to a different conclusion.

In another case from 1995,[3] a battery company ran a television commercial which featured mechanical toys dancing at a masked ball. The unicorn with the company's battery strapped to its back kept on going after the masked pink bunny collapsed and died. The general impression was clear: the advertiser's batteries outlasted the competitor's batteries. The court concluded that the advertiser did not have proper substantiation for this claim.

The court also raised, in a curious aside, the question of "puffery". In certain cases, statements can be literally untrue but can be acceptable as "mere puffery". However, "puffery" refers to self-congratulatory claims that are unlikely to be taken seriously. A battery performance claim does not fit within this category.

E.   SINS OF OMISSION

It is self-evident that ads can mislead by what they fail to say. A simple example is a "50% Off" banner that neglects to say that the sale is limited to certain merchandise. Or an ad which proclaims that a certain laundry detergent makes "whites whiter" but neglects to state that the performance benefit is only achieved on 100 per cent cotton fabrics in cold water.

2   *Maple Leaf Foods v. Robin Hood Multifoods Inc.*, [1994] O.J. No. 2165, 58 C.P.R. (3d) 54 (Ont. Gen. Div.).
3   *Eveready v. Duracell*, [1995] O.J. No. 3495, 64 C.P.R. (3d) 348 (Ont. Gen. Div.).

F.   MICE TYPE

It is a fundamental principle of advertising law that what the headline giveth the fine print cannot taketh away. As section 1 of the *Canadian Code of Advertising Standards* states: "Disclaimers and asterisked or footnoted information must not contradict more prominent aspects of the message..." There is a fine line to be walked with disclaimers. Certain industries are rife with them. For example, car financing ads, ads for internet service and airline ticket sales are always accompanied by lengthy footnotes. More problematic are the same ads in televised form where the disclaimers are full-screen supers which flash on screen for one or two seconds. If a super cannot be read, it is completely futile. As the Code states, disclaimers "should be located and presented in such a manner as to be clearly visible and/or audible".

This problem is easy to solve in print ads because consumers have time to read the fine print provided it is large enough. There are no strict size requirements, although the Ontario Motor Vehicle Industry Council guidelines are useful. They require disclaimers to be no smaller than the classified ads in the same publication.

In addition, fine print must not include critical information that "contradicts" the main message. "Critical information" will differ from ad to ad. For example, if a large down payment is required to obtain a featured lease payment, this should not be buried in the mice type, however legible. If an advertised product is not available yet, this should be stated in the body copy. You cannot assume that consumers will read the mice type. Anything that consumers need to know before calling a 1-800 line to order your product or taking another irrevocable step, should be communicated in the body copy.

1.   Examples

There are several misleading advertising cases that revolve around the use of disclaimers.

In 1995, Scott Paper sued a competitor regarding a comparative T.V. ad for a new brand of paper towels. The ad included a side-by-side absorbency demonstration. One critical component of the demo — that the new product was 25 per cent larger than the Scott Paper product — was buried in a difficult-to-read super. This factor, among others, led to an out-of-court settlement.

In a leading comparative advertising case from 1994,[4] Purolator sued another courier company for an advertising campaign where the Purola-

---

[4]   *Purolator Courier v. United Parcel Service Canada Ltd.*, [1995] O.J. No. 876, 60 C.P.R. (3d) 473 at 490 (Ont. Gen. Div.).

tor competitor claimed to provide guaranteed 10:30 a.m. overnight delivery service "usually at rates up to 40% less than other couriers charge".

Purolator argued that the ads were materially misleading because they conveyed the general impression that their competitor's rates were always or usually 40 per cent lower than Purolator's rates. In effect, Purolator contended that consumers did not register the qualifying words "usually" and "up to". The court disagreed. In its judgment, the court accepted that even though inattentive listeners might misunderstand the claim, this was not the test. The correct analysis of disclaimers required a two-part test: first, was the qualifying language properly part of the message and second, what was the impression conveyed to the average consumer in the target market? The court held that the ads were directed at sophisticated business customers who would understand that the opportunity for 40 per cent savings was limited. The judge adopted a remarkably laissez-faire approach to comparative advertising:

> Advertising…[b]y its nature…is one-sided and usually does not convey a full and balanced analysis. To do so, of course, might diminish its persuasive power…competitors may complain that the ad does not depict the whole picture; but they are just as equipped to tell their side of the story in the commercial marketplace of ideas…

G.   VISUAL INNUENDOS

An ad can mislead by visual innuendo as effectively as with words. For example, if fillers are used to make a mega-burger look substantially larger than the actual product or a wide-angle lens exaggerates the roominess of business class airline seats, these are wordless but misleading claims. Visual claims are particularly important when appearance is a key selling point of the advertised product or service. If your product is an "age defying" facial cream, the "before" and "after" shots should duplicate actual results. If you are advertising luxury hotel rooms, the furniture, fittings and size depicted in your ads should be representative of the actual hotel rooms.

Misleading visual claims frequently arise in the context of comparative advertising. The battery commercial which featured the premature death of a battery-operated pink bunny is a classic example. A more subtle case was a soft drink commercial from the mid-1980's where a truck bearing the logo of the number two brand was shown overtaking the number one brand's truck. The leading brand successfully argued that these visuals misrepresented both the rate of their competitor's sales growth and the market share it had gained.

H.   COMPARATIVE ADVERTISING

In reality, unless your advertising has crossed the line into outright deceit, the most likely parties to complain about misleading advertising are your competitors. If the ads contain misleading claims but are not comparative, competitors may complain to Industry Canada, Health Canada, Advertising Standards Canada or another regulator about your failure to comply with the relevant legislation or codes. If the ads are comparative, and thus directly damaging to their bottom line, competitors may bring a Trade Dispute before Advertising Standards Canada or in a worst-case scenario, launch legal proceedings.

Comparative advertising is so commonplace today that it is hard to remember a time (more than 25 years ago) when advertisers in Canada and the U.S. referred to competing products as "Brand X". That was before the U.S. Federal Trade Commission issued a policy statement in 1979 encouraging truthful comparative advertising which led to brand name comparative advertising in both the United States and Canada. What followed in both countries was a free-for-all when aggressive comparative ads became a common tactical weapon and several lawsuits helped define the rules of engagement.

I.   CRITICAL FACTORS

Because the case law involving comparative advertising is complex and contradictory, we will not attempt to analyze it. Instead, we will list the critical factors to consider if you are contemplating a comparative advertising campaign:

• The single most important factor is the truth. Every claim in a comparative ad — both about your product and your competitor's product — must be truthful and not misleading. Hyperbole is never appropriate in the comparative context. Every claim must be based on adequate and proper substantiation. This is not the occasion to exaggerate your product's merits. Any attempt at humour, self-congratulation or "harmless" puffery may backfire.

• Do not engage in excessive cherry-picking. While comparative ads are not required to be perfectly even-handed, if you ignore a significant defect in your product or service or overlook a significant advantage of your competitor's, you do so at your peril. At the end of the day, the comparison should involve similar products and not "apples and oranges".

• Do not disparage your competitor's products, services or business or engage in unfair disparagement. This is called trade libel and it is actionable. Disparagement can take many forms: a backhand reference to your competitor's product as "that old thing"; an actor who grimaces slightly when handling the competitive product; depicting your product in a halo of sunshine and your competitor's in shades of grey; dropping, tossing, discarding or otherwise abusing your competitor's product; using any visual or verbal device that depicts your competitor's product as shoddy, unfashionable, unsafe, unhealthy or otherwise second-rate.

- Do not depict your competitor's packaging, logos or mascots. This could constitute copyright infringement. Do not use a competitor's trade-marks if they are registered for services. Through a quirk in the *Trade-marks Act*,[5] trade-marks which are registered only for wares (the majority of packaged goods marks) can be used in comparative advertising whereas the use of service marks (such as Speedy Muffler which is registered for services such as "automobile repair") could trigger a claim. You should also be aware that unnamed competitors can complain about your advertising if they are readily identifiable, for example, "The fast food chain with the golden arches" identifies McDonalds without naming it. Unnamed competitors can also sue if they belong to the group that is targeted by your advertising. For example, if a wireless telephone company claims to have the best rates in Canada, any of its competitors could complain about this claim if the claim is untrue and damages their business.

- Timing is everything. Do not time your comparative ad to disrupt a competitor's product launch or to inflict unreasonable damage. If the case goes to court, a judge will have to decide which party will suffer greater "inconvenience": the competitor who is targeted by the advertising or the advertiser whose ads may be pulled. Aggressive timing may weigh against you.

J.   ENFORCEMENT: HOW MISLEADING ADVERTISING IS CURBED

1.   Complaints to Regulators

When advertising is false or misleading, a written complaint to the relevant regulator is often the simplest remedy. These complaints are typically made by competitors acting through their law firms. They are also made by consumer organizations. These regulators include the Competition Bureau for breaches of the *Competition Act*; Health Canada or the

---

[5]   R.S.C. 1985, c. T-13.

Canadian Food Inspection Agency for breaches of the *Food and Drugs Act* and related regulations and guidelines; the various provincial ministries for breaches of provincial legislation and the relevant trade associations. For example, in Ontario, false or misleading claims in car dealer advertising are usually dealt with by OMVIC.

In most cases, the government authorities will investigate problematic advertising of their own accord and pursuant to complaints from consumers and competitors.

While written complaints are a simple remedy, they have limitations. The complainant must have standing to make a complaint — for example, a party who is injured by the false or misleading advertising or a member of the applicable trade association. Second, having made the complaint, the complainant is typically out of the picture and will not be informed whether or when follow-up action is taken. Third, the ability of regulators to respond to written complaints is a function of staffing levels and current priorities. Some complaints may take months to process. Fourth, if you have a complaint pending before a government regulator, Advertising Standards Canada precludes a simultaneous Trade Dispute involving the same advertising.

2.   The Competition Bureau

The ultimate regulator of false or misleading advertising in Canada is the Competition Bureau which investigates problematic advertising of its own accord and pursuant to consumer and competitor complaints. Ordinary false or misleading advertising falls under section 74.01(1)(a) of the *Competition Act* and will be dealt with as a "reviewable matter" by the Competition Tribunal or the courts. The potential penalties include a cease and desist order lasting up to 10 years; a requirement that the advertiser publish an information notice describing the false or misleading claims and the subsequent court order; a monetary penalty of up to $50,000 for a first offence and the registration of a consent order detailing the resolution reached by the advertiser and the Bureau. There were proposed *Competition Act* amendments, which would dramatically increase the maximum monetary penalty for a corporation to $10 million for a first offence, that died on the order paper but may be reintroduced.

In serious cases of false or misleading advertising where there is substantial harm to the public interest and the advertiser has acted deliberately or recklessly, the Bureau may pursue a criminal prosecution under section 52(1)(a) of the Act. The maximum penalty for the criminal offence of misleading advertising is a $200,000 fine. If the Crown proceeds by way of indictment, directors and officers of the advertiser may face prison sentences and the fines may involve millions of dollars.

3.   ASC Trade Dispute Procedure

When comparative (and non-comparative) advertising involves false or misleading claims, the most cost-effective remedy is Advertising Standards Canada's Trade Dispute Procedure. The procedure is initiated by a written complaint to the Standards Division of the ASC alleging a breach of the *Canadian Code of Advertising Standards*. There is a minimum filing fee of $6,677 for members and $10,015 for non-members which includes the filing fee and the complaint analysis. GST must be added to all amounts. This fee is partially refundable: complainants will receive a refund of $5,240 if the complaint is not accepted for review. If the complaint is accepted, there is an additional Complaint Hearing Fee of $7,800 for members and $11,700 for non-members. This fee is also partially refundable if the Procedure is cancelled before the distribution of the evidence. If the complaint is determined to have merit, the Standards Division will convene a mandatory dispute resolution meeting. If the parties fail to reach a settlement at this meeting, a Trade Dispute Panel will be convened and a hearing date will be set with at least 10 working days notice.

In advance of the hearing, each party will submit its case in the form of written arguments and evidence. The five-member Trade Dispute Panel consists of one representative from each of the following groups: advertisers, agencies, media, consumers and the legal profession. The hearing itself is relatively informal.

The complainant presents its case and is questioned by the Panel and then the defendant advertiser presents its case. The Panel has five working days to reach a decision. If the complaint is upheld, and the advertiser refuses to voluntarily pull the ad, media members of the ASC will be informed and they will likely (although this has never been tested) pull the advertising in question. The entire procedure, from start to finish, can be concluded in five to six weeks for relatively little money if the parties, rather than their lawyers, handle most of the work. Because the Trade Dispute Panels are comprised of advertising industry members, their decisions are often more practical than a court's. Finally, the proceedings are confidential: a distinct advantage for defendants if not for complainants. Advertising Standards Canada also has a consumer complaint procedure which is described in the Appendix to Chapter 1. A single consumer complaint about a breach of the *Canadian Code of Advertising Standards* can result in an ad being pulled.

4.   Legal Proceedings

If a competitor makes false or misleading claims about your company or its products in any form of advertising (including packaging) or improper superiority claims about its own products, there are several grounds for legal proceedings, including breaches of the *Competition Act* and the *Trade-marks Act* (if applicable), trade libel and wrongful interference with economic relations. There are several major advantages to legal proceedings:

- If the advertising is very damaging, you may be able to obtain an interim injunction in as little as 10 days.
- Legal proceedings can be accompanied by press releases allowing you to win the battle of public opinion and correct any false impressions arising from the advertising.
- If the case proceeds to trial (an unlikely event), you could win a damages award.

There are also major disadvantages:

- Legal proceedings will almost invariably involve filing a Statement of Claim and applying for an interim injunction. The costs of preparing for an injunction in a straightforward case with little expert evidence could range from $100,000 to $200,000.
- The courts are unpredictable. Even cases which seem to overwhelmingly favour one side or another can be lost by that side.

If you are contemplating legal proceedings, there are several things to consider. You should act as quickly as possible: if you sit too long on your legal rights, this could weigh against you. Come to the court with "clean hands": if you have been guilty of making false or misleading claims — particularly about the competitor in question — this could damage your case. Do not time your case to inflict maximum damage, such as aborting a competitor's product launch. This will make it more difficult to obtain an injunction. And finally, if you are contemplating legal proceedings, be prepared to lose. This is a strategy that requires a back-up plan.

Chapter 3

SUBSTANTIATING ADVERTISING CLAIMS: WHAT YOU NEED AND WHEN YOU NEED IT

A. INTRODUCTION

How do you know when your product claim needs to be substantiated? In the highly competitive world of advertising, claims based on superiority or consumer preference are often integral to an aggressive marketing campaign. The role of the advertising lawyer is to segregate claims that fall under the heading of "puffery" or "hyperbole" and do not require substantiation from advertising claims that require support from technical or consumer research. There are four general categories of advertising claims:

(1) **Puffery**
A purely self-congratulatory statement of opinion, for example, the Barnum & Bailey claim that their circus is "The Greatest Show on Earth".

(2) **Hyperbole**
A "hyperbolic" claim is one that is so exaggerated that members of the public could not reasonably rely on it, for example, "this pain reliever works faster than a speeding bullet".

(3) **Efficacy or Comparative Efficacy Claims**
Claims that relate to the technical efficacy of the product require technical testing of the product, for example, "No other line of batteries lasts longer."

(4)   **Consumer Opinion or Performance Claims**
Consumer opinion or preference claims which require consumer research across a representative sample, for example, "90% of children love the taste of new Cinnamon Crunch waffles"; or "60% of
cola drinkers surveyed said they preferred the taste of our new
cola."

B.   THE LAW

As discussed in Chapter 1, until the new *Competition Act*[1] came into
force on March 18, 1999, misleading advertising was strictly a criminal
offence, subject to strict liability (meaning prosecutors did not have to
prove intent) and the defence of due diligence. Although misleading
advertising is still a residual criminal offence, the criminal justice system
will only deal with the most serious cases where misrepresentations are
made knowingly and recklessly.

Part VII.1 of the Act covers deceptive marketing practices which are
now reviewable civil matters subject to administrative remedies. The
pertinent section is section 74.01(1) which reads:

74.01 (1) A person engages in reviewable conduct who, for the purpose of promoting, directly or indirectly, the supply or use of a product or for the purpose of promoting, directly or indirectly, any business interest, by any means whatever,

(a) makes a representation to the public that is false or misleading in a material respect;

(b) makes a representation to the public in the form of a statement, warranty or
guarantee of the performance, efficacy or length of life of a product that is not
based on an adequate and proper test thereof, the proof of which lies on the person making the representation; or

(c) makes a representation to the public in a form that purports to be

(i) a warranty or guarantee of a product, or

(ii) a promise to replace, maintain or repair an article or any part thereof or to
repeat or continue a service until it has achieved a specified result,

if the form of purported warranty or guarantee or promise is materially misleading
or if there is no reasonable prospect that it will be carried out.

Further, section 74.02 states that other reviewable matters include:

74.02 A person engages in reviewable conduct who, for the purpose of promoting,
directly or indirectly, the supply or use of any product, or for the purpose of promoting, directly or indirectly, any business interest, makes a representation to the
public that a test has been made as to the performance, efficacy or length of life of
a product by any person, or publishes a testimonial with respect to a product,

_____

[1]   R.S.C. 1985, c. C-34.

unless the person making the representation or publishing the testimonial can establish that

(a) such a representation or testimonial was previously made or published by the person by whom the test was made or the testimonial was given, or

(b) such a representation or testimonial was, before being made or published, approved and permission to make or publish it was given in writing by the person by whom the test was made or the testimonial was given,

and the representation or testimonial accords with the representation or testimonial previously made, published or approved.

The term "representation" has been given a broad meaning. A representation has been held to include:

* verbal statements including what a salesman tells consumers;
* communications by illustration or photograph;
* auditory or visual effects; or
* omission of a material fact;

It is the "overall impression" of the advertisement that must be considered when assessing whether the advertisement is false or misleading in a material respect. These provisions of the *Competition Act* guard against advertisers taking advantage of the public by making representations that lack the support of adequate or proper testing.

A violation of any of these sections could result in an administrative remedy such as:

* an order not to engage in the unlawful conduct;
* an order to publish a notice bringing to the attention of those affected a description of the conduct; or
* an order to pay an administrative remedy: $100,000 on a first order, and $200,000 for subsequent orders.

It is important to note that reviewable conduct under Part VII.1 is not excluded from criminal review. Any listed matter may still be subject to criminal sanctions, provided that the *mens rea* (knowledge and recklessness) requirement is met.

C. TYPES OF CLAIMS AND SUBSTANTIATION

"Puffery", as described by Mr. Justice Jarvis in the case of *Church & Dwight Ltd. v. Sifto Canada Inc.*, is the "staple of the advertising industry and of marketers everywhere" and, therefore, in most cases does not require substantiation.[2] Similarly, "hyperbolic" claims do not require substantiation as the claims made are exaggerated to the point that the average consumer could not be misled. On the other hand, claims that relate to the performance of the product and in particular, superiority claims, whether they are comparative, absolute or opinion claims, must be proven through testing and/or consumer research prior to their publication. If these type of claims are not corroborated, not only can they be challenged by a competitor, but an advertiser could also face a criminal prosecution.

D.   HOW DO YOU SUBSTANTIATE?

Advertisers must know how to substantiate advertising claims in order to protect themselves from the very real possibility of criminal and/or civil actions for false or misleading advertising. A successful marketing campaign *must* include substantiation of claims prior to publication. However, the *Competition Act* itself does not provide any specific direction as to how "adequate and proper testing" can be achieved. Therefore, one must draw upon industry practices, court decisions on substantiating advertising claims, and recognized scientific and/or survey procedures to achieve "adequate and proper testing" and attempt to shield the advertiser from liability upon a challenge.

E.   GUIDING PRINCIPLES

1.   Governmental

In May 2005, ASC revised its *Guidelines for the Use of Comparative Advertising and its Guidelines for the Use of Research and Survey Data to Support Comparative Advertising Claims*. Previously, the Guidelines referred only to food advertising. Now, the Guidelines have general application.

Under the *Guidelines for the Use of Comparative Advertising*:

* Comparisons must involve similar products and be based on similar properties, features, ingredients, benefits or performance. An advertisement must not create an unsupportable negative impression of the "compared-to" product or service beyond the factual comparison being made.
* Other products or services must not be unfairly discredited or disparaged by a claim specifically made in an advertisement.

---

[2]   [1994] O.J. No. 2139, 20 O.R. (3d) 483 at 486 (Ont. Gen. Div.).

Advertisements should avoid visual imagery that might leave an unwarranted negative general impression of other products or services.

- Selected comparisons of specific features or attributes should not be used to claim or imply overall superiority without factual support that such a link is justified.
- Testimonials should be presented as individual opinion, unless there is valid research or survey data that supports it is a generalized view.
- Claims which rely on research or survey data should follow ASC's *Guidelines for the Use of Research and Survey Data to Support Comparative Advertising Claims*.
- Advertisers engaged in a trade dispute under ASC's Trade Dispute Procedure must provide ASC with adequate support for their advertising claims when requested to do so by ASC.

Under the *Guidelines for the Use of Research and Survey Data*:

- All comparative claims must be supportable:

  - Claims based on consumer preference require consumer survey data for support.
  - Claims of objective facts likely find support in other ways such as through laboratory test or sales data.

- Research to support a particular comparative claim should follow published standards of the market research industry or generally accepted industry practices.
- Comparative advertising research should be based on:

Validity
- The survey measures what it is supposed to measure.
- Blind testing is recommended for comparisons.
- Leading or loaded questions and other user biases should be avoided.

Reliability
- Research should be reliable, in that it should be reproducible.
- Research should be based on a representative sample of the pertinent population, with sufficient size to permit reasonably accurate inferences to be drawn.
- The research should be based on the population about whom the claim is made.
- Random sampling is almost always appropriate, but substitutes, such as mall sampling may be appropriate.

- An overall sample size of not less than 300 for large populations, which produces a margin for error plus or minus 6 per cent to a 95 per cent confidence level is recommended.
- A 95 per cent confidence level is the minimum recommended.
- Sub-sample sizes of 100 each for sub-groups to which the advertiser makes specific references are recommended.
- With a national claim, the desirable sample would include four out of five of Canada's major marketing regions (B.C., Prairies, Ontario, Quebec and Atlantic).
- Data must be reliable and valid at all times during which research-based comparative claims are made.

When a trade dispute is submitted under the Trade Dispute Procedure, all comparative claims should be accompanied by the appropriate documentation including: sampling methodology, population, questionnaires, survey results, margins of error and levels of confidence.

2.   The Canadian Code of Advertising Standards

Sections 1, 5, 6 and 7 of the *Canadian Code of Advertising Standards* also provide guidance on substantiating advertising claims under the following headings:

(a)   *Accuracy & Clarity*

- Advertisements must not contain inaccurate or deceptive claims, either direct or implied, with regard to price, availability or performance of a product or service.
- Advertisements must not omit relevant information in a manner which is deceptive.
- All pertinent details of an advertised offer must be clearly stated.

For example, an ad offered a fitness club membership during a nine-day promotional period. The ad contained a disclaimer that the offer was time limited and provided an expiry date. Actually, time limited meant that the membership could be used only three days per week during certain hours. However, the ad gave the impression that "time limited" applied to the duration of the promotion. This ad was found in violation of the *Code* for deceptive and vague claims.

- Disclaimers or asterisked information must not contradict more prominent aspects of the message and should be clearly visible.

EXAMPLE

UNLIMITED LONG DISTANCE CALLING*

*Subject to certain limitations and restrictions.

The footnoted copy which contradicts the more prominent "Unlimited" message in the headline violates the Code.

(b)   Guarantees

- No advertisement shall offer a guarantee or warranty, unless the guarantee or warranty is fully explained as to conditions and limits and the name of the guarantor or warrantor is provided, or it is indicated where such information may be obtained.

  EXAMPLE:

  Satisfaction Guaranteed, or Your Money Back!

This ad was found to be in violation of the Code because it did not fully explain the conditions of the guarantee. When a customer tried to return an item, the advertiser offered only to replace it and not to refund the purchase price!

(c)   Comparative Advertisement

- Advertisements must not discredit, disparage or unfairly attack other products, services, advertisements, or companies or exaggerate the nature or importance of competitive differences.

  EXAMPLE:

  DON'T TRUST THOSE ADS FOR XYZ ELECTRONICS! WE WILL OFFER YOU MUCH BETTER PRICES!

Comparative advertisements are also discussed in Chapters 1 and 2 of this book.

(d)   Testimonials

Testimonials must reflect the genuine, reasonably current opinion of the individual, group or organization making the statement and must be based upon adequate information about or experience with the product or service being advertised.

For example, an outdoor ad depicted a shirtless firefighter photographed through a clear bottle of an alcoholic beverage. This ad was featured on the outside wall of a building adjacent to a fire station and was found to be in violation of the *Canadian Code of Advertising Standards* because it implied an endorsement of the product by the firefighters and the Fire Department.

F.   GUIDING PRINCIPLES FOR SUBSTANTIATING CLAIMS

1.   Case Law

In the 1981 case of *R. v. Alpine Plant Foods*[3] the following guidelines for "adequate and proper tests" were described:

- Tests should be conducted under controlled conditions so that any external variables which might affect the results are excluded.
- Test results should be capable of replication in a randomized population to ensure that the advertiser can state with confidence that similar tests conducted at a later time would produce the same or substantially similar results.

The 1995 decision of the British Columbia Supreme Court in *BC Tel Mobility Cellular Inc. v. Rogers Cantel Inc.*[4] added the following guideline:

- The type of testing must be appropriate to the specific performance claim being made; that is the test should be designed to validate the claim as interpreted and understood by the average consumer, not as interpreted by the advertiser.

2.   Claim Substantiation

To comply with the *Competition Act* requirements, certain advertising preference claims must be based on a properly conducted survey using the appropriate population. The claim itself must accurately reflect the data received from the survey results. For example, the claim should not "stretch" or "tailor" the results of a survey to suit the needs of the advertiser. The claim made must be an *accurate reflection* of the survey results. Bias should be eliminated from the testing procedure. If the subjects become aware that they are being tested, they may adjust their behaviour according to what they believe is expected from them. Techniques such as "blind" or "double blind" testing can guard against bias.

---

[3]   June 11, 1981 (unreported).
[4]   [1995] B.C.J. No. 1999 (B.C.S.C.).

3.   Relevant and Recent Case Law Concerning Claim Substantiation

(a)   The Dead Bunny Case[5]

The defendant battery company broadcast a television commercial which claimed its batteries were superior to all other batteries, including the plaintiff's using the claim: "The Copper Top Tops Them All" and showing the competitor's mascot boogying on the dance floor.

The plaintiff commenced an action alleging that the ad violated the misleading advertisement provisions of both the *Competition Act* and the *Trade-marks Act*. They also sought an interlocutory injunction to prevent the defendant's ad from appearing on television.

Although the defendant had conducted earlier testing against the plaintiff's batteries, by the time the advertisement aired, the plaintiff had changed its product such that performance differences between the two batteries were not commercially or statistically significant. The defendant had failed to conduct any tests between their battery and the new version of the plaintiff's battery.

The court focused on the fact that the defendant had an obligation under the *Competition Act* to conduct its own adequate, proper and current testing prior to making a superiority claim.

The court ordered that the ad be withdrawn from the air.

(b)   Cell Phone Wars[6]

The defendant advertiser, conducted a sound quality survey whereby it retained a third party to compare the services of two cell-phone competitors. Following completion of the survey, they launched an ad campaign referring to the results of the survey by citing statistics to support its claims of superior service.

The plaintiff brought an action alleging that the ads offended the misleading advertising provisions of both the *Competition Act* and the *Trade-marks Act*. As in the Dead Bunny case, the plaintiff also sought injunctive relief.

The plaintiff challenged the methods used in conducting the survey and the criteria used, arguing that the advertisement and performance claims did not adequately reflect the results of the survey. Essentially it was a "stretch" of the survey. Specifically, the plaintiff alleged that the survey did not measure sound quality of the phone whereas the advertisement depicted a user commenting on the quality of the sound.

---

[5]   *Eveready Canada v. Duracell Canada Inc.*, [1995] O.J. No. 3495, 64 C.P.R. (3d) 348 (Ont. Gen. Div.).

[6]   *BC Tel Mobility Cellular Inc. v. Rogers Cantel Inc.*, [1995] B.C.J. No. 1999 (B.C.S.C.).

The court agreed with the plaintiff that there must be a "reasonable basis" on which the defendant could base its assertion that its services were superior to the plaintiff.

(c)   The Imperfect Pie Crust Case[7]

The defendant made performance claims stating that its frozen pie crusts were superior to those of its direct competitor. The plaintiff commenced a civil action claiming that the advertisements were misleading and unfair, and were in breach of section 7 of the *Trade-marks Act*. Injunctive relief was also sought. The court agreed with the plaintiff that the advertisements were misleading and granted an injunction.

Due to the nature of visual images used, the court held that the overall impression of the advertisements was false and misleading, despite the fact that the information contained in the advertisements was factually accurate (the plaintiff's product did only provide for a bottom pie crust which had to be re-shaped for the top). It was the disparaging depiction of the crusts in the advertisement, and the overall impression created that the court focused on.

(d)   The Purest Baking Soda Case[8]

The defendant launched an advertising campaign to promote its new baking soda. In the advertisements the defendant claimed to be producing "the purest possible baking soda" and that it was "the only naturally occurring baking soda on the market".

The plaintiffs, who produced the market leading baking soda, alleged that these advertisements offended the misleading advertising provisions of the *Competition Act* and the *Trade-marks Act* and that the performance claims told the public that the plaintiff's baking soda was not the purest possible.

The court held that even though the competitor was not specifically named in the advertisements, there was "identity by implication" as the plaintiff held 75 per cent of the market share.

The court concluded that the claims created the overall general impression that it would be unhealthy to use a baking soda not manufactured by the defendant.

The court also held that the differences between the two products were so slight as to make the products indistinguishable from one another and that the representations made by the defendant had not been substantiated through proper testing. The injunction was granted.

---

[7]   *Maple Leaf Foods v. Robin Hood Multifoods Inc.*, [1994] O.J. No. 2165, 58 C.P.R. (3d) 54 (Ont. Gen. Div.), leave to appeal refused [1994] O.J. No. 2461, 58 C.P.R. (3d) 54*n* (Ont. Div. Ct.).

[8]   *Church & Dwight Ltd. v. Sifto Canada Inc.*, [1994] O.J. No. 2139, 20 O.R. (3d) 483 (Ont. Gen. Div.).

(e) The Mother's Milk Case[9]

The parties were competitors in the field of infant formulas. The defendant made the following performance claim: "After many years of innovative research with thousands of infants, new [Product Name] has been proven to support infant growth and development, providing your baby with benefits that until now were only associated with breast milk".

The plaintiff attacked this statement on the grounds that the marketing claims were not reflective of the study and test results and were misleading and untruthful as they claimed benefits far greater than the study found. The court concluded that the defendant's claims had not been adequately substantiated and were not reflective of the study results.

(f) The Headache Case[10]

The defendant made a comparison between its pain relief product and a competitor's. The claim read: "[Product A] relieves headaches and other pain better than extra-strength [Product B]". The plaintiff commenced an action relying on the provisions of the *Competition Act*, the *Trade-marks Act* and the common law, stating that the claims were false and misleading.

The defendant led evidence that in addition to its own independent testing, it had also obtained pre-approval from the Health Protection Branch which had scientists and consultants evaluate the claim. The evaluation led the Branch to decide that their product's formulation was better than the competitor's formulation for the relief of headaches.

The claim had also been tested and approved by the Canadian Pharmaceutical Advertising Advisory Board which is an independent organization that reviews and clears pharmaceutical advertising directed to health professionals. It was only after these approvals that the defendant commenced the advertising campaign.

The court held that there was "ample evidence to support the defendant's superiority claims" relying on the "scientific scrutiny of the appropriate Canadian regulatory agencies" and that the defendant's materials were "virtually uncontradicted".

(g) The Moisture in your Bath Bar Case[11]

The defendant compared their new Bath Bar to the leading Beauty Bar. The advertisement claimed that Bath Bar A was superior to the leading beauty bar in terms of its effect on skin hydration. The plaintiff alleged

---

[9] *Mead Johnson Canada v. Ross Pediatrics*, [1996] O.J. No. 4342, 70 C.P.R. (3d) 417 (Ont. Gen. Div.).

[10] *Johnson & Johnson Inc. v. Bristol-Myers Squibb Canada*, [1995] O.J. No. 2230, 62 C.P.R. (3d) 347 (Ont. Gen. Div.).

[11] *UL Canada v. Procter & Gamble Inc.*, [1996] O.J. No. 624, 65 C.P.R. (3d) 534 (Ont. Gen. Div.).

that the claim constituted a direct comparison with their product and was false and misleading.

The court reviewed in detail the evidence of several experts including the defendant's expert who was responsible for the support of the claim and the development of the advertised Bath Bar.

In addition to scientific studies conducted in-house, the defendant also obtained clearance from Advertising Standards Canada. The plaintiff disputed the defendant's tests with respect to their methodology and lack of linear correlation between the rate of skin moisture loss and moisture content. The plaintiff also led evidence of their own that showed no statistically significant differences between the products as to moisture content or the rate of moisture loss.

In response, the defendant called an independent expert who confirmed that the defendant's testing had been scientifically conducted using sophisticated methodology which resulted in reliable and accurate measurements.

The court adopted the view of the independent expert and held that the defendant had adequately and properly tested its product prior to the advertisement of the superiority claim. The court denied the injunction request.

G.   SUMMARY

Hyperbolic claims and pure puffery do not require substantiation. Claims about the performance and attributes of your product, particularly comparative claims, require "adequate and proper" testing.

1.   Guidelines for Proper Substantiation

- Ensure your test is appropriate to the nature of the claim.
- Ensure your consumer survey sample reflects your actual consumers.
- Ensure your survey sample reflects the geographic nature of the claim.
- Ensure your test is statistically valid and controlled, with sufficient sample sizes and no intentional or inadvertent biases.
- Make sure that you have sufficient documentation and data to substantiate your claim.
- Make sure all relevant details are included in the claim and that the claim is accurately and clearly stated.
- Ensure that your testimonials and testing are current.
- DO NOT rely solely on tests done in the U.S. or elsewhere to support Canadian claims.

- DO NOT rely on apparent consumer satisfaction alone, without adequate testing or use.
- DO NOT make blanket statements of superiority, unless you have tested against all competitors.
- DO NOT begin advertising campaign unless testing is complete.
- DO NOT assume that someone has to prove your claims are false. Proof of substantiation rests with the party making the claim.
- DO NOT exaggerate differences between products.

2.   The Law

The requirement for "adequate and proper" claim support is set out in section 74.01 of the *Competition Act*.

Violations may result in criminal sanctions. More commonly, violations will result in administrative remedies such as fines or injunctions.

3.   Guiding Principles Found In:

- *Guidelines in the Use of Research/Survey Data in Support of Advertising Claims* (1996) issued by Industry Canada.
- Sections 1, 5, 6 and 7 of the *Canadian Code of Advertising Standards* which discuss Accuracy and Clarity, Guarantees, Comparative Advertising and Testimonials.
- Case Law:

  - *R v. Alpine Plant Foods*
  - *BC Tel Mobility Cellular Inc. v. Rogers Cantel Inc.*
  - *Eveready Canada v. Duracell Canada Inc.*
  - *Maple Leaf Foods v. Robin Hood Multifoods Inc.*
  - *Church & Dwight Ltd. v. Sifto Canada Inc.*
  - *Mead Johnson Canada v. Ross Pediatrics*
  - *Johnson & Johnson Inc. v. Bristol-Myers Squibb Canada*
  - *UL Canada v. Procter & Gamble Inc.*

Chapter 4

PRICE AND CREDIT ADVERTISING

A. INTRODUCTION

As far as areas of the law go, advertising law is perceived to be relatively interesting and almost fun! This chapter, however, will cover a less entertaining aspect of advertising law. Price and credit advertising, however complicated, must be tackled, particularly for those in the retail, automotive and banking sectors. This chapter begins with an outline of "free", "ordinary price" and "sales" claims which are particularly relevant for retailers. The second half focuses on credit and cost of credit disclosure for lease and financing advertising across Canada.

B. "FREE" OR "BONUS" OR "NO EXTRA CHARGE" CLAIMS

Not surprisingly, when manufacturers claim that an item is "free" or available at "no extra charge", consumers have an expectation that it won't cost them anything. If a "free" offer is made, the item must, in fact, be free and any attempt to recover the cost of the "free" item will contravene Canadian competition law.

In practice, certain marketplace factors such as electronic cash registers, a complicated tax structure and a law against manufacturers dictating the price of their products conspire to make this a challenge.

For example, if you supply a "free" bottle of conditioner shrink-wrapped to a bottle of shampoo, the retailer could choose to increase the price of the "bonus" pack at retail, thereby making the "free" claim false. For this reason, we recommend a disclaimer such as "Free — Supplied to retailers at no extra cost". Because of price fixing laws, you can't force the retailer to charge a certain price for the "bonus" pack, but you can encourage them not to inflate the price at which they would regularly sell the shampoo alone.

Timing is also crucial. If you introduce a bonus pack on the market at the same time as you ordinarily have a yearly price increase, this could also have the effect of making the "Free" or "Bonus" claim false. Similarly, if a "Bonus" or "Free" offer is in place continuously for over 90 days, it runs the risk of becoming the regular price for the two items combined, undermining the legitimacy of the "Free" or "Bonus" offer. See "Sales and Ordinary Price Claims" below for an explanation of the laws on "ordinary prices" in Canada.

As a final cautionary note, in Quebec, as discussed in Chapter 17, you cannot advertise a "premium" that takes up more than one-half of the space of an ad.

RULES OF THUMB

- DO ensure no price increase at wholesale or retail at time of offer.
- DO limit offer to 90 days or less.
- For on-pack claims DO include a disclaimer "Supplied to Retailer at No Extra Cost".
- In Quebec, DO ensure bonus offer takes up less than one-half the ad.
- DO make sure any hidden charges are fully disclosed (*e.g.*, free by mail with $2.00 shipping and handling).
- If tax must be charged on the item before deduction of free coupon value, DO ensure this is fully explained.

C. SALES/ORDINARY PRICE CLAIMS

The term "sale" implies something has been reduced in price, usually on a temporary basis. Sales claims are therefore inherently related to the regular or ordinary price of a product.

Both the former *Competition Act* and the 1999 amendments prohibit "a materially misleading" representation to the public concerning the price at which a product or like products have been, are or will be "ordinarily sold". Before the 1999 amendments, it was a criminal offence to misrepresent the ordinary selling price of an item. The amendments moved the misleading price claims provisions into the reviewable conduct provisions (the new Part VII.1 of the Act). The Act still contains a criminal offence provision that prohibits false and misleading representations to the public that are made "knowingly and recklessly" and this provision could extend to sales claims.

1.   What was the Test Under the Old Act?

Prior to the 1999 amendments to the *Competition Act*,[1] the Competition Bureau took the position that in order to make a valid comparison to the ordinary price of a product, at least 50 per cent of the volume of the stock must have actually sold at the "ordinary price". However, most retailers could not comply with this "volume" test. Due to the nature of the retail market and consumer behaviour, a larger volume of products are sold when items are on "sale". This was and remains particularly true for big-ticket items, as consumers are generally willing to wait until the retailer puts the item on sale.

2.   What is the Test Under the Current Act?

Under the current provision, a retailer must comply with either the old "volume" test, or the "time" test. For the time test, the retailer must "offer the product in good faith a substantial period of time" at the ordinary price. "Substantial" is defined in the Bureau Guidelines as 50 per cent or more of the time. The Bureau will generally look at a one year time period, either before or immediately after the representation as to "ordinary price". Therefore, the product must have been offered at the "ordinary price" for at least six months in order to meet the test. This time period may be shortened depending on the nature of the product.

Some examples of claims that fit within the "ordinary price" restrictions are as follows:

(1)   Save $2,000
(2)   10% Off
(3)   Was $20,000, now $18,000
(4)   MSRP $20,000, now $18,000
(5)   Regular Price $20,000 — Sale $18,000
(6)   Our Price $18,000 — Compare at $20,000
(7)   Manager's Special

---

[1]   R.S.C. 1985, c. C-34.

D.   ESTABLISHING A REGULAR PRICE

Certain rules must be followed in "regular price" comparisons:

(1)   The "regular" price must be established based on actual use prior to any comparison.

>   EXAMPLE:
>
>   New Item:
>
> | | |
> |---|---|
> | Intended New Price (socks with a "Sale Price" representation): | $ 5.00 |
> | Savings Representation: | 50% |
> | Claimed "Regular Price": | $10.00 |

Since this is a new item and you have *never* offered it for sale or sold it at $10, the "Sale Price", "Savings" and "Regular Price" representations would be considered violations.

(2)   There may be times when you wish to introduce a product at a lower price, then raise the price to a "regular" level. In these circumstances, use the terms "Introductory Price" and "After Sale Price" and ensure that there are sufficient quantities of the items available for sale at the After Sale Price.

(3)   Before claiming something is on sale as compared to a "regular" price, you must ensure that either (a) the regular price is offered in good faith a majority of the time prior to the sale ("Time Test"); or (b) a majority of the volume of the goods were actually sold at the "regular price" ("Volume Test").

(4)   "Good Faith" means that you genuinely offer the goods and genuinely expect people to buy them at the regular price. You should offer a broad selection of colours and sizes, in an upfront way (not hidden in the warehouse) over a period of time when customers would reasonably be expected to purchase them (*e.g.*, snow skis in July will be questionable, although children's ski suits in September should be acceptable since customers often purchase their ski suits prior to the season to ensure best selection.)

(5)   The term "regular price", is deemed to be the price of sellers generally in the marketplace. You will have a positive obligation to validate this claim, and it is virtually impossible to do so with a vast number of competitors. Therefore, you should always use "our regular price" as the basis for your comparison. Since "our regular price" will not always be the price at which a majority of goods are *actually* sold, it is prudent to include a disclaimer on your flyers (as

they do in the U.S.) which clarifies it is the price at which the goods are ordinarily *offered for sale*.

E.   SALES

Anytime a regular price is reduced temporarily, you have a "sale". The word "temporarily" is crucial since the case law indicates that continuous sales will effect a *new* "regular price", namely, the long-running "sale" price. For this reason, continuous sales in excess of 90 days must be avoided. At the other end of the spectrum are "clearances". Clearances are generally understood to be a firm markdown or a permanent discount in order to get rid of a discontinued item.

RULES OF THUMB

- DO NOT have a sale continue for more than 90 days.
- DO NOT use sale terminology (*i.e.*, savings, % off, discounted) unless you have established your reference price as "Our Regular Price" using either the Time or Volume Test.
- Always start and end sale events on the dates advertised. For the purpose of the Time Test, you must constantly tally and calculate the number of regular and sale priced days to ensure that you are offering "Our Regular Price" the majority of the time. Days in which the item is not advertised but is still offered or sold at the sale price must be counted as "sale days".

F.   WHAT HAPPENS WHEN THE RULES ARE BROKEN — IMPORTANT CASE LAW

In June 2003, the Commissioner of Competition and Suzy Shier Inc. filed a ten-year consent agreement with the Competition Tribunal. The Commissioner's investigation, which began in January 2001, revealed that Suzy Shier had violated the ordinary selling price provisions of the *Competition Act*[2] because of certain pricing practices related to the sale of its womens apparel. Specifically, the investigation revealed that in

---

[2]   R.S.C. 1985, c. C-34.

some of its stores, Suzy Shier had: affixed price tags to products that referred to regular prices when the products were in fact being promoted at a reduced price; overstated these regular prices given the nature of the products and the market; had not sold the garments in any significant quantity at the regular price within a reasonable time; and had not offered the products at the regular prices featured for a substantial period of time immediately before making the sales claims. Based on the results of the investigation, Suzy Shier had failed the time and the volume tests. Under the consent agreement, Suzy Shier agreed to: ensure all future regular price claims complied with the *Competition Act*; implement a price practices corporate compliance program; publish corrective notices on its corporate website; publish corrective notices in 16 different newspapers across Canada for three consecutive weeks; and pay an Administrative Monetary Penalty ("AMP") in the amount of $1 million.

In July 2004, the Commissioner of Competition and the Forzani Group Ltd. entered into a consent agreement. The Commissioner had investigated Forzani's practices in relation to price advertising promoting the sale of sporting goods at certain of its Sport Chek and Sport Mart retail locations. During the course of the investigation, the Commissioner found that Forzani had, in sales advertisements, overstated the ordinary selling price offered by suppliers generally in the relevant geographic market by using the terminology "compared to". Forzani did not meet the time test or the volume test for its sales claims versus the ordinary selling price offered by suppliers generally. Forzani also made sales claims versus its own regular prices. However, the investigation found that Forzani's ordinary selling prices were in fact inflated and were often higher than the manufacturer's suggested retail prices. Therefore, Forzani did not meet the time test or the volume test for sales claims made compared to its own regular prices. The Commissioner also asserted that Forzani failed to exercise sufficient due diligence in its efforts to ensure compliance with the Act in good faith. Under the terms of the ten-year consent agreement, Forzani agreed to: comply in the future with the ordinary selling price provisions of the *Competition Act*; publish corrective notices in newspapers across Canada, in Sport Chek and Sport Mart flyers, on its corporate web sites and in its retail stores across Canada; establish and maintain a corporate compliance program; indemnify the Competition Bureau for all costs and disbursements incurred during the course of its investigation which amounted to $500,000; and pay an AMP of $1.2 million.

The Competition Bureau's investigation of Sears Canada Inc. was litigated before the Competition Tribunal instead of settled by way of a consent agreement. In January 2005, The Competition Tribunal found that Sears had violated the ordinary selling provisions of the Competition Act by inflating the regular price of tires during a 1999 sales promotion.

In its sales advertisements, Sears used a misleading reference price in its sales advertisements and always referenced the price of a single tire. Sears had a "2For" price which was always lower than the regular price of one unit but the "2For" price was not used as a reference price in any ads. The Tribunal considered several factors in determining that the proper regular price must be for two tires instead of one, including that tires are usually sold in pairs, tire sales are stable over time, and consumers don't spend much time evaluating alternative products. The Tribunal found that Sears violated both the volume test and the time test. Sears admitted that it had failed the volume test since it had sold only 2 per cent of the tires at the regular price, but argued that it had met the time test. In determining that Sears had failed the time test, the Tribunal found that the relevant geographic area for evaluating compliance with the time test was Canada; it did not allow a regional split. The Tribunal also found that the proper reference period for the time test in this circumstance was six months before the sales claims. Finally, the Tribunal found that Sears could not have truly believed that the ordinary selling prices used in the ads were genuine prices offered in good faith since: Sears did not really expect it would sell many tires at the regular price; Sears did not expect to sell many single tires at the regular price; Sears referred to its practice of pricing tires in pairs as its everyday pricing strategy; and the regular prices Sears used were not comparable and were much higher than the regular prices of competitors such as Canadian Tire. Sears was ordered to pay an AMP of $100,000 which is the maximum corporate penalty for reviewable conduct under the Act. In addition, Sears had to pay $387,000 towards the Bureau's legal costs. The Tribunal also ruled that a ten-year prohibition order was appropriate.

G.   SPECIAL KINDS OF SALES

1.   Special Buys/Manufacturer's Clearance

There are times when your suppliers offer specials on certain items, and you order that item for the first time in a large quantity in order to pass special savings onto your customers. In the alternative, you may take advantage of the offer to buy additional quantities of an item you already carry. *A special buy or manufacturer's clearance should be referred to explicitly as such and no savings or percent off claims should be made.*

RULES OF THUMB

- DO NOT use the term "sale" or imply that a special buy or manufacturer's clearance item is off-priced.
- DO NOT make a percentage or dollars off savings claim.
- The item should not be replenished (*i.e.*, it must genuinely be a "one shot" purchase).
- Be sure that you will have sufficient quantities of the special buy item to meet the demand you reasonably expect. Document what demand you believe there will be and why.
- Note the requirement in Quebec that you must disclose the number of units available at the special price.
- In advertising, state that there are "limited quantities — no rain checks".

---

2.   Possible Exceptions: Ordering Extra Quantities of Existing Items

If you have carried the item for some time, the vendor discontinues it and you buy up the remainder at a special price to blow them out, it may be possible to refer back to "Our Regular Price" (established through the Time Test). However, this should be done only if the goods are of the same quality. In addition, this type of event will count as a "sale" for purposes of the Time Test.

3.   Bill C-19 – Amendments to the Competition Act

The hot topic in 2005 was Bill C-19. Bill C-19, *An Act To Amend The Competition Act And to Make Consequential Amendments To Other Acts*, had its first reading in the House of Commons on November 2, 2004. It proposed several significant revisions to the *Competition Act*. The most controversial proposal was substantial increases in the amount of Administrative Monetary Penalties ("AMPs") for deceptive marketing practices. AMPs for individuals found to have engaged in reviewable conduct would increase from $50,000 to $750,000 for the first offence and $1 million for each subsequent offence. AMPs for corporations would increase from $100,000 to $10 million for the first offence and to $15 million for each subsequent offence.

Bill C-19 also proposed that the courts and the Competition Tribunal should be given the power to order an advertiser to pay restitution to persons to whom products were sold, in an amount not to exceed the amount paid by consumers for the product that was the subject of the misrepresentation.

The proposed amendments were not well received by retailers and manufacturers. The majority of stakeholders who made submissions during the Competition Bureau's Public Policy Forum opposed the imposition of increased AMPs. Critics believed that the penalties should be limited to forward-looking remedies such as cease and desist orders. The civil provisions govern behaviour that is not inherently anti-competitive and is prohibited only after the Competition Tribunal determines it is anti-competitive. Critics also believed that the AMPs proposed were punitive in nature. Further, the Competition Bureau could not provide evidence that the current remedies were inadequate in achieving compliance goals. Higher AMPs could have a potentially chilling effect on the Canadian economy because they could place companies on the defensive through greater exposure to financial liability.

Bill C-19 was not passed before the minority government fell in January 2006. It remains to be seen if a similar version is revived once a new government is formed.

H.   CREDIT ADVERTISING

1.   The Challenge

Those working in the automotive financing and leasing, credit or credit card businesses are well aware of the intricacies and changing landscape for advertising of credit. Canadian law regarding cost of credit and lease advertising is currently undergoing significant revisions based on a harmonization Drafting Template (discussed below) agreed to by most provinces. Each provincial legislature has authority to pass its own legislation with respect to cost of credit disclosure, applicable to consumer transactions in that province. The provinces are currently adopting the harmonization rules in their own time and often in their own way. Difficulties arise because advertisers wish to advertise nationally, with cost of credit disclosure that complies with *all* provincial requirements instead of creating different versions of each ad to address provincial variations. The following is a discussion of the complexity of the cost of credit and lease advertising rules as they currently stand in Canada. Because of recent and significant changes to these rules, it is advisable that credit advertisers consult their advertising lawyer for updates and for review and approval of credit and lease advertisements.

(a)   Harmonized Cost of Credit

(i)   A Brief History

In the late 1980's, the Alberta Law Reform Commission began looking into the possibility of harmonizing cost of credit disclosure laws. It consulted with stakeholders, including consumer groups, credit grantors and law reform advocates in other provinces. Many of the important issues had been analyzed by the time the project came under the aegis of the Agreement on Internal Trade (the "AIT") in 1995. Under the AIT, the federal and provincial governments agreed in principle to the harmonization of cost of credit disclosure legislation. Over the next year, the Consumer Measures Committee, comprised of representatives from Industry Canada and each provincial consumers affairs ministry, prepared the first harmonization proposals. These proposals were submitted to a meeting of federal and provincial Consumer Affairs ministers in September 1996. The ministers agreed in principle with the proposals and assigned the Consumer Measures Committee (the "CMC") the task of preparing a template for harmonized cost of credit disclosure legislation. The final 50-page Drafting Template released in June 1998 is entitled, the *Agreement for Harmonization of Cost of Credit Laws in Canada*.

Once the Drafting Template was published in 1998, the provinces agreed to enact legislation that covers the core issues, but they have been slow to adopt new rules. The current status is outlined below:

- Alberta was the first to enact harmonized legislation based on the Drafting Template in 1999 as part of the *Fair Trading Act*[3] and *Cost of Credit Disclosure Regulations.*[4]
- Ontario has adopted the harmonized rules in the Ontario *Consumer Protection Act, 2002,*[5] and corresponding regulations which came into force July 30, 2005.
- B.C. has also adopted new rules in its new *Business Practices and Consumer Protection Act*[6] and *Disclosure of the Cost of Consumer Credit Regulation.*[7] Cost of credit provisions and corresponding regulations came into force in July, 2006.
- Saskatchewan has tabled Bill 24, *The Cost of Credit Disclosure Amendment Act, 2005*, which contains amendments to *The Cost of Credit Disclosure Act, 2002.*[8] New regulations are currently

---

[3]   R.S.A. 2000, c. F-2.
[4]   AR 198/1999.
[5]   S.O. 2002, c. 30, Sch. A.
[6]   S.B.C. 2004, c. 2.
[7]   B.C. Reg. 273/2004.
[8]   R.S.S. 1978, c. C-41.

being finalized. The proposed in-force date for the new Saskatchewan Act and regulations is October 1, 2006.

- Manitoba amended its *Consumer Protection Act*[9] in June 2005,
  but the amended Act has yet to be proclaimed into force. Draft
  regulations have been released for comment. The amended Act
  will not likely come into force until the corresponding regulations are finalized. The consultation period for the new regulations ended March 20, 2006. At the time of writing, no in-force
  date for the new Manitoba legislation had been proposed.

- The New Brunswick *Cost of Credit Disclosure Act, 2002*[10] was
  assented to in June 2002, but has not yet been proclaimed into
  force. There are currently no regulations to accompany this Act.

- Nova Scotia's amended *Consumer Protection Act*[11] received
  royal assent on November 30, 2000, but has not been proclaimed
  into force and there are currently no corresponding amended
  regulations.

Harmonized credit, finance and lease advertising requirements are an
exciting prospect for advertisers who, to date, have been stuck drafting
different disclosures for each province. However, when the provinces
agreed to harmonize, they did not agree to adopt the exact proposed
language. Since the provinces retain regulatory powers over the credit
legislation they enact, each province's harmonized rules can and do contain some differences in language and scope which can have a significant
effect on the interpretation and application and in turn may defeat the
purposes of harmonization. As each province gets on board with harmonization, it remains to be seen whether the final harmonized legislation across the country will be sufficiently similar to allow for national
harmonized credit, financing and leasing advertising.

(b) The Quebec Disclosure Rules

Quebec has a different approach to cost of credit advertising disclosure
rules. The Quebec *Consumer Protection Act*[12] provides unique rules for
financing and lease advertising. Although they were quite innovative
when adopted, today they appear somewhat archaic and can lead to a lot
of uncertainty with respect to their application.

The Quebec *Consumer Protection Act* distinguishes ads concerning
goods from ads concerning credit. In ads concerning credit, it is prohibited to incite consumers to purchase goods on credit or to illustrate a

---

[9]   C.C.S.M., c. C200.
[10] S.N.B. 2002, c. C-28.3.
[11] R.S.N.S. 1989, c. 92.
[12] R.S.Q., c. P-40.1.

good or a service available on credit. In ads concerning credit, it is also prohibited to disclose terms and conditions of credit, except the credit rate, unless all prescribed particulars are included. These particulars are set out in section 86 of the Regulations and include an example of financing as well as a table of examples of credit charges.

With respect to ads concerning goods, the *Consumer Protection Act* prohibits advertising for credit other than mentioning the availability of credit in the manner prescribed by section 86 of the Regulations (as detailed above). In practice, however, retailers and manufacturers will mention the available financing rate and the maximum term offered without other elements in order not to trigger other disclosure obligations. For example, "2.9% financing up to 60 months" does not in practice trigger the table of examples of credit charges.

If an interest rate is disclosed in an ad, be it with respect to goods or credit, the rate calculated in accordance with the *Consumer Protection Act* should be disclosed with the same prominence. The rate calculated in accordance with the Act should take into consideration all credit charges, including any rebate a consumer would be entitled to if he or she paid cash. In practice, however, retailers and manufacturers will likely choose to disclose only the rate calculated in accordance with the Act.

The lease advertising rules are much more straightforward. Any ad concerning a true long term lease must contain all of the following elements if one element is disclosed:

(a) all payments required before the beginning of the leasing period;
(b) the number and duration of the payment periods;
(c) the amount of the (monthly) instalments; and
(d) any limit on the degree to which the goods may be used and the cost of any use beyond that limit, if there is such a cost;

Finally, although revisions to the Regulations were discussed to provide exceptions for limited media, no amendments were ever tabled. Therefore, the same rules will apply to advertising in print or on billboards, television and radio. In practice, however, full disclosure is not always made in radio ads, but this is one area where the advertiser should use great caution.

(c)   Harmonized Legislation In Canada

The harmonized legislation has been adopted in Alberta, B.C. and Ontario and will soon be in force in B.C. and Saskatchewan. The Manitoba, New Brunswick and Nova Scotia legislation will hopefully be in force sometime in 2006 or 2007. The harmonization rules significantly revise how providers of fixed credit financing, open credit, credit cards and leases advertise to consumers. One of the most significant changes is the requirement to calculate and disclose the Annual Percentage Rate ("APR"). For leases, this rate is called the Lease APR. The harmonized rules provide a specific new formula for calculation of the APR. The APR differs from traditional interest rates because it requires inclusion of interest and non-interest finance charges. Non-interest finance charges include administrative charges, service fees and rebates offered only to cash customers (see discussion on rebates below). Another significant change is the new equal prominence rules applicable to disclosure of the APR in relation to other credit information disclosed in an ad, including any other interest rate. The disclosure of an interest rate together with the APR in one advertisement will inevitably cause confusion and therefore the equal prominence rules, in effect, cause the replacement of traditional interest rates with the APR.

Advertising disclosure requirements have been significantly revised under the new cost of credit disclosure rules and the following disclosure must now be made in advertisements published in provinces which have brought the new rules into force:

(i)   Fixed Credit Advertising

One of the most familiar forms of fixed credit advertising is vehicle purchase financing ads with headlines such as "Visit Ted's Auto Today! All our vehicles are available for 1.9% purchase financing for a limited time only!" followed by line after line of complex mice-type set out at the bottom of the page.

The harmonization rules have somewhat simplified the basic requirements for fixed credit finance advertising. An advertisement that offers fixed credit and discloses the interest rate payable or the amount of any payment to be made must disclose the following:

(1)   the APR for the credit agreement;
(2)   the term of the credit agreement; or

If the advertisement applies to a specifically identified good:

(3)   the cash price; and
(4)   the cost of borrowing of the product.

If the ad applies to a range of goods, the ad must disclose the cash price and cost of borrowing of a representative transaction and must identify the transaction as a representative transaction. "Representative transaction" means an example of a credit agreement that fairly depicts the credit agreements to which the ad applies.

In Ontario, Alberta and the proposed legislation in Saskatchewan and New Brunswick, there is an exemption from the disclosure of the total cost of borrowing for broadcast, radio and other time and space-limited advertisements. There is currently no similar exemption in the proposed B.C. or Manitoba legislation.

The equal prominence requirements for fixed credit advertising are as follows: the APR must be disclosed in equal prominence to any other information which necessitates the disclosure of the APR. For example, if a monthly payment is disclosed in the body of the ad, the APR must be disclosed in equal prominence to such payment.

(ii) Open Credit Advertising

The open credit advertising rules are applicable to such things as certain loans and lines of credit.

In Alberta and B.C., and in the proposed legislation in New Brunswick, if the open credit is not associated with a credit card, the APR must be disclosed, in equal prominence to any other information regarding the cost of open credit.

In Ontario, and the proposed legislation in Manitoba and Saskatchewan, the same rules apply to open credit advertising, whether associated with a credit card or otherwise. Open credit advertisements in Ontario and Saskatchewan must disclose:

(1) The annual interest rate payable under the credit agreement.
(2) The amount of any initial non-interest finance charge and any periodic non-interest finance charges. Initial non-interest finance charges include sign-up or joining fees. Periodic charges are monthly fees. NSF or withdrawal fees, which are not charged initially or on a periodic basis, are not required to be disclosed in advertising.

In Manitoba, open credit advertisements must state the annual interest rate and any non-interest finance charges for credit.

It is important to note that the annual interest rate required to be disclosed in Ontario, Saskatchewan and Manitoba is not the APR and does not need to be calculated based on the prescribed harmonized formula.

(iii) Credit Card Advertising

The Alberta and B.C. and proposed New Brunswick credit card advertising requirements are the same as those in force in Ontario and proposed in Saskatchewan and Manitoba. An advertisement which gives specific information about the cost of credit must disclose:

(1)   the current annual interest rate; and

(2)   any initial or periodic non-interest finance charges.

(iv) Advertising Interest-Free Periods

When advertising interest-free periods, advertisers must disclose whether the period is unconditionally interest-free, or whether interest accrues during the period but will be forgiven if certain conditions are met. In the latter case, the advertisement must state the conditions to be met and what the APR would be if the conditions are not met. For credit card advertising, the annual interest rate applicable if the conditions are not met must be disclosed. An ad that does not disclose any conditions or APR/annual interest rate if the conditions are not met, is deemed to represent that the transaction is unconditionally interest-free.

(v)   Lease Advertising

Under the harmonized regime, uniform disclosure requirements apply to lease advertising for the first time. Over the past few years, leasing has become very popular and now accounts for many new vehicle "purchases". The attraction of leases is short-term gain: a new and better car more often with monthly payments that are typically lower than finance payments for the same vehicle. However, over the long term, the cost of vehicle "ownership" is usually higher with leasing. Long term leases are a form of financing but until the harmonization rules were proposed, had not been treated as such by provincial cost of credit disclosure laws.

The harmonized lease disclosure requirements only apply if the lease: (a) is for a fixed term of 4 months or more; (b) is for an indefinite term or is renewed automatically until one of the parties takes positive steps to terminate it; or (c) is a residual obligation lease.

The biggest change imposed by the harmonized rules is the requirement that all lease ads which give specific information about the cost of a lease (for example, monthly payments, down payments) must disclose the lease APR. Lease advertising has traditionally focused on and disclosed down payments and monthly payments. Lenders may evaluate their lease offers in terms of APR but historically, consumers have not. Consumers will now need to be educated to think of leases as credit, and to comparison shop on the additional basis of APRs.

A lease advertisement must disclose:

(1)   That the transaction is a lease.

(2)   The lease APR.

(3)   The length of the lease term.

(4)   The amount of each pre-inception payment other than the monthly payments.

(5)   The fact that the payments are monthly and the amount of the monthly payment.
(6)   The nature and amount of any other payments required to be paid by the lessee in the ordinary course of events.
(7)   In Ontario and Alberta for a lease with a kilometre allowance of less than 20,000 km per year, the excess kilometre charge.

In the proposed legislation in Manitoba, the kilometre allowance and excess kilometre charge must always be disclosed, regardless of the actual allowance. In B.C. and in the proposed Saskatchewan legislation, there are currently no prescribed requirements for disclosure of excess kilometre charges.

Equal prominence rules apply to leases as well. The lease APR must be displayed as prominently as any other disclosed element of the cost of borrowing. As discussed above, lease advertisements have traditionally disclosed monthly payments. The equal prominence rules now require the lease APR to be disclosed in equal prominence to such monthly payments.

Advertisements that apply to a range of leases must disclose all required information for a representative lease. A representative lease refers to a lease that fairly depicts the leases to which the ad applies.

Television, radio and small space ads must disclose:

(1)   the fact that the agreement is a lease;
(2)   the amount of each pre-inception payment other than the monthly payment;
(3)   the length of the term; and
(4)   the lease APR.

Television, radio and small space ads must also disclose a toll-free telephone number or concurrent print ad where information about the length of the lease term and the APR can be obtained. In the proposed Manitoba legislation, it is sufficient to disclose an internet URL instead of the lease term and APR. There are no small space lease advertising exceptions in the B.C. rules.

(d) Disclosure Statements

The harmonized rules set out specific new requirements for disclosure in fixed credit, open credit, credit card and lease initial disclosure statements. There are also new prescribed requirements for credit card applications and open credit and credit card monthly statements.

(e) Other Fundamental Changes Under The Harmonized Rules

Under the harmonized rules there is a new cap on consumer liability under residual obligation leases. Residual obligation leases are leases under which the lessor is required to pay the difference, if any, between the estimated residual value of the leased goods and the actual realizable value of the leased goods at the end of the lease term. The cap is the estimated residual value of the leased goods at lease end minus the greater of:

(1)   the price at which the goods are sold;
(2)   80 per cent of the estimated residual value; and
(3)   the estimated residual value minus three monthly payments.

In Alberta, where this provision has been in force since 1999, finance companies are typically no longer offering residual obligation leases to consumers.

Under the harmonized rules, there is a right of cancellation and rebate for "optional services" of a continuing nature offered by a credit company or an associate of a credit company. An optional service is a service that is offered to a borrower in connection with a credit agreement that the borrower does not have to accept in order to enter into the agreement. In Ontario, B.C. and Manitoba, "associate" is not defined and therefore the application of this provision is untested.

(f) Rebates and the Wrye Decision

Prior to the new harmonized legislation coming into force, rebate/low financing programs were popular with car manufacturers and dealers. Under these incentive programs, buyers were given a choice between a rebate off the advertised cash price and a low financing rate. Choosing the low financing meant foregoing the cash rebate.

In the 1988 decision, *Re Motor Vehicle Manufacturers' Association and Wrye*,[13] the Ontario High Court took the position that the true cost of borrowing should include the amount of the rebate. Following this decision, rebate/low financing advertising in Ontario included an interest rate and cost of borrowing together with an "effective" interest rate with the foregone rebate factored in. The "effective" interest rate was always higher than the advertised low financing rate.

The *Wrye* analysis spread to other provinces and within 2-3 years, an "effective" interest rate and "effective" cost of borrowing were required across Canada. Nova Scotia went further and prohibited the advertise-

---

[13]   [1988] O.J. No. 265 (Ont. H.C.J.).

ment of anything other than the "effective" interest rate if the amount of the rebate was stated.

The *Wrye* decision and subsequent provincial guidelines (except in Nova Scotia) only dealt with the disclosure of the "effective" interest rate in advertisements which featured both the rebate and the low interest rate alternative. The provincial guidelines did not deal with ads which featured only one component of the alternative offer, nor did they deal with unadvertised rebates. Further, the guidelines only required the "effective" rate to be disclosed in mice type.

The new harmonized fixed credit financing APR calculation takes the *Wrye* decision one step further. The APR approximates previous "effective" interest rates in traditional rebate/low financing alternative offers. The harmonized rules now mandate that financing APRs be calculated based on the cash price at which the goods are sold to cash customers in the ordinary course of business, less any rebate offered only to cash customers. When the rebate is factored into the APR calculation, the APR is higher than the APR would be had there been no rebate offered to cash customers.

What makes the harmonized rules different from the previous provincial requirements based on *Wrye*, is that whether the rebate is advertised or not is not determinative for disclosure of the APR. If the promotion is structured such that it is a rebate/low financing alternative offer, the rebate must be factored into the financing APR and the APR must be disclosed in the ad. Further, the APR may not be disclosed in mice type. As discussed above, the APR must be disclosed in equal prominence to any other interest rate and therefore, in a rebate/low financing advertisement, the APR must be disclosed in equal prominence to the advertised low financing rate. Rebate/low financing alternative offers are not prohibited *per se* under the harmonized rules, but are now less valuable incentive programs because an advertiser must either (1) disclose only a higher and less attractive APR factoring in the rebate or; (2) advertise the low financing rate, with the higher APR shown in equal prominence with the resulting risk of confusing consumers with the display of two interest rates.

The same rules are applicable to leases. Although rebates are not specifically described in the formula for calculation of lease APR, the formula requires inclusion of the cash price of the goods sold to cash customers in the ordinary course of business. If in the ordinary course of business, dealers sell goods to cash customers at discounted prices, the discounted price must form part of the calculation of lease APR. Lease APR must be disclosed in equal prominence to any other disclosed element of the cost of borrowing.

The result is that instead of offering rebate or low interest rate alternative programs, manufacturers and dealers are making cash rebates "stackable". "Stackable" means that cash rebates traditionally offered only to cash customers are now also available to finance and lease customers in addition to special rates. A stackable offer might now be advertised with a headline which reads "$2,000 cash back and 1.9% APR!"

(g) The Current Status — National Advertising

Until all provinces have brought the harmonized rules into force, there will still be differences in required disclosures. Ideally, advertisers will one day be able to advertise nationally using one credit or lease disclaimer appropriate for all provinces. As a general rule, a national advertisement that is compliant in the province with the most onerous requirements, should be compliant nationally. However, with the current state of provincial cost of credit and lease advertising requirements, several issues arise with national advertising.

First, there will likely never be true national finance or lease advertisements because of the unique rules in Quebec and because Quebec does not intend to harmonize. Therefore, the best an advertiser can do in advertising credit and leasing nationally is to formulate unique Quebec disclaimers and attempt to formulate disclaimers applicable to the rest of Canada.

Second is the significant issue of disclosure of an interest rate under the harmonized rules versus the "old" rules still in force in several provinces. Finance or lease APR calculated in accordance with the prescribed formulas in Ontario, B.C. and Alberta is not the same as, for example, the financing rate currently disclosed in Nova Scotia. For now, national advertisers will have to consider disclosing at least two interest rates when the APR and any other interest rate are not the same.

The third issue pertains to the different list of required advertising disclosures in harmonized provinces versus the required disclosures in provinces with "old" credit advertising rules. For instance, under the "old" rules, monthly payments and total obligation for financing are required. A true national advertisement for financing should disclose interest rate and/or APR, term, cash price, monthly payments, cost of borrowing and total obligation in order to comply with existing rules and with the harmonized rules.

(h) Additional Disclosure

An interesting issue that arises out of the coming into force of the harmonized rules is whether the harmonized advertising disclosure requirements are sufficient to inform consumers making purchase (and lease) decisions.

Since, in most provinces, there were no previous legislative requirements pertaining to lease advertising, the consensus is that the harmonized lease advertising requirements provide for significantly more uniform disclosure to inform consumer decisions. However, certain useful information such as total lease obligation is not mandated by law.

This issue also arises with fixed credit finance advertising which, as stated above, requires disclosure of APR, term, cash price and cost of borrowing. Other disclosures which are potentially important to consumers, but which are not mandatory under the harmonized laws, are total obligation and monthly finance payments. Advertisers must consider whether disclosure of the minimum statutory requirements is enough to inform consumers and ensure that advertisements contain all material information.

(i) Provincial Self-Regulation

The motor vehicle dealer laws in several provinces delegate the regulatory power governing dealer licensing and advertising to a provincial motor dealer council. Typically, the jurisdiction of these councils extends only to dealers and dealer associations in the province, but not manufacturers. Several provincial motor dealer councils have published advertising guidelines. The guidelines often require additional disclosures beyond what is required by the basic cost of credit rules discussed above.

The B.C. Motor Dealer Council has published updated *Advertising Guidelines*, which were in force as of November 2005. The *Advertising Guidelines* provide detailed direction for dealers regarding price, financing, leasing and other vehicle advertising issues. Under the *Advertising Guidelines*, credit advertisements must disclose all that is required under the new cost of credit disclosure legislation in B.C., and in addition, the number and amount of the monthly payments and the total obligation under the credit offer. For lease advertising, the terms required in the legislation must be included and, in addition, the total lease obligation and the buy-out amount where applicable. Oddly, total obligation for both lease and finance must include taxes, and the "tax-in" total obligation must be disclosed at least as prominently as the monthly payments in advertising. Other highlights from the *Advertising Guidelines* include that O.A.C. is no longer an acceptable abbreviation. "On approved credit" must be spelled out. The Guidelines permit advertising the fact that extended warranties are available, but the disclosure of any other information regarding the extended warranty triggers extensive additional disclosure such as a clear description of the coverage, the term of coverage, that the extended warranty is optional and has a limited cancellation policy. Also, the Guidelines prohibit advertising a vehicle unless the photo exactly matches the advertised vehicle. Even for minor differences, the disclaimer "vehicle may not be exactly as shown" is likely insufficient.

The Ontario Motor Vehicle Industry Council ("OMVIC") also has published detailed advertising guidelines as part of its *Standards of Business Practice*. The latest version was published in 2000, and has not been updated since the Ontario *Consumer Protection Act, 2002*, came into force. Like the B.C. Motor Dealer Council *Advertising Guidelines*, the OMVIC guidelines provide detailed direction regarding price, finance, lease and general vehicle advertising issues for Ontario motor vehicle dealers.

The Manitoba Motor Dealers Association has published *Advertising and Marketing Guidelines* updated to January 2000.

The Alberta Motor Vehicle Industry Council has also published basic advertising guidelines. As of March 1, 2006, the amended *Automotive Business Regulation*[14] to the *Fair Trading Act* is in force. The amended Regulation contains a detailed advertising Code of Conduct applicable to dealers in the province. Highlights from the Code of Ethics include that a dealer ad:

*   Must not use a font that due to its size or other visual characteristics is likely to materially impair the legibility or clarity of the advertisement and, without limiting the generality of the foregoing, in no case uses a font size smaller than eight points.
*   Include in the advertised price for any vehicle the total cost of the vehicle, including, but not limited to, all fees and charges such as the cost of accessories, optional equipment physically attached to the vehicle, transportation charges and any applicable taxes or administration fees, but not including GST or costs and charges associated with financing.
*   Must not use the words, or words similar to, "savings", "discount", "percentage off the purchase price", "free", "invoice price", "below invoice", "dealer's cost", "at cost" or a price that is a specified amount above or below invoice or cost unless the claims represented by the words can be substantiated.
*   Should not imply a warranty exists with respect to a vehicle or a repair or service unless such a warranty with respect to the vehicle, repair or service exists and is available at the price advertised.
*   Cannot offer a guaranteed trade-in allowance for any vehicle regardless of make, year or condition.
*   Should include the stock number of the specific vehicle that is advertised as being available for sale at the time the advertisement is placed.

---

[14]   AR 192/1999.

(j)   A Note On Total Price

Several provinces, including B.C., Alberta, Saskatchewan, Manitoba and Newfoundland, have provisions in their consumer protection or business practice legislation which state that it is deceptive to give less prominence to the total price of goods when advertising the price of a unit or installment. Some provinces, including B.C., have interpreted this to mean that known charges, specifically freight and pre-delivery inspection ("PDI") costs should be included in the advertised price of a vehicle.

The B.C. *Motor Dealer Act Regulation*[15] and the amended Alberta *Automotive Business Regulation*, including the advertising Code of Conduct (as discussed above), specifically require that when dealers advertise a vehicle price it must include freight and PDI and the cost of accessories and optional equipment physically attached to the vehicle shown.

I.   CLASS ACTIONS IN QUEBEC

In October 2002, the Union des Consommateurs of Quebec/Billette filed a petition for leave to bring a class action against 11 major car manufacturers in Canada that lease or finance automobiles. The petitioner leased an automobile and was invoiced $46 by the company for a security registration fee. The petitioner claimed that the fee was not disclosed in any written or broadcast advertising by the company, and as such, amounted to an illegal commercial practice under the Quebec *Consumer Protection Act*. The Quebec Consumer's Association estimated that there were 800,000 people affected by the advertising in question. The petition claims a refund of the $46 expense, $100 in damages and $100 in exemplary damages for each member of the affected class. The petition for leave to bring the class action has been granted by the Superior Court of Quebec.

In November 2002, the Union des Consommateurs of Quebec and its designated class member, Christian Contat, brought another petition for leave to bring a class action suit against eight automobile manufacturers and their credit companies under the Quebec *Consumer Protection Act*. It is alleged that car manufacturers offered incentive programs whereby consumers were offered low financing rates, or a price reduction on the vehicle if they paid cash. The petition alleges that the cash reduction actually represented undisclosed credit charges and should be included in the advertised interest rate. The Consumer's Association estimated that practically everyone who purchased or leased a new vehicle from the

---

[15]   B.C. Reg. 447/78.

defendant companies since November 1999 was affected by the advertising. The Petitioner seeks to indemnify consumers by way of a reimbursement equivalent to the hidden credit charges as well as general damages and punitive damages. The action has not yet been certified as a class action by the Courts, but a hearing took place in October 2005, on the motion for leave to bring the class action.

Another petition for leave to bring a class action has recently been brought by Petitioner Danielle Fournier against eight Canadian banks on behalf of all individuals in Quebec who, from December 16, 2002 until final judgment, had to pay fees for the Registry of Personal and Movable Real Rights ("RPMRR") in excess of the actual cost, to one of the respondent banks. Petitioner Fournier alleges that on May 28, 2004, she financed a vehicle through the Bank of Nova Scotia and was charged a $56.30 RPMRR fee. The actual fee for registration was $34 and as such, she was charged $22.30 in excess and without justification. She seeks, for each member of the class, a reimbursement of the $22.30 or any excess amount charged, $100 damages and $100 in punitive damages. The action has not yet been certified.

The Quebec class actions are a warning to all advertisers that disclosure requirements must be taken seriously, not just in Quebec, but in all provinces where class actions are a right of action available to consumers.

Chapter 5

CONTESTS AND PROMOTIONS

A. INTRODUCTION

Contests, promotions and loyalty programs take up a growing share of marketing budgets as retailers and manufacturers compete to attract and hold the attention of consumers. From the time-honoured $1 off coupon to talking beer cans and complicated online auctions, incentive offers are everywhere, and the legal issues multiply as the offers get more complicated.

This is an area of marketing law that involves many cautionary tales of promotions gone horribly wrong. The legal rules that govern contests are not particularly complex. There are the "illegal lotteries" provisions in the *Criminal Code*,[1] the disclosure requirements in the *Competition Act*,[2] Quebec's *Act respecting lotteries, publicity contests and amusement machines*[3] and the common law of contracts. Unfortunately, minor oversights in legal compliance can have major repercussions.

Many marketers assume they know the essentials of promotion law. In order to shatter any illusions of security, this chapter is structured differently. It opens with disaster stories and goes on to explain the rules that will help you avoid them.

B. TEN TALES OF CONTEST AND PROMOTION NIGHTMARES

1. "Just Kidding"

In 1997, Pepsi launched a massive rewards program called "Pepsi Stuff". The merchandise was the usual branded teenage stuff like clothing, baseball caps and drinking glasses. A television commercial announcing the program featured various rewards and their value in Pepsi Points. The

---

[1] R.S.C. 1985, c. C-46.
[2] R.S.C. 1985, c. C-34.
[3] R.S.Q., c. L-6.

commercial closed with a shot of a Harrier jet and the superimposed punchline: "Harrier Fighter: 7,000,000 Pepsi Points".

Under the program, you could order Pepsi Stuff with a combination of Pepsi Points acquired from specially marked Pepsi bottles and Pepsi Points purchased at a cost of ten cents each.

A Seattle resident set out to acquire the Harrier jet. He collected a certain number of points and submitted a cheque for the remainder of the 7 million required points. His lawyers contacted Pepsi to arrange delivery of the jet.

Pepsi took the case to court for a declaratory judgment. The court obliged with a 1999 decision that declared that no reasonable person could have concluded that Pepsi was really giving away a Harrier jet. Although Pepsi won, it was an expensive lesson. When Pepsi ran the commercial in Canada, they added a precautionary super opposite the Harriet jet: "Just kidding".

Moral: there are many "professional contestants" who will exploit any loophole in your contest.

2.   Thrilla In Manilla

In the Philippines in 1992, in an under-the-bottle-cap promotion called "Number Fever", Pepsi intended to award one $50,000 prize. However, due to "computer errors", some 800,000 bottle caps were distributed with the winning number 349.

Pepsi offered to pay $20 to anyone with a winning cap. The offer fizzled. Bombs were thrown into Pepsi bottling plants, two people died in "Coalition 349" riots and all foreign-born Pepsi executives were withdrawn from the country. Twenty-two thousand people filed lawsuits for fraud and deception and "Coalition 349" candidates even ran in subsequent parliamentary elections. Pepsi ended up paying approximately $10 million dollars in goodwill gestures. Although all of the lawsuits were dismissed, the damages to Pepsi's reputation were incalculable. Pepsi's share of the soft drink market in the Philippines dropped from 25 per cent to 16 per cent and "Number Fever" is still a vivid (and presumably bitter) memory to many Filipinos.

Moral: Even with iron-clad contest rules which protect promoters from a legal standpoint, when printing or production errors result in too many prizes being seeded, the rules cannot prevent massive public relations problems when a game goes wrong.

3.   The Ticking Milk Bomb

Several years ago, the Dairy Farmers of Ontario launched an innovative "talking pack" contest called "Moo You Win". Milk drinkers had a chance to win prizes such as ski vacations and snowboard gear if their carton "Moo'd" when it was opened.

An employee at Toronto's Eaton Centre called security when she noticed the two wires on a winning carton. The Metro Police arrived, took one look at the carton and ordered the immediate evacuation of the mall. A bomb squad expert x-rayed the carton, saw the wiring and the microchip and ordered that the carton be blown up. The mall was closed for three hours and more than 35 police officers, firemen, and ambulance workers were deployed before someone was able to convince officials that they were dealing with a promotional device.

Despite this unfortunate incident, "Moo You Win" was a very successful promotion and still continues to this day.

Moral: Anticipate the absolute worst case scenario.

4.   He Shoots! He Scores!

In 1994, Coca-Cola ran a sweepstakes with the Florida Panthers. The Grand Prize was the chance to win $1 million by shooting a hockey puck across the full length of the hockey rink into a "special small goal" at a Florida Panthers home game.

Randy Giunto was one of the Grand Prize winners. Prior to taking his shot, Mr. Giunto signed an agreement which included a stipulation that the puck had to "pass completely through" the goal. From a distance of 118 feet, he managed to shoot the puck partly through a very small opening. The contest judge declared his shot invalid. Mr. Giunto sued the contest sponsors for the million dollar prize. The case hinged on the agreement he had signed. In particular, a clause that declared that the contest judge was the final arbiter as to whether a shot had passed "completely through" the goal. Giunto lost his case and Coca-Cola's lawyers were doubtlessly very happy about the fine print in their contract.

Moral: There is a reason for lawyers and fine print.

5.   The Clever Contestant

The prize for "Cleverest Contestant" should go to a Mr. Johnson of California. In 1989, a gas company ran a contest called "Licence Plate Jackpot". Every week a randomly selected licence plate number was posted in service stations. If your licence plate number exactly matched the posted number, you could win a new BMW 325.

Mr. Johnson used public records to track down the owner of the car with one of the winning licence plate numbers. He bought the car for $650 and used it to claim the BMW. The promotion house learned of these maneuvers and claimed that Johnson's claim was not "legitimate" within the meaning of the contest rules. The case went to court. The Court found that a reasonable person applying the Official Rules to these facts could not fairly conclude that Johnson had failed to meet the "obtain legitimately" provision. Johnson was awarded damages for breach of contract equal to the value of the BMW.

Moral: There are many professional contestants who will exploit any loophole in your contest.

6. Popsicle Points

In the summer of 1990, Popsicle Industries ran a "Popsicle Points" program with Nintendo games offered as the ultimate reward if you accumulated 15,000 points. Nintendo games were extremely popular among the Popsicle crowd. Despite the fact that the hurdles were high — you had to collect as many as 750 Popsicle sticks to amass the required points — the demand far exceeded Popsicle's estimate of 2,000 Nintendo games. Popsicle Industries stopped honouring the Nintendo game requests when the number exceeded 3,700 and offered other less expensive rewards in their stead. Not surprisingly, there were many complaints. To the target group, there was no acceptable substitute for a Nintendo game. Popsicle was charged under section 74.06 of the *Competition Act*, which requires timely distribution of prizes in a promotional contest. Following its guilty plea, Popsicle Industries was fined $200,000 and required to offer its approximately 4,500 unhappy customers a choice of three video games free of charge. In the end, Popsicle Industries had underestimated demand for the Nintendo game rewards by a factor of four or five. The public relations fiasco was predictable. The legal consequences were equally predictable given Popsicle's remarkable failure to deliver on its promise.

Moral: Always overestimate demand and be prepared to meet unexpected demand.

7. Charity Scam

Big-ticket hospital lotteries have become a favourite fund-raising device. Luxury cars, exotic vacations and "dream homes" are the incentives, along with the opportunity to make a charitable donation. In 1998, The Children's Hospital of Eastern Ontario held a lottery in which the Grand Prize was a "dream home". Tickets cost $100 but when the winner was selected, the Hospital discovered that he had paid with an NSF cheque. Because other selected entrants who had "paid" with NSF cheques were allowed to make good on their payments, the same opportunity was extended to the Grand Prize winner. He paid his $100 in cash and won a dream home. The Hospital changed the official rules for subsequent lotteries to void any ticket that had not been paid in full before the draw.

Moral: Experience is a great teacher. Many things that go wrong with contests could not have been anticipated.

8. Scratch & Save 10%

The Hudson's Bay Company has a long-standing tradition of Scratch & Save Days where shoppers can "win" a discount ranging from 10 per cent to 25 per cent off the purchase price of selected merchandise. The discounts are awarded through game cards with a special scratch area revealing the "prize": a 10, 15, 20, or 25 per cent discount.

In 1998, Simpson's (since acquired by The Bay) was prosecuted under the *Competition Act* and fined $100,000 for a similar promotion. The one day event featured "mini casino" cards with four tabs; under each tab was a certain percentage discount. Advertising for the promotion promised savings of "10% - 25% on practically everything in the store". Although the appearance of the casino cards implied a range of discounts under the tabs, 90 per cent of the cards had the 10 per cent discount printed under all four tabs. Simpson's was convicted under *The Competition Act* for failing to disclose information that materially affected the odds of winning on the actual game card: *i.e.*, that only 10 per cent of the game cards had a chance of containing more than a 10% discount.

Moral: In every seeded contest, the odds of winning each kind of prize must be stated on promotional pieces and not just "buried" in the contest rules.

9. 15 Big Chances to Win!

Thirty years ago, when Canadian contest law was in its infancy, Kraft conducted a contest in which it advertised "15 Big Chances to Win!" Although the contest was nationally advertised, the prizes were awarded on a regional basis — three each for Quebec and Ontario, two for British Columbia and one for each of the remaining provinces/territories. Draws were conducted over time in each province but Kraft failed to disclose the regional prize allocation and continued to advertise "15 Big Chances to Win!" after some of the prizes had been awarded. In fact, the best placed contestants — those in Ontario and Quebec — had only three "Big Chances to Win!" at the outset of the contest. On these facts, Kraft was convicted of misleading advertising and fined.

Moral: Regional allocation of prizes must be clearly stated. This is a *Competition Act* requirement. In addition, contest materials must clearly state that the number of prizes will diminish as prizes are claimed.

The preceding cautionary tales only skim the surface. Many U.S. contest lawyers spend much of their time in court. To avoid that possibility, it is important to understand the law as set out in the following section.

10. The Ground Rules

Every contest and incentive program is a contract between the promoter and participants. The terms of the contract are set out in either the contest rules or the terms and conditions of the offer. Most advertisers wouldn't sign a business contract without careful attention to the legal side, but many people in marketing do not realize the legal implications of the contracts they regularly extend to consumers in the form of contests and premium offers.

Contest rules must be comprehensive, unambiguous and clearly communicated to consumers. The same applies to the terms and conditions of other incentive programs. If these contracts are incomplete or poorly drafted and you have to rely on them in court, be aware of the legal rule of *contra preferendum*. Any ambiguity in a contract is interpreted against the party who drafted the contract: in this case, the promoter or advertiser.

To assist in understanding the potential issues and weeding through the legal boilerplate, there are draft contest rules set out later in this chapter. In a good set of rules or terms and conditions, every word is there for a reason.

Equally important is the applicable legislation. Promotional contests are governed by the *Competition Act*, the *Criminal Code* and Quebec's *Act respecting lotteries, alcohol, publicity contests and amusement machines*.

Before discussing the law, we will briefly define some terms. Contests can be divided into two broad categories: skill contests and contests where prizes are awarded at random. Skill contests — where winners are selected by experienced judges based on the contestants' skill at storywriting, photography, *etc.* — are rare. Much more common, in fact ubiquitous, are contests where winners are randomly selected.

These include sweepstakes — where prizes are awarded by random draw; seeded games (including Coke's "under the bottle cap" promotions and Tim Hortons' "Roll Up the Rim to Win") where prizes are randomly seeded on game cards or on-pack and participants must scratch, unpeel or otherwise reveal the prize area to discover whether they have won a prize; on-line instant win games where consumers enter a code number (usually obtained on-pack); "match and win" games where participants must collect game pieces to spell specific words or match the pieces of a puzzle. "Match and win" games are usually structured to include "rare pieces" which make the odds of winning a major prize astronomical. There are as many varieties of random contests as imaginative marketers can devise.

C. THE CRIMINAL CODE

Sweepstakes, scratch and win games and other contests where prizes are awarded by chance are classified as "lotteries" by the *Criminal Code*. The common law defines a lottery as a scheme with the following three elements: a prize, an award by chance and money or other consideration paid by participants. Lotteries have been illegal for several hundred years, unless they are government sponsored. In 1802, *The English Gaming Act* addressed the problem as follows:

> Whereas evil disposed Persons do frequently resort to Public Houses and other Places, to set up certain mischievous Games or Lotteries ... and to induce Servants, Children, and unwary Persons to play at the said Games and thereby... most fraudulently obtain great sums of Money from Servants, Children and Unwary Persons, to the great Impoverishment and utter Ruin of many Families...

In order to avoid being classified as an illegal lottery, you have to remove either chance *or* consideration from your promotion. (You could also remove the prize or prizes, but that would probably defeat your purpose.)

There are two ways to deal with the question of chance. The most straightforward is to eliminate chance altogether by conducting a pure skill contest. A juried art show is at the high end of skill contests but there are many other skill contests which are accessible to a broad range of consumers. For example, Kodak frequently conducts photography contests to showcase its cameras and film; mass-market magazines hold writing contests; software companies hold contests to select creative applications of their products.

The good thing about skill contests is that in most cases purchase requirements are perfectly legal. Contestants can be required to buy and use your products (*e.g.*, Canon cameras, Corel Draw) as part of their contest submissions. Technically, you could even charge entry fees.

The difficult thing about skill contests is the selection process. The judging criteria must be clearly communicated to contestants and the judge or judges must painstakingly and fairly apply those criteria to hundreds or thousands of entries.

The other way to deal with the question of chance is by adding an element of skill to a random selection process. Hence the ubiquitous skill-testing question requirement. The most common skill question is a three or four part mathematical question. The question is often found on entry forms in a contest where many prizes will be awarded. In a contest with relatively few prizes, the skill-testing question is typically administered by telephone, mail or e-mail.

The preference for mathematical questions has two sources. First, it is the easiest solution to the contest promoter's dilemma: skill is required but promoters do not want contestants to get the answer wrong. Second, there is a long line of old Canadian cases that hold that various non-mathematical feats — such as shooting a turkey from a distance of 50 yards — do not constitute sufficient "skill" to avoid the "illegal lottery" prohibition.

The other "illegal lottery" element that must be eliminated in most (but not all) cases is a purchase requirement — what lawyers call "consideration". This is a complicated question. There are circumstances in which a purchase requirement may be legal, for example, where a contest's prizes consist exclusively of cash and/or other intangibles like vacations or tickets to a concert. A purchase requirement is also legal where contestants have made their purchase before the fact; *e.g.*, a contest restricted to current Chrysler owners.

There is also considerable debate about what constitutes a "purchase requirement". For example, does an internet contest involve a purchase requirement in the form of internet access fees? The answer is probably no, because the internet is so widely available in Canada.

In most cases, the simple answer to the purchase requirement issue is to add a No Purchase option. If game cards are distributed with the product, you should have a write-in address for "free" game cards. If contest submissions require a UPC, facsimiles of the UPC should be accepted.

It is difficult to define with clarity the parameters of legal and illegal lotteries. In part, this is due to the case law. Canadian contest cases are relatively rare and frequently contradictory. In large part, the difficulty stems from the obtuse language used in the "illegal lotteries" provisions of the *Criminal Code*. These provisions are reproduced below. After reading them, you will understand why contest lawyers are necessary.

206(1) Every one is guilty of an indictable offence and liable to imprisonment for a term not exceeding two years, who

(a) makes, prints, advertises or publishes, or causes or procures to be made, printed, advertised or published, any proposal, scheme or plan for advancing, lending, giving, selling or in any way disposing of any property by lots, cards, tickets or any mode of chance whatever;

(b) sells, barters, exchanges or otherwise disposes of, or causes or procures, or aids or assists in, the sale, barter, exchange or other disposal of, or offers for sale, barter or exchange, any lot, card, ticket or other means or device for advancing, lending, giving, selling or otherwise disposing of any property by lots, tickets or any mode of chance whatever;

(c) knowingly sends, transmits, mails, ships, delivers or allows to be sent, transmitted, mailed, shipped or delivered, or knowingly accepts for carriage or transport or conveys any article that is used or intended for use in carrying out any device, proposal, scheme or plan for advancing, lending, giving, selling or otherwise disposing of any property by any mode of chance whatever;

(d) conducts or manages any scheme, contrivance or operation of any kind for the purpose of determining who, or the holders of what lots, tickets, numbers or chances, are the winners of any property so proposed to be advanced, lent, given, sold or disposed of;

(e) conducts, manages or is a party to any scheme, contrivance or operation of any kind by which any person, on payment of any sum of money, or the giving of any valuable security, or by obligating himself to pay any sum of money or give any valuable security, shall become entitled under the scheme, contrivance or operation to receive from the person conducting or managing the scheme, contrivance or operation, or any other person, a larger sum of money or amount of valuable security than the sum or amount paid or given, or to be paid or given, by reason of the fact that other persons have paid or given, or obligated themselves to pay or give any sum of money or valuable security under the scheme, contrivance or operation;

(f) disposes of any goods, wares or merchandise by any game of chance or any game of mixed chance and skill in which the contestant or competitor pays money or other valuable consideration;

(g) induces any person to stake or hazard any money or other valuable property or thing on the result of any dice game, three-card monte, punch board, coin table or on the operation of a wheel of fortune;

(h) for valuable consideration carries on or plays or offers to carry on or to play, or employs any person to carry on or play in a public place or a place to which the public have access, the game of three-card monte;

(i) receives bets of any kind on the outcome of a game of three-card monte; or

(j) being the owner of a place, permits any person to play the game of three-card monte therein.

. . .

(4) Every one who buys, takes or receives a lot, ticket or other device mentioned in subsection (1) is guilty of an offence punishable on summary conviction.

. . .

(7) This section applies to the printing or publishing, or causing to be printed or published, of any advertisement, scheme, proposal or plan of any foreign lottery, and the sale or offer for sale of any ticket, chance or share, in any such lottery, or the advertisement for sale of such ticket, chance or share, and the conducting or managing of any such scheme, contrivance or operation for determining the winners in any such lottery.

D. THE COMPETITION ACT

Assuming your contest has been structured to comply with the *Criminal Code*, you still have to deal with section 74.06 of the *Competition Act*. This section prohibits contests, lotteries, games of chance or skill and games of mixed chance and skill unless organizers can ensure that:

(a) there is adequate and fair disclosure of the number and approximate value of the prizes, of the area or areas to which they relate and of any fact within the knowledge of the advertiser that materially affects the odds of winning;

(b) distribution of the prizes is not unduly delayed; and

(c) selection of participants or distribution of prizes is made on the basis of skill or on a random basis in any area to which prizes have been allocated.

The third requirement appears to be irrelevant to all legitimate contests. It does, however, prohibit deliberately selecting a friend or family member as a winner.

The other two requirements are more problematic.

The first requirement deals with "adequate and fair" disclosure to consumers of certain contest information: the number and value of the prizes, and regional allocation of prizes (if your contest is structured to award one second prize per province, for example, and one grand prize nationally, this must be properly disclosed) and any facts that materially affect the odds of winning. In a sweepstakes, the odds of winning are dependent on the number of eligible entries received. Arguably, this is self-evident and doesn't need to be disclosed. With scratch and win games and other seeded promotions, however, the odds of winning a particular prize can be stated with precision. If a scratch and win game has multiple prizes, the easiest way to make disclosure is with a chart which describes each prize and the number, value and odds of winning that prize. This information should always be disclosed in "mini-rules" on packaging, point of sale materials and on the back of game cards.

The Commissioner of Competition takes the position that disclosure should be made in a *reasonably conspicuous manner prior to the potential entrant being inconvenienced in some way*. The onus should not be on consumers to obtain further details which, by statute, are required to be disclosed by the contest sponsor nor should consumers be required to visit a particular retail outlet in order to become "adequately and fairly" informed.

The conservative view is that the disclosure required by the *Competition Act* (prize information and odds of winning) should be in all contest advertising. This is often not feasible — a radio spot has time constraints; billboards and television advertisements are not appropriate media for communicating details of a typical scratch and win game. An acceptable compromise is posting the official contest rules on a website and including the website address and a write-in address or a toll-free number in all contest advertising. Most Canadians have access to the internet, so when contest information is available online or through a write-in address, consumers can access it before they visit a store or make a purchase decision.

The second *Competition Act* requirement[4] is that prize distribution not be unduly delayed. This requirement has rarely been an issue. However, Popsicle Industries was convicted under the predecessor section in 1990 for a Popsicle Points promotion in which the company ran out of the advertised Nintendo game awards.

The other *Competition Act* section which is frequently applied to contests is the prohibition against false or misleading advertising. It goes without saying that the general principles of advertising law — that all representations be truthful and not misleading — apply to contest advertising.

E.   CONTESTS, COUPONS, INCENTIVE PROGRAMS, REBATES AND OTHER PROMOTIONAL OFFERS

1.   A through Z

Alcohol: Every province has different guidelines concerning the kinds of contests and promotions that alcohol manufacturers and licensees are allowed to conduct. These are long and complicated and are summarized in Chapter 11. However, alcohol promotions require pre-approval by several of the provincial liquor boards and should not be attempted without a careful review of the latest provincial requirements.

Automatic Entry: There are several common mechanisms for automatic contest entry. Scratch and win prize claimants can be automatically entered in a second tier sweepstakes; consumers who complete an online questionnaire can be automatically in a contest. The most common form of automatic entry is through use of a credit card. The problem with "swipe and enter" contests is no purchase entry. Non-purchasers must be allowed to enter approximately as often as the typical card user will use their card during the contest period.

Bonds: Quebec's *Lotteries Act* allows the Régie des alcools, des courses et des jeux (the "Régie") to require a security bond for contests open to Quebec residents if the contest sponsor does not have a place of business in Quebec or the value of any single prize exceeds $5,000 or the total prize value exceeds $20,000. The security bond is a one-page document that is sent to sponsors after registration with the Régie. It provides security for the prizes until they have been awarded or until the Régie has been notified that there are no winners from Quebec. The security bond is typically completed by the sponsor's bank or insurance company.

---

[4]   Section 74.06(b).

Cancellation: Sometimes a contest goes horribly wrong. A printing error results in thousands of Grand Prize claims; an online game crashes because of a software glitch or the intervention of hackers. The contest rules should anticipate these situations and allow the sponsor to cancel the contest (with the approval of the Régie in Quebec). The cancellation should be announced at point-of-sale, in print and broadcast advertisements if appropriate and on the sponsor's website. Moreover, if there are legitimate prize claimants before the cancellation is announced, the contest rules should allow you to award the advertised number of prizes by random draw among those claimants.

Cash Prizes: The wonderful thing about cash prizes is they may, in certain circumstances, allow you to have a purchase requirement (provided no other prizes consist of "goods, wares or merchandise" and your contest can stay out of 206(1)(e)). The other advantage of cash is that it is not an inherently dangerous prize.

Charities: Charities (such as hospital foundations) can obtain a licence from the province or municipality to hold a lottery or run a casino as a fund-raising event. The number of licences for any type of event is usually limited and the application process is long and complicated. Allow plenty of lead-time and consider hiring a consultant who is familiar with the process.

Child-directed Contests: Contests directed at children should include, on the entry form, space for the name and signature of a parent or legal guardian. This ensures that a responsible adult has consented to the child's participation in the contest. It also ensures that you have a contact for the winning entrants. The prizes should be awarded to the parent/legal guardian of the winners who should also sign the release forms on behalf of the winning children. Child-directed advertising, including contest advertising, is prohibited in Quebec with certain exceptions. In-store displays, on-pack advertising and advertisements in children's magazines are all permitted provided you follow the Regulations under the *Consumer Protection Act*. Quebec defines "children" as anyone under the age of 13. If you are planning a children's contest for Quebec you *should proceed with caution* and expert advice.

Closed Universe: There are situations in which a purchase can be required of a closed universe of participants if the purchase was made without any knowledge of the contest. For example, a car company could restrict a contest to current owners of its vehicles. In this scenario, the purchase was not made in order to participate in the contest. Similarly, you can hold a contest at a fair, trade show or amusement park that has an entry fee provided you do not advertise the contest outside that venue.

Competition Act: The *Competition Act* regulates contests conducted by telemarketers (see below) and requires that all contest advertising be truthful and not misleading. In addition, there are specific provisions governing proper disclosure of certain contest information (the number, value and odds of winning each type of prize; any regional allocation of prizes) and requiring that the distribution of prizes not be unduly delayed.

Coupons: Coupons are a relatively simple device. The complications usually arise with fraud in the redemption process. The typical in-store coupon features a prominent savings claim on the front: ("Save 50$^¢$ now on the purchase of any Dove® beauty bar") along with a beauty shot of the featured product and a statement that details are on the back. The offer should be clear. Do not use the word "any" if certain SKU's are excluded. On the back, there is dealer and consumer copy. The following language is standard:

> TO THE DEALER: Price Co. will reimburse you for the coupon's face value plus our specified handling fee provided it is redeemed by your customer at the time of purchase of any item(s) specified. Other applications may constitute fraud. Failure to send in, on request, evidence that sufficient stock was purchased in the previous 90 days to cover coupons submitted will void coupons. Coupons submitted become our property. Reproduction of this coupon is expressly prohibited. For redemption, mail to: [address].

> TO THE CONSUMER: Provincial Law may require the retailer to charge the applicable tax on the full value of the purchase(s) before the reduction in coupon value. GST, HST, QST and PST are included in face value, where applicable. Limit: one coupon per purchase. No facsimiles. Offer valid in Canada only and may not be combined with any other offers. COUPON EXPIRY DATE: _____ .

This coupon language is definitely not elegant but it works. One word of caution: OTC drug coupons are prohibited by Quebec's *Pharmacy Act*.

Deadline Extension: Occasionally, sponsors want to extend the contest deadline. This is usually a desperate measure when contest participation has been lower than expected. Ordinarily, we would never recommend extension of a typical "sweepstakes" contest. If the contest rules do not allow you to change the rules, extending the deadline amounts to a breach of contract and prejudices those contestants who met the original deadline. Even if the rules allow the deadline to be extended, the approval of the Régie will be required in Quebec; the extension must be prominently featured in all contest advertising and point of sale materials; and there is still a risk of a class action.

Distribution of Prizes: The *Competition Act* requires that the distribution of prizes not be unduly delayed. This section has been applied to incentive programs which fail to deliver advertised rewards. The Régie in Quebec requires a winners' list (or final report) to be filed 60 days after the draw date. If some of the prizes have not been awarded, the Régie requires an explanation: *i.e.*, how many times did you attempt to contact a winner, by what means, *etc.* In general, 60 days is a good "rule of thumb". If prizes have not been awarded within this time, either you have a major problem on your hands or you have not been very diligent.

Eligibility: Except in Quebec, there is no legal requirement that employees, officers and agents of the contest sponsor be excluded from contests. This restriction is typically added to contest rules to prevent prizes being awarded to "inappropriate" winners. In Quebec, the *Lotteries Act* requires that the following people be precluded from participating in contests:

> A person for whom a publicity contest is carried on, his employee, representative or agent, a member of the jury and the persons with whom they are domiciled.

In drafting eligibility clauses, you should take certain factors into account:

(a)   consider whether or not to include Quebec residents;

(b)   consider whether to limit the contest to people over the age of majority. Are the prizes appropriate for children? Do you want to obtain a release from the parents of winners who are under the age of majority?;

(c)   if the contest excludes employees "and family members of employees", "family member" should be defined. Further, it is possible that exclusion of family members might be discrimination based on family status. It may be simpler to exclude people living in the same household as the employees;

(d)   contests should not directly discriminate against any of the categories of people protected by human rights legislation. For example, a clause such as "This contest is not open to same-sex couples" will invariably invite a complaint. Many contests indirectly discriminate against one or more of the protected categories. For example, "Young Writers" contests or contests offering a "Family vacation" as a prize. Whether or not this kind of "adverse impact" discrimination is unlawful will depend on the circumstances and the evolving case law.

Fraud: There is no limitation on the creativity of so-called "professional contestants" and others who want to "win" a contest at any cost. The problem of outright fraud arises with seeded games such as scratch and win games, when winning game pieces can be stolen or forged. To prevent this, anti-counterfeiting measures should be used for valuable game pieces and contest rules should specify that all prize claims are subject to verification and that the decisions of the contest judges with respect to the authenticity of prize claims are final and binding. The most common problems with sweepstakes are multiple entries by the same contestant and prizes which are claimed by ineligible participants. Most contest rules limit the number of entries per person, address and/or e-mail address. This limitation is fine provided it is enforceable. It is difficult, however, to weed out multiple entries when a contest involves many thousands of entries. At a minimum, contest rules should prohibit mechanically reproduced entries and should require that every mail-in entry be separately mailed with sufficient postage.

In terms of eligibility, no major prizes should be awarded before the winner's eligibility has been verified. It is difficult, although not impossible, to retract a prize that has been wrongly awarded to a store manager's husband or wife. Many contest sponsors require potential winners to sign an affidavit of eligibility. Contest rules should include a clause that allows the sponsor to terminate the contest or alter the contest rules at any time without notice. This may allow you to close a loophole that professional contestants have discovered. The best protection against fraud and bad faith entrants is a carefully drafted set of contest rules. That said, there is no such thing as bulletproof contest rules.

Gambling: Gambling is illegal in Canada, unless it is government-sanctioned. Apart from government-run lotteries and licensed casinos, the only legal gambling is conducted by charities and fairs pursuant to licences granted by the municipality in which the event will be held. The number of licences for any type of event is limited and the application process is complicated.

Incentive Programs: Employee incentive programs have a great deal in common with contests. However, they are not contests, and contest language, such as "prizes" and "winners", should be avoided. Incentive programs involve "rewards" that employees receive when they meet certain performance criteria. These criteria are usually sales related. Incentive programs often involve several benchmarks with increasingly more valuable rewards. Like contests, incentive programs involve a contract between the sponsor (or employer) and participants. The terms of this contract should be clearly and comprehensively set out in the program rules.

Insurance: Every contest sponsor should have insurance coverage to protect against contest disasters (*e.g.*, printing or production errors, website failure, lawsuits by contestants). In addition, sponsors should ensure that their agents — in particular, promotion, fulfilment and printing companies — have adequate insurance. In the last few years, insured contests have become interestingly common. These are contests with valuable prizes (such as $1 million cash) which are next to impossible to win: the odds may approach one in 1 billion. Sponsors purchase insurance to protect against the remote possibility of a winner. The insurance companies providing this coverage are sophisticated risk-takers. Their contracts should be carefully reviewed to ensure that, if there is a $1 million winner, the insurer will pay out in all circumstances. Similarly, sponsors must ensure that the rules of the contest and the terms of the insurance contract are followed strictly or the insurers may have the right to deny coverage.

Judging Organization: There is no legal requirement that a contest be run by an independent judging organization unless you have contractually obligated yourself to do so by stating it in the contest rules. This job is usually handed to a promotion house to take advantage of their expertise. That said, if a contest is run internally, procedures should be carefully documented and an independent party requested to handle the draw. This is particularly advisable for a high profile contest with major prizes. If a "professional contestant" challenges the selection process, it is helpful to have independent evidence.

Legal Review: No matter how many promotions you have managed, there are good reasons for submitting contest rules for legal review. For one thing, your lawyer should know about recent developments in the law and technical solutions for safeguarding new promotional concepts. For another thing, legal pre-approval is a safe and sensible means of passing the buck. If the promotion implodes, you will not be blamed. However, promotion law is a "specialized area". If you do not choose an expert (see the listings at <http://www.lexpert.com>) you may be throwing your money away.

Loyalty Programs: Loyalty programs range from coffee card programs to VISA's Aerogold® air miles program. Coffee card programs are simple to administer. Six holes punched and your coffee is free. The reward is small enough that retailers do not worry about transferred or falsified cards.

Programs like Hbc Rewards and Aerogold VISA®, on the other hand, are enormously complicated. It would take a book-length chapter to describe the potential legal issues. Consider, for example, what happens if you want to cancel the program (the GM Card) or merge it into a larger program (from Club Z to Hbc Rewards). How do you change the program rules or the value of program points? How do you protect against fraud and address consumer privacy issues? Once your marketing objectives are clearly defined, you will need experienced counsel to draft a contract that will give you sufficient flexibility as your loyalty program matures and sufficient protection against the many contingencies that can arise in a long term contractual relationship with hundreds or hundreds of thousands of consumers.

Mini-Rules: "Mini-rules" or short form rules are appropriate for contest vehicles such as statement stuffers, ad pads, print advertisements (particularly those that include an entry form) and the back of scratch and win cards. They should be used whenever it is important to communicate the essential details of a contest but space limitations prevent publication of the official contest rules. Mini-rules should include the following information:

- how to enter and any limitations on the type or number of entries;
- how to enter without purchase;
- how to obtain complete contest rules;
- the number, approximate value and a description of each prize;
- any regional allocation of prizes;
- the odds of winning each prize (in a scratch and win or other seeded game);
- a statement that in order to win, a mathematical skill-testing question must be correctly answered;
- the contest closing date;
- the date, time and place of the contest draw; and
- unusual eligibility restrictions.

These mini-rules are based on a straightforward contest with no unusual twists. If your contest is more complicated, the mini-rules will be longer. If space is very limited, the on-pack disclosure described below may be sufficient.

Minors: People under the age of majority (which is 18 in all provinces except British Columbia, Nova Scotia, New Brunswick and Newfoundland and all the Territories where it is 19) can participate in contests and win prizes. They cannot, however, sign legally binding contracts. Therefore, whenever a prize is won by a minor or a minor will be the travelling companion of a contest winner, the applicable liability/publicity release should be signed by the minor's parent or legal guardian.

Odds of Winning: The *Competition Act* requires "adequate and fair" disclosure of the odds of winning. In a sweepstakes, the odds depend on the number of entries received. In a seeded game, the odds depend on the number of each type of prize seeded among the total number of game cards. In a collect and win game, the odds depend on the odds of receiving each required game piece multiplied by the odds of receiving all other required pieces. In a seeded game, the odds of winning each type of prize should be available to consumers before they make a purchase, preferably on point of sale materials and all game cards and through a 1-800 number or a website.

Online Contests: Most well trafficked websites feature at least one contest at any given time. The rules of the offline world apply to internet contests. However, certain considerations are specific to online contests. The rules should begin with a prominent statement regarding eligibility, *e.g.*, "This contest is only open to residents of Canada and is governed by Canadian law." The exact deadline for entry should be stated: "Contest closes with entries received at 11:59 p.m. (Eastern Time), November 20, 2007."

The number of entries per e-mail address should be limited to one per person or e-mail address (per day, per week, *etc.*). In addition, there should be a mechanism for determining who submitted an online entry in the event of a dispute: this is usually deemed to be the holder of the e-mail account.

To protect against system crashes and other technical problems, internet contest rules should include a comprehensive "glitch" clause denying liability for entries that are lost in cyberspace and for damages to any user's computer caused by bugs or other online hazards and allowing the sponsor to cancel the contest if software problems, hackers or simple internet congestion interfere with the proper conduct of the contest. It is a good idea to require participants to read the contest rules before they play and to click on an icon to indicate that they have read and agree to be bound by the rules.

It is still early days for internet contest law. The next few years will give a better idea of the legal hazards of this medium.

On-pack Disclosure: If game cards are distributed in-pack or a UPC is required for contest entry, a prominent front panel flash should state, at a minimum: "No purchase required. For no purchase option and complete contest rules, visit <http://www.abc.com> or call 1-800-xxx. Contest closes with entries [or prize claims] received on [date]." Further on-pack disclosure (for example, prize details and odds of winning) may be required, depending on the contest, the claims being made and whether the information is included on point of sale materials.

Premiums: A premium is something given away to consumers on the purchase of a particular product or service. It is not a "prize" within the meaning of Canadian law because there is nothing random about premiums. Everyone who fulfils the promotion's criteria receives the same item. Premiums range from free products — often a new product in the manufacturer's lineup — to movie tickets, baseball caps and Thanksgiving turkeys. Any "free with purchase" offer must be clearly stated. What is the premium (name, variant, quantity) and what must be purchased to obtain it? Is the offer limited to certain locations? What is the expiry date? In almost every case, the expiry date should be qualified by the statement "or while quantities last" in case the program's popularity exceeds expectations. If the offer will be advertised in Quebec, be aware that Quebec's *Consumer Protection Act* prohibits placing undue emphasis on premiums. In any print or broadcast advertising, the amount of space or time devoted to the premium must be less then half of the total advertisement.

Purchase Requirement: Section 206 of the *Criminal Code* prohibits purchase requirements for all "games of chance or mixed chance and skill" where the prizes consist of "goods, wares or merchandise". In all such cases, you must have a non-purchase means of entry. Usually, this is a hand-drawn facsimile of the entry form and/or of the UPC. You can also require a short (50-100 words) hand-written essay. Non-purchase entrants should be treated with "equal dignity": this means that you cannot require non-purchase entrants to inconvenience themselves in a major way or expend considerably more effort than "purchase" entrants.

You *can* generally have a purchase requirement in two situations:

(a)   in a skill contest, *i.e.*, a contest where winners are determined solely on the basis of skill such as a photography or writing contest; and

(b)   where *none* of the contest prizes fall into the category of "goods, wares or merchandise". Exempt prizes include cash, services (such as a car lease or a health club membership) and trips.

We note however that some lawyers take the position that section 206(1)(e) of the *Criminal Code* also applies. This provision prohibits a scheme whereby the winner would receive a larger amount of "valuable security" than the sum paid by reason of the participation of others. This is a broad prohibition, and the Supreme Court of Canada has held that it applies to contests of pure skill. It is generally advisable therefore to have a no purchase form of entry to avoid the potential application of section 206(1)(e).

Quebec: Whether or not to include Quebec residents in a contest is often determined by whether you want to deal with the Régie. The Régie has jurisdiction over all contests which are "launched to the public" in Quebec. Thus, employee contests are not governed by the Régie but trade promotions are. In most cases, the Régie does not have jurisdiction over skill contests. All "public contests" which are open to Quebec residents must be registered with the Régie unless the total prize value is less than $2,000. You should note however, that if the prize pool is less than $2,000 but more than $100, the "duty" will still have to be paid to the Régie.

Complete information on registering your contest with the Régie is available at www.racj.quebec@racj.gouv.qc.ca. If you need to deal with the Régie, you should consider the following:

(a)   Who should file the registration documents? If anyone other than the sponsor or the sponsor's lawyer registers the contest, they will have to file a proxy.

(b)   Contest rules and contest-related advertising must be filed with the Régie 10 days before the start date. These should be filed in French unless the contest will be carried only in English media.

(c)   The Régie assesses taxes at the rate of 3 per cent of total prize value for a national contest or 10 per cent of the value of prizes allocated to Quebec residents. If the contest is a scratch and win or otherwise seeded, you only have to pay taxes on the value of the prizes you estimate will be redeemed. Taxes and the registration documents are due 30 days before the contest start date. The usual penalty for late filing is interest on the late payment of taxes.

(d) If the value of any prize offered to Quebec residents exceeds $5,000 or the total prizes offered to Quebec residents exceed $20,000, you will have to file a security bond.

(e) Within 60 days of the contest's draw date, you have to file a final report (*i.e.*, a winners' list) with the Régie.

(f) You cannot amend or withdraw a contest in Quebec without the Régie's approval.

(g) The Régie requires you to keep all contest entry forms for 120 days following the draw date.

(h) If a contest falls within the Régie's jurisdiction, the rules and advertising must include specific clauses that are not required in the rest of Canada. These are set out in sections 5 and 6 of the "Rules respecting publicity contests".

Rebates/Mail-In Offers: There are many kinds of rebates and mail-in offers but they all have certain things in common. Consumers are asked to submit their contact information along with one or more proofs of purchase in order to receive a rebate cheque or merchandise. If merchandise is involved, it is frequently branded merchandise (a plush Energizer® Bunny; vintage Coca-Cola® glasses). There are several legal issues to consider. The terms of the offer should specify what kinds of proofs of purchase are required: *i.e.*, original UPC codes and/or original dated sales receipts. Dated sales receipts are required if the offer only applies to purchases made between certain specified dates. If an on-pack rebate form is used, is it necessary to submit the original form? What is the deadline for receipt of rebate requests? Is there a limit to the number of rebate requests per person or household? Is the offer open to groups and organizations? How long will delivery of the rebate take? If the mail-in offer involves merchandise, the merchandise should be specifically described. The manufacturer should forecast demand as accurately as possible, because legal problems can arise if demand for an advertised offer exceeds supply. If shipping and handling and/or additional money are required to order the merchandise, consider the Quebec *Consumer Protection Act* which requires a security bond to be posted if pre-paid mail-in offers are open to Quebec residents.

Régie des alcools, des courses et des jeux (see Chapter 17, *Uniquely Quebec Issues*)

Regional Allocation: The *Competition Act* requires "fair and adequate" disclosure of any regional allocation of prizes. If a certain number of prizes will be awarded per province or other region, this information should be featured in all contest-related advertising. If Quebec has a separate prize pool, the Régie will assess taxes on those prizes alone (at the rate of 10 per cent of the value of the Quebec prizes).

Releases: Contest winners (and the travelling companions of trip winners) should be required to sign a standard release confirming that they have read and complied with the contest rules, that they agree to the use of their name, photograph and comments in any contest-related publicity and release the sponsors and prize suppliers from any liability associated with the contest or their prize. This document should be signed before the prize is awarded, but releases are not required for prizes of minor value (under $50) unless they are inherently dangerous, *e.g.*, a skateboard, tickets to rides at Canada's Wonderland.

Skill Contests: Skill contests are competitions. The winners are chosen exclusively on the basis of their skill and creativity in the designated activity: story writing, photography, recipe creation, drawing *etc*. The rules for skill contests should clearly describe the requirements for entry submissions, the judging process and the criteria for selecting winners. The rules should also indicate that entry submissions will not be returned.

If the contest involves a range of skill levels — for example, a child's drawing contest — it may be appropriate to separate entries into different age categories. If the winning entries will be published or otherwise used by the contest sponsor, the winner(s) should sign a copyright assignment and warrant that their entry is entirely original and does not infringe any third party rights.

Skill-testing Question: All contests must have an element of skill. This requirement is inherently met by skill contests. Other contests satisfy this requirement with a mathematical question. Check with your lawyer before you use any other kind of skill. Canadian case law is quite bizarre on what constitutes sufficient skill. For example, identifying the characters in a sitcom or the products in a catalogue would probably not involve sufficient skill. Mathematical skill-testing questions should consist of a 4-part equation with 2 to 3 digit numbers which either follows the order of mathematics (x, ÷, +, -) or uses brackets. We do not know how difficult the math must be but Grade 6 level is probably not enough (unless the contest is aimed at children).

Store Visits: The Competition Bureau discourages contest advertisements that direct consumers to retail outlets for complete contest information. Consumers should not be inconvenienced in order to obtain the information required by the *Competition Act*. Depending on the medium, it may be acceptable to say "Complete contest details available in-store" provided those details are also available online or through a 1-800 number.

Sweepstakes: The American term for a contest where prizes are awarded in a random draw.

Taxes: In Canada, winners are not taxed on their contest winnings except in the case of employee contests where prizes may be taxed as an employment benefit or the prize consists of an annuity which is taxable in the hands of the recipient. Moreover, it is unusual to require winners to pay any prize-related expenses, such as installation or monthly service fees. If winners will be responsible for any such charges, this should be clearly specified in contest advertising and in the rules.

Telemarketing: Over the past 20 years, telemarketing fraud has grown to a multi-billion dollar a year industry in North America. Fraudulent telemarketers work from lists of vulnerable consumers — often senior citizens — who have fallen for their pitches in the past. In order to deal with this problem, which often involves cross-border operations, Industry Canada has established a joint task force with the Federal Trade Commission in the United States. In addition, the 1999 amendments to the *Competition Act* introduced new criminal provisions dealing with deceptive telemarketing. These provisions prohibit telemarketing contests in which payment is required to receive a prize (the typical fraud involves a major prize, *e.g.*, a luxury car that the "winner" will allegedly receive once they have sent the telemarketer thousands of dollars in applicable taxes). This prohibition is also directed at multi-level 1-900 contests where consumers can incur significant telephone charges before becoming eligible for a prize.

The telemarketing provisions require disclosure of certain contest information during the telemarketing call or within a reasonable time prior to the call. The disclosure required is the same as for other contests: the number and approximate value of the prizes, any regional allocation of prizes and the odds of winning. The problem is disclosing the information during the course of a telephone call — which can make for a long and awkward conversation — or in an appropriate manner before the telephone call occurs. If the information is mailed to a targeted list before the telemarketing begins, it must be mailed within a "reasonable time". Presumably, the direct mail contest piece must be received in close enough proximity to the telemarketing call that consumers can find or remember the required information during the telephone call. It is important to remember that the telemarketing provisions involve criminal law sanctions. Telemarketers should govern themselves accordingly. There have been many prosecutions under this section and significant fines and jail terms have been imposed.

Television Advertisements: A contest television advertisement should include a prominent super with certain minimum information: "No purchase required. Contest closes [date]. Full contest details available in-store or at <http://www.abc.com>". Official rules should be posted on the inter-

net and/or available through a 1-800 number. If the television advertisement will be broadcast in Quebec, the super should include the value of the
prizes or the range in value. Additional supers, or audio disclaimers, may
be triggered by the content of the commercial. For example, a statement
such as "Win a Trip to Disneyland Instantly" may require a qualifying
super such as "skill-testing question must be correctly answered. Three one
week trips for 2 available to be won. Approx. value: $7,000 each."

Trade Promotions: Most of the principles and regulations that apply
to consumer contests apply to trade promotions. There must be proper
disclosure of prize details, odds of winning and regional allocation of
prizes, there must be a skill-testing question and complete contest rules.
In fact, there are no short cuts for trade promotions.

Trademarks: Contest headlines and advertising should not use third
party trademarks and other intellectual property (logos, product shots)
without permission. This is particularly risky if the third party is a company like Disney which actively licenses its brands. Under no circumstances should the word "Olympics" or any other Olympics trademark be
used without permission from the Canadian Olympic Committee. If you
have developed a catchy title for your program, consider a trademark
search to ensure that the phrase is available for use.

United States: U.S. contest law follows the same basic principles as
Canadian contest law with some major exceptions. For example, in the
U.S. there is no skill-testing question requirement and winners must pay
income tax on their prizes. Moreover, every state in the U.S. has specific
contest legislation. Therefore, running a contest in the United States is
like dealing with 50 different versions of Quebec's Régie. DO NOT
ATTEMPT THIS without the advice of an experienced U.S. lawyer. And
be forewarned. There are hundreds of professional contestants in the U.S.
They will find and exploit any weakness in your contest.

Winners: Once you have selected a winner, several potential problems can arise. First, you may not be able to contact your winner. He or
she may have moved or be on vacation. The couriered prize notification
envelope may be undeliverable. Your contest rules should always state
how many and what kind of attempts will be made to contact a winner
before their prize will be forfeited and an alternate winner selected. Once
a winner has been contacted, he or she may fail to return the release and
other documentation in a reasonable time. Again the contest rules should
state that the contest documents must be signed and returned within a
certain number of days of notification or the prize will be forfeited.
Finally, there are the reluctant winners who do not want their prizes.
They want the cash instead. Contest rules almost always state that prizes
must be accepted as awarded and are not convertible to cash. Moreover,
the contest sponsor has usually paid for the prize. It is a bad idea —

unless the reluctant winner has a very compelling story — to deviate from the contest rules and award a cash equivalent prize.

SAMPLE OFFICIAL CONTEST RULES
(WITH ANNOTATIONS)

Perfect Cuppa Coffee Contest
Official Rules

THIS CONTEST IS INTENDED FOR RESIDENTS OF CANADA ONLY AND WILL BE INTERPRETED ACCORDING TO CANADIAN LAW

HOW TO ENTER: Purchase any 1 pound package of Perfect Cuppa coffee and find the 12 number UPC code on the packaging. To enter online go to <http://www.coffeebreak.com> and click on the "Perfect Cuppa Contest" link. Complete and submit the online registration form, including your Perfect Cuppa UPC code and the answer to the mathematical skill-testing question. The contest ends with entries submitted by 11:59 p.m. (EST) on November 20, 2007. Limit: one e-mail entry per person or e-mail address per day.

NO PURCHASE NECESSARY. You may also enter by printing on a 3" x 5" piece of paper your name, complete address, daytime phone number, age and the answer to the following skill-testing question: $(112 \times 54) \div 756 + 816 - 824$. Mail your entry in a separate envelope bearing sufficient postage to: "Perfect Cuppa Coffee" contest, Suite 4900, Commerce Court West, Toronto, Ontario, M5L 1J3. Entries must be postmarked by November 20, 2007 and received by November 28, 2007. Mechanically reproduced entries will not be accepted. Perfect Cuppa Ltd. (the "Sponsor") is not responsible for lost, late, illegible, incomplete, misdirected or postage due mail entries.

ONLINE PLAY: The Sponsor is not responsible for any problems or technical malfunctions of any telephone network or lines, computer online systems or servers, computer software problems or traffic congestion on the internet or at any website and assumes no liability for damage to entrant's or any person's computer resulting from participating in the game. In the event of a dispute as to the identity of a winner based on an e-mail address, the winning entry will be deemed to be made by the authorized account holder of the e-mail address at time of entry. "Authorized account holder" is the natural person who is assigned an e-mail address by an internet service provider or other organization responsible for assigning e-mail addresses for the domain associated with the e-mail address in question.

CONTEST DRAW: Winners will be selected from among all eligible entries received in a random draw conducted by an independent judging organization at 12 noon in Toronto, Ontario on December 7, 2007. Odds of winning depend on the total number of eligible online and mail entries. Limit: one prize per person or household.

PRIZES: One Grand Prize will be awarded consisting of a trip for a family of four (2 adults, 2 children) to Disney World in Orlando, Florida. Trip includes round trip economy class airfare to Orlando from the international airport closest to the winner's residence, 6 nights standard hotel accommodation (two rooms, double occupancy), 7 days rental of a mid-level rental car, 5 day passes for four people to Disney World and Epcot Center and $1,500 (CDN) spending money. Winner and his/her travelling companions are responsible for proper travel documentation, travel insurance, meals, gas, excess insurance and mileage for the rental car and all other expenses that are not specifically included. Trip must be completed by December 31, 2008 and is subject to availability at the time of booking. Certain blackout periods may apply. Approximate retail value of trip based on Vancouver departure is $9,500.

There will be five First Prizes awarded each consisting of a year's supply of Perfect Cuppa coffee. This prize will be awarded in the form of 52 gift certificates for 1 pound of Perfect Cuppa coffee, flavour and grind to be determined by winner, redeemable at participating retailers.

Prizes must be accepted as awarded and are not transferable or convertible to cash. No substitutions except at Sponsor's option. Sponsor reserves the right to substitute a prize or prize component for one of equal or greater value.

In order to win, selected entrants must first correctly answer a time-limited mathematical skill-testing question to be administered by mail or telephone. Winners will be notified by mail or telephone and will be required to sign and return an affidavit of eligibility and a liability/publicity release within 10 business days of notification. If a selected entrant cannot be contacted by mail or telephone or fails to return the contest documents within the specified time, he/she will forfeit their prize and an alternate winner will be selected. The travelling companions of the Grand Prize winner (or their parent/legal guardian for travelling companions who are under the age of majority) will also be required to sign a standard liability/publicity release. All prizes will be delivered to confirmed winners.

ELIGIBILITY: This contest is open to residents of Canada who are over the age of majority in their province or territory of residence except employees (and persons with whom they are domiciled) of Perfect Cuppa Ltd., its affiliated companies, advertising and promotion agencies and the independent judging organization.

GENERAL: This contest is subject to all applicable federal, provincial and municipal laws and regulations. By entering the contest, participants agree to be bound by these official rules and by the decisions of the contest judges, which shall be final on all matters relating to this contest. All entries become the property of the Sponsor and none will be returned. For information on Sponsor's use of personal information in connection with this contest, see the privacy policy posted on our website at <http://www.coffeebreak.com>.

If for any reason the online portion of this contest is not capable of being completed as planned including, but not limited to computer virus, bugs, tampering, technical failures or other causes beyond the control of the Sponsor, Sponsor reserves the right, subject to the approval of the Régie in Quebec, to cancel, suspend or modify the online portion of the contest.

FOR RESIDENTS OF QUEBEC, any litigation concerning the conduct or administration of this publicity contest may be submitted to the Régie des alcools, des courses et des jeux for a ruling. Any litigation concerning the awarding of a prize may be submitted to the Régie only for the purpose of helping the parties reach a settlement.

Chapter 6

ADVERTISING TO CHILDREN

A.   INTRODUCTION

We all learn about the power of advertising to children first-hand when our toddlers start waving and pointing wildly in the back seat every time we pass the "Golden Arches". This powerful force reaches new heights in adolescence when our children refuse to wear any clothing unless it is made by one of the approved labels.

Children are, by definition, young and more vulnerable than any other segment of society. The law recognizes that children require some insulation from high-pressured advertising. The degree of protection varies by jurisdiction and media. This chapter will highlight the most important provincial and self-regulatory restrictions concerning children's advertising and will give you practical tips on traps to avoid.

B.   FEDERAL REQUIREMENTS

1.   The Broadcast Code for Advertising to Children

While there are no federal statutes or regulations that specifically regulate advertising to children, broadcast advertising that is child-directed is subject to the Broadcast Code for Advertising to Children (the "Code").

Although compliance with the Code is "voluntary", the fact that the Code is published by the Canadian Association of Broadcasters in association with Advertising Standards Canada and is endorsed by the CRTC, means that no child-directed advertising will get to air unless it is in compliance with the Code.

According to the Code, "children's advertising" is any advertising during children's programming as well as any "child-directed" advertising during other programming. The Code acknowledges that parents occasionally control the T.V. agenda and that a child who is bored by their parent's show will immediately perk up when a Nintendo spot comes on. A "child", for the purposes of the Code, is anyone under the age of 12.

The Code's prohibitions are easy to summarize. You cannot lead a child to covet a product through exaggerated demos, endorsements by *Spiderman*, *Digimon* and the like, heavily-promoted giveaways, calls to action, implicit social pressure ("You need this. All your friends have it. You will be so uncool if you only have the old version of that game.") You cannot encourage a child to pressure his or her parents to buy. Finally, you cannot brainwash a child through repetition (the limit is one broadcast of the same commercial per 30 minute time-slot).

Within these limits it is still easy to create a compelling ad. It may interfere with the creative to have to show a product's relative size by placing it in a child's hand. Or to have to state in the audio and in a super "You have to put this toy together" or "Batteries not included". It requires some tinkering to ensure that a premium offer — a contest, rewards program, package insert — takes up no more than 50 per cent of your spot. This requirement is strict. Every second that your "free tattoos" are featured counts towards the "premium" half. It may be annoying to abandon superiority claims when you know for a fact that your product is the best.

The Code, however, leaves many avenues open. You can feature a cartoon or fantasy character if it was created for the product: *Tony the Tiger* and *Ronald McDonald*, for example. You can use all the laudatory non-superlative words in a child's vocabulary (words that parents don't know the meaning of). You can sometimes circumvent the Code by appealing to parents while casting the net wide enough to potentially catch the child. "Hey mom, remember what fun you had with *Barbie?*" In English Canada, you can certainly get your message across.

RULES OF THUMB

- A child is anyone under 12.
- Children's advertising includes ads during children's programming and ads directed at children.
- Although the Code is technically "voluntary", television and radio ads will not be accepted for broadcast unless they comply.
- You cannot pressure a child to buy or use your products.
- Premium offers can only take up 50 per cent of the ad.
- You can use fantasy characters if they were created for the product.

---

2.   Canadian Code of Advertising Standards

In addition to the *Children's Broadcast Code*, Advertising Standards Canada's *Canadian Code of Advertising Standards*, available at

<http://www.adstandards.com/en/Standards/canCodeOfAdStandards.asp>, has a specific provision that applies to all advertising. Section 12 of this Code states:

> Advertising that is directed to children must not exploit their credulity, lack of experience or their sense of loyalty, and must not present information or illustrations that might result in their physical, emotional or moral harm.

> Child-directed advertising in the broadcast media is separately regulated by the *Broadcast Code for Advertising to Children*, also administered by [Advertising Standards Canada]. Advertising to children in Quebec is prohibited by the Quebec *Consumer Protection Act*.

As with the other ASC Code provisions, this section is broad and extremely subjective in its interpretation. The most common example of an ASC Code violation in child-directed media is an ad which encourages unsafe or dangerous behaviour. Some examples are obvious — showing a child diving off the roof into the neighbour's swimming pool is an obvious violation. Others are more subtle — would showing a child telling a "white lie" to a teacher cause them moral harm? What is clear is that many parents are disturbed if their children see a commercial that contains sexual innuendo, even if it is at 10 p.m. during the hockey game. We personally think that kids should be in bed by 10 but you should know that such commercials, whether they are child-directed or not, will generate enough complaints to burn up the client's phone lines.

RULES OF THUMB

- You cannot exploit a child's innocence or lack of knowledge.
- Ads cannot encourage unsafe behaviour.
- There is a complaint procedure in place for violations of the Code.

---

3. Quebec

If there is a common theme in this book, it is that Quebec is in its own world of advertising law. Children's advertising is no exception.

In Quebec, the issues are challenging because children's advertising is expressly prohibited by section 248 of the *Consumer Protection Act*.[1] The definition of section 252 of the Act states that the definition of "to advertise" is as follows: "to prepare, utilize, distribute, publish or broadcast an advertisement, or to cause it to be distributed, published or broadcast". This definition is not only broad but it is circular.

---

[1] R.S.Q. c. P-40.1.

Some guidance can be had from section 249 of the Act which provides three factors which help determine whether or not an ad is directed at children under 13. These factors are "nature and intended purpose of the goods advertised, the manner of presenting the ad, and the time and place it is shown". As well, the overall context and the presentation of the ad must be considered.

Because the regulation of children's advertising in Quebec is complex, we have reproduced key excerpts from the *Consumer Protection Act* and Regulations below:

248. Subject to what is provided in the regulations, no person may make use of commercial advertising directed at persons under thirteen years of age.

249. To determine whether or not an advertisement is directed at persons under thirteen years of age, account must be taken of the context of its presentation, and in particular of

    (a)   the nature and intended purpose of the goods advertised;
    (b)   the manner of presenting such advertisement;
    (c)   the time and place it is shown.

The *Regulation respecting the application of the Consumer Protection Act* states:

90. An advertisement directed at children is exempt from the application of section 248 of the Act, if it is constituted by a store window, a display, a container, a wrapping or a label or if it appears thereon, provided that the requirements of paragraphs a to g, j, k, o and p of section 91 are met.

91. For the purposes of applying sections 88, 89, and 90, an advertisement directed at children may not:

    (a)   exaggerate the nature, characteristics, performance or duration of goods or services;
    (b)   minimize the degree of skill, strength or dexterity or the age necessary to use goods or services;
    (c)   use a superlative to describe the characteristics of goods or services or a diminutive to indicate its cost;
    (d)   use a comparative or establish a comparison with the goods or services advertised;
    (e)   directly incite a child to buy or to urge another person to buy goods or services or to seek information about it;
    (f)   portray reprehensible social or family lifestyles;
    (g)   advertise goods or services that, because of their nature, quality or ordinary use, should not be used by children;
    (h)   advertise a drug or patent medicine;
    (i)   advertise a vitamin in liquid, powered or tablet form;
    (j)   portray a person acting in an imprudent manner;
    (k)   portray goods or services in a way that suggests an improper or dangerous use thereof;

(l) portray a person or character known to children to promote goods or services, except:

  i.   in the case of an artist, actor or professional announcer who does not appear in a publication or programme directed at children;
  ii. in the case provided for in section 89 where he is illustrated as a participant in a show directed at children.

For the purposes of this paragraph, a character created expressly to advertise goods or services is not considered a character known to children if it is used for advertising alone;

  (m) use an animated cartoon process except to advertise a cartoon show directed at children;
  (n) use a comic strip except to advertise a comic book directed at children;
  (o) suggest that owning or using a product will develop in a child a physical, social or psychological advantage over other children his age, or that being without the product will have the opposite effect;
  (p) advertise goods in a manner misleading a child into thinking that, for the regular price of those goods, he can obtain goods other than those advertised.[2]

Applying a legal mind to these complex provisions results in the following:

RULES OF THUMB

• DO ensure that product/service claims are true, clear and can be understood by children (*e.g.*, "Some assembly required. GI Joe sold separately.")

• DO NOT exaggerate product characteristics or performance or minimize the skill, strength or dexterity needed to use them (*e.g.*, "You can put this Ferris Wheel together in 10 minutes flat!")

• DO NOT use superlative terms such as "BEST" or "ULTIMATE" to describe a product or diminutives such as "ONLY" or "JUST" to describe its cost (*e.g.*, "You can have the most powerful MP3 Player around for just $299.")

---

[2] R.Q. P-40.1, r. 1.

- DO NOT use comparisons (*e.g.*, "Did your Mom buy you those cheap dry-tasting hot dogs?")

- DO NOT incite a child to buy or to urge others to buy the product or to seek further information about it (*e.g.*, "Ask your Mom for these jeans today!")

- DO NOT portray a reprehensible social or family lifestyle (*e.g.*, "Why write your own essays when our easy download service can write them for you!")

- DO NOT advertise goods to kids which are not suitable for kids (*e.g.*, "This cigarette lighter is perfect for your next rock concert.")

- DO NOT show a person acting in an imprudent manner (*e.g.*, "These delicious candies are great for playing mouth catch.")

- DO avoid portraying goods in a way that suggests improper or dangerous use.

- DO NOT suggest that kids will have an advantage (physical/social/psychological) over other kids by owning a product or that they will be at a disadvantage if they don't have one (*e.g.*, "Don't be the only kid in your class without a cellphone this year.")

- DO NOT suggest that a child will get free extra goods for regular price (*e.g.*, "Get free fries today only* (with purchase of a regular hamburger and drink).")

4.   Permitted Media in Quebec Child-directed Ads

- in-store/wrapper advertising if it meets the requirements of section 91 of the Regulations
- print — only if it is in a children's magazine/insert which is offered for sale at least quarterly and if it meets section 91 requirements

5.   Privacy Issues

Privacy becomes relevant in advertising law as marketers engage in contests and promotions. Many contests are directed mainly or entirely at children. These activities usually involve the collection of some contact and personal information. The collection and use of personal information obtained from children is subject to particular standards.

The collection and use of personal information is regulated under different legislative schemes. There are five provinces which have enacted Privacy Acts. The most strict of these is Quebec's *Act respecting access to documents held by public bodies and the protection of personal information.*[3]

In the Quebec statute, "personal information" is information which relates to a "natural person" and allows that person to be identified. This does not limit the definition of "personal information" to Quebec residents.

Section 17 of the Quebec Act is the only section dealing directly with personal information about Quebec residents. It requires companies carrying on business in Quebec and communicating information about Quebec residents to businesses outside Quebec to "take all reasonable steps to ensure" (1) that the information will not be used for purposes not relevant to the matter or communicated to third parties without the consent of the persons involved, except for nominative lists (names, addresses and phone numbers of existing clients or employees); and (2) in the case of nominative lists, that people have a valid opportunity to refuse that personal information concerning them be used for commercial or philanthropic solicitation and can have their personal information deleted from the list.

Section 13 states that, subject to the exceptions listed in section 18, a company must have the express consent of a person before it may use that person's personal information or communicate it to a third party. Section 18 provides an exception for among other things, "nominative lists". A company may communicate a "nominative list" to a third party without the consent of the persons on the list if certain conditions are met.

The Canadian Marketing Association has also instituted a *Code of Ethics and Standards of Practice* which governs privacy and children's privacy issues. Recently, the Code has been significntly revised. The revisions will come into force January 1, 2007. All CMA members are required to adhere to this Code (published online at <http://www.the-cma.org/regulatory/codeofethics.cfm>).

Section K3.1 of the CMA Code provides:

> Except as provided below in Section K4, *Contests Directed to Children*, all marketing interactions directed to children that include collection, transfer and requests for personal information require the express consent of the child's parent or guardian.

---

[3]   R.S.Q., c. A-2.1.

In addition:

> When marketing to persons between 13 years and the age of majority (teenagers), marketers are strongly cautioned that children may be exposed to these communications and, in such cases, these interactions with children are governed by the preceding guidelines concerning consent.

The CMA therefore, requires express parental consent for the collection of personal data from children under 13. This could be accomplished by having the parent/guardian of children under 13 fax back the questionnaire and consent.

The CMA also prescribes guidelines for contests directed at children under 13. In the contest context, marketers may collect personal information from children without obtaining the parent or guardian's express consent, only if the marketer:

- Collects a minimal amount of personal information, sufficient only to determine the winner(s);

- Deals only with the winner(s)' parent or guardian and does not contact the winner(s);

- Does not retain the personal information following the conclusion of the contest or sweepstakes;

- Makes no use of the personal information other than to determine the contest winner(s); and

- Does not transfer or make available the personal information to any other individual or organization.

The CMA has developed guidelines in Section L of the Code for marketing to teens. The *CMA Guidelines* emphasize that marketing to teens imposes a special responsibility requiring discretion and sensitivity by taking into consideration the age, knowledge, sophistication and maturity of teens. Specifically, the *CMA Code* requires that marketers should not portray sexual behaviour or violence that is inconsistent with community or industry standards.

Furthermore, the CMA has created special rules for the collection of information from teenagers. Marketers must not use or collect personal information from teens in order to acquire further household information, and shall not solicit information about a third party from a teenager.

Information is divided into two categories; (1) contact information which includes name, address, e-mail, home and mobile telephone numbers; (2) personal information which consists of any general information other than contact information which identifies the individual.

For teenagers between 13 and 16, marketers may collect and use contact information with the teenager's express consent. However, marketers must obtain express parental consent before disclosing a teenager's contact information to a third party, or collecting, using or disclosing the teenager's personal information. For teenagers over 16, marketers must obtain their express consent for the collection, use and disclosure of both their contact and personal information. Generally, marketers must provide teenagers with an easy means to withdraw consent and to end a marketing relationship.

In the U.S., CARU (the Children's Advertising Review Unit) has issued a policy that requires parental consent for e-mail disclosure. In our view, this policy should be considered in Canada as well.

Section J of the CMA *Code of Ethics and Standards of Practice* outlines ten privacy principles from the National Standard of Canada and five additional CMA privacy requirements. The principles endorse more individual control over the type of information held and used by companies. All of these provisions should be strictly observed when dealing with children. Particular attention is required in keeping such information from third parties.

6.   Product Liability Issues

In addition to complying with the various Codes and statutes, child-directed advertisers should avoid advertising that encourages unsafe or dangerous practices in children. Following various U.S. lawsuits in which parents of teens who committed suicide or injured themselves brought legal action against rock and rap performers for disturbing lyrics which allegedly pushed their child over the edge, Canadian advertisers may be found liable for commercials which encourage a child to do something harmful. Ironically, Advertising Standards Canada is less than satisfied by supers which state "DON'T TRY THIS" stating that children often do the opposite of what they are told.

Media placement is often crucial in assessing whether the adult message could be misinterpreted by a naive child and cause serious harm.

Chapter 7

PACKAGING AND LABELLING

A. INTRODUCTION

Packaging and labelling requirements are the nuts and bolts of marketing. There is nothing particularly catchy about the *Consumer Packaging and Labelling Act*,[1] the *Hazardous Products Act*,[2] the *Consumer Chemical Container Regulations, 2001*[3] or the *Marking of Imported Goods Order*.[4] However, if you distribute packaged goods in Canada which incorrectly state "product identity" or "net quantity" or which fail to include appropriate hazard symbols or country of origin statements, you risk having your products pulled from the shelf and having to be relabelled, an expensive proposition in itself, plus the possibility of fines and product liability lawsuits.

The applicable legislation includes requirements which apply to most categories of packaged goods — as set out in the *Consumer Packaging and Labelling Act* — as well as product-specific requirements — for example, those described in the *Textile Labelling Act* and the *Tobacco Act*.

In addition, all labels and packaging are subject to laws of general application. Before examining the specific information that must be included on labels, we will review some fundamental issues.

B. CLAIMS

All product claims made on packaging and labels must be truthful, non-misleading and properly substantiated. In other words, label claims are subject to the same standards as other advertising claims. However, label claims are potentially more powerful than other claims because they are

---

[1] R.S.C. 1985, c. C-38.
[2] R.S.C. 1985, c. H-3.
[3] SOR/2001-269.
[4] C.R.C., c. 535.

presented at point of sale and because, in many cases, they continue to have an impact throughout the life of a product. Think, for example, of the hundreds of impressions made by a "Softer. Stronger" claim on a box of facial tissues.

Therefore, label claims are often subject to greater scrutiny, and there are specific guidelines for label claims made for food, drugs and cosmetics. The Canadian Food Inspection Agency's *Guide to Food Labelling and Advertising* is a comprehensive document that deals with the wide variety of claims on food labels. This Guide, and other food labelling issues, are discussed in another chapter of this book.

Health Canada's *Consumer Drug Advertising Guidelines* describes, in general terms, the kinds of claims that are permitted on the labels of over-the-counter drugs. The requirements for drug labels and natural health products are discussed elsewhere in this book.

The *Guidelines for the Labelling of Cosmetics* is a comprehensive handbook which, in conjunction with the Cosmetics Regulations under the *Food and Drugs Act*,[5] describes the specific labelling requirements for cosmetics, including the warning symbols and caution statements required for aerosol products, hair dyes and other potentially hazardous products, as well as the list of "acceptable" cosmetic claims. Whether or not a cosmetic claim is "acceptable" depends, in most cases, on whether the claim is confined to cosmetic benefits, that is, cleaning or improving the appearance of hair, skin, teeth and nails, or whether it deals with biological or therapeutic benefits which cannot be attributed to cosmetics. For example, "eliminates wrinkles" is a drug-type claim and prohibited for cosmetics. Cosmetics, however, can claim to "reduce the appearance of wrinkles".

Similarly, cosmetics cannot claim SPF (Sun Protection Factor) levels, anti-bacterial action, anti-oxidant or vitamin benefits. The list of acceptable and unacceptable cosmetic claims is an exercise in careful semantics and should be read and reread by all cosmetics manufacturers.

1.   Environmental Claims

Consumers continue to be concerned about the impact of products and packaging on the environment. Therefore, Environment Canada has published guidelines regulating the use of claims such as "biodegradable", "recyclable", "environmentally friendly" and symbols such as the Mobius loop recyclable icon.

---

[5]   R.S.C. 1985, c. F-27; C.R.C., c. 869.

C.   CONTESTS

Many consumer contests are advertised on-pack. In fact, many contests include game cards or contest entry forms which are packaged with the product. In all such cases, there are minimum disclosure requirements. At a minimum, you must prominently disclose that "No Purchase is Required", include a contest closing date and provide a mechanism, such as a 1-800 number, a website and/or a write-in address, where consumers can obtain full contest details (including a free game card, if applicable) without purchase. If the contest includes in-pack seeded game cards, the package should state the odds of winning. Further information is provided in Chapter 5, *Contests and Promotions*.

D.   MADE IN CANADA

"Made in Canada" can be a powerful selling point. In order to make this claim, the following requirements must be met. More than 51 per cent of the cost of the raw materials and the production costs must be incurred in Canada and the product must come into being in Canada. In addition to the statement "Made in Canada", the use of the 11 point maple leaf is subject to the same requirements. (In order to use the Canadian flag, or any other official symbol or coat-of-arms on-pack, you require the permission of Heritage Canada or the applicable government authority.)

E.   TRADE-MARKS AND COPYRIGHT

Logos and other elements of label design are protected by copyright. This means that you cannot reproduce or substantially copy third party labels in any medium. It also means that highly original labels are an important and protectible feature of branding.

Trade-mark law protects other elements of packaging. If the design of your product or the packaging of your product is unusual and distinctive such that it has acquired "secondary meaning" as a trade-mark — meaning that consumers can identify the source of the product by its shape/design or by its packaging — the *Trade-marks Act* will protect these so-called "distinguishing guises" in the same way that other trade-marks are protected. Examples of famous distinguishing guises which function as trade-marks include the original Coca-Cola bottle, the Tiffany box and the Perrier bottle.

The protection of brand names and other trade-marks is an important packaging consideration. Registered trade-marks should be followed by a ® symbol, unregistered trade-marks by a "TM/MC" notation (for "Trade-mark/Marque de commerce") and the packaging should include a trade-mark ownership line: "® Registered trade-mark of the Coca-Cola Company."

F.   THE CHARTER OF THE FRENCH LANGUAGE

No other statute has had as big an impact on Canadian packaging as the infamous Bill 101 — Quebec's *Charter of the French Language.* Section 51 of the Charter requires that all text on products sold in Quebec and on materials accompanying the products, such as warranty statements and in-pack instructions for use, must be translated into French of equal prominence. This essentially cuts in half the amount of meaningful information that can be included on packaging and makes it difficult to include even minimal information on very small products such as batteries.

The French "equal prominence" requirement means that non-mandatory information is often omitted. "Equal prominence" does not necessarily mean that the same size type must be used for French copy (although the Office de la langue francaise has occasionally asserted this requirement). This would be onerous because French is more verbose than English and often requires up to 30 per cent more words. Therefore, it is our view that smaller type can be used for the French text provided the French text occupies at least as much space as the English. In addition, the French text should not be downplayed through poor colour contrast or poor placement. There are a few exceptions to section 51 of the Charter, such as inscriptions which are permanently engraved on a product. Generally, these exceptions have limited application. However, it is important to note that English-only trade-marks are permitted under the Charter.

G.   THE MARKING OF IMPORTED GOODS ORDER

The Marking of Imported Goods Order is a protectionist scheme administered under the *Canada Customs and Revenue Agency Act*[6] which requires a permanent "country of origin" statement on 37 categories of goods imported into Canada. These categories include toys, batteries and printed paper. The "country of origin" statement must be a legible statement such as "Made in China". The purpose of the Order is to communicate to end users that certain products are *not* made in Canada. The requirements differ for NAFTA and non-NAFTA countries.

---

[6]   S.C. 1999, c. 17.

H.   TEXTILE LABELLING ACT

The type and the quantity of fabrics used in consumer textile products, for example, socks, shirts, blankets, as well as the registered manufacturer or importer number, must be included on permanent labels pursuant to the *Textile Labelling Act*. This information is usually set out on tags sewn into collars and other seams. The Act describes the manner in which this information must be declared, the abbreviations which are acceptable, the placement of the label and the process for obtaining the required manufacturer's number. There are also provincial regulations regarding stuffed and upholstered items which should be considered.

I.   THE HAZARDOUS PRODUCTS ACT

The single most complicated statute that affects marketing in Canada is the *Hazardous Products Act* and its associated regulations. This Act deals with products that are inherently hazardous such as poisonous chemicals; products that are packaged in potentially hazardous containers, such as aerosol cleaners; and products, such as toys and cribs, which are intended for use by children and are therefore subject to additional safeguards. If your product falls into one of the regulated categories, you may be required to include a prominent hazard symbol — such as the "Explosive", "Inflammable" or "Poison" symbols — on the front of your package as well as prescribed "warnings" and "caution statements", in English and French, on the front and back labels. Be warned that although most of the potentially hazardous products covered by the Act are obvious, some are not.

Controlled products within a Canadian workplace must be properly labeled in order to provide workers with relevant information about the product. The *Controlled Products Regulations* under the *Hazardous Products Act* include formulas and tests for establishing the level of specific hazards, for example, the "flashback" caused by certain explosions, to allow for the proper classification of the controlled product. These regulations also mandate the size, placement and language of the required hazard symbol and other information. This is a component of Canada's country-wide Workplace Hazardous Materials Information system known as WHIMS which also requires that workers be provided with a Material Safety Data Sheet (MSDS) for each controlled product. Corresponding product labels must also include a statement indicating that the product's MSDS is available.Other statements including risk phrases, precautionary measures for product handling, use or exposure, and first aid measures may also be required.

J.   PRODUCT LIABILITY

Many categories of products are covered by legislation which mandates that specific warnings and/or caution statements appear on the outer and/or inner labels and, in some cases, on package inserts. The *Hazardous Products Act* and WHMIS Regulations are discussed above. Mandatory warning statements are prescribed for all drugs and pest control products and for many cosmetics. It is important to remember, however, that compliance with these statutory requirements does not necessarily let manufacturers off the hook. Product liability law requires manufacturers to warn of all reasonably foreseeable hazards. This is a branch of the common law tort of negligence which was formulated in a 1928 Scottish case when a woman successfully sued a ginger beer manufacturer because she discovered a slug in her ginger beer. Since that case, the law has required adequate warnings to all parties who might reasonably be affected by known or potential hazards.

In terms of product liability, certain things are clear. If a manufacturer knows of a potential hazard — *e.g.*, combustibility, incompatibility of certain chemicals with other commonly used chemicals, sharp edges — these hazards should be clearly described on the label. This is particularly true if the product is intended for or could be used by vulnerable parties including children, senior citizens and pregnant women.

What is less clear is whether manufacturers need to warn of obvious and well-known hazards. For example, is anything accomplished by including the warning "This coffee is very hot" on take-out coffee cups?

K.   THE CONSUMER PACKAGING AND LABELLING ACT

The *Consumer Packaging and Labelling Act* (the "CPLA") and Regulations are the fundamental regulatory scheme for labelling in Canada. This federal statute applies to all pre-packaged products sold or offered for sale to consumers. There are some exemptions, for example, drugs, textile products and artists' supplies, but the Act has wide application.

There are three basic labelling requirements set out in the CPLA:

(1)   the name and address of the manufacturer or Canadian dealer must be included on the package;
(2)   the "identity" of the product in terms of its common or generic name must be stated on the "principal display panel" in English and French; and
(3)   the "net quantity" or numerical count of the product must be included on the principal display panel in English and French.

The CPLA Regulations contain partial exemptions for test market and specialty products, special requirements for net quantity declarations for consumer paper products, the tolerances for incorrect quantity declarations, lists of products for which the net quantity must be stated by weight, by volume or by numerical count and many other variations on and additions to the basic labelling regime.

LABEL CHECKLIST

To illustrate the many issues which must be considered in devising labels that comply with Canadian requirements, following is a basic checklist. This checklist does not cover the specific requirements for drugs, cosmetics, food, natural health products and pest control products.

• Is the generic or common name of the product stated in English and French on the principal display panel (the "PDP")?

• Is the type height of the generic name 1.6 mm. where only upper case letters are used or if lower case letters are used, does the height of the letter "o" meet the 1.6 mm. requirement or if the PDP is less than 10 cm. sq., is the minimum height requirement of 0.8 mm. met?

• Does the generic name exemption that applies to products sold by count and packaged in a manner that is visible and identifiable apply? Or is there an accurate pictorial representation of the product on the label such that the generic name is not required?

• Is the net quantity of the product stated metrically (bilingually) on the principal display panel?

• Unless an established trade practice exists, are the measurements by volume if the product is a liquid, gas or viscous? Or by weight if the product is solid? Or by numerical count if the product is sold by numerical count?

• Is the net quantity declaration in bold type? Are the minimum height requirements for the numerical portion of the net quantity met? [1.6 mm. where the area of the PDP is less than 32 cm.^{2}; 3.2 mm where the area of the PDP is more than 32 cm.^{2} but less than 258 cm.^{2}; 6.4 mm where the area of the PDP is more than 258 cm.^{2} but less than 645 cm.^{2} and so on.]

• Are there exemptions from the net quantity declaration requirement such as for a pre-packaged non-food product which is visible, identifiable and sold by count?

• Is the name and address of the manufacturer or Canadian dealer stated in English or French on the package (anywhere but on the bottom)?

• Have the minimum height requirements (1.6 mm.) been met for the manufacturer's/dealer's name and address?

• Does the product have both an inner and an outer label? If so, does the outer label correctly state the "product identity", the net quantity and the dealer's name and address? Does the inner label correctly state the product identity and the dealer's name and address?

• Is the product subject to standardized size requirements? Does it comply?

• Does the product contain hazardous ingredients or does its container pose a hazard? Are the appropriate warnings included on the label as required by the *Hazardous Products Act* and the *Consumer Chemical Container Regulations*?

• Is the product imported? If so, does the statement "Imported by/importé par" or a country of origin statement precede the name and address of the Canadian dealer? Alternatively, does the label include the name and address of a foreign dealer?

• Does the product require a country of origin statement pursuant to the *Marking of Imported Goods Order*?

• Does the product make a disinfecting or pest control claim? If so, does the label comply with the *Pest Control Products Act*?

• Is the product a "controlled product" intended for use in a Canadian workplace? If so, does the label comply with the *Controlled Products Regulations*?

• Will the product be marketed in Quebec? Does the label give equal prominence to English and French text?

- Do any environmental claims comply with the *Guiding Principles for Environmental Claims*?

- Does the label refer to a contest or premium? If so, are the minimum disclosure requirements met pursuant to the *Criminal Code* and the *Competition Act*?

- Are trade-marks/industrial designs/patents properly marked on the label?

- Does the product contain a guarantee? Does the guarantee comply with provincial legislation (*e.g.*, *Sale of Goods Act*)?

- Is the product used by children? Does the label comply with the *Hazardous Products Act*?

- If the product is a textile, does it comply with the *Textile Labelling Act*?

- Is the product subject to specific legislation (*e.g.*, *Tobacco Act*, *Liquor Licensing Acts*)?

Chapter 8

DRUGS AND NATURAL HEALTH PRODUCTS

Contributed by Joel B. Taller and Lewis Retik

A.   INTRODUCTION

Over the past decade, there has been considerable reflection on the nature of human health, the factors that affect it and what steps consumers can take to enhance their well-being. It is almost impossible to pick up a newspaper without reading a story about the positive or negative effects of some substance, drug, Natural Health Product ("NHP") or food. Consumers look at the array of information with confusion and often frustration, unable to make informed choices about their own well-being. This phenomenon occurs against a backdrop of rapid scientific change and debate over its appropriate limits in some areas, as, for example, with respect to genetically modified foods.

There is a growing desire among Canadians to assume greater control over their own well-being. In order to do so, consumers often seek out relevant information on their own. This has led to a resurgence of products bearing "natural" claims, including products marketed as traditional, herbal or homeopathic remedies, vitamin and mineral supplements and foods that are recognized as contributing to good health.

The federal government has recognized this trend and has undertaken major reviews of its policies regarding NHPs, nutritional labelling, nutrient content claims, diet-related health claims and product-specific health claims for foods. These reviews have led to two sets of regulatory reforms: (1) regulations for NHPs (the "*NHP Regulations*");[1] and (2) regulations for Nutritional Labelling, Nutrient Content Claims and Diet-related Health Claims. These changes are intended to allow consumers to make more informed choices about the products they purchase.

---

[1]   The *Natural Health Products Regulations* came into force on January 1, 2004.

B.   NATURAL HEALTH PRODUCTS

1.   Overview

(a)   General

NHPs generate divergent views. Some believe in a traditional science-based approach to establishing the safety and efficacy of products intended to provide health benefits. Others believe that natural substances offer us what our bodies need in order to stay healthy and that traditional science cannot always measure their benefits.

This point of view also recognizes that NHPs may contain a host of substances which together produce the beneficial effect, making it difficult to isolate a single active substance. In addition, the effectiveness of a herbal NHP may depend on the time of the year the plant is harvested.

There are many examples of natural substances which have been traditionally used by various cultures. Honey, for example, has a time-honoured use as an antibacterial agent. Laboratory studies support this effect and there is scientific discussion about the use of honey on micro-organisms referred to as "super bugs". What evidence should be supplied to support such a claim? Although we think of honey as a benign substance, is it necessary that honey-based products be regulated to ensure their safety and efficacy? These are the fundamental issues involved in regulating NHPs.

C.   FORMER REGULATORY STATUS OF NHPS

The federal *Food and Drugs Act*[2] and the *Food and Drug Regulations*[3] were the primary legislative and regulatory framework governing the sale of NHPs. Only two definitions were relevant: the section 2 definitions of a "food" and of a "drug". A "food" is defined to include "any article manufactured, sold or represented for use as food or drink for human beings, chewing gum, and any ingredient that may be mixed with food for any purpose whatever". A "drug" is defined in part to include "any substance or mixture of substances manufactured, sold or represented for use in the diagnosis, treatment, mitigation or prevention of a disease, disorder, or abnormal physical state, or its symptoms", or "for restoring, correcting or modifying organic functions".[4]

---

[2]   R.S.C. 1985, c. F-27.

[3]   C.R.C., c. 870.

[4]   A drug includes any substance or mixture of substances manufactured, sold or represented for use in the diagnosis, treatment, mitigation or prevention of a disease, disorder or abnormal physical state, or its symptoms, in human beings or animals; restoring, correcting or modifying

Generally, NHPs sold without health claims fell within the "food" definition. However, the presence of certain ingredients (*i.e.*, amino acids, vitamins, or minerals) would have likely resulted in the NHP being classed as a drug. An NHP was also regulated as a drug where a medicinal or health claim was made for the product.

If an NHP was classified as a drug, this entailed regulatory requirements which restricted the ability to market the product. In addition, drugs were required to satisfy a pre-market approval process, comply with Health Canada mandated Good Manufacturing Practices, be labelled in a specific manner and meet a variety of other requirements.

1.   The Need for Change in the Regulation of NHPs

(a)   Regulatory Factors

For years, NHPs had been inconsistently regulated causing confusion for suppliers as well as consumers. Consumers were confronted with products containing identical ingredients, side by side on the store shelf, one marketed as a drug with claims and the other as a food without claims. Some highlighted an ingredient while others mentioned only the raw herb. Consumers were left to wonder which product was more effective and in many cases, what the product was used for.

(b)   Public Opinion

In addition to the regulatory factors, there has been a substantial change in consumer attitudes.

- In 1995, Statistics Canada reported that about 15 per cent of adult Canadians, or 3.3 million people, reported using some form of alternative medicine in the past year;[5]
- In 2001, the *Regulatory Impact Analysis Statement* which accompanied the proposed *NHP Regulations*, it was noted that, "recent surveys have shown that more than one-half of Canadian consumers regularly take vitamins and minerals, herbal products, homeopathic preparations, and the like".[6]

---

organic functions in human beings or animals; or disinfection in premises in which food is manufactured, prepared or kept. *Food and Drugs Act*, R.S.C. 1985, c. F-27, s. 2.

[5] Statistics Canada, *National Population Health Survey Overview* (Ottawa: Statistics Canada, 1994-1995).

[6] SOR/2003-196, C. Gaz. II 1571.

(c)   The Beginning of the Review

In 1997, the Minister of Health asked the Standing Committee on Health to conduct a public review of the regulation of NHPs. The Minister commented:

> As a government, we must respect and allow room for Canadians' freedom of choice when it comes to natural health products. Canadians should have the broadest range of options available to them.

> At the same time, we must keep in mind our fundamental role as a regulator. The public relies upon Health Canada to prevent and correct dangers associated with health products, to ensure their quality and safety.[7]

The Standing Committee consulted extensively with over 150 associations and coalitions. In November 1998, the Standing Committee published its report[8] containing a list of 53 recommendations including:

* establishment of a separate regulatory body for NHPs;
* the need for a definition of an NHP;
* product licensing, including a pre-market review to establish safety and efficacy of all NHPs;
* claims permitted for NHPs; and
* labelling criteria.

The federal government subsequently announced the creation of a new Office of NHPs (now the Natural Health Products Directorate of the Health Products and Food Branch of Health Canada ("NHPD")). The Minister of Health noted that "for the first time, there will be a dedicated group of professional experts who will treat the evaluation of health products with the distinctiveness and flexibility it deserves".[9]

2.   The NHP Regulations

(a)   Overview

On June 18, 2003, the new *NHP Regulations* were published. These Regulations contain provisions regulating the manufacture, packaging, labelling, storage, importation, distribution and sale of natural health products and oversight of the clinical trial process.

---

[7]   Health Canada, News Release, "Allan Rock halts new regulation of natural health remedies and announces public review" (4 October 1997).

[8]   Report of the Standing Committee on Health, *Natural Products: A New Vision* (November 1998).

[9]   Health Canada News Release (26 March 1999).

Most provisions of the *Food and Drug Regulations* governing the sale of vitamins and minerals as drugs were repealed. Vitamin and minerals are regulated as NHPs and the strict limitations on claims permitted for vitamins and minerals have been repealed. Therefore, it should be possible to make expanded claims about the effects of vitamins and minerals provided that evidence is submitted to the NHPD, supporting the expanded claims.

NHPs are essentially classed as a subset of drugs. However, the *NHP Regulations* exempt NHPs from most provisions of the *Food and Drug Regulations*. Some of the provisions in the *Food and Drug Regulations* that apply to drugs also apply to NHPs, *i.e.*, child-resistant packaging.

(b) *Definition of an NHP*

The definition of an NHP is comprised of two components, a "substance component" and a "function component". The substance component includes homeopathics, traditional medicines, or one of the following alone or in combination as a medicinal ingredient:

Item 1	A plant or a plant material, an alga, a fungus or a non-human animal material
Item 2	An extract or isolate of a substance described in item 1
Item 3	Any of the following vitamins, their salts or derivatives: biotin, folic acid; niacin; pantothenic acid; vitamin A; vitamin B_1 or thiamine; vitamin B_2 or riboflavin, B_6 or pyridoxine, vitamin B_{12} or cyanocobalamin; vitamin C or ascorbic acid; vitamin D; vitamin E
Item 4	An amino acid
Item 5	An essential fatty acid
Item 6	A synthetic duplicate of a substance described in any of items 2 to 5
Item 7	A mineral
Item 8	A probiotic

Conjugates or salts of natural compounds remain within the definition, however those substances that are derived from nature but are chemically altered (*i.e.*, new molecular structure), would fall outside the definition of an NHP.

The function component follows the first two parts of the definition of a drug, referring to substances which are manufactured, sold or represented for use in:

(a) the diagnosis, treatment, mitigation or prevention of a disease, disorder or abnormal physical state or its symptoms in humans;

(b) restoring or correcting organic functions in humans; or

(c) maintaining or promoting health or otherwise modifying organic functions in humans.

Excluded from the definition of an NHP are antibiotics made from microorganisms, tobacco products, radionucleotides and biologics (*i.e.*, blood or blood derivatives). Also excluded are prescription drugs. Unlike drugs, NHPs only apply to humans, not animals.

It appears possible that a party wishing to avoid compliance with the *NHP Regulations* could use the same approach currently used to avoid the drug regulations, *i.e.*, make the product available without claims. However, there is a statement in the *Regulatory Impact Analysis Statement* which indicates the intention of government to formulate a list of substances which will not be permitted to be sold as food. To date no such list has been formulated.

(c)   Product Licensing (Part 1 of the NHP Regulations)

(i)   Product Licence Application

In order to obtain pre-market authorization for an NHP, an application for a product licence will have to be made. The formal requirements for a product licence are extensive; the application must provide sufficient information to enable the Minister to assess the safety and efficacy of the NHP. This requirement extends not only to the ingredients in the NHP and evidence supporting the safety and efficacy of those ingredients, but also to the product specifications and assurance that Good Manufacturing Practices will be adhered to.

The name, address, *etc.* of the applicant as well as all parties involved in manufacturing, packaging, labelling and distributing must be listed, as well as the site licence number for each. The medicinal and non-medicinal ingredients must be listed as must the strength, source and composition of the medicinal ingredient if it is manufactured synthetically. The purpose of the non-medicinal ingredient(s) must be given. The application must also list all brand names under which the product will be sold. The recommendations for use of the NHP and all copy to be used on the label must also be disclosed for the pre-market review.

(ii)   Issuance of Product Licence

Following the review of application, the Minister will issue a Product Licence and assign a product number to the NHP ("NPN"). The Product Licence will include the information submitted in the application, and the sale of the NHP must be in accordance with the Licence and the criteria set out therein.

Similar to drugs for which an established Labelling Standard or a Category IV Monograph exists, the *NHP Regulations* provide for the establishment of a Compendium of Monographs. The Compendium of Monographs provide support for the safety and claim of the medicinal ingredient of the NHP. If the applicant can show in support of the safety and efficacy of the NHP that the medicinal ingredient(s) is/are already contained in the Compendium of Monographs, then the Minister must dispose of the Application within 60 days without requiring additional safety and efficacy data. The NHPD is accepting as support for the safety and efficacy of certain NHPs, compliance with established Labelling Standards and Category IV Monographs that previously applied to certain NHPs when classed as drugs. Unfortunately, only compliance with the NHPD monograph will provide a "fast track" 60-day review.

The review process has been slow; a very limited number of NPNs have been issued to date, representing a very small percentage of the thousands of applications that have been submitted. This has placed added emphasis on the need to look carefully at transition provisions and the impact these provisions have on the sale of non-compliant NHPs.

(iii) Adverse Reaction Reporting

Under the *NHP Regulations*, the Licensee must provide the Minister with a case report for each serious adverse reaction in respect of an NHP that occurs within 15 days of becoming aware of the reaction.

Beyond these reporting obligations, the Minister may request further case studies or additional information where warranted.

(iv) Phasing in of Product Licensing

All NHPs sold prior to January 1, 2004, while not legal, may continue to be sold without complying with the product licensing provisions in accordance with the NHPD's Compliance Guide and Policy on non-compliant NHPs. Compliance will be required through a staged process for such products, which began in June 2004. The sale of all NHPs must comply with the *NHP Regulations* by January 1, 2010. Full compliance would be required when a Product Licence Application for the NHP is disposed of or withdrawn. The *NHP Regulations* also include transition provisions, however those provisions only apply to products which have a DIN. NHPs that are not required to comply with the *NHP Regulations* that have a DIN must, be sold in compliance with the *Food and Drug Regulations*.

(d) *Site Licensing (Part 2 of the Regulations)*

While Product Licensing deals with the efficacy and safety of the NHP, Site Licensing is intended to ensure that all levels of manufacturing, packaging and labelling of an NHP are performed with a level of control and oversight to ensure that the NHP is manufactured on a consistent basis, containing only what is intended to be included. This is achieved through the linkage of a Site Licence and compliance with Part 3 of the *NHP Regulations*, which deals with Good Manufacturing Practices. As of January 1, 2006, a Site Licence is required for all importers, manufacturers, packagers and labellers of NHPs. The Site Licence will be specific to any building in which any of the regulated activities are carried out.

(e)   *Good Manufacturing Practices (Part 3 of the Regulations)*

Good Manufacturing Practices ("GMPs") ensure quality control by setting appropriate standards regarding manufacturing, storage, handling and distribution of NHPs. All manufacturers, packagers, labellers, importers and distributors of NHPs must comply with GMPs. In fact, NHPs may not be sold unless they have been manufactured, packaged, labelled and stored in accordance with GMPs.

GMPs deal with product specifications, the manufacturing/labelling sites, equipment used in the manufacturing/labelling/storage process, personnel, sanitation, operation procedures, quality assurance, stability, record keeping, sampling and recall reporting. GMPs are drafted broadly without specificity. The NHPD has issued a GMP Guidance Document which suggests different ways in which compliance can be achieved. Good Manufacturing Practices, which is tied to Site Licensing, became a hot topic as of January 1, 2006. It is felt by many within the NHP industry that the GMP Guidance Document has gone beyond that which was envisioned for the industry, making compliance exceedingly difficult. This has caused a number of foreign manufacturers to re-think whether or not Canada will continue to fit within long term marketing plans. The added cost of compliance may result in a reduction of foreign products available to Canadian importers and consumers. It has been suggested that a detailed review of the manner in which the NHPD is interpreting Part 3 of the *NHP Regulations* is necessary. In light of the relative safety associated with most NHPs, this review is necessary to ensure that reasonable GMPs are implemented.[10]

(f)   *Clinical Trials (Part 4 of the Regulations)*

The level of detail and complexity regulating clinical trials in the *NHP Regulations* is similar to that provided in the *Food and Drug Regulations*, with respect to "Drugs".

In order to conduct a clinical trial using an NHP in Canada, approval must be sought from the Minister. This will entail:

- the submission of an application;
- the development of a protocol and informed consent;
- authorization of a Research Ethics Board;

---

[10]   Report of the Standing Committee on Health, *Natural Products: A New Vision* (November 1998), p. 24.

- selection of a qualified Clinical Trial Investigator;
- the development of an Investigator's Brochure;
- Clinical Trial Labelling;
- adverse reaction reporting;
- adherence to Good Clinical Practices; and
- record keeping.

(g) *Labelling and Packaging (Part 5 of the Regulations)*

(i) Requirements

Section 86 of the *NHP Regulations* states that no person is permitted to "sell a natural health product unless it is labelled and packaged in accordance" with the Regulations. This requirement does not apply to NHPs sold to a manufacturer or distributor.

The information required on the label must be in either English or French with the exception of the following, which must be in French *and* English:[11]

- recommended use or purpose;
- recommended route or administration;
- recommended dose;
- recommended duration of use; and
- risk information, including cautions, warnings, contra-indications or known adverse reactions.

Section 88 of the *NHP Regulations* states that the information required on an NHP label must be "clearly and prominently displayed; and readily discernible to the purchaser under customary conditions of purchase and use".

If there is only one label, then all the required information must be shown on that label.

Subject to the provisions for small container sizes, the inner and outer label must show the following information on the principal display panel:[12]

- the brand name;
- the product number;
- the dosage form;
- if the product is sterile, the words "Sterile" and "Stérile";
- the net amount of the immediate container in terms of weight, measure or number;

---

[11] See s. 93(1)b of the *NHP Regulations*.
[12] *Ibid.*, s. 93(1)(a).

and on any other panel:[13]

- the name and address of the product licence holder;
- if the product is imported, the name and address of the importer;
- the proper name and the common name of each medicinal ingredient;
- the strength or potency of each medicinal ingredient as contained in each dosage unit;
- recommended use or purpose;
- recommended route of administration;
- recommended dose;
- recommended duration of use, if any;
- risk information including any cautions, warnings, contra-indications, or known adverse reactions associated with the product's use;
- recommended storage conditions;
- lot number;
- expiry date; and
- a description of the source material of each medicinal ingredient.

In addition to the prescribed content for the inner and outer labels, the outer label must show:[14]

- a list of all non-medicinal ingredients contained in the natural health product; and
- if the product contains mercury or any of its salts or derivatives, a quantitative list by proper name that sets out all preservatives contained in the product.

As many NHPs are sold in small packages the *NHP Regulations* provide that if the container is too small to accommodate an inner label with all the required information, the inner label may contain only the following:[15]

- brand name;
- list by proper name that sets out in descending order of quantity all medicinal ingredients;
- recommended dose;
- recommended duration of use, if any;
- lot number;
- expiry date;
- product number;

---

[13] *Ibid.*, s. 93(1)(b).
[14] *Ibid.*, s. 93(2).
[15] *Ibid.*, s. 94(1)(a).

- if the product is sterile, the words "sterile" and in French "stérile";
- the net amount of the container;
- recommended use or purpose; and
- if the product does not have an outer label, a statement that refers the purchaser or consumer to a leaflet.

The outer label is required to have all the information required for outer labels regardless of the size of the container. If the product does not have an outer label, the information must be shown in a leaflet that is attached to the container.

(h)   Transition/Compliance

The *NHP Regulations* provides for a step wise, but generally helpful approach for the transition of NHPs not compliant with the *NHP Regulations*. In all cases, the transition provisions of the *NHP Regulations* require that the non-compliant NHPs comply with the previously applicable provisions of the *Food and Drug Regulations*. In many cases this is an impossibility as many present day non-compliant NHPs were also not compliant with the *Food and Drug Regulations*, particularly those provisions that apply to drugs. The NHPD in the *Regulatory Impact Analysis Statement* in Canada Gazette, Part I indicated an administrative compliance and enforcement approach would be followed for those NHPs that were marketed before the implementation of the *NHP Regulations*, and were not compliant with the *NHP Regulations* and the *Food and Drugs Act*. While this was not repeated in the *Regulatory Impact Analysis Statement* in Canada Gazette, Part II which accompanied the publication of the *NHP Regulations*, the NHPD nonetheless maintained that a compliance and enforcement approach would be followed with respect to NHPs not compliant with the *NHP Regulations* and the *Food and Drug Regulations*. This compliant and enforcement approach would be based on safety and risk. Ostensibly, this would mean that, while not legal to sell, where no safety concern exists, enforcement activity would likely not be directed to non-compliant NHPs, whether non-compliant with the *NHP Regulations* or the *Food and Drug Regulations*. Health Canada's *Compliance Policy for Natural Health Products* (the "Policy") centres on the issue of safety and focuses on bringing NHPs into compliance, in successive time frames, starting with those NHPs comprising ingredients that were previously characterized as a new drug. The approach requires the manufacturer of non-compliant NHPs that are being sold, to submit a Product Licence Application and receive a submission number by a date specified in the Policy, after which time enforcement activity will be directed at that class of NHPs where no submission number has been issued. Once the date specified in the Policy has passed, a manufacturer can still bring itself within the scope of the Policy by submitting a Product Licence Application, receiving a submission number and complying with any other aspects of the Policy. It is important to read the Policy in conjunction with the *Natural Health Products Compliance Guide* (the "Guide"). The Guide sets out the two-stage approach, that of risk and product categorization, the latter referred to above in the discussion on the Policy. The Guide sets out a series of questions that if answered in the positive will mean that there is an unacceptable risk associated with the sale of the non-compliant NHP, without an NPN. This determination could very well lead to a recall, *i.e.*, is the product one of those not exempt and directed to children 12 and under and, if so, then unless an NPN is assigned to the product, enforcement action will likely result if the product is brought to the attention of Health Canada.

D.   DRUG ADVERTISING

Any person who wants to promote drug products is subject to a variety of advertising and promotional restrictions. Existing Canadian regulatory requirements and/or policies limit the way drugs can be advertised to the general public and to health professionals.

That being said, not all drugs are treated equally under Canadian law. Certain drugs, due to their potential harm, types of conditions they are intended to treat, or the potential risk of abuse, are subject to more restrictions than other drugs. For example, subject to the proposed regulatory amendment, referred to hereinafter, where a drug is a scheduled drug as provided for in the *Food and Drug Regulations*, that drug and its purpose is prohibited from being advertised to the general public.[16]

Where a drug is a new drug,[17] it cannot be sold or advertised to the general public unless the manufacturer of the new drug has filed with the

---

[16]   *Food and Drug Regulations*, C.R.C., c. 870, s. G.01.007 and s. C.01.041.

[17]   The term "new drug" is defined as:

(a) a drug that contains or consists of a substance, whether as an active or inactive ingredient, carrier, coating excipient, menstruum or other component, that has not been sold as a drug in Canada for sufficient time and in sufficient quantity to establish in Canada the safety and effectiveness of that substance for use as a drug;

(b) a drug that is a combination of two or more drugs, with or without other ingredients, and that has not been sold in that combination or in the proportion in which those drugs are combined in that drug, for sufficient time and in sufficient quantity to establish in Canada the safety and effectiveness of that combination and proportion for use as a drug; or

(c) a drug, with respect to which the manufacturer prescribes, recommends, proposes or claims a use as a drug, or a condition of use as a drug, including dosage, route of administration, or duration of action and that has not been sold for that use or condition of use in Canada, for sufficient time and in sufficient quantity to establish in Canada the safety and effectiveness of that use or condition of use of that drug.

Food and Drug Regulations, C.R.C., c. 870, s. C.08.001.

Minister of Health, to the Minister's satisfaction, a New Drug Submission for the new drug; the Minister of Health has issued a Notice of Compliance to the manufacturer of the new drug in respect of the New Drug Submission; the Notice of Compliance has not been suspended; and the manufacturer of the new drug has submitted to the Minister of Health specimens of the final version of any labels, including packaging inserts, product brochures and file cards, intended for use in connection with the new drug and a statement setting out the proposed date on which those labels will first be used.

1.   Section B — Schedule A

Regardless of whether or not a drug meets the definition of a new drug, section 3 of the *Food and Drugs Act* restricts advertising of drugs to the general public with respect to any diseases, disorders, and abnormal physical states set out in Schedule A of the *Food and Drugs Act*. It has been the position of the Government of Canada, that with respect to these listed conditions, there is either no treatment or preventative or the listed conditions are inappropriate for self-treatment and require the intervention of a practitioner for treatment.

On November 19, 2005, proposed amendments to the *Food and Drug Regulations* and the *Natural Health Product Regulations* were released ("Proposed Amendments"). The Proposed Amendments, if they become law, would exempt non-prescription drugs and NHPs from the restriction against advertising claims relating to the prevention and treatment of Schedule A diseases. These claims would still require proper evidentiary support and be part of the market authorization that results from the pre-market review.

2.   Name, Price and Quantity

There are certain drug products that may be advertised to the public, but are limited to claims regarding the name, price and quantity of the drug. The logic behind this limitation is that drugs bound by such limitations are intended for conditions that are deemed to be unsuitable for self-diagnosis and/or self-treatment by members of the general public. As a result, these drugs require the intervention of a medical professional. Advertising the name, price, and quantity of such drugs allows consumers to make value decisions based on comparisons.

The types of drugs that may only be advertised to the general public in terms of name, price, and quantity can be divided into two basic categories: (1) limit dose drugs, and (2) Schedule F drugs.

Limit dose drugs (prescription) are listed in section C.01.021 of the *Food and Drug Regulations*. Limit dose drugs are listed in the form of a maximum single or daily dosage or in statements of concentration whereby a drug is limited to a maximum level of concentration. A limit dose drug with a dose above the maximum single or daily dosage or with a level of concentration that exceeds the level of concentration provided in section C.01.021 is deemed not to be suitable for self-medication by the general public.

Schedule F drugs are those drugs listed in Schedule F to the *Food and Drug Regulations*. Schedule F contains a list of drugs that may be sold for human use only when a medical practitioner provides a prescription. As a prescription is required, these drugs are not considered suitable for self-medication by the general public.

3.   Child Resistant Packaging and Labelling

Sections C.01.029 to C.01.031 require various cautionary statements and child resistant packaging where the drugs are known to be of concern when used by children. For example, where a package contains more than the equivalent of 250 mg. of elemental iron, a cautionary statement is required to the effect that the drug should be kept out of the reach of children, and that there is enough drug in the package to seriously harm a child. This cautionary statement must be preceded by a prominently displayed symbol that is octagonal in shape, conspicuous in colour and on a background of contrasting colour.

4.   Scientific Information in Advertising

Not all communications between drug manufacturers and the public are considered advertising for the purpose of the *Food and Drugs Act* and the *Food and Drug Regulations*. As such, there are methods drug manufacturers may employ to communicate with the public, or particular members of the public, without consideration of whether a drug is a limit dose drug or a Schedule F drug. Consideration of whether a message falls within the definition of advertising depends on the context of the message, whether the target audiences are limited or unlimited in scope, who delivers the message (*i.e.*, the drug manufacturer or an independent third party), who sponsors the message, the drug manufacturer's influence on the message, the content, and the frequency that the message is delivered. These factors are not exhaustive and are not determinative. Each message would be evaluated based on its own merit and may involve other factors.

There are various examples of messages that may not be considered advertising. For example, a patient support group that publishes information regarding the better understanding of a disease or its treatment may not be considered advertising, even where a drug manufacturer sponsors the publication of such a brochure. Such publications would be non-promotional material where the content of the information is disease-related and not product-related, the treatment options (whether drug or non-drug) are discussed in an objective manner, there is no emphasis on a single drug product, no reference is made to an unauthorized drug, other than to confirm that research is occurring in a particular area, and no reference is made to the availability of an unauthorized drug through the Therapeutic Products Directorate's ("TPD") Special Access Program.[18]

Another example is the use of 1-800 telephone numbers that appear in "Help Seeking Announcements". Where a member of the general public calls such a 1-800 line, the information provided by the sponsor may not be considered advertising if the information provided meets the same criteria as with patient support group publications. However, such information may be advertising where these conditions are not met or where other factors indicate that the 1-800 number exists for the primary purpose of promoting the sale of a particular drug.

5.   False, Misleading, Deceptive or Likely to Create an Erroneous Impression

The *Food and Drugs Act* also prohibits the advertising of drugs in a manner that is false, misleading, or deceptive or likely to create an erroneous impression regarding its character, value, quantity, composition, merit, or safety. Drug advertisers can avoid non-compliance with Canadian regulatory requirements by providing accurate and concise information so that the consumer can identify the availability and the effects of medical products for self-medication.

Drug advertising should indicate that the product is a drug and should not create the impression that the product is either a food or a cosmetic. Drug advertisements should not promote the unnecessary use of a drug. Examples of how an erroneous impression can be created by a drug advertisement include the use of seals of approval, quotations from the press, and testimonials. Seals of approval without a specific description of the type and degree of recognition accorded by the approving organization may create a false impression regarding the safety or value of a drug product. Quotations from the press raise concern where the publication of an article does not necessarily reflect the overall consensus of the professionals in a particular field, but is merely the opinion of a particular author. Testimonials may be limited to individual cases and therefore create a biased impression.

The TPD has stated that the issues affecting the benefits and risks associated with drug use is complex. As such, the TPD has expressed

---

[18] The TPD is accessible through Health Canada's website <http://www.hc-sc.gc.ca/english/index.html>.

concern that comparisons between drugs could result in the advertisement misleading members of the general public. It takes this position based on the belief that members of the general public usually lack the necessary expertise required to evaluate the comparisons of therapeutic properties and make educated decisions based on these comparisons.

Comparisons may also be misleading because they may be incomplete, overstate the advantages of the promoted product and the disadvantages of the competing products, exaggerate the importance of such advantages, and ignore the difference of opinions with regard to the impact of various qualities. Comparative advertising is not limited to direct comparisons between two specific products, but may include terms that imply a comparison without identifying the other product. Such terms include words such as "better", "richer", and "stronger".

Comparative advertising also includes negative statements with regard to competitive products such as implying that another product has a negative effect. Concerns are also raised by the use of negations, such as "non-toxic". Negations can lead consumers to consider a drug to be safe. This is a concern because the reality is that all drugs can be harmful if used improperly.

The TPD has published a series of consistent standards for advertisers to consult with regard to comparative claims relating to therapeutic aspects of drugs. Such comparative claims may not relate to drug products and ingredients that have not been authorized for sale in Canada. As such, advertisers must observe the following principles in making comparative claims:

1. the compared drugs/products have an authorized indication for use in common, and the comparison is related to that use; or, in addition to the common indication for use, a second authorized indication is claimed as an added benefit of the advertised drug;

2. the comparison is drawn between drugs under the same conditions of use, e.g., at equivalent part(s) of their authorized dose ranges (e.g., maximum vs. maximum dosage), in a similar population;

3. the claim does not conflict with the terms of market authorization of the compared products;

4. the claim is of clinical relevance in humans, i.e., relevant to treatment selection, and, where this is not readily apparent, its clinical relevance can be justified by the sponsor;

5. the evidence generated to substantiate the claim is conclusive and based on:

    i.   consideration of all relevant data;
    ii. scientifically accurate, unbiased, reproducible data obtained from studies conducted and analyzed to current scientific standards using established research methodologies and validated end points;
    iii. appropriate interpretation of the data; and

6. the claim and its presentation should:

  i.   identify the compared entities; and
 ii.   the medicinal use related to the claim where this is not readily apparent; and
iii.   not obscure the therapeutic use of the advertised product/ingredient; and
 iv.   not attack the compared drug product(s)/ingredient(s) in an unreasonable manner; and
  v.   be expressed in terms, language and graphics that can be understood by the intended audience.[19]

Under certain conditions, comparison claims can be made with respect to non-therapeutic aspects of non-prescription drugs. As with comparative claims, this only applies to non-prescription drugs because prescription drugs cannot be advertised to the public, expect for names, price and quantity. Such comparison advertising may occur where non-therapeutic aspects of non-prescription drug products are being compared to other non-prescription drug products or to products in other categories (*i.e.*, cosmetics). However, such advertising may not be false, misleading, or deceptive with regard to the therapeutic effects, value, quantity, composition, merit or safety of the product. In accordance with existing TPD policy, the following principles apply to such comparison advertising:[20]

  I.   Comparison between drug products in terms of comparability or superiority with respect to non-therapeutic attributes can be made under the following conditions:

    1.   the advertised product is primarily represented as a drug as defined in the Food and Drugs Act;
    2.   the compared products have an authorized indication for use in common with the advertised product;
    3.   the information provided may be of some benefit to some or most consumers, e.g., relevant to product selection;
    4.   the claim is supported by adequate, up to date, unbiased and statistically valid data;
    5.   the claim does not obscure information on the authorized indication(s) or intended medicinal use(s) of the advertised drug product;
    6.   any comparison of non-therapeutic characteristics should also include a reference to therapeutic characteristics; and
    7.   messages with comparison of non-therapeutic characteristics should carry a statement to the effect that superiority in these areas does not mean better compliance and/or better therapeutic characteristics, unless such a claim can be substantiated by scientific data.

. . .

 II.   Comparison between a drug product and products in other product categories (i.e. cosmetics) in terms of comparability or superiority with respect to non-therapeutic attributes can be made under the following conditions:

---

[19]   Therapeutic Products Directorate (TPD) Special Access Program, *Therapeutic Comparative Advertising: Directive and Guidance Document*, Part I, Section E.
[20]   TPD, *Principles for Claims Relating to Comparison of Non-therapeutic Aspects of Non-prescription Drug Products*, Section 5, Policy.

1. the advertised product is primarily represented as a drug, and the other product's identity/function/purpose is clearly identified (e.g. food, cosmetic...);
2. there is no implication of therapeutic activity attributed to the non-drug product(s);
3. the compared products are intended for use on or in the same body organ, e.g., hair, skin, mouth, teeth;
4. the information provided may be of some benefit to some or most consumers, e.g., relevant to product selection;
5. the claim is supported by adequate, up to date, unbiased and statistically valid data;
6. the claim does not obscure information on the authorized indication or intended medicinal use of the advertised drug product; and
7. the overall impression of the advertisement does not mislead the consumer as to the overall character, merit, composition, identity, function etc of the drug or non-drug product.

Where a drug is like a cosmetic, comparative advertising may be used with respect to non-therapeutic characteristics of the drug, such as taste, appearance and cleansing ability. Using surveys to indicate public preference for non-therapeutic aspects of a cosmetic-like drug is also acceptable as long as such statements can be statistically supported.

Other ways of misleading consumers are through the use of "accepted opinions", the use of information about the therapeutic properties of drugs derived from survey data, undue emphasis on particular claims (*i.e.*, through print size, colour, bold), and the use of misleading terminology. Care should be taken to avoid extreme descriptions (*i.e.*, "fantastic", "amazing", or "unbelievable") and scare advertising that could induce fear by suggesting, for example, that the consumer will suffer from a particular ailment if they do not use a drug. Advertising should avoid appealing to children through the use of cartoon characters and other forms of animation.

In a recent consultation document posted on TPD's website entitled *Consumer Advertising Guidelines For Marketed Health Products*, it is proposed that any advertising of non-prescription drugs or NHPs should contain information with respect to serious adverse drug reactions associated with the advertised product, to enable the consumer to make an informed decision. The consultation document provides that if the advertised product, when used according to the directions, has known serious adverse reactions (in terms of severity and clinical importance), or is contraindicated for a known group of people because it could cause serious adverse reactions, an appropriate warning of those reactions must be included in the advertisement. While this consultation document is currently in draft, it will be interesting to see what form the final document takes and what obligations are imposed on advertisers to include warning information about a drug within an advertisement, or to require a reference to review the label of the drug product.

6. Category IV Monographs/Labelling Standards

In addition to the foregoing, there are specific restrictions with respect to advertising drugs for which there are Category IV Monographs or Labelling Standards published by the TPD. Drugs subject to such restrictions include analgesics, antacids, antiperspirants, antiseptics, cold and allergy remedies, dental preparations, diuretics, laxatives, diet sedatives, skin preparations, smoking deterrents, vitamin and mineral products. For example, antacids may not be advertised in a manner that would promote overeating, careless eating habits, or the consumption of food identified as unsuitable for certain individuals. Laxatives should be promoted to the general public for occasional use, as regular use of laxatives may cause dependence. No advertisement should imply that vitamins and minerals are suitable substitutes for a healthy diet and that the results of a poor eating habit can be avoided by the use of such vitamins or minerals.

Regardless of the TPD's review of a DIN Application that is submitted in compliance with Category IV Monographs or Labelling Standards, which application includes a product label, the DIN applicant is responsible for ensuring that the labelling and advertising of the product complies with the Category IV Monograph and the Labelling Standard. Where such a label and/or application contains a claim not provided for in the Category IV Monograph or Labelling Standard, then it is likely that any advertisement with the same claim submitted for review by the TPD's designated entities will be refused. A number of the products that were the subject of either a Labelling Standard or Category IV Monograph are now regulated as NHPs. In many cases, the NHPD is accepting Product Licence Applications citing compliance with either of these TPD documents.

7. Drug Labelling

In addition to the advertising restrictions above, there are specific labelling requirements with regard to drug products. It should be noted that the same restrictions that apply to advertising also apply to labelling. For example, care must be taken to avoid misleading consumers, such as through the use of comparative claims.

Under the *Food and Drug Regulations*, the following labelling requirements are outlined:

(1)   All information on a label must be clearly and prominently displayed, and readily discernible to the purchaser or consumer under the customary conditions of purchase and use. The lettering on a label must be of a size that can be easily read by a person with normal vision.

(2)   Abbreviations should not appear on labels for products and ingredients, however, variations may appear where provided by the TPD, specifically permitted under the *Food and Drugs Act* or the *Food and Drug Regulations*, and may also appear for units of weight, volume, or potency.

(3)   When a product has a proper or common name, the name should appear on the main panel of the inner and outer labels, in the case of a proper name, should be at least half the size of the brand name, and should immediately proceed or follow the brand name. Where there is no brand name, the proper name must be on the main panel of the product label. This proper name is the name assigned to the drug in one of the pharmacopoeias listed in Schedule B to the *Food and Drugs Act*. The applies primarily in the case of single ingredient drug products.

(4)   The Drug Identification Number ("DIN") provided by the TPD must appear on the main panel of both the inner and outer labels. It should be noted that a DIN does not indicate, in the case of a product compliant with a Labelling Standard or Category IV monograph, that a product label is satisfactory but indicates that the information required has been filed with Health Canada.

(5)   Regardless of under what standard a drug has been manufactured, the standard used must appear on the main panel of the outer and inner label of the drug product.

(6)   The inner and outer labels of the product must indicate the quantities of all medicinal ingredients by their proper names, and if proper names do not exist, by their common names. Medicinal ingredients must be mentioned in a prescribed manner depending on whether the product is in the form of tablets, capsules, suppositories, powders, liquids, creams, lotions, or ointments.

(7)   The name and address of the manufacturer must appear on the inner and outer label. It should be noted that the manufacturer does not necessarily mean the fabricator of the product. It is the person who, under their own name or trademark or trademark controlled by that person, sells the drug. If the address of the manufacturer is not in Canada, the name and address of the Canadian importer must also be included on the product label. Interestingly, country of origin is not required for drug products.

(8) The inner and outer label must also include a lot number, expiration date, net contents, adequate directions for use, warnings and cautions as prescribed by the *Food and Drug Regulations*.

(9) Another issue that has recently surfaced as part of the TPD review of a DIN application is the placement on the label of the product name. Often, the product name may appear on the label with intervening words, often stressing a cosmetic aspect of the drug product. In a number of cases, TPD reviewers have insisted that either the name be revised on the DIN application to correspond to the way the name is shown on the label, *i.e.*, including the fragrance mentioned on the label, or require that the intervening language be moved on the label to either precede or follow the product name. For cosmetic-like drugs with multiple fragrances, this means ensuring the fragrance does not fall within the name on the label to avoid the requirement for multiple DINs where the name varies by fragrance only.

The *Food and Drug Regulations* address the issue of labelling products that are packaged in small containers. As such, where a drug is packaged in a container that is too small to bear all the information required by the *Food and Drug Regulations*, the requirements that normally apply are varied.

The *Food and Drug Regulations* outline that any statement, information or declaration that is required to appear on a drug label appear in either French or English, in addition to any other language on the label. Further, the adequate directions for use required to appear on the inner and outer label, as described in item 6 above, must appear in French and English where the drug is available for sale without prescription in an open self-selection area.

E.   ADVERTISING CLEARANCE

Advertising Standards Canada (the "ASC") has been designated by Health Canada to pre-screen drug and NHP advertisements for compliance with the *Food and Drugs Act* and its accompanying regulations. Advertisements that require pre-screening include radio and television and mass media. The process for submitting a request for approval is simple. The sponsor of the advertisement must submit an ASC clearance submission form by fax, mail or courier. The advertisement review process conducted by the ASC takes four business days from the receipt of the completed clearance form. A priority service is available to advertisers at an extra cost, with a turnaround of two business days from receipt of the completed clearance form. The charges for regular services for non-prescription drugs range from $50 to $235, depending on the type of media and whether the sponsor of the advertisement is an ASC member. The ASC will consult the *Food and Drugs Act*, the *Food and Drug Regulations*, Health Canada's Consumer Drug Advertising Guidelines, the authorized product information available from Health Canada, and other relevant Health Canada policies and guidelines and ASC clearance policies for the advertisement review.[21] Recently, ASC issued a statement that it would begin reviewing "no claim" NHP advertising copy that has received a submission number based on the submission of a Product Licence Application but not an NPN. A "no claim" advertisement is advertising in which no therapeutic claim is made. In those cases, the advertisement cannot (i) identify the product as an NHP; (ii) make any direct or indirect reference to the NHPD or Health Canada; or (iii) be directed to children or pregnant or nursing women (two of the risk questions in the Guide).

Advertising limitations also exist for advertisements directed to health care professionals. The Pharmaceutical Advertising Advisory Board ("PAAB") plays a role in the advertising of drugs to health care professionals. PAAB has the responsibility of reviewing all drug advertisements directed to health care professionals. PAAB is a multidisciplinary body which provides an independent review and preclearance of drug advertising and promotion materials. Part of PAAB's role is to include an evaluation of marketing claims that make a direct or implied comparison between two or more drug products. PAAB has the authority to clear such information where the manufacturer provides support of such marketing claims provided that such claims or supporting data does not extend beyond the limits of the terms of market authorization. It should be noted that PAAB's role is quite broad and applies to letters issued by manufacturers that are directed to doctors and pharmacists.[22]

---

[21] Accessible online at: <http://www.adstandards.com>.

[22] Accessible online at: <http://www.paab.ca>.

Appendix B

SCHEDULE "A": DISEASES SECTION 3 OF THE FOOD AND DRUGS ACT

Alcoholism	Gout
Alopecia (except hereditary androgenetic alopecia)	Heart disease
Anxiety state	Hernia
Appendicitis	Hypertension
Arteriosclerosis	Hypotension
Arthritis	Impetigo
Asthma	Kidney disease
Bladder disease	Leukemia
Cancer	Liver disease (except hepatitis)
Convulsions	Nausea and vomiting of pregnancy
Depression	Obesity
Diabetes	Pleurisy
Disease of the prostate	Rheumatic fever
Disorder of menstrual flow	Septicemia
Dysentery	Sexual impotence
Edematous state	Thrombotic and Embolic disorders
Epilepsy	Thyroid disease
Gall bladder disease	Tumor
Gangrene	Ulcer of the gastro-intestinal tract
Glaucoma	Venereal disease

Chapter 9

COSMETICS ADVERTISING AND LABELLING

Contributed by Shelley Samel

A. INTRODUCTION

The cosmetics industry is a multi-billion dollar industry in Canada. In an era of aging baby boomers, cosmetic companies are constantly trying to pitch miracle cures to keep people from looking their age. Cosmetic companies are continuously reformulating, repackaging and inventing new products to meet (and create) consumer demand. In promising cures and miracles, cosmetic companies must tread a fine line, as cosmetic claims have to be just that — related to the cosmetic benefits of a product. Claims are not allowed to cross the line and make drug-like claims, unless they are in fact registered with Health Canada as drug products.

Cosmetics are defined in the *Food and Drugs Act*[1] as any substance or mixture of substances that is manufactured, sold or represented for use in cleansing, improving, or altering the complexion, skin, hair or teeth, and include deodorants and perfumes. At this point, it is worth reviewing the section 2 definition of "drug" in the *Food and Drugs Act*:

"drug" includes any substance or mixture of substances manufactured, sold or represented for use in

(a) the diagnosis, treatment, mitigation or prevention of a disease, disorder or abnormal physical state, or its symptoms, in human beings or animals,

(b) restoring, correcting or modifying organic functions in human beings or animals, or

(c) disinfection in premises in which food is manufactured, prepared or kept.

The key distinction between cosmetics and drugs is the intended use of the product.

---

[1] R.S.C. 1985, c. F-27.

This chapter will provide an overview of the regulations and guidelines that are specific to the marketing of cosmetics in Canada.

B.   THE LAW

The *Food and Drugs Act*, and specifically the *Cosmetic Regulations*,[2] govern cosmetics. Not only do these pieces of legislation detail specific labelling requirements, they also set out the requirements for mandatory filings by cosmetic manufacturers or distributors.

A Cosmetic Notification must be filed with Health Canada prior to importation of a cosmetic into Canada or within ten days of the first sale of the product if it is manufactured in Canada. Unlike the drug submission process, the cosmetic process is *not* an evaluation or approval of the product.

Section 16 of the *Food and Drugs Act* prohibits, amongst other things, the sale of any cosmetic that has in or on it any substance that may cause injury to the health of the user when the cosmetic is used according to the directions on the label or for such purposes and by such methods as are customary for such a cosmetic. To that end, Health Canada produces a Cosmetic Ingredient Hot List that lists prohibited and restricted ingredients. Some ingredients on the list can be included in certain products and in certain concentrations (and prescribed cautions may be mandated), whereas other ingredients are prohibited outright. The list is frequently updated and Health Canada has mechanisms in place to deal with products that contain ingredients included on the Hot List, which are outlined in its guidance documents.

While some aspects of cosmetic labelling are set out in the *Cosmetic Regulations*, the *Consumer Packaging and Labelling Act*[3] and its corresponding Regulations as well as the *Hazardous Products Act*[4] and its *Consumer Chemicals and Containers Regulations* (as they read on September 30, 2001), also govern the labelling of cosmetics.

Further, the overarching requirement to produce truthful advertising that includes claims that can be substantiated stems from the *Competition Act*, as described in more detail in Chapters 1, 3 and 14.

C.   CLAIMS

The key to making claims for cosmetics is to ensure that the claims relate to cosmetic benefits and do not cross the line and become drug claims.

---

[2]   C.R.C., c. 869.
[3]   R.S.C. 1985, c. C-38.
[4]   R.S.C. 1985, c. H-3.

To that end, Advertising Standards Canada, Health Canada and CCTFA (Canadian Cosmetic, Toiletry and Fragrance Association) publish the Guidelines for Cosmetic Advertising and Labelling Claims.

The Guidelines (which can be found on the Advertising Standards Canada website) include lists of acceptable and unacceptable claims for various forms of cosmetics, as well as by claim type. It is meant to provide an overview of what types of claims would be considered acceptable — although, since it is a guideline, it does not have the force of law. Basically, the acceptable claims are ones where the benefit is clearly cosmetic. Unacceptable claims include those that imply that the cosmetic in question works on the cellular level or is able to treat an abnormal skin condition. Even words like "treatment" and "therapy" are generally reserved for drugs and should be used with caution. The Guidelines address how these terms can be used for cosmetic products in specific circumstances.

The Guidelines have been revised several times in the last few years. Draft revised guidelines were published in the summer of 2005, however, the draft revisions have yet to be formally accepted.

Some of the more popular claim types and their treatment in the Guidelines are canvassed below.

(1) **Antioxidants**

Antioxidants seem to be the buzzword of the cosmetic industry, as they are believed to protect the skin by attaching themselves to free radicals, minimizing the harm free radicals can do to the skin. For a time, Canadian cosmetic manufacturers or distributors could only mention that a product contained antioxidants as a product preservative. Now, the presence of antioxidants may be claimed without reference to a product preservative provided no benefit is linked to that ingredient. For instance, the claim "Product X contains antioxidants and vitamin E. The product evens out skin tone and makes skin look firm" would be acceptable.

It is unacceptable to make a claim concerning the therapeutic effect of antioxidants (such as free radical scavenging). It is also unacceptable to claim that a product contains vitamins that act as antioxidants — likely because the claim implies that antioxidants have a therapeutic benefit.

Cosmetics manufacturers and distributors can go even further than mentioning the presence of antioxidants. According to the Guidelines, antioxidants can be directly linked to a cosmetic benefit. In order to directly attribute any benefits to the presence of antioxidants, however, two conditions must be met. First, the benefits claimed must be cosmetic in nature (*i.e.*, reduces the appearance of wrinkles, or moisturizes); and, written attestation is required for broadcast pre-clearance. This latter condition requires the advertiser to have data on file to support the claim that the stated benefits are directly attributable to the presence of the antioxidant (undoubtedly a tall order). These same two conditions apply for claims relating to a benefit attributed directly to vitamins, minerals or other active ingredients as well.

(2) **Anti-Aging**

Anti-aging claims are another type of claim that inundates the media. Anti-aging claims are permitted for cosmetics provided the claims relate to the look of aging. For instance, "slows the look of aging" and "reverses the signs of aging" are acceptable, but "anti-aging" or "anti-wrinkle" in an unqualified sense are not. In essence, the take-away from the claim cannot be that the product will prevent aging or slow the onset of aging.

(3) **Firming**

Firming claims are permitted for moisturizing products provided the claims are modified by the fact that the firming is from an appearance perspective, *i.e.*, skin looks firmer. Unqualified firming claims are on the list of unacceptable claims.

(4) **Healthy**

This is another popular claim, particularly for U.S. cosmetics. In Canada, cosmetic products can make your hair or skin *healthy-looking* but cannot make them healthy *per se*.

(5) **Nourish**

A cosmetic product can only claim to nourish via moisturization. So, any claims that a product is nourishing must be clearly linked to the moisturizing aspect of the product. Copy writers can work their magic on the beauty copy provided it is clear that the nourishing aspect of the product is a result of moisturization.

As set out above, the Guidelines' listings are merely examples. Have your lawyer review all on-pack and advertising claims to ensure that your cosmetic product does not become characterized as a drug as a result of the claims you are making or your product may be recalled. If a claim causes the product to be characterized as a drug, it must comply with the *Food and Drug Regulations*,[5] including all drug submission and labelling requirements, and cannot be sold without a DIN number.

---

[5]   C.R.C., c. 870.

D. LABELLING

Some aspects of the labelling of cosmetics are set out specifically in the *Cosmetic Regulations* and others stem from the *Consumer Packaging and Labelling Act* and its Regulations. The reference to the *Hazardous Products Act* and the *Consumer Chemicals and Containers Regulations* (affectionately referred to as the "CCCRs") applies in respect of cosmetic products sold in pressurized metal containers. Interestingly, the *Cosmetic Regulations* incorporate by reference a version of the CCCRs that is no longer in force.

While the requirements listed below are those under Canadian federal law, if a product is sold in Quebec (and most are, since Quebec accounts for such a large percentage of our economy and distribution in health and food channels tends to be national), all elements of the product label — with the exception of INCI ingredient names as discussed below — must be translated into French and the French text must be at least of equal prominence to the English text.

Different labelling requirements apply to inner and outer labels of cosmetic products. Font size and typefaces used are prescribed in certain circumstances and may depend on the package size. Also, specific provisions apply with respect to the placement of mandatory information on ornamental containers, such as perfume bottles, which are popular within the cosmetics industry.

An ornamental container is defined in the *Consumer Packaging and Labelling Regulations* as a container that, except on the bottom, does not have any promotional or advertising material, other than a trade mark or common name and that, because of any design appearing on its surface or because of its shape or texture, appears to be a decorative ornament and is sold as a decorative ornament in addition to being sold as the container of a product. For most cosmetics, certain mandatory information must appear on the principal display surface which is customarily in view to the consumer, and the name and address of the manufacturer or distributor of a cosmetic is not permitted to appear on the bottom of a label. Neither of these requirements applies to ornamental containers, for which the bottom of the container or an attached tag is a permitted surface for such information.

1. Requirements for Outer Labels

(a) Product Identity — must be included in English and French on the principal display panel of the product. There are exceptions where the product is bubble-packed and you can see the contents or where an accurate pictorial representation is used. Generally, this must be in a font size of at least 1.6 mm in height.

(b)   Net Quantity — must be included in metric units in English and French on the principal display panel. Most abbreviated versions of the metric units are considered bilingual — such as g, kg, L, l, mL and ml. The numerical portion must be in bold face font and meet minimum height requirements (for most cosmetics, this will be at least 1.6 mm in height). Volume is generally used for liquid, gas or viscous substances and weight is used for solids. This is to be contrasted with the U.S. situation, where typically, the volume versus weight declaration will depend on viscosity. Where supplementary information is given, it cannot be misleading. For instance, U.S. fluid ounces are slightly larger than Canadian fluid ounces (the reason for this eludes me). Where a harmonized label is being used, it is important to be clear that the fluid ounces declared are American, *i.e.*, 591 mL, 20 fl. oz. (U.S.) Note there is some risk in not translating the term "U.S." into French if the product is being sold in Quebec, although this risk seems to be assumed by many distributors of cosmetics in Canada. There are specific rounding rules that apply, as well as rules that detail the number of figures in the decimal system that must be declared.

(c)   Domicile — According to the *Consumer Packaging and Labelling Act*, the name and address of the dealer must be included and can appear anywhere except for the bottom of the package, in either French or English or both. If the product is not manufactured in Canada, the words "imported by/importé par" or "imported for/importé pour" or a statement of origin must be set out next to the domicile. Font type must be at least 1.6 mm height.

(d)   Avoidable Hazards & Cautions — The *Cosmetic Regulations* set out required disclosures in English and French for specific product types, such as hair dyes, genital deodorants, pressurized metal containers and flammable pressurized metal containers. Some of the elements must be on the principal display panel and others can go on the back panel. In addition, there is an obligation to warn consumers in English and French of all avoidable hazards and how these hazards can be avoided. From a product liability perspective, any hazards should be thoroughly considered and appropriately described.

(e)   Ingredients — As of November 17, 2006, all cosmetics will have to carry an ingredient listing on the product's outer label. The listing of ingredients is preceded by the words "Ingredients/Ingrédients:" These requirements are canvassed in more detail below.

2.   Requirements for the Inner Label

Assuming the product contains an outer label that complies with the above-noted requirements (if there is only one label, all requirements apply to the inner label), the following is a list of the requirements for the inner label:

(a) Product Identity — required to be set out on the principal display panel in English and French and in sizing set out above unless the identity is obvious.

(b) Domicile — under the *Cosmetic Regulations*, the name and address of the manufacturer or distributor listed in the Cosmetic Notification is required to be set out in English, French or both in font that is easily readable and can appear anywhere except for the bottom of the package. The same rules as outlined above for the outer label in respect of imported products apply here.

(c) Avoidable Hazards & Cautions — some of the regulated language is required on inner labels and in some circumstances, the requirement will depend on product sizing. As a rule, all inner labels must warn of all known hazards as well (in both English and French).

3. Mandatory Ingredient Labelling

In November 2004, new labelling requirements were enacted by way of amendment to the *Cosmetic Regulations* requiring mandatory ingredient labelling on cosmetic products. As of November 17, 2006, *all* cosmetics must comply (including samples and hotel cosmetics). The only exemption appears to be cosmetic-counter demos.

Under the amended Regulations, ingredients must be listed on the outer label of a cosmetic package. If there is only one label, the list must be on that label. The list of ingredients (like all other mandatory labelling requirements for cosmetics) must be clearly legible and remain so throughout the useful life of the cosmetic under normal conditions of sale and use. Inclusion of the ingredient list on a peel-away tab would likely not comply with these requirements.

Ingredients are defined to mean any substance that is one of the components of a cosmetic and includes colouring agents, botanicals, fragrance and flavour, but does not include substances that are used in the preparation of the cosmetic but that are not present in the final product as a result of a chemical process.

Ingredients must be listed using the International Nomenclature Cosmetic Ingredient ("INCI") name assigned to an ingredient in what is known as the ICI Dictionary — International Cosmetic Ingredient Dictionary and Handbook. The 11th edition is the current version, although the most current edition must be used. INCI is multilingual, multinational and based on Latin. It is the mandatory nomenclature in the United States, the European Union and (soon to be) Canada.

The amended Regulations require that each ingredient must be listed:

- by its INCI name (except where there are trivial names, as described below);
- botanicals must be listed *at least* by the genus and species portions of the INCI name (this can also include the common name, plant part and preparation method); makeup, nail polish and enamel sold in a range of colour shades can list all colouring agents used in the range if "+/-" or "±" or "may contain/ peut contenir" are used;
- if there is no INCI name, then the chemical name from a recognized source must be used; and
- the Schedule to the Regulations lists about 60 EU Trivial Names and their English and French equivalent. If an ingredient falls in this list, the EU Trivial Name can be used *or* both the English and French name can be used. Trivial names are the Latin version of the INCI names as assigned by the European Union. For instance, cosmetics that are to be sold in Canada and the United States must list the ingredient of water as "water" to comply with U.S. labelling requirements. To meet Canadian requirements, the ingredient can be listed as either "aqua" or "water/eau". Since "water" is mandatory for the U.S., most such products will opt to use "water/eau".

Additionally:
- fragrances that are used to produce or mask odour can be listed as "parfum"; and
- flavours that are used to produce or mask flavours can be listed as "aroma".

Descriptive or promotional terms are not permitted in front of an ingredient name in the ingredient list.

A major concern arose as a result of Quebec's *Charter of the French Language*'s requirement that all elements of a package that are included in a language other than French must be included in French as well and that the French must be at least as prominent as the other language. This requirement applies on its face to all INCI ingredients, as they are not in French. Fortunately, as a result of extensive lobbying by the cosmetics industry, the Quebec government has agreed that INCI is sufficient to meet labelling laws under the *Charter of the French Language*. We have been advised that in May, 2006, the Quebec legislature passed a law which will allow for the *Charter of the French Language* to be revised to respect the INCI and ensure harmonization with the *Cosmetic Regulations'* ingredient labelling requirements.

Ingredients must be listed in descending order of predominance, in concentration by weight. The following exceptions apply:
- Where concentrations are 1 per cent or less those ingredients can be listed after all ingredients present at more than 1 per cent in random order.

- All colouring agents (regardless of concentration) can be listed at the end of the list in random order.
- "Parfum" and "aroma" can be inserted at the end of the list (or each fragrance/flavour ingredient can be listed following the rules for all other ingredients) or at the appropriate point in the ingredient list.

Many cosmetic manufacturers and distributors were concerned about the impact this would have on their packaging. For instance, one can easily imagine that it would be no easy task to physically fit a list of all ingredients onto a lipstick or eyeliner package.

This situation has been accounted for in the Regulations. If the package is so small that the ingredients cannot be clearly legible, then the list can appear on a tag, tape or card affixed to the container. Further, if there is no outside package and the size, shape or texture make it impractical to label the ingredients, then the list must be in a leaflet that must accompany the package at point of sale.

E.   PRE-CLEARANCE

Broadcast advertising copy can be pre-cleared by Advertising Standards Canada ("ASC") or Broadcast Clearance Advisory ("BCA") on a fee-for-service basis. Pre-approval is not mandated by Health Canada, however, practically speaking, Canadian broadcasters will not run a cosmetic ad without prior approval.

Chapter 10

FOOD ADVERTISING AND LABELLING

Contributed by Shelley Samel

A.   INTRODUCTION

You may notice when watching American television or vacationing in the United States that there appears to be more healthy food choices available to our neighbours to the south. The reality is that in Canada there are not necessarily fewer healthy choices, rather, Canadian food manu-facturers face restrictions on their ability to convey the health benefits of foods.

The labelling and advertising of foods is a highly regulated field. This chapter is meant as an overview of some of the issues that, in our experience, most frequently arise in food labelling and advertising as well as a brief overview of new regulations that now govern most of this field. We strongly advise that you seek the assistance of your advertising lawyer before preparing any food labels or food advertising campaigns.

B.   STATUTORY FRAMEWORK

Food advertising and labelling is governed generally by two statutory regimes: the *Competition Act*[1] and the *Food and Drugs Act*.[2]

As discussed in greater detail in Chapters 1 and 2, the *Competition Act*, administered by the Competition Bureau, is the keystone of advertising law. Under the *Competition Act*, advertisers are prohibited from, among other things, making representations in advertising that are "false or misleading in a material respect". Unlawful advertising occurs when a false or misleading representation could influence a consumer to buy the product or service advertised. The *Competition Act* also requires that an

---

[1]   R.S.C. 1985, c. C-34.
[2]   R.S.C. 1985, c. F-27.

advertiser possess "adequate and proper" testing for any claim made in advertising *before* the claim is published.

The *Food and Drugs Act* and its Regulations strictly control the advertising, packaging and labelling of food, prohibit certain claims and mandate the inclusion of certain information.

We are currently at a pivotal point in the regulation of food. Recent amendments to the *Food and Drug Regulations* made expansive changes to the landscape of Canadian food labelling and advertising.

The *Food and Drugs Act* is administered by Health Canada. However, the Canadian Food Inspection Agency ("CFIA") is also charged with administering the food-related elements of the Act and Regulations.

The *Guide to Food Labelling and Advertising* ("the Guide") was issued by Health Canada as a reference for food manufacturers and advertisers to ensure compliance with the *Food and Drugs Act*. The amended Guide, which was issued on December 31, 2003, one year after the amendments to the Act and its Regulations, sheds some light on how the CFIA interprets the new Regulations.

While the Guide sets out Health Canada's position on many "grey" areas, it does *not* have the force of law.

However, since broadcast advertisements relating to food products (with the exception of "no claim" ads) must receive prior approval from Advertising Standards Canada ("ASC") or Broadcast Clearance Advisory ("BCA"), the *Guide to Food Labelling and Advertising*, which is used by both the ASC and BCA, has the effect of law for broadcast ads for food. "No claim" advertisements are those that do not make any direct or indirect reference to quality; ingredients or composition; nutrition; nutritional properties; health, safety or weight management; or production and processing.

There is also additional legislation that should be consulted for various types of foods. For instance, the *Canada Agricultural Products Acts* regulates, amongst other things, the grading, packing and marking of processed agricultural products including eggs, fruits, vegetables, honey and dairy. Some provincial governments have also enacted legislation that may be relevant, such as edible oil legislation and dairy regulations.

Further, in the past, natural health products were regulated either as foods or as drugs. As described in Chapter 8, if a product meets the substance and function definition of natural health products (which are considered drugs), it will be regulated exclusively by the *Natural Health Products Regulations*, regardless of the fact that the product could also be characterized as a food.

C.   GENERAL LABELLING REQUIREMENTS

The *Food and Drugs Act* and the *Consumer Packaging and Labelling Act* establish the general labelling requirements for food, which will be canvassed in this chapter.

1.   Required Information

(a)   Appearance and Position

As a rule of thumb, all required information must be easily read and clearly and prominently displayed. Unless otherwise specified in the legislation, the Act stipulates that the minimum type height is 1.6 mm. — based on the lowercase letter "o" — for certain required information. The Guide suggests that *all* required information (with the exception of the Nutrition Facts table which has its own font requirements explained below) adopt this minimum height requirement.

With the exception of information that must appear on the principal display panel and the Nutrition Facts box as discussed below, all required information may appear on any panel except the bottom.

(b)   Bilingual Requirements

All required information must be stated in both official languages, with the exception of the identity and principal place of business of the manufacturer or distributor (frequently referred to as the "domicile") which may be in either English or French. Note that shipping containers not offered to consumers do not need to be labelled in both languages. Similarly, local products sold in an area in which one of the official languages is the mother tongue of less than 10 per cent of the residents can be labelled exclusively in the other official language.

However, if a food is offered for sale in Quebec, the *Charter of the French Language* requires that all elements of the package must be bilingual and the French copy must be at least as prominent as the English.

(c)   Required Elements — Specific to Foods

The common name of a food must appear on the principal display panel of the food. The common name is set by regulation (*e.g.*, "mayonnaise" or "milk chocolate") or, if no name is prescribed by the Regulations, the common name is the name by which the food is commonly known (*e.g.*, vanilla cookies or chocolate cake). The common name cannot be misleading. Therefore, it cannot incorporate words which are not justified by the composition of the food (*e.g.*, "butter cookies" for cookies made with vegetable oil) or improperly suggest a place of origin (*e.g.* "Champagne" for Canadian sparkling wine). Also, the common name should not resemble (and this includes phonetic resemblance) the name of another product for which it is an imitation or substitute.

The net quantity must also appear on the principal display panel. There are some exceptions to the net quantity requirement, and declarations of net quantity for foods that are not prepackaged for retail sale (*e.g.*, fruits and vegetables) are governed by the *Weights and Measures Act.*

Prepackaged multi-ingredient foods, with few exceptions, must contain an ingredient list (in both English and French) which lists the ingredients in descending order of proportion by weight. Certain ingredients, such as spices, seasonings, artificial flavours, vitamin and mineral nutrients, can be shown at the end of the ingredient list in any order. There are various guidelines concerning the listing of ingredients by common names and the inclusion of ingredient components (ingredients of ingredients).

If an illustration on a food label suggests a natural flavour source, such as a picture of a strawberry, where an artificial flavour has been added to a food (either alone or with a natural flavour source), the label must state in both English and French and adjacent to the illustration that the added flavouring ingredient is imitation or artificial.

Best before dates are required, with a few exceptions, on pre-packaged goods that have a durable life of 90 days or less. The durable life of a food is the period (from the date the food is packaged) during which food will retain its normal palatability and nutritional value, if stored under appropriate conditions. The best before dates and storage instructions (if other than room temperature) must be in English and French on any panel other than the bottom, unless there is a clear indication elsewhere on the package that the best before date is on the bottom.

Nutrition Fact tables including certain minimum nutrient declarations became mandatory on December 12, 2005 for most companies. A discussion of Nutrition Facts tables is included below.

Certain foods have other mandatory information requirements that are beyond the scope of this chapter. For instance, the label of any food sweetened with artificial sweeteners and meal replacements commonly used as dietary products must display certain information and have specific compositional requirements. One should always check the *Food and Drugs Act* and its Regulations to ensure that the food in question does not have labelling requirements specific to the food or category.

D.   NUTRITIONAL LABELLING

A major change now in effect (and warranting a detailed discussion in this chapter) is that it has become mandatory for most manufacturers to include Nutrition Facts tables on prepackaged food products sold in Canada. Prior to December 12, 2005 (unless early compliance was triggered by certain claims[3]), including a nutrition information table was voluntary and the words "Nutrition Facts" were prohibited (as they were thought to be misleading and confusing with the U.S. system which uses a different basis for many calculations).

The Regulations now set out in great detail the form and content of the mandatory Nutrition Facts tables.

1.   Mandatory Nutrition Facts

A "Nutrition Facts" table is *required* for all pre-packaged foods,[4] unless the food meets one of the following exemptions:

- beverages with an alcohol content of more than 0.5 per cent;
- fresh fruits or vegetables;
- single ingredient meats, meat by-products, poultry meats or poultry meat by-products that are raw and not ground;
- raw single ingredient marine or fresh water animal products;
- food sold in the retail establishment where the product is prepared and processed;
- food sold at a roadside stand, craft show, flea market, fair, farmers' market or sugar bush by the individual who prepared and processed the food;
- an individual serving of food sold for immediate consumption which has not been subjected to a process to extend its shelf life;
- a food sold only in retail establishments where it is packaged if the product has a sticker and less than 200 cm² of display surface;
- one-bite confections; a prepackaged individual portion of food served by a restaurant or other commercial enterprise with meals or snacks; or
- milk sold in a refillable glass container.

Since there are already specific food labelling requirements for infant formulas, meal replacements, nutritional supplements, human milk substitutes, foods represented for use in a very low energy diet and formulated liquid diet, these foods are also excluded from the mandatory nutritional labelling requirements.

Generally, where a food is otherwise exempt from the mandatory nutrition labelling requirements, the product may lose its exemption if:

- a vitamin or mineral is added to the product;

---

[3]   If manufacturers took advantage of certain of the newly permitted claims before compliance became mandatory, their food labels had to be compliant as soon as the claims were made.

[4]   Other than foods sold by small manufacturers who had gross revenues from sales in Canada of food of less than $1 million in the 12-month period prior to December 12, 2002 — in which case they have until December 12, 2007 to comply.

- the product or its ingredients (other than flour) contains a declared vitamin or mineral;
- the product contains added aspartame, sucralose or acesulfame-potassium;
- the label of, or any advertisement for, the product contains a reference to the energy value, a nutrient or a constituent of a nutrient;
- a statement, claim or representation is made that suggests that the product has a particular nutritional or health-related property, including any of the nutrient content claims discussed above, biological role claims or diet-related health claims;
- a health-related name, statement, logo, symbol, seal of approval, or mark is used on the packaging; or
- the phrase "nutrition facts", "valeur nutritive" or "valeurs nutritives" is used.

2.   Content

The Nutrition Facts table must always include certain core information in a prescribed order. In addition to the core list, manufacturers may include certain additional information in the Nutrition Facts table as permitted in the Regulations. Only the core list and permitted additional information may be included in the Nutrition Facts table. The elements required in the core list are the following:

- the serving of stated size;
- energy value in calories;
- amount of fat;
- amount of saturated fatty acids;
- amount of *trans* fatty acids;
- the sum of saturated fatty acids and *trans* fatty acids;
- amount of cholesterol;
- amount of sodium;
- amount of carbohydrate;
- amount of fibre (which can be spelled "fibre" or "fiber");
- amount of sugars;
- amount of protein;
- amount of the following vitamins and minerals:
  - vitamin A;
  - vitamin C;
  - calcium; and
  - iron.

These values must be expressed in the units of measure and according to the rounding rules set out in a table in the Regulations.

The following permitted or optional nutritional information may be included in the Nutrition Facts table:

- servings per container;
- energy value measured in kilojoules;
- energy value from fat;
- energy value from the sum of saturated and *trans* fatty acid;
- amount of polyunsaturated fatty acids;
- amount of omega-6 polyunsaturated fatty acids;
- amount of omega-3 polyunsaturated fatty acids;
- amount of monounsaturated fatty acids;
- amount of potassium;
- amount of soluble fibre;
- amount of insoluble fibre;
- amount of sugar alcohol;
- amount of starch;
- amount of additional vitamin and minerals:

Vitamin D	Vitamin E
Vitamin K	Thiamine
Riboflavin	Niacin
Vitamin B6	Folate
Vitamin B12	Biotin
Pantothenic Acid	Phosphorus
Iodide	Magnesium
Zinc	Selenium
Copper	Manganese
Chromium	Molybdenum
Chloride	

- basis of the percent daily values; and
- energy conversion factors.

Certain of the permitted or optional nutrition information may become mandatory, in the following circumstances:

- if the amount of any omega-6 polyunsaturated fatty acid, omega-3 polyunsaturated fatty acid or monounsaturated fatty acid is included on the label of the food or in any ad placed by the manufacturer, the amount of each of those fatty acids must be included in the Nutrition Facts table;
- if the amount of polyunsaturated fatty acids is included in the Nutrition Facts table or on the label or in any ad placed by the manufacturer, the amount of omega-6 polyunsaturated fatty acids and omega-3 polyunsaturated fatty acids and monounsaturated fatty acids must also be included in the Nutrition Facts table;

- if the label or any advertisement for a pre-packaged product contains a statement, claim or representation which includes information that is set out as an optional nutritional item;
- if the pre-packaged product contains added potassium and the label of any product refers to reduced sodium content, then the amount of potassium in the product must be included in the Nutrition Facts table;
- if the pre-packaged product contains an added sugar alcohol or added vitamin or mineral, the amount of the sugar alcohol or vitamin or mineral nutrient must be included in the Nutrition Facts table; or
- if a vitamin or mineral is declared as a component of any ingredient other than flour, the amount of that vitamin or mineral must be declared.

Information on amounts of other nutrients or food components not listed above may be provided outside the Nutrition Facts table, as discussed later in this chapter.

3.   Basics of Nutrition Labelling

In order to provide for standardization of the information provided to consumers, the information in the Nutrition Facts table must be based on the pre-packaged product as it is offered for sale. If, however, the pre-packaged product:

- contains separately packaged ingredients or foods that are to be consumed together, the information in the Nutrition Facts table may be set out for each ingredient or food or for the entire product;
- contains separately packaged food intended to be consumed individually, the information in the Nutrition Facts table shall be based on each food;
- contains an assortment of the same type of food (such as a box of cookies), the information in the Nutrition Facts table may be set out for each food or for a stated quantity of the food; or
- contains a food that is to be prepared according to directions provided with the package or that is commonly combined with other ingredients or cooked before being consumed, the Nutrition Facts table may also set out the information for the food as consumed.

The information in the Nutrition Facts table may also be set out for different serving sizes that reflect different uses of the food.

The nutrition information is to be calculated based on a serving of stated size, which is defined to include the entire contents of a package of food in certain situations, including when the quantity of the food can reasonably be consumed by one person at one time. The serving size should be declared in a common household measurement, or as a fraction of the package when no practical household measurement can be provided, as well as in grams or millilitres.

4. Location and Look of the Nutrition Facts Table

The information in the Nutrition Facts table must be standardized and easily legible so that consumers can readily compare the nutritional content of different products.

The Nutrition Facts table can be on the bottom of a pre-packaged product provided that the food will not leak out and the package will not be damaged when the package is turned over.

If a pre-packaged product contains separately packaged ingredients or foods, the Nutrition Facts table must be located on the outer container or the retail package. If, on the other hand, two or more pre-packaged products are combined together in such a manner that no common outer container is used, or no outer label is available, each product must have its own Nutrition Facts table.

Certain rules ensure uniformity of information and display between products. Schedule L to the Regulations illustrates examples of the Nutrition Facts table in English, French and in a bilingual format, including various shapes and sizes for different packaging sizes. Following are the "standard" English and bilingual Nutrition Facts tables.[5]

---

[5] The Nutrition Facts tables in this chapter are not reproduced according to scale. The tables are reprinted from Health Canada's Compendium of Templates for "Nutrition Facts" tables with the permission of Health Canada. See the complete Compendium of Templates for the introductry notes referenced within the tables.

Standard Format

• For the provision of nutrient information solely for the food as sold.

Figure 1.1

Normal width font
Heading in 13 point bold type
Nutrients in 8 point type
with 12 point leading
Thin rules – 0.5 point
Rules centred between text

When to Use
• If selected format
  (See introductory note 2.1)
• If there is sufficient space

Total surface area: 61.2 cm²

Nutrition Facts Per 125 mL (87 g)		
Amount		% Daily Value
Calories 80		
Fat 0.5 g		1 %
Saturated 0 g + Trans 0 g		0 %
Cholesterol 0 mg		
Sodium 0 mg		0 %
Carbohydrate 18 g		6 %
Fibre 2 g		8 %
Sugars 2 g		
Protein 3 g		
Vitamin A 2 %	Vitamin C	10 %
Calcium 0 %	Iron	2 %

4.7 cm x 6.5 cm = 30.6 cm²

Valeur nutritive par 125 mL (87 g)		
Teneur		% valeur quotidienne
Calories 80		
Lipides 0,5 g		1 %
saturés 0 g + trans 0 g		0 %
Cholestérol 0 mg		
Sodium 0 mg		0 %
Glucides 18 g		6 %
Fibres 2 g		8 %
Sucres 2 g		
Protéines 3 g		
Vitamine A 2 %	Vitamine C	10 %
Calcium 0 %	Fer	2 %

4.7 cm x 6.5 cm = 30.6 cm²

Figure 1.2

Normal width font
Heading in 13 point bold type
Nutrients in 7 point type
with 11 point leading
Thin rules – 0.5 point
Rules centred between text

When to Use
• See introductory note 3

Total surface area: 49.2 cm²

Nutrition Facts Per 125 mL (87 g)		
Amount		% Daily Value
Calories 80		
Fat 0.5 g		1 %
Saturated 0 g + Trans 0 g		0 %
Cholesterol 0 mg		
Sodium 0 mg		0 %
Carbohydrate 19 g		6 %
Fibre 2 g		8 %
Sugars 2 g		
Protein 3 g		
Vitamin A 2 %	Vitamin C	8 %
Calcium 0 %	Iron	2 %

4.1 cm x 6.0 cm = 24.6 cm²

Valeur nutritive par 125 mL (87 g)		
Teneur		% valeur quotidienne
Calories 80		
Lipides 0,5 g		1 %
saturés 0 g + trans 0 g		0 %
Cholestérol 0 mg		
Sodium 0 mg		0 %
Glucides 18 g		6 %
Fibres 2 g		8 %
Sucres 2 g		
Protéines 3 g		
Vitamine A 2 %	Vitamine C	8 %
Calcium 0 %	Fer	2 %

4.1 cm x 6.0 cm = 24.6 cm²

Figure 1.3

Condensed font
Heading in 13 point bold type
Nutrients in 7 point type
with 11 point leading
Thin rules – 0.5 point
Rules centred between text

When to Use
• See introductory note 3

Total surface area: 38.4 cm²

Nutrition Facts Per 125 mL (87 g)		
Amount		% Daily Value
Calories 80		
Fat 0.5 g		1 %
Saturated 0 g + Trans 0 g		0 %
Cholesterol 0 mg		
Sodium 0 mg		0 %
Carbohydrate 18 g		6 %
Fibre 2 g		8 %
Sugars 2 g		
Protein 3 g		
Vit A 2 %	Vit C	10 %
Calcium 0 %	Iron	2 %

3.2 cm x 6.0 cm = 19.2 cm²

Valeur nutritive par 125 mL (87 g)		
Teneur		% valeur quotidienne
Calories 80		
Lipides 0,5 g		1 %
saturés 0 g + trans 0 g		0 %
Cholestérol 0 mg		
Sodium 0 mg		0 %
Glucides 18 g		6 %
Fibres 2 g		8 %
Sucres 2 g		
Protéines 3 g		
Vit A 2 %	Vit C	10 %
Calcium 0 %	Fer	2 %

3.2 cm x 6.0 cm = 19.2 cm²

Standard Format

• For the provision of nutrient information solely for the food as sold.

Figure 1.4

Condensed font
Heading in 10 point bold type
Nutrients in 7 point type
with 10 point leading
Thin rules – 0.25 point
Rules centred between text

When to Use
• See introductory note 3
• More sophisticated printing process may be required to meet the legibility criteria (B.01.450(3)(a)).

Total surface area: 33.0 cm²

Nutrition Facts Per 1 cup (264 g)		
Amount		**% Daily Value**
Calories 260		
Fat 13 g		20 %
Saturated 3 g + Trans 2 g		25 %
Cholesterol 30 mg		
Sodium 660 mg		28 %
Carbohydrate 31 g		10 %
Fibre 0 g		0 %
Sugars 5 g		
Protein 5 g		
Vit A 4 %	Vit C	2 %
Calcium 15 %	Iron	4 %

3.0 cm x 5.5 cm = 16.5 cm²

Valeur nutritive par 1 tasse (264 g)		
Teneur		**% valeur quotidienne**
Calories 260		
Lipides 13 g		20 %
saturés 3 g + trans 2 g		25 %
Cholestérol 30 mg		
Sodium 660 mg		28 %
Glucides 31 g		10 %
Fibres 0 g		0 %
Sucres 5 g		
Protéines 5 g		
Vit A 4 %	Vit C	2 %
Calcium 15 %	Fer	4 %

3.0 cm x 5.5 cm = 16.5 cm²

Figure 1.5

Condensed font
Heading in 10 point bold type
Nutrients in 6 point type
with 10 point leading
Thin rules – 0.5 point
Rules centred between text

When to Use
• See introductory note 3

Total surface area: 32.0 cm²

Nutrition Facts Per 1 cup (264 g)		
Amount		**% Daily Value**
Calories 260		
Fat 13 g		20 %
Saturated 3 g + Trans 2 g		25 %
Cholesterol 30 mg		
Sodium 660 mg		28 %
Carbohydrate 31 g		10 %
Fibre 0 g		0 %
Sugars 5 g		
Protein 5 g		
Vit A 4 %	Vit C	2 %
Calcium 15 %	Iron	4 %

2.9 cm x 5.5 cm = 16.0 cm²

Valeur nutritive par 1 tasse (264 g)		
Teneur		**% valeur quotidienne**
Calories 260		
Lipides 13 g		20 %
saturés 3 g + trans 2 g		25 %
Cholestérol 30 mg		
Sodium 660 mg		28 %
Glucides 31 g		10 %
Fibres 0 g		0 %
Sucres 5 g		
Protéines 5 g		
Vit A 4 %	Vit C	2 %
Calcium 15 %	Fer	4 %

2.9 cm x 5.5 cm = 16.0 cm²

Figure 1.6

Condensed font
Heading in 10 point bold type
Nutrients in 6 point type
with 9 point leading
Thin rules – 0.25 point
Rules centred between text

When to Use
• See introductory note 3
• More sophisticated printing process may be required to meet the legibility criteria (B.01.450(3)(a)).

Total surface area: 28.6 cm²

Nutrition Facts Per 1 cup (264 g)		
Amount		**% Daily Value**
Calories 260		
Fat 13 g		20 %
Saturated 3 g + Trans 2 g		25 %
Cholesterol 30 mg		
Sodium 660 mg		28 %
Carbohydrate 31 g		10 %
Fibre 0 g		0 %
Sugars 5 g		
Protein 5 g		
Vit A 4 %	Vit C	2 %
Calcium 15 %	Iron	4 %

2.8 cm x 5.1 cm = 14.3 cm²

Valeur nutritive par 1 tasse (264 g)		
Teneur		**% valeur quotidienne**
Calories 260		
Lipides 13 g		20 %
saturés 3 g + trans 2 g		25 %
Cholestérol 30 mg		
Sodium 660 mg		28 %
Glucides 31 g		10 %
Fibres 0 g		0 %
Sucres 5 g		
Protéines 5 g		
Vit A 4 %	Vit C	2 %
Calcium 15 %	Fer	4 %

2.8 cm x 5.1 cm = 14.3 cm²

Bilingual Standard Format

• For the provision of nutrient information solely for the food as sold.
• May be useful when there is only one panel available for nutrition labelling.

Figure 3.1

Normal width font
Heading in 13 point bold type
Nutrients in 8 point type
with 12 point leading
Thin rules – 0.5 point
Rules centred between text

When to Use
• If selected format
  (See introductory note 2.1)
• If there is sufficient space

Total surface area: 42.1 cm²

Nutrition Facts Valeur nutritive		
Per 125 mL (87 g) / par 125 mL (87 g)		
Amount Teneur	% Daily Value % valeur quotidienne	
Calories / Calories 80		
Fat / Lipides 0.5 g	1 %	
Saturated / saturés 0 g + Trans / trans 0 g	0 %	
Cholesterol / Cholestérol 0 mg		
Sodium / Sodium 0 mg	0 %	
Carbohydrate / Glucides 18 g	6 %	
Fibre / Fibres 2 g	8 %	
Sugars / Sucres 2 g		
Protein / Protéines 3 g		
Vitamin A / Vitamine A	2 %	
Vitamin C / Vitamine C	10 %	
Calcium / Calcium	0 %	
Iron / Fer	2 %	

5.2 cm x 8.1 cm = 42.1 cm²

Valeur nutritive Nutrition Facts		
par 125 mL (87 g) / Per 125 mL (87 g		
Teneur Amount	% valeur quotidien % Daily Val	
Calories / Calories 80		
Lipides / Fat 0,5 g	1	
saturés / Saturated 0 g + trans / Trans 0 g	0	
Cholestérol / Cholesterol 0 mg		
Sodium / Sodium 0 mg	0	
Glucides / Carbohydrate 18 g	6	
Fibres / Fibre 2 g	8	
Sucres / Sugars 2 g		
Protéines / Protein 3 g		
Vitamine A / Vitamin A	2	
Vitamine C / Vitamin C	10	
Calcium / Calcium	0	
Fer / Iron	2	

5.2 cm x 8.1 cm = 42.1 cm²

Figure 3.2

Normal width font
Heading in 13 point bold type
Nutrients in 7 point type
with 11 point leading
Thin rules – 0.5 point
Rules centred between text

When to Use
• See introductory note 3

Total surface area: 34.5 cm²

Nutrition Facts Valeur nutritive		
Per 125 mL (87 g) / par 125 mL (87 g)		
Amount Teneur	% Daily Value % valeur quotidienne	
Calories / Calories 80		
Fat / Lipides 0.5 g	1 %	
Saturated / saturés 0 g + Trans / trans 0 g	0 %	
Cholesterol / Cholestérol 0 mg		
Sodium / Sodium 0 mg	0 %	
Carbohydrate / Glucides 19 g	6 %	
Fibre / Fibres 2 g	8 %	
Sugars / Sucres 2 g		
Protein / Protéines 3 g		
Vitamin A / Vitamine A	2 %	
Vitamin C / Vitamine C	10 %	
Calcium / Calcium	0 %	
Iron / Fer	2 %	

4.6 cm x 7.5 cm = 34.5 cm²

Valeur nutritive Nutrition Facts		
par 125 mL (87 g) / Per 125 mL (87 g)		
Teneur Amount	% valeur quotidienne % Daily Value	
Calories / Calories 80		
Lipides / Fat 0,5 g	1 %	
saturés / Saturated 0 g + trans / Trans 0 g	0 %	
Cholestérol / Cholesterol 0 mg		
Sodium / Sodium 0 mg	0 %	
Glucides / Carbohydrate 19 g	6 %	
Fibres / Fibre 2 g	8 %	
Sucres / Sugars 2 g		
Protéines / Protein 3 g		
Vitamine A / Vitamin A	2 %	
Vitamine C / Vitamin C	10 %	
Calcium / Calcium	0 %	
Fer / Iron	2 %	

4.6 cm x 7.5 cm = 34.5 cm²

Bilingual Standard Format

• For the provision of nutrient information solely for the food as sold.
• May be useful when there is only one panel available for nutrition labelling.

Figure 3.3

Condensed font
Heading in 13 point bold type
Nutrients in 7 point type
with 11 point leading
Thin rules – 0.5 point
Rules centred between text

When to Use
• See introductory note 3

Total surface area: 30.8 cm²

Nutrition Facts / Valeur nutritive		
Per 125 mL (87 g) / par 125 mL (87 g)		
Amount / Teneur	% Daily Value / % valeur quotidienne	
Calories / Calories 80		
Fat / Lipides 0.5 g		1 %
Saturated / saturés 0 g + Trans / trans 0 g		0 %
Cholesterol / Cholestérol 0 mg		
Sodium / Sodium 0 mg		0 %
Carbohydrate / Glucides 19 g		6 %
Fibre / Fibres 2 g		8 %
Sugars / Sucres 2 g		
Protein / Protéines 3 g		
Vitamin A / Vitamine A		2 %
Vitamin C / Vitamine C		10 %
Calcium / Calcium		0 %
Iron / Fer		2 %

4.1 cm x 7.5 cm = 30.8 cm²

Valeur nutritive / Nutrition Facts		
par 125 mL (87 g) / Per 125 mL (87 g)		
Teneur / Amount	% valeur quotidienne / % Daily Value	
Calories / Calories 80		
Lipides / Fat 0,5 g		1 %
saturés / Saturated 0 g + trans / Trans 0 g		0 %
Cholestérol / Cholesterol 0 mg		
Sodium / Sodium 0 mg		0 %
Glucides / Carbohydrate 19 g		6 %
Fibres / Fibre 2 g		8 %
Sucres / Sugars 2 g		
Protéines / Protein 3 g		
Vitamine A / Vitamin A		2 %
Vitamine C / Vitamin C		10 %
Calcium / Calcium		0 %
Fer / Iron		2 %

4.1 cm x 7.5 cm = 30.8 cm²

Figure 3.4

Condensed font
Heading in 10 point bold type
Nutrients in 6 point type
with 10 point leading
Thin rules – 0.5 point
Rules centred between text

When to Use
• See introductory note 3

Total surface area: 24.5 cm²

Nutrition Facts / Valeur nutritive		
Per 125 mL (87 g) / par 125 mL (87 g)		
Amount / Teneur	% Daily Value / % valeur quotidienne	
Calories / Calories 80		
Fat / Lipides 0.5 g		1 %
Saturated / saturés 0 g + Trans / trans 0 g		0 %
Cholesterol / Cholestérol 0 mg		
Sodium / Sodium 0 mg		0 %
Carbohydrate / Glucides 19 g		6 %
Fibre / Fibres 2 g		8 %
Sugars / Sucres 2 g		
Protein / Protéines 3 g		
Vitamin A / Vitamine A		2 %
Vitamin C / Vitamine C		10 %
Calcium / Calcium		0 %
Iron / Fer		2 %

3.6 cm x 6.8 cm = 24.5 cm²

Valeur nutritive / Nutrition Facts		
par 125 mL (87 g) / Per 125 mL (87 g)		
Teneur / Amount	% valeur quotidienne / % Daily Value	
Calories / Calories 80		
Lipides / Fat 0,5 g		1 %
saturés / Saturated 0 g + trans / Trans 0 g		0 %
Cholestérol / Cholesterol 0 mg		
Sodium / Sodium 0 mg		0 %
Glucides / Carbohydrate 19 g		6 %
Fibres / Fibre 2 g		8 %
Sucres / Sugars 2 g		
Protéines / Protein 3 g		
Vitamine A / Vitamin A		2 %
Vitamine C / Vitamin C		10 %
Calcium / Calcium		0 %
Fer / Iron		2 %

3.6 cm x 6.8 cm = 24.5 cm²

Bilingual Standard Format

• For the provision of nutrient information solely for the food as sold.
• May be useful when there is only one panel available for nutrition labelling.

Figure 3.5

Condensed font
Heading in 10 point bold type
Nutrients in 6 point type
with 9 point leading
Thin rules – 0.25 point
Rules centred between text

When to Use
• See introductory note 3
• More sophisticated printing process may be required to meet the legibility criteria (B.01.450(3)(a)).

Total surface area: 21.4 cm²

Nutrition Facts / Valeur nutritive
Per 125 mL (87 g) / par 125 mL (87 g)

Amount / Teneur	% Daily Value / % valeur quotidienne
Calories / Calories 80	
Fat / Lipides 0.5 g	1 %
Saturated / saturés 0 g + trans / trans 0 g	0 %
Cholesterol / Cholestérol 0 mg	
Sodium / Sodium 0 mg	0 %
Carbohydrate / Glucides 18 g	6 %
Fibre / Fibres 2 g	8 %
Sugars / Sucres 2 g	
Protein / Protéines 3 g	
Vitamin A / Vitamine A	2 %
Vitamin C / Vitamine C	10 %
Calcium / Calcium	0 %
Iron / Fer	2 %

3.5 cm x 6.1 cm = 21.4 cm²

Valeur nutritive / Nutrition Facts
par 125 mL (87 g) / Per 125 mL (87 g)

Teneur / Amount	% valeur quotidienne / % Daily Value
Calories / Calories 80	
Lipides / Fat 0,5 g	1 %
saturés / Saturated 0 g + trans / Trans 0 g	0 %
Cholestérol / Cholesterol 0 mg	
Sodium / Sodium 0 mg	0 %
Glucides / Carbohydrate 18 g	6 %
Fibres / Fibre 2 g	8 %
Sucres / Sugars 2 g	
Protéines / Protein 3 g	
Vitamine A / Vitamin A	2 %
Vitamine C / Vitamin C	10 %
Calcium / Calcium	0 %
Fer / Iron	2 %

3.5 cm x 6.1 cm = 21.4 cm²

Figure 3.6

Condensed font
Heading in 10 point bold type
Nutrients in 6 point type
with 8 point leading
Thin rules – 0.25 point
Rules centred between text

When to Use
• See introductory note 3
• More sophisticated printing process may be required to meet the legibility criteria (B.01.450(3)(a)).

Total surface area: 20.0 cm²

Nutrition Facts / Valeur nutritive
Per 125 mL (87 g) / par 125 mL (87 g)

Amount / Teneur	% Daily Value / % valeur quotidienne
Calories / Calories 80	
Fat / Lipides 0.5 g	1 %
Saturated / saturés 0 g + Trans / trans 0 g	0 %
Cholesterol / Cholestérol 0 mg	
Sodium / Sodium 0 mg	0 %
Carbohydrate / Glucides 19 g	6 %
Fibre / Fibres 2 g	8 %
Sugars / Sucres 2 g	
Protein / Protéines 3 g	
Vitamin A / Vitamine A	2 %
Vitamin C / Vitamine C	10 %
Calcium / Calcium	0 %
Iron / Fer	2 %

3.5 cm x 5.7 cm = 20.0 cm²

Valeur nutritive / Nutrition Facts
par 125 mL (87 g) / Per 125 mL (87 g)

Teneur / Amount	% valeur quotidienne / % Daily Value
Calories / Calories 80	
Lipides / Fat 0,5 g	1 %
saturés / Saturated 0 g + trans / Trans 0 g	0 %
Cholestérol / Cholesterol 0 mg	
Sodium / Sodium 0 mg	0 %
Glucides / Carbohydrate 19 g	6 %
Fibres / Fibre 2 g	8 %
Sucres / Sugars 2 g	
Protéines / Protein 3 g	
Vitamine A / Vitamin A	2 %
Vitamine C / Vitamin C	10 %
Calcium / Calcium	0 %
Fer / Iron	2 %

3.5 cm x 5.7 cm = 20.0 cm²

Figure 3.7

Condensed font
Heading in 9 point bold type
Nutrients in 6 point type
with 7 point leading
Thin rules – 0.25 point
Medium rules – 0.75 point
Thick rules – 1.5 point
Outer box – 0.25 point
Text inset – 1 point
Rules centred between text

When to Use
• See introductory note 3
• More sophisticated printing process may be required to meet the legibility criteria (B.01.450(3)(a)).

Total surface area: 16.8 cm²

Nutrition Facts / Valeur nutritive
Per 125 mL (87 g) / par 125 mL (87 g)

Amount / Teneur	% Daily Value / % valeur quotidienne
Calories / Calories 80	
Fat / Lipides 0.5 g	1 %
Saturated / saturés 0 g + Trans / trans 0 g	0 %
Cholesterol / Cholestérol 0 mg	
Sodium / Sodium 0 mg	0 %
Carbohydrate / Glucides 19 g	6 %
Fibre / Fibres 2 g	8 %
Sugars / Sucres 2 g	
Protein / Protéines 3 g	
Vitamin A / Vitamine A	2 %
Vitamin C / Vitamine C	10 %
Calcium / Calcium	0 %
Iron / Fer	2 %

3.3 cm x 5.1 cm = 16.8 cm²

Valeur nutritive / Nutrition Facts
par 125 mL (87 g) / Per 125 mL (87 g)

Teneur / Amount	% valeur quotidienne / % Daily Value
Calories / Calories 80	
Lipides / Fat 0,5 g	1 %
saturés / Saturated 0 g + trans / Trans 0 g	0 %
Cholestérol / Cholesterol 0 mg	
Sodium / Sodium 0 mg	0 %
Glucides / Carbohydrate 19 g	6 %
Fibres / Fibre 2 g	8 %
Sucres / Sugars 2 g	
Protéines / Protein 3 g	
Vitamine A / Vitamin A	2 %
Vitamine C / Vitamin C	10 %
Calcium / Calcium	0 %
Fer / Iron	2 %

3.3 cm x 5.1 cm = 16.8 cm²

The Regulations strictly regulate the appearance of the Nutrition Facts table itself, including requirements that the table be set out:

- in order of presentation contained in the illustrations in the new Regulations;
- in a visual equivalent of 100 per cent solid black type on a maximum 5 per cent tint of colour;
- in a single strand sans serif font that is not decorative;
- using type of a single colour;
- using upper and lower case letters as shown in the illustrations in the Regulations;
- in such a manner that the characters never touch; and
- in English and in French, unless otherwise provided for in the *Food and Drugs Act* (note that there are very limited exceptions for certain local market foods in unilingual communities).

A single Nutrition Facts table, whether bilingual or unilingual, must appear on one continuous surface. The Guide defines this to mean "a single flat surface or slightly curved surface that is unbroken or uninterrupted by defined edges, large angles, rims, sides, corners, seams, etc.".[6]

As mentioned above, Schedule L to the Regulations provides for several formats of the Nutrition Facts table, *i.e.*, standard, horizontal and linear, the use of which is determined on the basis of the amount of available label space. As a general rule, the Nutrition Facts table does not have to be displayed on more than 15 per cent of the available display surface. If there is insufficient label space for the standard or horizontal format, then a manufacturer is permitted to abbreviate certain of the statements contained in the Nutrition Facts table, and reduce the size of the font to no less than six points. If the label space is still inadequate, the manufacturer may use the linear format.

In the event that a pre-packaged product meets certain specifications, the information in the Nutrition Facts table may be set out on a tag attached to the package, the inner side of the label, a fold-out label or a package insert. In each case, the type size must be no less than six points. If the information is on the inner side of a label or on a package insert, then the outside label must indicate where the information is located. For packages with an available display surface of less than 100cm², the manufacturer can include the information separate from the product. In that case, the label must clearly indicate, in no less than eight point font, how consumers may obtain the information, including, at the least, a postal address or a toll-free telephone number.

---

[6] *Guide to Food Labelling and Advertising*, s. 5.5.4.

E.   GENERAL FOOD ADVERTISING REQUIREMENTS

As a general rule, no food can be labelled, packaged or advertised "in a manner that is false, misleading or deceptive or likely to create an erroneous impression regarding its *character, quality, value, quantity, composition, merit or safety*".[7]

Section 2 of the *Food and Drugs Act* defines "advertisement" to include "any representation by any means whatever for the purpose of promoting, directly or indirectly, the sale or disposal of any food, drug, cosmetic or device". This definition covers everything that a manufacturer or retailer communicates to the public about food products.

An discussed in detail below, an essential element in Canadian food advertising is that foods can only be advertised to the general public as a treatment, preventative, or cure for any of the diseases, disorders or abnormal physical states listed in Schedule "A" to the *Food and Drugs Act* in limited circumstances.

Certain issues are unique to the advertising of food, such as the following:

- As a general rule, unacceptable label information is not permitted in advertising. Therefore you cannot use a mocked-up package that contains unacceptable information in a beauty shot of the product, although you can omit certain required information from this label.
- A food should be described by its common name (as discussed above), at least on first reference in an advertisement. Therefore, do not refer to a food as "orange juice" if it is really "orange juice from concentrate".
- As with food labels, it is important to be careful about the use of illustrations implying an ingredient is present when it is not.
- Do not scare the public by suggesting that any one food is essential to health or nutritional well-being.
- Ads should not associate guilt with the consumption of foods.
- If a picture of the food being advertised is used, make sure you actually use the product sold in the marketplace. Also, if the food must be prepared, the picture should show the product as prepared according to the directions.
- Generally, statistics and references from technical literature are unacceptable in food ads.

---

[7]   *Food and Drugs Act*, s. 5 (emphasis added).

F.   REGULATED DESCRIPTIVE TERMS

The *Guide to Food Labelling and Advertising* and other government policies define the use of certain descriptive terms. This section of the chapter will canvass some of the more frequently used terms and the requirements that must be met before these terms are used.

"Fresh" can be used to describe the nature, age, and sensory qualities (flavour, texture, appearance and smell) of a food. "Fresh" may also be used for an ingredient or food that has not been processed or preserved in any way.

"Natural" may be used for foods that do not contain any artificial flavours, synthetic substances or added colours and have not been processed.

"New" is generally permitted to describe a product for one year from its launch.

G.   NUTRIENT CONTENT CLAIMS

Nutrient content claims are "statements or expressions that describe, directly or indirectly, the level of a nutrient in a food or group of foods".[8] They include such terms as "low in sodium", "low fat" and "high in [a specified nutrient]". Terms such as "low", "high" and "a source of" as well as comparative claims such as "less", "more" and "reduced" must meet certain regulatory requirements. The amended Regulations revise the prior nutrient content claim regime and include certain previously prohibited claims, such as "free of trans", and omega-3 and omega-6 claims. The Regulations expressly prohibit the making of a representation, express or implied, that characterizes the energy value of the food or the amount of nutrition contained in the food. One of the limited exceptions applies where the claim is expressly permitted in the Regulations. The Regulations also stipulate the wording of the permitted claim, the conditions that the food must meet in order to make the nutrient content claim and the disclosure required on the label or in the ad where the claim is used. Nutrient content claims that are not expressly allowed in the Regulations cannot be made. According to the Guide, it is clear that basic statements of fact as to the nutrition content of a food without any characterization (express or implied) will be permitted provided they are declared on the basis of a serving of a stated size in the units stipulated by the Guide. For instance, "4 calories per 250 ml serving" is permitted. Interestingly, the Guide provides that the word "contains" is a qualifying term. As a result, the claim "0g carbohydrates" is

---

[8]   *Guide to Food Labelling and Advertising*, s. 7.1.

acceptable but not "contains 0g carbohydrates".[9] At this point, it is unclear whether this analysis would stand if challenged in court.

According to a government issued policy statement, the Regulations with respect to nutrient content claims have the following goals:

- Consumers should be able to make informed dietary choices in order to reduce the risks to their health;
- The claims should be consistent, accurate and non-misleading;
- The claims should be based on recognized health and scientific criteria; and
- The claims should take into account economic and trade considerations where possible, when not in conflict with health and safety concerns.

The Regulations include a table to section B.01.513 which sets out in a column format the subject matter of the claim, the actual language of the claim, the conditions which must exist for the claim to be permissible and the disclosure that must be included on the label or in the advertisement.

The compositional criteria for nutrient content claims must be based on a regulated standardized "reference amount" for each particular food (set out in Schedule M of the Regulations). For instance, any claims relating to bagels must be based on a 55g serving of bagel. This was not required by the previous Regulations and is in addition to the requirement that the food must meet the compositional criteria based on a serving of a stated size, which is determined for the most part, by the food manufacturer.

Interestingly, for certain claims, where the reference amount of a food is 30 grams or less, not only does the food have to meet the compositional criteria for that serving size, but it also must meet the criteria based on 50 grams of that food.

Since nutrient content claims are based on reference amounts, a manufacturer cannot make a nutrient content claim for a food that does not have a reference amount listed in Schedule M.

A nutrient content claim which includes the words "more", "light", "reduced" or "lower", in addition to meeting certain compositional requirements, requires a reference on the labelling and advertisement to:

- the reference food;
- the amount of the food and the reference food being compared, if those amounts are not equal; and

---

9   *Ibid.*, s. 7.4.

- the differences in the nutrient contained in the food and in the referenced food expressed as a percentage or a fraction or in grams.

Nutrient content claims can only be made in the manner set out in the Regulations. No words can be inserted between the wording used in the Regulations and no words can be used to qualify the nutrient content claim. Specifically, the words "very", "ultra" and "extra" may not be used, unless expressly set out in the Regulations.

If a food that meets the compositional requirements for a nutrient content claim has not been processed or formulated to meet the conditions of the claim, then the claim cannot be made in a manner that implies that claim applies to the particular brand of food because all foods of that type would meet the claim requirements. In such a case, the claim must indicate that it applies to all foods of that type and not only to the specific food. For instance, brand X applesauce should state "applesauce is low in fat", rather than "Brand X applesauce, naturally low in fat".

There are limited claims that are permitted for foods for children under two years of age. The Regulations also set out specific requirements that must be met to claim that a food is for use for certain specific diets, such as "energy reduced diets" and "sodium restricted diets".

Any information required on the label or in the advertisement when a nutrient content claim is used must be prominent and readily discernible, adjacent to the most prominent statement or claim and in letters of at least the same size and prominence as the claim. In a broadcast ad, the required information must be clearly linked to the claim. The Regulations are detailed with respect to how the information is conveyed in print, radio and television advertisements (depending on whether the claim is made in the audio or visual portion of the T.V. ad). There are also specific disclosure requirements where claims are made by a third party who is not the manufacturer of the food.

1.   Vitamins and Minerals

Along with the changes to the Regulations, the term "Daily Value" (DV) is now used in the Nutrition Facts table instead of the term "Recommended Daily Intake" (RDI) which had previously been used in nutrition information tables. Despite the change to nomenclature, the terms have the same meaning.

According to the Guide, in order to claim that a food is a "source" of any vitamin or mineral nutrient, a serving of the food must include 5 per cent or more of the daily value of that particular vitamin or mineral. A claim that a food is a "good source" can only be made if a serving of the food contains at least 15 per cent of the daily value, or at least 30 per cent in the case of vitamin C. Finally, for a claim that a food is an "excellent source" of a particular vitamin or mineral, the food must contain at least 25 per cent of the daily value, or at least 50 per cent in the case of vitamin C. Claims can only be made for vitamins and mineral nutrients for which an RDI has been established by Regulation.

The Guide sets certain restrictions on the vitamin and mineral nutrient content claims permitted for fortified foods.

2. Fat

Since so many Canadians are concerned about their fat intake, food manufacturers and advertisers frequently promote their products as low-fat, reduced-fat or fat-free. It is interesting to see how far this has been stretched (for example "fat-free apples").

Fortunately, in order to avoid fat claims being used haphazardly, there are specific requirements that must be met before fat claims are permitted.

For a food to be "low-fat", it must contain three grams or less of fat per serving and per reference amount.

If a comparative claim is made, such as "reduced in fat", then the food must contain at least 25 per cent less fat than the reference food, and the reference food cannot meet the criteria of a "low-fat" food. Where a reduced fat claim is used, the food label and any advertising which includes the claim must set out the difference in fat content between the food and the referenced food and the amounts of the food and reference food compared if the amounts are not the same.

Claims that were previously prohibited without an Interim Marketing Authorization from Health Canada relating to *trans* fatty acids and omega-3 and omega-6 polyunsaturated fatty acids, are now permitted provided that the specified conditions are met.

3. Energy

The circumstances under which claims can be made regarding "low calorie" foods have changed under the new Regulations. A "low calorie" claim can only be made if the food has 40 calories or less per reference amount and serving of a stated size. If the reference amount is 30 grams (or mL) or less, then the food must have 40 calories or less per 50 gram (or mL) serving. For instance, for rice cakes with a reference amount of 15 grams, a serving must have no more than 40 calories per 50 gram serving (more than three times the reference amount) to support a "low calorie" claim.

Sometimes claims are made regarding food as a source of "energy". These claims, such as "helps give a lift" or "for people on the go", are permitted provided the claims do not imply that:

- the food in question provides "instant" pep, vitality, vigour, power or strength;
- the food provides all the energy necessary to carry people through certain physical activities;
- the food provides all the energy necessary to carry one through until the next meal; and
- a food, consisting mainly of carbohydrates, provides food energy which lasts over many hours of hard work or play.

Be careful that the visuals in a food ad or on the label do not convey any of these prohibited implications.

Any claim relating to the fact that a food is a source of "energy" should not be made unless the food contains at least 100 calories per serving and per reference amount.

4. Carbohydrates

In a world that seems to be extremely carbohydrate aware, it is interesting that the new Regulations do not permit the making of any claims concerning the content of carbohydrates in a food. According to an Information Letter issued on the topic by the CFIA, since implied claims are also prohibited, "[t]his means that other statements about the presence or absence of carbohydrates, including the use of brand names and trade-marks, are subject to these regulations."

As mentioned above, according to the Guide, food packaging and advertising can note the number of carbohydrate grams per serving size or the percentage of the DV per serving, provided the word "contains" is not used.

5. Light

The nutrient content claim "light" is only allowed for foods that meet the criteria for either "reduced in fat" or "reduced in energy". Previously, there had been various uses of "light" — it could refer to calories, fat, saturated fatty acids, cholesterol, sugars or sodium.

The amended Regulations are much more stringent in the manner in which the claim is made as well. As mentioned earlier, conditions that must be included in the advertisement or on the label must be in the same size and prominence as the most prominent appearance of the permitted claim without any intervening print, written or graphic material. Therefore, a "light" claim could only look like this: "LIGHT 50% LESS FAT THAN OUR REGULAR ICE CREAM." This applies equally to use of "lite". As one of the Regulations' idiosyncrasies, this severely restricts manufacturers in the design of their packaging, despite the fact that it would be grammatically correct, and more aesthetically pleasing to include a dash between the word "light" and the required condition.

"Light" can also be used to refer to a sensory or physical characteristic, such as "light in texture" or "light tasting". However, even these uses are circumscribed by detailed conditions set out in the Regulations. For instance, the term "light" should not be used in the common or brand name of the food where "light" refers to sensory or physical characteristics unless that characteristic is also included in the name *e.g.*, "Light tasting cola". The sensory characteristic must be adjacent to the word "light" (in its most prominent occurrence) without any intervening print and in the same size and prominence as the word "light". Specific regulations exist to explain how to achieve this on radio and in television ads.

H.   DIET-RELATED HEALTH CLAIMS

Foods that make claims relating to curing or mitigating diseases or disorders contravene the *Food and Drugs Act* because such claims can only be made for "drugs". As mentioned above, in Canada, there is also a general prohibition against making a claim that a food is a treatment, preventative or cure for a Schedule "A" disease.

Schedule "A" includes: Alcoholism; Alopecia (except hereditary androgenetic alopecia); Anxiety state; Appendicitis; Arteriosclerosis; Arthritis; Asthma; Bladder disease; Cancer; Convulsions; Depression; Diabetes; Disease of the prostate; Disorder of menstrual flow; Dysentery; Edematous state; Epilepsy; Gall bladder disease; Gangrene; Glaucoma; Gout; Heart disease; Hernia; Hypertension; Hypotension; Impetigo; Kidney disease; Leukemia; Liver disease (except hepatitis); Nausea and vomiting of pregnancy; Obesity; Pleurisy; Rheumatic fever; Septicemia; Sexual impotence; Thrombotic and Embolic disorders; Thyroid disease; Tumor; Ulcer of the gastro-intestinal tract; and Venereal disease.

The diseases, disorders or physical abnormalities listed in Schedule "A" either have no known cure and/or require the intervention of a health professional.

A major change has occurred in the amended Regulations. Companies can now make limited diet-related health claims that mention certain Schedule "A" diseases. Diet-related health claims are statements that characterize the relationship between a nutrient or a food and a specified disease or condition.

Health Canada concluded that risk reduction claims for food should be permitted while therapeutic claims should continue to be regulated as drugs. To this end, the Regulations now permit certain diet-related health claims on food labels and in food advertising. Such claims are contingent on foods meeting certain criteria. The wording of diet-related health claims is mandated by the Regulations in order to ensure consistency and accuracy, and must be used exactly as provided. Further, where a diet-related health claim is used, it must appear in both English and French.

The relationship between certain health risks and dietary characteristics are set out in the chart below.

Characteristics of the Diet:	May Reduce Risk of:
Low in sodium and high in potassium	High blood pressure, a risk factor for stroke and heart disease
Adequate source of calcium and vitamin D in combination with regular physical activity	Osteoporosis and help strengthen bones
Low in saturated fat and *trans* fat	Heart disease
Rich in fruits and vegetables	Some types of cancer
Low in fermentable carbohydrates or that do not result in a lowering of plaque pH below 5.7 during 30 minutes after consumption	Tooth decay

Three of these diet-related health claims relate to Schedule A diseases: heart disease, hypertension and cancer are all listed in Schedule A. In order to allow these claims, the Regulations exempt the prohibition in the *Food and Drugs Act.*

In the United States, there are currently ten health-related claims permitted on food products (including the five now permitted in Canada). However, Health Canada has concluded that only the five claims listed above are supported by adequate science at the present time. Interestingly, Health Canada has determined that there is insufficient evidence to support the claim that there is a relationship between dietary fat and cancer.

In order to make one of the health-related claims, the food must meet the compositional requirements referred to for that specific claim. In the case of claims with respect to high blood pressure, osteoporosis and heart disease, these claims will be permitted if they are followed by a statement that the food associated with the claim contains the characteristics of the relevant diet. For example "A diet low in saturated and *trans* fats may reduce the risk of heart disease. [*Naming the food*] is low in saturated and *trans* fats."

An essential element of the claim is the link between the reduced risk of disease and a healthy diet with particular characteristics. The claim then sets out the characteristic of the food that contributes to the risk reduction statement. The statements are meant to ensure that consumers are aware that it is not a particular food, but rather the consumption of the food as part of a healthy diet, that may lead to the risk reduction.

As canvassed in further detail in Chapter 8, there is a movement afoot to permit claims relating to Schedule A diseases for certain drugs, including natural health products.

Similarly, the use of the heart symbol, the word "heart" and the word "healthy" are strictly regulated by the Guide. A food cannot be described as "healthy" since that implies that health will be obtained or maintained from the consumption of a particular food. A food can, however, be referred to as being a "healthy choice" or "part of healthy diet/eating" if it is accompanied by a linking statement that relates the food to a recommended pattern of eating.

Describing a product as a "heart smart choice" is not permitted because it suggests that the food prevents a Schedule A disease. Health Canada has released a policy regarding the use of heart symbols and "heart health" statements which sets out specific conditions for use of such symbols and statements. For instance, heart symbols can be used in a manner to indicate affection. Heart symbols are also permitted if: (a) they do not convey the impression that the food may help prevent heart disease; and (b) the use of a health organization's name or logo which includes a heart symbol satisfies the conditions set out in the *Policy on the Use of Third-Party Endorsements, Logos and Seals of Approval*.[10]

Logos and seals of approval can be used if the following conditions are met:

(a)   the name, statement, logo, symbol (the "Endorsement") do not imply that the food, on its own, is healthy, superior in terms of health, safety or nutrition to any food not containing that logo, or is a treatment, preventative or cure for a disease; and

(b)   one of the following criteria is met:

    (i)   the reason for the Endorsement should be clearly explained. If use of the Endorsement requires financial support, that fact must be declared; or

    (ii)   it is clearly indicated that use of the Endorsement does not constitute an endorsement of the food; or

    (iii)   the name of the third party whose Endorsement is used should appear in conjunction with that party's nutrition recommendations or dietary guidelines.

Food labels that meet these guidelines must also include a Nutrition Facts table even if the food would otherwise be exempt from including the table.

---

[10]   *Ibid.*, s. 8.11.

1. Biological Role Claims of Nutrients

Claims as to the effect of the food's energy value or a nutrient contained in the food can be made where it is generally recognized as an aid in maintaining the functions of the body necessary to the maintenance of good health and normal growth. For instance, the Guide provides that the following claim is permissible: "Energy is a factor in the maintenance of good health."

In addition, there are certain biological role claims that are permitted for nutrients, provided that the claim does not refer directly to the treatment, mitigation or prevention of any disease, disorder or abnormal physical state. The claims are also prohibited from referring directly or indirectly to correcting, restoring or modifying organic functions.

Foods that contain at least five per cent of the recommended daily intake of a vitamin or mineral or a food that contains a protein rating of at least 20, are permitted to make claims that the particular nutrient is "a factor in the maintenance of good health", or "a factor in normal growth and development". The following is a table summarizing the biological role of nutrient claims that are permitted:

Acceptable Biological Role Claims for Nutrients[11]

PROTEIN	– helps build and repair body tissue – helps build antibodies
FAT	– supplies energy – aids in the absorption of fat-soluble vitamins
CARBOHYDRATE	– supplies energy – assists in the utilization of fats
VITAMIN A	– aids normal bone and tooth development – aids in the development and maintenance of night vision – aids in maintaining the health of the skin and membranes
VITAMIN D	– factor in the formation and maintenance of bones and teeth – enhances calcium and phosphorous absorption and utilization
VITAMIN E	– protects the fat in body tissues from oxidation

---

[11] *Ibid.*, s. 8.5.6. Reprinted with the permission of the Canadian Food Inspection Agency.

VITAMIN C	— factor in the development and maintenance of bones, cartilage, teeth and gums
THIAMINE (VITAMIN B1)	— releases energy from carbohydrates — aids normal growth
RIBOFLAVIN (VITAMIN B2)	— factor in energy metabolism and tissue formation
NIACIN	— aids in normal growth and development — factor in energy metabolism and tissue formation
VITAMIN B6	— factor in energy metabolism and tissue formation
FOLACIN	— aids in red blood cell formation
VITAMIN B12	— aids in red blood cell formation
PANTHOTHENIC ACID	— factor in energy metabolism and tissue formation
CALCIUM	— aids in the formation and maintenance of bones and teeth
PHOSPHOROUS	— factor in the formation and maintenance of bones and teeth
MAGNESIUM	— factor in energy metabolism, tissue-formation and bone development
IRON	— factor in red blood cell formation
ZINC	— factor in energy metabolism and tissue formation
IODINE	— factor in the normal functioning of the thyroid gland

While these claims are permitted, the wording of the claims cannot imply that the consumption of the food by itself will have the effect attributed to the nutrient. For instance, the Guide gives examples of acceptable and unacceptable claims. An acceptable claim would be:

Milk is an excellent source of calcium which helps build strong bones and teeth.

An unacceptable claim would be:

Milk helps build strong bones and teeth.

If one of the permitted claims is made, the nutrient content must be per stated serving of that food.

I.   HARMONIZATION WITH THE UNITED STATES

Given the size of the Canadian market, many manufacturers would like to be able to package and label a product for sale across North America. The recent amendments to the *Food and Drug Regulations* indicate that Canada is moving closer towards the U.S. system for nutritional labelling. Specifically, Health Canada has noted the benefits to be derived from the U.S. approach and Canadian consumer acceptance of this approach. A stated objective of Health Canada's nutrient content claims review was "to harmonize with the United States to the greatest extent possible, except where there were compelling health-related reasons to retain the current, or develop new compositional criteria". Health Canada has also recognized that an updated regulatory framework for nutrient content claims would facilitate meeting the requirement for Canada to work toward compatibility in food labelling standards with the United States.

While we are on the way to harmonizing with the United States, we are not all the way there. A food manufacturer is still not able to use a U.S. label for a food product in Canada. There remain differences between the Canadian system and the U.S. system. Some examples of differences include:

- the recommended daily intakes for vitamin and minerals as provided for in Part D of the *Food and Drugs Regulations* are different than those provided in the U.S.;
- *trans* fatty acid claims are permitted in Canada, but not in the U.S.; and
- only five of the ten diet-related health claims that are now acceptable in the United States have been accepted in Canada.

J.   VIOLATION OF THE FOOD LABELLING AND ADVERTISING REQUIREMENTS

Violations of the various requirements discussed in this chapter, as well as other requirements of the *Food and Drugs Act* and the *Competition Act*, will be dealt with either by Health Canada (on its own or through its agent, the Canadian Food Inspection Agency) or by the Competition Bureau. The following is a brief summary of the penalties that apply.

Health Canada — infringement of the *Food and Drugs Act* or its Regulations amounts to a criminal offence. It is a hybrid offence — one that can be prosecuted on summary conviction or as an indictable offence, at the option of the Crown. On summary conviction, the penalty is a fine not exceeding $500 and/or a prison term of not more than three months for the first offence. Subsequent offences can incur a fine of not more than $1,000 and/or imprisonment for a term of not more than six months. On conviction for an indictable offence, the penalty is a fine not exceeding $5,000 and/or imprisonment for not more than three years. As is the case with all criminal offences, the wording of the legislation will be read narrowly and the *mens rea* element (*i.e.*, intentional wrongdoing) must be established.

Competition Bureau — The Competition Bureau can challenge advertising claims as a reviewable matter in a hearing before the Competition Tribunal. If the criminal misleading advertising prohibition is violated, the Competition Bureau will proceed before the Tribunal or in the Federal Court or a Provincial Superior Court. In order for the criminal offence to be established, the accused must have the necessary *mens rea* (mental) element, which means that the accused must have "knowingly or recklessly" made a false or misleading statement in a material respect. The criminal offence provisions of the *Competition Act* also constitute a hybrid offence that can be prosecuted by way of a summary conviction offence or as an indictable offence (at the option of the Crown). On summary conviction, the maximum penalty is a fine not exceeding $200,000 and/or up to one year in prison. By way of indictment, the potential penalty is a fine at the discretion of the court (with no cap) and/or up to five years in prison. Most cases are prosecuted under the civil track, which carries potential penalties that include the requirement not to engage in certain conduct; the requirement to publish a "correction" notice and fines not to exceed $50,000 (first offence) and $100,000 (each subsequent offence) for individuals and $100,000 (first offence) and $200,000 (each subsequent offence) for corporations.

Chapter 11

REGULATION OF SPECIFIC SECTORS

Contributed by John Leckie, Sarah Chenoweth and Stephen A. Pike

A. INTRODUCTION

Many products and sectors are subject to specific regulation. These include child-directed advertising, food, drugs, natural health products and credit advertising, all of which are covered in other chapters of this book. This chapter will deal with advertising restrictions in three highly regulated sectors: the alcohol, automotive and tobacco industries.

B. ALCOHOL ADVERTISING

Alcohol advertising is extensively and strictly regulated in Canada. It is allowed only within certain categories if it meets stipulated content criteria and, in certain provinces, is approved by the applicable regulatory board. While alcohol advertising is generally regulated under provincial liquor licensing and control Acts, it is also subject to federal broadcast regulations under the jurisdiction of the Canadian Radio-television and Telecommunications Commission (CRTC).

   Alcohol is more strictly regulated than other consumer products because of the social and health consequences associated with excessive alcohol consumption. These concerns have given rise to the complex legislative framework and the requirements that, for the most part, alcohol advertising must: (a) meet each province's unique guidelines regarding advertising content; (b) be pre-approved by certain provincial liquor control boards; and (c) comply with the CRTC *Code for Broadcast Advertising of Alcoholic Beverages*. The result for national advertisers is an onerous process of ensuring compliance with a maze of federal and provincial requirements.

1.   Alcohol Advertising and ASC

Alcohol advertising may be submitted to Advertising Standards Canada (ASC) for review. Although submission is not mandatory, ASC will review alcohol broadcast advertising copy for compliance with the CRTC *Code for Broadcast Advertising of Alcoholic Beverages.*

ASC began reviewing alcohol advertising at the request of manufacturers and broadcasters in 1997, when the CRTC disbanded its clearance unit. In 1999, following regulatory changes in British Columbia, ASC was requested by BC advertisers to expand its copy clearance services to include print and out-of-home advertisements.

ASC will:
- review alcoholic beverage advertising copy for radio and television;
- review print and out-of-home advertising copy (British Columbia only);
- provide consultation services for new product launches or new advertising concepts; and
- upon request, will obtain Telecaster numbers and/or preliminary CBC clearances.

2.   Legislation and Guidelines

The following table sets out a summary of the provincial legislation and applicable guidelines on a per-province basis.

TABLE OF LEGISLATION

PROVINCE	STATUTES	REGULATIONS/ GUIDELINES
Alberta	*Gaming and Liquor Act*, R.S.A. 2000, c. G-1	Policy Guidelines published by the Gaming and Liquor Commission: (1) Liquor Advertising for Liquor Suppliers, Liquor Agencies and Licensees; and (2) Product Promotion in Licensed Premises
British Columbia	*Liquor Control and Licensing Act*, R.S.B.C. 1996, c. 267	*Liquor Control and Licensing Regulations*, B.C. Reg. 244/2002 B.C. Liquor Distribution Branch, *Beverage Alcohol Promotions Program*
Manitoba	*Liquor Control Act*, C.C.S.M. c. L160	*Liquor Advertising Rules of Conduct Regulation*, Man. Reg. 125/95 *Occasional Liquor Permits Regulation*, Man. Reg. 12/2002
New Brunswick	*Liquor Control Act*, R.S.N.B. 1973, c. L-10	*Advertising of Liquor Regulation*, N.B. Reg. 90-10 New Brunswick Liquor Corporation *In-Store Merchandising Policy*
Newfoundland and Labrador	*Liquor Control Act*, R.S.N.L. 1990, c. L-18	*Liquor Licensing Regulations*, C.N.L.R. 1162/96

PROVINCE	STATUTES	REGULATIONS/ GUIDELINES
Nova Scotia	*Liquor Control Act*, R.S.N.S. 1989, c. 260	*Nova Scotia Liquor Corporation Regulations*, N.S. Reg. 22/91, amended to N.S. Reg. 98/2001 *Liquor Licensing Regulations*, N.S. Reg. 156/83, amended to N.S. Reg. 158/2004
Ontario	*Liquor Licence Act*, R.S.O. 1990, c. L.19	*General*, R.R.O. 1990, Reg. 718, amended to O. Reg. 434/04 *Manufacturers Licenses*, R.R.O. 1990, Reg. 720, amended to O. Reg. 283/02 *Licences to Sell Liquor*, R.R.O. 1990, Reg. 719, amended to O. Reg. 8/05 *Social Occasion Permits*, O. Reg. 389/91, amended to O. Reg. 404/05 *Brew on Premise Facilities*, O. Reg. 58/00, amended to O. Reg. 286/02 *Advertising Guidelines* published by the Alcohol and Gaming Commission LCBO *Merchandising Programs*
Prince Edward Island	*Liquor Control Act*, R.S.P.E.I. 1988, c. L-14	*Regulations*, P.E.I. Reg. EC704/75 Licensee Policy Manual published by the P.E.I. Liquor Control Commission

PROVINCE	STATUTES	REGULATIONS/ GUIDELINES
Québec	*Act Respecting Offences Relating to Alcoholic Beverages,* R.S.Q. I-8.1	*Regulation Respecting Promotion, Advertising and Educational Programs Relating to Alcoholic Beverages,* c. P-9.1, r.7.1
Saskatchewan	*Alcohol and Gaming Regulations Act,* 1997, S.S. 1997, c. A-18.011	*Manufacturers' Media Beverage Alcohol Advertising Policy Manual,* published by the Liquor and Gaming Authority

RESTRICTIONS COMMON TO MOST PROVINCES

RULES OF THUMB

- DO note that alcohol advertising guidelines tend to be directed at manufacturers, suppliers, licensees, government stores and licensed restaurants and bars.

- DO confirm whether provincial regulatory approval is required, including for any of the activities which are acceptable in some provinces and not in others.

- DO comply with the CRTC *Code for Broadcast Advertising of Alcoholic Beverages* in addition to the provincial legislation and guidelines.

- DO run any advertising during programs directed at an audience of legal drinking age or in publications which have an adult readership.

- DO ensure that advertising is in good taste and consistent with the principle of responsible and safe consumption of liquor. Advertising may not depict excessive or prolonged drinking.

- DO promote certain brands or types of alcohol, but NOT the consumption of alcohol in general.

- DO employ sponsorships using a corporate or brand name, as long as the event is not geared towards minors.

- DO use on-site signs during sponsored events, but any advertising should be about the event or activity being sponsored and should be limited to corporate or brand identification or brand slogans.

- DO use contests as long as they are limited to individuals over the legal drinking age in their province of residence and the prize is not alcohol.

- DO NOT make claims of healthful, curative or stimulative benefits for alcohol.

- DO NOT imply that consumption of alcohol is required for:
  - Social acceptance or professional achievement
  - Personal success and the realization of a desired lifestyle

- • Athletic prowess
- • Sexual opportunity
- • Enjoyment of activities or fulfilment of any goals
- • Resolution of problems

• DO NOT appeal directly or indirectly to people under the legal drinking age, include an underage person in an advertisement or place an advertisement in media that is targeted at young people. This does not apply to educational or public service messages.

• DO NOT use a well-known personality, for example, a celebrity, fictional character, cultural or religious figure, who may appeal directly or indirectly to young people.

• DO NOT use children's songs, jingles, rhymes or fairy tales.

• DO NOT depict a person holding or drinking an alcoholic beverage prior to or while engaged in any activity which involves care, skill or danger, such as skiing, hunting or surfing.

• DO NOT associate the consumption of liquor with driving a motor vehicle.

• DO NOT depict illegal sale, purchase, or consumption of alcohol.

• DO NOT require purchase or consumption of alcohol for entry into a contest.

3. Some Notable Restrictions and Requirements

(1) Ontario

• Motor vehicles involved in races, competitions or contests may be used in alcohol advertisements but the ads may not include images of the product (*i.e.*, bottles, cans, glasses) or specific references to alcohol content.

• No person may offer a gift or the opportunity to receive a gift which requires the purchase of alcohol, except for a gift of nominal value in relation to the regular purchase price of the product. Nominal value is defined to mean 20 per cent of the retail price of the alcohol to a maximum of $5.00. Therefore, in-pack premiums such as t-shirts or beer cosies may be worth no more than $5.00.

- Any benefits to purchasers must be provided at the time of purchase and must be related to a single purchase. "Frequent Buyers Clubs" are not permitted.
- Suppliers to the Liquor Control Board of Ontario ("LCBO") must have pre-approval from the LCBO of all contest rules and advertising in advance of the contest start date. Contests may be advertised in-store, on-pack, on-shelf or as part of a display program. The LCBO requires specific language be included in contest rules before they are approved including:

  - "To be eligible to win the entrant must not be an employee or a member of the immediate family of, or domiciled with an employee of the Liquor Control Board of Ontario ("LCBO"), an employee of the Alcohol and Gaming Commission of Ontario ("AGCO") or of any licensees authorized by AGCO, or of the independent contest organization."
  - "The winner will be required to sign a document in a form acceptable to the Liquor Control Board of Ontario ("LCBO") releasing the LCBO, its directors, officers, employees and agents from all liability of any kind in connection with the contest, or occurring as a result of the prize being awarded."
  - "The LCBO and AGCO are not connected to this contest in any manner whatsoever and are not liable in any way for any matter related to this contest."

(2) British Columbia

- Notice must be given of a sponsorship that is worth more than $1,500.
- Suppliers to the B.C. Liquor Distribution Board ("LDB") must obtain pre-approval from the LDB for all contests promoted in B.C. Liquor Stores. The LDB requires specific language be included in contest rules including:

  - "Employees and contractors of the provincial liquor agencies, liquor licensees, their employees and members of their immediate families are not eligible."
  - "The provincial liquor agencies are not connected with this contest in any manner whatsoever, and are not liable in any way whatsoever in regard to any matter which relates to the contest."

(3)   Saskatchewan

- All advertising must be approved by the Saskatchewan Liquor and Gaming Authority.
- Advertising of liquor prices is not permitted.
- The Liquor and Gaming Authority will not approve advertising by a manufacturer on billboards, radio, TV or in print unless satisfied that at least 15 per cent of the total message will be devoted to educational content.

(4)   Alberta

- Alberta has five different classes of licensees, A through E, and different advertising requirements for each.
- The existence of a "Happy Hour" may be advertised but free liquor or drink specials (e.g., "2 for 1" or "all you can drink") may not be advertised.

(5)   Manitoba

- Advertising on outdoor signs, billboards or transit shelters is prohibited unless the purpose is to encourage responsible use of alcohol or to promote a socially or environmentally responsible message. Actual liquor products may not be displayed in responsible use ads.
- Advertising on the exterior of motor vehicles is prohibited with the exception that a manufacturer may advertise on its cars or trucks using only corporate name or logo.
- Coupons issued by a manufacturer may be offered to customers at point of sale, or on packaging, but may not be otherwise advertised.
- Brand identified inflatables, such as those in the shape of a bottle, may be displayed at promotional events but not near a school or a house of worship.
- "Happy Hour" or "Shooter Night" may be advertised as long as there is no mention of price.

(6)   Prince Edward Island

- Motorized vehicles cannot appear in scenes where a liquor product is shown.

(7)   Nova Scotia

- All alcohol advertisements, including radio, television, billboards, signs and sponsorship programs must be submitted to the Nova Scotia Liquor Corporation for approval before they are published or communicated.

- A manufacturer is not permitted to display any form of advertising, other than its corporate name, on any motor vehicle unless prior approval is obtained.
- Radio and television advertising by a manufacturer is restricted to brand, public service or corporate advertising only.

(8) New Brunswick

- The New Brunswick Liquor Corporation/Alcools NB Liquor ("ANBL") *In-Store Merchandising Program* mandates that all in-store promotional material, including on-pack advertising, posters, contest ballots and other support material be submitted to the ANBL for pre-approval before the in-store promotion is launched. This requirement should be strictly complied with since the ANBL Program specifically states "the fact that materials are already printed will not impact the decision on whether or not they may be used…".
- The ANBL also requires that all promotional materials, including on-pack advertising, must be presented in both English and French and on the same side of any advertising material. The ANBL interprets this to mean that French must be presented on the same side as any material and in equal prominence to English. There are limited exceptions to the "same side" rule. For example, a neck tag, recipe card or ceiling dangler may present English on one side and French on the other.
- Any draw for an in-store contest prize valued at $500 or more must be managed by a third party. Draws for prizes worth less than $500 may be done in-store by a representative of the supplier witnessed by an ANBL employee.

(9) Quebec

- Manufacturers must submit all advertising for pre-approval at least five days before publication.
- No person may advertise alcoholic beverages where the ad directly or indirectly portrays consumption of the beverage.
- A manufacturer may not advertise alcohol products on clothing or equipment intended for use by a minor. Advertising on baseball caps may be prohibited.
- At no time may a holder of a permit that authorizes consumption on the premises offer or advertise a reduced selling price on drinks, or free drinks.
- Manufacturers must, individually or as a group, implement educational programs relating to alcoholic beverages. These programs must be submitted no later than March 1st of each year.

Subsequent advertising approval will be refused unless the educational program is submitted on time.

C.   AUTOMOTIVE ADVERTISING

The rules governing automotive advertising come from a number of sources — federal, provincial and, in some cases, industry associations. It should be noted that statutes of general application, such as the *Competition Act*[1] and the various consumer protection laws, are discussed elsewhere in this book.

Each provincial government has passed legislation applicable to automotive advertising and motor vehicle dealers in the province. For example, all provinces require motor vehicle dealers to be licensed or registered in that province and most provinces require that dealer ads include the name of the dealer and their licence or registration number. In addition, various industry associations, including the B.C. Motor Dealer Council, the Ontario Motor Vehicle Industry Council ("OMVIC") and the Alberta Motor Vehicle Industry Council ("AMVIC") have published applicable advertising and marketing codes.

At the end of this section is a table of legislation, regulations and online materials to assist advertisers.

1.   The General Rules

In addition to the legislation specific to motor vehicle dealers and advertising, the general misleading advertising rules dictated by the federal *Competition Act* and Advertising Standards Canada's *Canadian Code of Advertising Standards* (discussed in previous chapters in this book), are also applicable to automotive advertising in Canada.

2.   Overall Impression

The *overall impression* given by the advertisement must be truthful. Canadian courts have determined that the average person feels they are at a disadvantage when purchasing a car. The consumer can be overwhelmed by variations in price, credit and lease terms, different offers and differences in models, features and options. As a result, automotive ads are often subject to greater scrutiny than other kinds of advertising.

Ads must be both contextually and technically correct; in other words, the visual impression of the ad and the wording of the text cannot be contradictory. Pertinent information cannot be omitted if it changes the

---

[1]   R.S.C. 1985, c. C-34.

meaning or impression of the ad. Advertisers must remember that the visual component of ads plays a large role in the general impression formed by consumers.

If an ad is ambiguous, then it is quite possible that the general impression will be false or misleading. For example, "Big Bob's Car Emporium" has advertised a special financing rate and has included pictures of five different car models. However, the advertisement does not clarify that the special rate only applies to one of the five models. Without further clarification, this advertisement may well be found to be false or misleading because it is only partially true.

RULES OF THUMB

* DO NOT show the base model price underneath a picture of a fully loaded model, unless you state "starting from" and also state the price of the vehicle shown.
* DO ensure that all options and accessories are appropriately described as "optional" or "available" or they will otherwise be understood to be standard.
* If price or lease terms are advertised, DO disclose specifics regarding additional charges such as freight, pre-delivery inspection ("PDI"), registration and PPSA.
* If a price is quoted, DO ensure that the vehicle is available at that price. An ad cannot quote a manufacturer's suggested retail price ("MSRP") of $25,000 when that model is only available with a $2,000 option package.
* DO have permission before referring to safety awards (such as the U.S. National Highway Traffic Safety Administration's 5 Star Safety Awards) or other awards given by car magazines and other organizations.

---

3.   Do Not Mislead the Average Purchaser

An ad may be considered false and misleading if it would mislead the average vehicle purchaser in a material respect. This average person ("Mr. X") does not actually exist — he is a figment of the court's imagination. A charge of false and misleading advertising does not require anyone to actually be misled by the advertisement — only that it could mislead the fictional Mr. X. The courts, in determining whether an ad is false or misleading, have given Mr. X the following characteristics:

* of average intelligence;
* lack of sophisticated knowledge of vehicles;

- only a very general knowledge of the characteristics, performance and categories of vehicles;
- no specialized knowledge of the technical features of the vehicle;
- not a sceptical reader; and
- reads the advertisement in its entirety, including qualifications and disclaimers.

In other words, Mr. X knows that a Chevy Cavalier is a compact domestic car available in a number of different colours, option packages and models. Mr. X does not know the exact differences between the models, or, for example, why a model with one particular engine is more expensive than another. Further, if Mr. X saw a (hypothetical) advertisement that read "The Gryphon — Enough Power to Pull Five Boats at a Time!", he would consider it to be a fair statement of the Gryphon's abilities. Mr. X would then continue to read the advertisement to see if the statement was qualified or if the advertised price included any optional features. If Mr. X reads a financing offer, he is deemed to understand the required qualifications and limitations of the offer.

4.   Disclaimers

A disclaimer should be used only to clarify ambiguous or incomplete language. The particular language that needs clarification should be followed by an asterisk indicating that there is a disclaimer. For example, if the body copy only mentions the MSRP or the base price, further disclosure in a disclaimer of costs such as freight and PDI, PPSA, and any options shown in the featured car must be made.

A disclaimer cannot be used to save false or misleading advertising. For example, if a luxury car advertisement showed a picture of the car with the words "Could be yours for only $15,000*!" and the disclaimer read "$15,000 was the price offered to the daughter of the owner of the company. MSRP base price is $85,000 plus freight, delivery, PDI, air-conditioning tax ...", this disclaimer obviously would not correct the misleading headline.

Disclaimers must be clear and legible. This rule is often broken on TV ads by automotive manufacturers. Ideally, TV supers with lease, finance or price legal mice-type should be large enough and on-screen long enough for consumers to actually read them.

5.   Claim Substantiation

As stated in previous chapters, the *Competition Act* requires that claims relating to the performance, efficacy and length of life of products be based on adequate and proper tests. Tests to substantiate such claims must have been conducted before the claims are published.

The applicable substantiation required to support a claim will vary depending on the type of claim:

- Consumer preference claims, such as "Voted sportiest re-design!", require proper survey evidence.
- Performance claims require proper technical data:
  - Claims about a manufacturer's own vehicle or vehicle services, such as "For 2007 we use shinier and scratch-proof paint", may be based on internal data from technical and other departments.
  - Comparative claims versus competitor's vehicles, such as "Most powerful new vehicle in its class!", should generally be based on independent third party tests and data.

In many cases, disclaimers should identify the basis for a claim. For example, if an ad claims that a certain model of car has a specific fuel consumption rating, then the basis of the testing should be disclosed, such as "Comparative rating based on Transport Canada test methods. Actual results may vary."

6. Comparative Claims

Comparative and superiority claims are the riskiest type of claims to make because, particularly in the automotive sector, such claims are the subject of intense scrutiny by competitors.

Even if an ad does not directly mention a competitor by name, the competitor may be targeted by implication by comparative statements mentioning, for example, "the largest domestic manufacturer".

RULES OF THUMB

- DO NOT unfairly disparage a competitor (by name or by implication) or exaggerate the differences between your vehicles and your competitor's.
- DO NOT engage in excessive cherry picking. This means that you should not highlight where your vehicle is superior to a competitive vehicle without mentioning material similarities or even superiorities of such competitive vehicle.
- DO compare apples to apples. The vehicles compared should be in the same class with the same options, features and packages and pricing. If lease or finance rates or offers are being compared, down payments, security deposits, excess kilometre charges, *etc.*, should be very similar as between the vehicles.
- The basis of a comparative price claim must be disclosed. Often such claims are based on MSRP. If actual selling prices differ greatly from MSRP, it is better to base price comparisons on advertised prices. The disclaimer must state which models are being compared and if the vehicles are similarly equipped.

---

7.   Price and Savings Claims

As discussed in Chapter 4, the Competition Bureau diligently enforces the provisions of the *Competition Act* related to price and savings claims. In order to comply with the *Competition Act* when making "savings" claims, the regular price of the product must be established based on the "time test" or the "volume test" (see Chapter 4 for further details on these tests). Unlike most consumer goods, vehicles don't have a typical "regular price" since they are very rarely sold at the MSRP. An ad cannot claim a savings of $10,000 from an MSRP of $35,000 if the vehicle normally sells for $25,000. Since dealers almost always sell below MSRP, advertising a savings as measured against MSRP is usually risky.

If the savings is a dollar amount in relation to the MSRP, the advertiser should be careful to relate the amount to MSRP and ensure there is a real savings. In general, terms like "save", "was" and "value" should be avoided since they imply an actual and exact savings amount. However, it might be acceptable to claim for example, "Up to $1,000 discount off the MSRP".

8.   Price Fixing

As discussed in Chapter 14, price fixing is a criminal offence under the *Competition Act*. It is an offence to influence prices upward or discourage reductions by way of agreement, threat or promise. In the automotive industry, manufacturers cannot reach an agreement with dealers regarding minimum prices. "Suggested" prices are permissible which is why price ads state: "Manufacturer's Suggested Retail Price (MSRP)". Every price advertisement should include a statement such as "dealer may sell for less" or "dealers are free to set individual prices".

9.   Non-availability

The *Competition Act* prohibits bait and switch advertising. Products cannot be advertised at a bargain price unless the advertiser has reasonable quantities of the product to meet expected demand. This is a particular problem for automotive advertisers who may advertise a special price on a vehicle, but may have none of the advertised vehicles available on dealership lots. In these circumstances, stating "limited supplies" or "dealer order may be necessary" will not insulate an advertiser from being charged with bait and switch.

10.   Offers

All advertisements for special offers should set out material details of the offer including:

*   Who is eligible. For example, "On Approved Credit" or "Offer available only to current lease customers whose lease contracts expire in December 2007".
*   What vehicles are eligible. For example, "Offer available on select 2007 models". If the offer is only applicable to a specific model, such model should be given, *e.g.*, "Offer available only on the GT 750".
*   How to take advantage of the offer. For example, "Lease or finance a vehicle before December 31, 2007 and get $2,000 cash back".
*   When the offer expires.
*   Whether the offer can be combined with any other offers.

Certain offers are specifically regulated under consumer protection and cost of credit laws, including "No Interest" offers. Under the harmonized cost of credit rules, a "No Interest" advertisement must state whether the period of the offer is unconditionally interest free or whether interest accrues but is forgiven under certain conditions. If conditions exist, they must be stated, and the APR if the conditions are not met must also be included in the ad (see Chapter 4 for further details on APR and the harmonized cost of credit rules).

11. Free and No Charge

"Free" cannot be used as a term in an offer where a consumer is required to make a purchase in order to obtain the "free" item unless the "free with purchase" qualification is clearly made.

If the advertiser offers "free" or "no extra charge" optional features, then any value identified for the offered features should be the actual retail price. For example, if air-conditioning is an advertised bonus and has an MSRP value of $1,000, this should be stated.

If words such as "free" or "no charge" are used, the advertiser should ensure that that the normal selling price, after negotiations, is not adjusted or increased to reflect the fact that the free item has been added and that bonus offers do not exceed 90 continuous days.

12. Fuel Efficiency

Fuel efficiency claims made in Canadian advertising must be based on Transport Canada testing figures published in the EnerGuide. Both highway and city fuel efficiency figures should be included in advertising. Fuel efficiency disclaimers should specify the publication date of the EnerGuide figures, *i.e.*, ...: "EnerGuide 2006". Further, such figures should also be accompanied by a disclaimer which states that EnerGuide figures should be used for comparison purposes only and which clarifies that actual fuel efficiency may vary based on driving conditions and the addition of certain vehicle accessories.

TABLE OF LEGISLATION, REGULATIONS AND ONLINE ADDRESSES FOR MOTOR VEHICLE ADVERTISING LAW

1.   Federal Legislation

STATUTE	NOTABLE SECTIONS
Competition Act, R.S.C. 1985, c. C-34	Sections 50-52, 54 and 74.01-74.09

2.   Provincial Legislation and Regulations

PROVINCE	STATUTES/ REGULATIONS	NOTABLE SECTIONS
Alberta	• *Fair Trading Act*, R.S.A. 2000, c. F-2	Sections 6, 7 and 9
	• *Cost of Credit Disclosure Regulations*, AR 198/99	Sections 4, 6,7, 12 and 18
	• *Automotive Business Regulation*, AR 192/99	Sections 2, 3 and 11
British Columbia	• *Motor Dealer Act*, R.S.B.C. 1996, c. 316	Sections 1, 3 and 13
	• *Motor Dealer Act Regulation*, B.C. Reg. 447/78	Sections 26, 26.1 and 27
	• *Business Practices and Consumer Protection Act*, S.B.C. 2004, c. 2	Sections 4-6
Manitoba	• *Business Practices Act*, C.C.S.M. c. B120	Sections 2, 3 and 9
	• *Highway Traffic Act*, C.C.S.M. c. H60	Section 19
	• *Consumer Protection Act*, C.C.S.M. c.200	Sections 26 and 27

PROVINCE	STATUTES/ REGULATIONS	NOTABLE SECTIONS
New Brunswick	• *Motor Vehicle Act*, R.S.N.B., 1973 c. M-17	Sections 54-57
Newfoundland and Labrador	• *Automobile Dealers Act*, R.S.N.L. 1990, c. A-21 • *Automobile Dealers Regulations*, C.N.L.R. 984/96 • *Trade Practices Act*, R.S.N.L. 1990, c. T-7	Section 19 Section 11 Sections 5 and 7
Nova Scotia	• *Motor Vehicle Act*, R.S.N.S. 1989, c. 293	Sections 26 and 53-56
Ontario	• *Consumer Protection Act, 2002*, S.O. 2002, c. 30, Schedule A • *Consumer Protection Act, 2002*, O. Reg. 17/05, amended to O. Reg. 200/05 • *Motor Vehicle Dealers Act*, R.S.O. 1990, c. M.42 • *Motor Vehicle Dealers Regulations*, R.R.O 1990, Reg. 801, amended to O. Reg. 23/05	Sections 14, 15, 17, 88 and 109 Sections 61 and 73 Sections 1, 5 and 19 Section 18
Prince Edward Island	• *Business Practices Act* R.S.P.E.I. 1998, c. B-7	Section 2
Quebec	• *Consumer Protection Act*, R.S.Q., P-40.1	Sections 1, 41, 43, 46, 219-225, 227, 228, 231-233, 238, 239, 241-247, 247.1, 311 and 312
Saskatchewan	• *Motor Dealers Act*, R.S.S. 1978, c. M-22 • *Consumer Protection Act*, S.S. 1996, c. C-30.1	Sections 2 and 29 Sections 5-8

3.   Industry and Government Web Sites

ORGANIZATION	INTERNET ADDRESS	APPLICATION
Advertising Standards Canada's *Canadian Code of Advertising Standards*	<http://www.adstandards.com/en/Standards/canCodeOfAdStandards.asp>	Code sets the criteria for acceptable advertising and forms the basis for evaluation in response to consumer, trade or special interest group complaints.
Alberta Motor Vehicle Industry Council	<http://www.amvic.org>	Alberta's self-regulatory body which enforces the rules under the Alberta *Fair Trading Act*. AMVIC publishes *Advertising Compliance Guidelines*.
Association of International Automobile Manufacturers of Canada	<http://www.aiamc.com>	Legal sub-committee which focuses primarily on consumer protection and liaison with provincial governments.
Automobile Protection Association	<http://www.apa.ca>	Consumer watchdog for the automotive industry.
British Columbia Automotive Retailers Association	<http://www.ara.bc.ca>	Deals with the auto-motive after-market. Mandate is to enhance the image and competitive status of Association members.
Motor Dealer Council of British Columbia	<http://www.mdcbc.com/>	Publishes the Motor Dealer *Advertising Guidelines*, latest version: November 2005.
Canada Competition Bureau	<http://www.competitionbureau.gc.ca/>	Publishes guidelines on the interpretation and application of the *Competition Act*.

Organization	Internet Address	Application
Ontario Motor Vehicle Industry Council	<http://www.omvic.on.ca>	Self-management body of registered dealers and salespersons in Ontario. Publishes OMVIC *Standards of Business Practice*, latest version: November 2000.
Manitoba Motor Dealers Association	<http://www.mmda.mb.ca>	*Advertising and Marketing Guidelines*: January 2000

D. TOBACCO ADVERTISING

The *Tobacco Act*[2] came into force on April 25, 1997. This legislation was passed in the wake of a narrow five to four majority decision of the Supreme Court of Canada in *RJR-MacDonald v. Canada (Attorney General)* ("*RJR-MacDonald*")[3] in 1995 which struck down the Federal *Tobacco Products Control Act* ("TPCA").[4] The TPCA had prohibited advertising of tobacco products in an attempt to reduce tobacco consumption in Canada.

In general, the *Tobacco Act* is less restrictive towards informational and brand name advertising and is more lenient towards corporate sponsorship than the TPCA. The less restrictive approach of the law has led critics to deem this legislation as ultimately less effective. The TPCA attempted to remove tobacco advertising from Canadian society by targeting lifestyle, informational, and brand name tobacco advertising. The *Tobacco Act* only prohibits lifestyle advertising and advertising clearly directed at youth and does not restrict sponsorship *per se*, but only the advertising of such sponsorships.

Many aspects of the tobacco industry are contentious, and the advertising of tobacco products is no exception. Before discussing the effect of the current *Tobacco Act*, it is useful to take a look at its history and why the TPCA was struck down in order to better understand the situation.

---

[2] S.C. 1997, c. 13.
[3] [1995] S.C.J. No. 68, [1995] 3 S.C.R. 199.
[4] R.S.C. 1985, c. 14 (4th Supp.) (repealed by S.C. 1997, c. 13, s. 64).

1.   History of the Tobacco Act

In *RJR-MacDonald*, the tobacco companies challenged the TPCA on two grounds: (1) as being *ultra vires* (or outside of the jurisdiction) of the Parliament of Canada, and (2) as a violation of their constitutionally guaranteed right to freedom of expression under s. 2(b) of the *Canadian Charter of Rights and Freedoms*. The Court ruled that the TPCA was, in essence, criminal law and could therefore be validly enacted by the federal government. However, in a surprising victory for the tobacco companies, the Supreme Court held that the legislation infringed freedom of expression. The decision is complex, but the ultimate question was whether this violation of the Charter was a justifiable violation of a Charter right. This was where the justices of the Court differed.

Madame Justice McLachlin (now Madame Chief Justice McLachlin) wrote the majority decision and explained in her judgment that the Supreme Court clearly supports restrictions on tobacco advertising. Nevertheless, in the Court's opinion, a less restrictive law would have achieved the government's objectives. The Supreme Court declared the provisions relating to advertising, trade-mark usage and unattributed health warnings unconstitutional.

Two important factors contributed to the downfall of the TPCA. The first was the finding that there was no direct scientific evidence showing a causal connection between advertising bans and reduced tobacco consumption. The second factor was that it is generally more difficult to justify a complete, rather than a partial, ban on freedom of expression. The majority of the Court found that not all forms of tobacco advertising stimulated consumption and ruled that the government could have imposed a partial ban on lifestyle advertising only, since this would have constituted a reasonable limitation of freedom of expression.

2.   Tobacco Act

Following *RJR-MacDonald*, the federal government passed the *Tobacco Act*, a law that attempts to come within the parameters set by the Supreme Court. The government introduced the legislation into Parliament in January 1997. It was immediately met with strong opposition. This time, the tobacco industry did not attempt to fight the legislation on constitutional grounds but used an economic argument, threatening to remove all direct sponsorship from cultural and sporting events in Canada. This imperiled events such as the Montreal International Jazz Festival, the Grand Prix, and various tennis and golf tournaments. Thus, the federal government made two concessions in the Bill. First, sponsor identification on racing cars, drivers and transportation equipment would be allowed to ensure the continuation of these events. Also, the *Tobacco Act* restrictions on advertising at cultural and sporting events did not take effect until Oct. 1, 1998 in order to give event planners time to find new sponsors.

3.   Advertising and Promotion

The *Tobacco Act* imposes a general prohibition on the promotion of tobacco products and tobacco product-related brand elements. The Act also contains a number of specific prohibitions including the following:

- false, deceptive or misleading claims about tobacco products;
- endorsement of any kind by a person, character or animal, whether real or fictional, subject to certain grandfathered exceptions;
- "lifestyle advertising", or advertising that could be construed on reasonable grounds to appeal to young people. Lifestyle advertising is defined in section 22 as "advertising which associates a product with, or evokes a positive or negative emotion about or image of, a way of life" or an aspect of living that includes "glamour, recreation, excitement, vitality, risk or daring"; and
- advertising depicting tobacco products, packaging or brand elements.

An exception to the general prohibition on advertising is informational and brand-preference advertising (but not lifestyle advertising) contained within:

- direct mailings addressed to an adult identified by name;
- publications with not less than 85 per cent adult readership; and
- in places where minors are not permitted by law.

Promotion of non-tobacco products bearing brand elements, excluding accessories (i.e. lighters), may be undertaken in certain publications and places. Note that a retailer may post signs that indicate the availability of tobacco products and their price.

The prohibitions on advertising and promotion referred to above do not apply to promotions directed at tobacco growers, manufacturers, distributors and retailers.

4.   Sponsorship

A person may not display a tobacco product-related brand element or the name of a tobacco manufacturer in a promotion directly or indirectly connected with the sponsorship of a person, entity, event, activity or permanent facility.

5. Games, Lotteries and Contests

No tobacco manufacturer or retailer may offer a bonus, premium, cash rebate or right to participate in a game, lottery or contest in connection with the purchase of tobacco products. Additionally, no one may give away tobacco products for free or along with the purchase of other goods or services (this applies equally to a tobacco accessory featuring a tobacco product-related brand element).

6. Enforcement

Enforcement provisions are set out in Part V of the *Tobacco Act*. For the purposes of ensuring compliance with the *Tobacco Act*, inspectors are given broad search powers except in relation to vehicles and houses. Inspectors may also seize certain goods if they believe on reasonable grounds that a provision of the *Tobacco Act* has been violated.

Penalties for packaging and promotion offences under Part VI of the *Tobacco Act* include:

(1) On summary conviction, fines not exceeding $100,000 and/or imprisonment for one year; or
(2) On indictment, fines not exceeding $300,000 and/or imprisonment not exceeding two years.

There are specific penalties for sale to minors, offences by retailers and offences by manufacturers. Section 50 of the Act also states that directors or officers of corporations can be convicted even if the corporation is not prosecuted. Employees and agents can commit offences on behalf of the accused, even if the employee or agent cannot be specifically identified. However, the accused has a defence if they are able to show that the offence was committed without their knowledge or consent, and that they exercised all due diligence to prevent the offence.

7. Health Warnings and Information

The *Tobacco Products Information Regulations* (the "Regulations")[5] sets out requirements for health warnings and health information. Notable aspects of the Regulations include:
- Section 4: a manufacturer may attribute the health information to "Health Canada" or "Santé Canada".
- Subsection 5(1): every manufacturer of tobacco products shall display the applicable health warnings on every package.

---

[5] SOR/2000-272.

• Subsection 5(2): the warnings must:

(a) be in English on one principal display panel and in French on the other;

(b) occupy at least 50 per cent of the principal display surface and be parallel to the top edge of the package;

(c) be displayed on the surface in a manner that ensures that none of the words are severed when the package is opened;

(d) be selected from the formats provided by the Minister for each health warning; and

(e) use the prescribed pitch, colour, font and size of text (subsection 5(2)).

The Regulations provide a list of warnings for each type of tobacco product. There are slightly different warnings for chewing tobacco, bidis, nasal snuff, and pipe tobacco. An example of a chewing tobacco warning is "THIS PRODUCT CAUSES MOUTH DISEASES". The Regulations also set out specifications for required health, toxic emission and toxic constituent information.

8. Provincial Tobacco Legislation

A number of provinces have Acts pertaining to tobacco and almost all of the provinces have Tobacco Tax or Taxation Acts. Advertising, marketing and the sale of tobacco products in a province must also comply with applicable provincial legislation. Many provinces have Acts pertaining to tobacco sales and access by minors to protect young people and to prevent consumers from being misled. In general, these Acts state that in order to sell tobacco to any person, that person must present proper age identification. It is no defence for the vendor that the person simply *appeared* to be of legal age. Signs must be posted in a conspicuous manner that refer to the prohibition against selling or supplying tobacco to minors. These signs must conform to specific regulations. For example, under the Nova Scotia *Tobacco Access Regulations*, retailers are required to post a Tobacco Access Act Door Decal, a Point of Purchase Identification Sign, a Cash Register Sticker and a Health Warning sign of a specific size, in specific locations and with specific content. Another example is the New Brunswick Regulations under the *Tobacco Sales Act* which specify the messages that may be used on the signs. Vendors may be charged and their licences may be suspended or cancelled if they are found to be in violation of these Acts.

The British Columbia *Tobacco Sales Regulations*[6] states that if a vendor is convicted under the *Tobacco Sales Act*[7] and its licence is sus-

---

[6] B.C. Reg. 216/94.

pended, the vendor must post a sign which reads "NOTICE: WE CANNOT SELL TOBACCO BECAUSE WE WERE CONVICTED OF TOBACCO SALES OFFENCES, INCLUDING SELLING TOBACCO TO A MINOR. SMOKING IS A MAJOR HEALTH HAZARD."

Many provincial statutes pertaining to tobacco also specify where tobacco can and cannot be sold. For example, in Ontario, section 4 of the *Smoke-Free Ontario Act*[8] specifies that tobacco cannot be sold in various places including public or private hospitals, pharmacies or charitable institutions.

The *Smoke-Free Ontario Act* also regulates the manner in which tobacco products may be sold, displayed, promoted and marketed. For example, it is prohibited to promote the sale of tobacco products in any place where they are sold through product association, product enhancement or any type of promotional material, including decorative panels associated with a particular brand, backlit or illuminated panels, promotional lighting, three-dimensional exhibits or any other device, instrument or enhancement.[9] A sign in any place where tobacco products are sold or offered for sale that refers to tobacco products and/or tobacco product accessories is considered promotional material under the *Smoke-Free Ontario Act* if the text of the sign is visible from outside the place where tobacco products are sold or offered for sale; the size of the sign exceeds 968 square centimetres; the background of the sign is a colour other than white and the text of the sign is a colour other than black; the sign includes text or a graphic that identifies or reflects a brand of tobacco or tobacco-related product or any element of such a brand; or the sign is one of more than three signs in that place that refer to tobacco products or tobacco product accessories or both. Signs that are required to be displayed by the *Smoke-Free Ontario Act* or the Regulations made thereunder are excluded from the foregoing provision.

The Quebec *Tobacco Act*[10] is another example of comprehensive provincial legislation with regard to advertising and promotions. Part IV of the Act deals exclusively with promotion, advertising and packaging. Many of the provisions are similar to the sections in the federal *Tobacco Act*. Points of note include:

• Section 21: a business or manufacturer may not supply tobacco free of charge, or offer reduced prices, gifts, rebates or the right to participate in a lottery or contest if consumers must, in return, provide information on tobacco or their tobacco consumption, purchase a tobacco product or present proof of purchase of a tobacco product.

[7] R.S.B.C. 1996, c. 451.
[8] S.O. 1994, c. 10.
[9] *Ibid.*, s. 3.1.
[10] R.S.Q., c. T-0.01.

- Section 22: any direct or indirect sponsorship that is associated with the promotion of tobacco, a brand or manufacturer of tobacco is prohibited.
- Section 23: no name, logo, brand element, design, image or slogan, except a colour, that is associated with tobacco products or manufacturers, may be associated with a sports, cultural or social facility, or a health facility.
- Section 24: all direct and indirect advertising for the promotion of tobacco, a brand of tobacco or a manufacturer of tobacco products is prohibited where the advertising is: directed at minors; is false or misleading; associates tobacco with a particular lifestyle; contains a testimonial or endorsement; uses a slogan; contains a text that refers to real or fictional persons, characters or animals; contains anything apart from text, with the exception of an illustration of the package or packaging of a tobacco product occupying not more that 10 per cent of the surface area of the advertising material; is disseminated other than in a printed newspaper or magazine of not less than 85 per cent adult readership (ad must include health warning and must be forwarded to Quebec government upon publication); or is disseminated otherwise than by means of displays visible only from the inside of a tobacco retail outlet. Indirect advertising for the promotion of tobacco includes, among other things, the use on a facility, a sign or an object that is not a tobacco product of a name, logo, design, image or slogan or brand element that is not directly associated with tobacco, a tobacco product, a brand of tobacco products or a manufacturer of tobacco products but that may reasonably be said to evoke a brand of tobacco product or a manufacturer of tobacco products because of its graphic design, presentation or association with a tobacco display stand or a tobacco retail outlet.
- Section 27: the sale, giving or exchanging of an object that is not a tobacco product is prohibited if a name, logo, design, brand element, image or slogan directly associated with tobacco, a tobacco product, a brand of tobacco product or a manufacturer of tobacco products, except a colour, appears on the object.

Chapter 12

TRADE-MARKS, COPYRIGHT AND OTHER FORMS OF INTELLECTUAL PROPERTY

A. INTRODUCTION

The term "intellectual property" refers to the bundle of intangible property rights which may be much more valuable than the physical assets of a business: intangible rights such as goodwill, trade secrets, know-how, patents, industrial designs, trade-marks and copyright. There are many compelling examples of the importance of intellectual property. Specialists in business valuation estimate that the trade-marks **Coca-Cola** and **Microsoft** are worth $70 billion and $65 billion respectively. The fortunes of many blue chip companies are built on patents. One of the most compelling business dramas of the early 21st century was the patent infringement case brought against RIM in the United States which threatened to deprive the U.S. government and millions of other addicts of their cherished BlackBerries.

In this chapter, we will concentrate on the two forms of intellectual property critical to the advertising industry: trade-marks and copyright. Trade-mark law protects a company's efforts at building its brands. Copyright protects the creative materials produced by agencies, promotion houses and advertisers.

Given that trade-marks and copyright are essential to an industry based on the packaging and selling of ideas, it is surprising how little they are understood. Many marketing people seem to believe that trade-marks and copyright can be intuitively understood. They are wrong. Trade-mark and copyright law is complex, very technical and sometimes unforgiving.

This chapter sets out the basic principles of trade-mark and copyright law. If you think your ideas have value, you should understand how to protect them.

B.   TRADE-MARK LAW

A trade-mark is always and fundamentally an indicator of origin. It is used to tell consumers and dealers that particular goods or services are supplied by a particular party. The trade-mark **Coke**, for example, tells consumers that the soft drink was made by the Coca-Cola Company or a licensee. This is intended to guarantee consistency.

Consumers care about trade-marks. They want a product labelled **Coke** to be the drink they always buy, with the taste and level of carbonation they prefer — not a counterfeit version. Manufacturers care about trade-marks for exactly the same reason. If they have built a reputation for their brand name, they do not want trade-mark infringers trading on that reputation by selling counterfeit products. Similarly, they do not want the value of their trade-mark damaged by second-rate knock-offs.

If you start with the principle that trade-marks function as an indicator of the source of particular goods or services, it is clear that trade-marks are not restricted to brand names. Many things can perform this identifying function. The three-note NBC chime is a trade-mark because it tells you which network you are watching. The colour and shape of a pharmaceutical pill can be a trade-mark if they are distinctive enough to denote the brand-name drug. The shape of a package, for example the Perrier bottle; or a product's appearance, for example, the "copper-topped" Duracell battery, are trade-marks because they immediately signify which companies they are produced by.

(As an aside, "grey market goods" are products made by the trade-mark owner or his licensee in another country and imported into Canada. As these are made to local standards, they may be even more unpalatable than counterfeit products, as anyone who has tried the French version of Diet Coke can attest.)

The Canadian Intellectual Property Office maintains a database of registered trade-marks and pending trade-mark applications. The database is available online at <http://strategis.ic.gc.ca/app/cipo/trademarks/search/tmSearch.do?language=eng> and makes for instructive reading. Some recent registrations demonstrate the infinite possibilities of trade-marks:

- Pepperidge Farm has registered the shape of its Gold Fish crackers
- The Labatt Company has registered the blue tab on its beer cans
- A tire company has registered a distinctive tire tread
- Pizza Pizza has registered its telephone number: 967-11-11
- A clothing company has registered a stitching pattern on a pocket
- A manufacturing company registered the colour pink applied to the whole visible surface of the wares (foam insulation)
- Nalge Nunc International Corp. registered the shape of the Nalgene plastic water bottle

The limits of trade-marks are constantly expanding. There is no reason, in principle, that a perfume, a menu-board or the shape of a chair could not be registered as trade-marks. Why is this important? Because you may protect, through trade-mark registration or at common law, much more than the name of your product.

C. TRADE-MARK REGISTRATION

The protection of a trade-mark leads to a fundamental question — why register a trade-mark? The common law will protect any brand name or other trade-mark which is sufficiently well-known as the "brand" of a particular trader. For example, McDonalds' "Golden Arches" have a worldwide reputation as the symbol of a particular fast food chain. McDonalds would not need trade-mark registrations to prevent a third party from using the Golden Arches without permission and trading on the goodwill of this symbol.

The common law provides protection to unregistered trade-marks only to the extent of their commercial reputation. For example, if your trade-mark is well-known in Toronto only, you cannot stop a Montreal company from adopting the identical trade-mark. Second, to succeed in protecting a common law trade-mark you have to prove that members of the public could be confused by the "infringing" trade-mark and that this could damage your business.

A trade-mark registration, on the other hand, gives you the exclusive right to use your trade-mark anywhere in Canada, regardless of where the mark is actually being used, in association with the goods and/or services covered by the registration. This is an important point in that the same trade-mark can be registered by many different parties for different goods or services provided there is no confusion between the co-existing registrations. For example, **Skippy** could be registered by different parties for both peanut butter and for motorcycles. It could not be registered by different parties for peanut butter and peanut flavoured candy because consumers would assume that these products were made by the same company, leading to confusion for the purchaser.

The second advantage of trade-mark registration is that enforcement proceedings are simpler. You are not required to prove the "reputation" of your mark. Finally, registration acts as a potential block to any subsequent party's application for a confusingly similar trade-mark. The Trade-marks Office polices its Register and does not permit the registration of confusing marks.

1.   Costs

It costs about $2,000 (including government fees) to obtain a trade-mark registration. The process can take at least two years, depending on staffing levels at the Trade-marks Office and whether the application encounters procedural problems or third party opposition. Once obtained, a trade-mark registration is valid for 15 years, and can be renewed thereafter for 15-year periods on payment of a renewal fee. The whole process of seeing a trade-mark application through to registration is called "trade-mark prosecution".

You can apply to register a trade-mark which is already in use or one which you are planning to use. A "proposed use" application allows you to "reserve" a trade-mark for five years or more. Eventually, you will be required to use the proposed trade-mark or abandon your application.

Because of the time, effort and money involved, registration does not make sense unless you have a long-term commitment to the brand.

2.   Limitations

Certain trade-marks are unregistrable, notably place names and surnames and descriptive trade-marks — such as **Soft And White** for facial tissues or **Bubbly** for soft drinks. One of the fundamentals of trade-mark law is that no one is allowed to monopolize words which are needed by other traders to describe particular goods or services. Descriptive trade-marks may be registrable in combination with a distinctive word, but the applicant will be required to disclaim any exclusive right to the descriptive words. The exception to this — and it is a very limited exception — is descriptive trade-marks which through long-term and extensive use have become so closely associated with a particular company's product that they acquire the "distinctiveness" necessary to function as trade-marks. A trademark cannot be functional. In a case decided by the Supreme Court of Canada in 2005, Lego was unsuccessful in preventing a competitor from manufacturing Lego-like bricks. The court held that the unique characteristics of the pegged building blocks were functional and could not be protected under trademark law after Lego's patents had expired.

The strongest trade-marks are coined words which do not describe any feature of the products they cover, trade-marks such as **Reebok**, **Bic** or **Kodak**. The more unique your trade-mark, the easier it will be to build customer recognition and to prevent other parties from acquiring rights to similar trade-marks. Before beginning to use any new trade-mark (and this includes contest titles and advertising tag lines), it is important to conduct clearance searches to determine if the trade-mark is available for use. A "locate" search to identify identical or highly similar marks can be done quickly and inexpensively. If you launch a new product or advertising campaign using trade-marks that infringe a competitor's rights, you may be enjoined from using the infringing marks. Obviously, this would involve the loss of considerable time and expense in the development and marketing of the abandoned brands, not to mention the risk of significant legal expenses.

In general, trade-mark protection extends only to the goods or services covered by the registration. A trade-mark is registered for the products and services marketed under that trade-mark at the time the registration issues. Registration does not confer a monopoly to prevent other parties from using the same trade-mark in other categories provided, always, that there is no confusion. The Trade-marks Register contains thousands of examples of the same word or phrase registered by different parties for unrelated goods or services. However, if you have a "famous mark", for example, **Kodak** or **Coca-Cola**, the law gives you a virtual monopoly. Because **Kodak**, for example, is universally recognized, consumers might assume that **Kodak** hotels were related to the camera company and Kodak Canada Inc. can therefore prevent hotels, food, software and any other products or services from being marketed under its brand.

3.   Some Interesting Technicalities

Trade-mark registration must be done on a country by country basis except for the European Community trade-mark, which covers all member countries of the European Union and the Madrid Protocol, to which Canada is not yet a signatory. Generally, the date of first use of a trade-mark is the priority date if a dispute arises between different parties. However, many trade-mark applications are filed on a prospective "proposed use" basis and the filing date establishes priority between competing "proposed use" applications. From the date of filing your trade-mark application in Canada (or in any of the approximately 169 countries which adhere to the Paris Convention), you have six months to file an application in other countries based on your Canadian filing date.

The Canadian *Trade-marks Act*[1] permits an anomalous category of so-called "official marks". These are marks or symbols associated with the Canadian and foreign governments, for example, national flags and coats-of-arms; with international organizations, such as the "Red Cross" symbol, as well as words or phrases which have been adopted and used in Canada by provincial governments, Crown corporations and other officially sanctioned, non-commercial publicly funded organizations such as the Canadian Olympic Committee ("COC"). Official marks are either set out in section 9 of the *Trade-marks Act* or advertised by an

---

[1]   R.S.C. 1985, c. T-13.

appropriate "public authority" or other qualifying organization in the Trade-marks Journal.

As soon as notice of an official mark is given in the Trade-marks Journal, no third party can use the same or a similar trade-mark in any category without the permission of the owner of the official mark. This confers a very effective monopoly and allows organizations like the COC and the provincial lottery corporations to exact licensing fees for any use of their staples of official marks.

4. Marking and Policing

Trade-marks should always be marked the first and/or the most prominent time they appear in an advertisement or on packaging. The symbol ® is typically used for registered marks; "TM/MC" for unregistered marks ("MC" is the abbreviation for "Marque de commerce"). On packaging, brochures and wherever possible, the trade-mark ownership line should appear at the bottom of the page, for example: "TM/MC **Good Eats** is a trade-mark of Barney's Food Co."

Trade-marks should be bolded, italicized or otherwise set apart from the rest of the copy whenever they appear. In addition, it is important to remember that trade-marks are proper adjectives and should always be followed by the noun they modify (**Bic** pens, **Kodak** cameras). Do not use them as a noun ("**Bic** is the best-selling disposable razor in Canada") or as a verb ("Xerox twenty copies of your presentation"). The danger is that your trade-marks will lose their trade-mark status and fall into the public domain. There are many common words which used to be trade-marks and have lost this status: for example, "jujubes", "brassiere", "cellophane" and "escalator". There are many other trade-marks which are widely used to refer to the product rather than the brand and are therefore in danger of becoming genericized: Jeep®, Aspirin® and Kleenex®, for example. In fact, Canada is the only country in the world where Aspirin® is still a protectable trade-mark.

It is also important to protect the validity of your trade-mark registration by using the mark as registered, by maintaining use of the trade-mark (trade-marks which have not been used in commerce for three or more years are vulnerable to third party expungement proceedings) and by policing the marketplace to ensure that other parties are not infringing your trade-marks.

5. Self-Help

For complete instructions on registering a trade-mark in Canada, visit <http://www.strategis.gc.ca>. However, proceed cautiously. There are more potential pitfalls in the one-page trade-mark registration document than in most legal forms. It is usually cheaper to retain a trade-mark lawyer from the start.

A better use of this website is to review the Trade-marks Journal where pending trade-mark applications are advertised. This gives you a preview of the trade-marks and line extensions your competitors are planning. It also provides a window of opportunity to prevent registration of a confusing trade-mark by a competitor.

6. Domain Names

In a perfect world, the owner of a well-known brand would have presumptive rights to Famousbrand.com or Famousbrand.ca. Not so in cyberspace. Domain names are assigned on a first come first served basis. A domain name can be pirated by a cybersquatter or by an innocent third party who shares the name. In many, but not all cases, the owner of the famous brand will have remedies that allow him or her to recover, at considerable expense, the domain name that corresponds to the famous brand.

Trade-mark owners need to protect the use of their trade-marks on the internet. Domain name registration is cheap compared to the costs of dealing with confusingly similar names which front competitors' websites or internet pornography. Trade-mark owners should identify the brands which are vital to their business and register all of them as domain names in the relevant generic top level domains (.com, .info, .biz, *etc.*) and in the country domains (.ca, .uk, *etc.*) where they carry on business. In addition, likenesses of the brand names and obvious misspellings (*e.g.* Barbi.com, Motarola.ca) should be registered.

You do not need to use each and every domain name. They can all be linked to your primary website. This is simply a strategy for brand protection. The acquisition and management of domain names is an increasingly important part of intellectual property protection.

7. Ambush Marketing

From a legal standpoint, the term "ambush marketing" has come to mean the practice of trading off the goodwill associated with a particular event, product or organization without paying for the right to do so. Ambush marketing is an extension of the tort of "passing off". "Passing off" arises when Party A uses without permission, Party B's name, design or other trademark, or one so closely resembling it as to be mistaken for it and causes consumers to think that Party A's product or service is actually that of Party B.

In a sense, ambush marketing is similar to misappropriation of personality (see Chapter 13). Implying that one is a sponsor or otherwise connected with an event, for example, is not much different than using, without permission, the name, voice, image or other characteristic of a famous person for the purpose of promoting one's product or service.

How do you sue someone for ambush marketing? In other words, what is the legal "cause of action"? Normally, in these situations, law-suits allege trademark infringement; passing off; depreciation of the goodwill associated with one's name, event, *etc.*; and interference with contractual relations.

(a) Extension of the Law

Traditionally, passing off required you to prove that the defendant had named or packaged or described its product or service in such a way as to lead the public to think that their product or service is actually yours — in other words, trading off your trademark's goodwill by literally making their product look like yours. While that traditional model of the law of passing off requires the plaintiff to establish a likelihood of confusion, the courts in recent years have broadened the definition. It is now suffi-cient to prove that a defendant has promoted its product or business in such a way as to create the false impression that its product or business is somehow approved, authorized or endorsed by the plaintiff or that there is some business connection between the plaintiff and the defendant. The law of ambush marketing proceeds on similar grounds.

(b) Court Decisions

While reported court decisions in this area are rare, there are a few cases of note. In the case of *National Hockey League v. Pepsi-Cola Canada Ltd.*,[2] the NHL sued Pepsi for implying a connection to the NHL by advertising during broadcasts of *Hockey Night in Canada* (which right it had sublicensed from Molson Breweries). The NHL alleged that the Pepsi commercials were causing confusion because the NHL had granted Coca-Cola Ltd. the right to be the "official soft drink of the NHL". The NHL sued Pepsi for passing off, trademark infringement and interference with contractual relations and, after detailed analysis, the court rejected the NHL's claims on the basis that there was no misrepresentation (and therefore no passing off), there was no trade-mark use (and therefore no trade-mark infringement) and that the NHL's agreement with Coca-Cola could not allow them to prohibit Pepsi-Cola from advertising in a lawful manner (and therefore no wrongful interference with contractual rela-tions).

The case of *Walt Disney Productions v. Fantasyland Hotel Inc.*[3] was similar and also referred to the "extended" law of passing off. However, as

---

[2] [1992] B.C.J. No. 1221, 92 D.L.R. (4th) 349 (B.C.S.C.), affd. [1995] B.C.J. No. 310, 122 D.L.R. (4th) 412 (B.C.C.A.).

[3] [1994] A.J. No. 484, [1994] 9 W.W.R. 45 (Alta. Q.B.), affd. [1996] A.J. No. 415, [1996] 6 W.W.R. 403 (Alta. C.A.).

in *NHL v. Pepsi*, the court in *Walt Disney v. Fantasyland Hotel* was unable to conclude that passing off had occurred. In the words of the Alberta Court of Appeal, "the allegation or even the belief that the respondent is benefiting from the use of the name Fantasyland is not enough to found the tort of passing off". The court found that Walt Disney's contention that its goodwill in the name "Fantasyland" for an amusement park was diminished by the operation of a hotel in Edmonton, adjacent to a mall in which there is an amusement park, was too much of a "stretch". The Fantasyland hotel did not create a false impression that it was authorized by or connected with Walt Disney.

(c)   Ambush Ads and the Olympics

Another area in which ambush marketing frequently emerges is the Olympics. The International Olympic Committee, and its national counterparts like the Canadian Olympic Committee, are very aggressive in protecting their rights and in pursuing legal action against anyone who implies, no matter how remotely, some connection with the Olympic Games. The rationale, not surprisingly, is that sponsorship is the Olympics' most lucrative source of revenue.

Moreover, Olympic sponsors, who have paid millions of dollars for their sponsorships, inevitably pressure Olympic organizations to prevent their competitors from wrongly implying an association with the Olympics. The list of parties against whom the Olympics have pursued legal action is very long. In some cases they have been successful, and in others they have not. Advertisers need to know that the Olympic associations are very litigious.

In one New Zealand case, Telecom New Zealand ran a print ad where the word "ring" appeared three times across the top of the ad and twice in the line immediately below, between the gaps in the upper three. The colours of the "ring" words were the same as those in the Olympic symbol. The International Olympic Committee took legal action and ultimately was unsuccessful, with the judge concluding that the Telecom design was simply too different from the actual Olympic symbol to create deception. However, because it was clearly arguable that there was an implication made about Olympic sponsorship, the court acknowledged that the case came close to the line and specifically stated that Telecom New Zealand came close to crossing the line.

With the approach of the 2010 Olympic Winter Games in Vancouver, the value to Canadian companies of an Olympic sponsorship is bound to increase. At the same time, the Canadian Olympic Committee will become increasingly aggressive in pursuing ambush marketing.

RULES OF THUMB

- DO create your own concept;
- DO avoid the use of concepts in which others may claim proprietary rights;
- DO NOT decide that the best way to promote your product or service is by pretending you have some connection with, or by referring to another party;
- DO NOT associate yourself with some person, place or thing without carefully assessing whether that person may be in a position to contest an implied endorsement; and, finally
- DO carefully consider who it is that might sue you and how aggressive they are likely to be.

D.   COPYRIGHT

Copyright protection is the birthright of every original creative "work". Copyright protects almost every form of human expression that is not predominantly utilitarian. The format of telephone directories is protected by copyright. As are architectural drawings, Pokemon cartoons, family photographs, and great works of art — such as Gershwin's "Rhapsody in Blue" and Henry Moore's sculptures — which are not in the public domain. Because copyright confers a limited monopoly, most works of art are in the public domain. In most cases, copyright expires 50 years after the death of the "author". Essentially, copyright tries to balance the need to encourage artists and the importance of public access to the arts. Artists are granted a limited term within which to exploit their talent. After copyright expires, the public has unrestricted access to their works of art (provided they are not part of a private collection).

Copyright is an important form of intellectual property in the marketing business. Almost everything in the marketing cycle from the "secret recipe" for your product, to the package design, to all elements of the advertising campaign including the shelf-talkers is protected by copyright. Two important issues are who — as between the advertiser and the advertising agency — owns the copyright and who is responsible for ensuring that the copyright in creative materials is not infringed? These are discussed below.

Copyright is simple and widely misunderstood. It arises automatically whenever an original idea is given concrete expression. This leads to several distinct and important attributes. Copyright protection is automatic. In Canada, there is no need to register "works of art" to obtain copyright protection — the laws differ in this respect from country to country. There are procedural advantages to registration in the event of a lawsuit. However, registration is generally delayed until a lawsuit is imminent. In certain industries, where copyright infringement is rife, copyright registration is commonplace. However, this is the exception rather than the rule.

In addition, there is no particular need in Canada to include a copyright notice on advertising materials. The familiar footnote — © 2006 LexisNexis Canada Inc. — is included as a footnote or a super in many U.S. advertisements for technical reasons. It is not required in Canadian advertisements.

1.   Copyright Protection

Copyright extends to the concrete expression of original ideas. Ideas, themselves, cannot be protected. This makes sense. Without concrete form, the nature, scope and timing of ideas would be impossible to prove. Moreover, copyright protects "original" works. It does not necessarily confer a monopoly. If a third party independently creates an identical "original" work, the two are allowed to co-exist. What copyright prevents is deliberate copying or other exploitation, for example, the translation into another language, of a protected work.

To properly discuss copyright issues, a few definitions are in order. The term "author" applies to the creator of any creative work. Author, therefore, subsumes writer, illustrator, composer, cinematographer, architect, photographer and many others. An original creation, no matter the category, is described as a "work". An "artistic work" can include paintings, sculptures or packaging graphics. A "literary work" can include a 500 page novel or a 50 word print advertisement (Interestingly, titles are explicitly *not* protected by copyright). "Copyright" means exactly what it says — the sole right to copy or authorize the copying of a work. In addition, a copyright owner has the sole right to make or authorize the making of derivative works or translations.

2.   Copyright Ownership

Determining who owns a copyright can get very complicated. In most cases, the author of a work is the owner of the original copyright. However, there are times when it is the client or entity who commissioned the work who owns the right. For example, works created in the course of employment. Creative materials produced at an advertising agency are owned by the agency. The agency, in turn, typically assigns copyright to its client after the creative materials have been paid for.

Depending on the work, there may be multiple authors. A motion picture, for example, consists of many protectable elements: the screenplay, the score, the cinematography, the direction and so on. The authors of each element will typically assign their copyright to the studio. Copyright can be the subject of a partial assignment (for a specified territory, for example), a licence (which allows use of the work for particular purposes such as an advertising campaign but the author retains all other rights) or a total buyout.

Advertisers and agencies frequently do not ensure that copyright issues are properly addressed. Copyright assignments and licences should be in writing and should be executed by all freelancers and independent contractors. These agreements should specifically address what territories and media are covered. Is the author assigning worldwide rights including the right to translate "literary works" into other languages? Are electronic media covered by the agreement, in particular, the internet and electronic products such as DVDs?

The advertising agency agreement should specifically cover copyright ownership of creative materials. However, even when the advertiser clearly owns copyright, the "authors", including agency employees, retain the "moral right" to protect the integrity of their work. For example, the artist Michael Snow exercised his moral rights when he enjoined the Toronto Eaton Centre from decorating his snow geese sculptures with Christmas bows. Moral rights cannot be sold. They can, however, be waived. Therefore, waivers of moral rights should be signed by all contributing "authors".

3.   Copyright Infringement

Copyright infringement involves the "substantial copying" of a protected work. Section 9 of the *Canadian Code of Advertising Standards* contains a similar prohibition: "No advertiser shall imitate the copy, slogans or illustrations of another advertiser in such a manner as to mislead the consumer." In both cases, the test is qualitative rather than quantitative: has the infringer copied the "essence" of a protected work?

The "essence" of any particular work may be small. Consider the famous case of George Harrison's song "My Sweet Lord".[4] Harrison was sued by The Chiffons on the basis that the three note chorus of "My Sweet Lord" infringed the copyright of the 1963 Chiffons' hit "She's So Fine". In fact, both songs featured identical and prominent choruses. Harrison denied copyright infringement. He was a gifted songwriter. Why would he deliberately and unlawfully "borrow" from another band? The court found that Harrison had "unintentionally" infringed the Chiffons' copyright. He had been exposed to "She's So Fine" and had unconsciously borrowed its chorus. This was sufficient to justify a $1,600,00 award in favour of the Chiffons.

---

[4]   420 F. Supp. 177.

Copyright infringement arises in many potential and actual lawsuits. There is the "nothing new under the sun" variety where an advertising campaign "borrows" too heavily from third party creative materials. Sometimes this is unintentional. Sometimes it is deliberate and cynical: an idea is adopted from a successful advertising campaign in another country, hopefully at a sufficient remove in time and space that no one will notice the similarities.

You need to be very aware of copyright issues whenever you are creating advertising, packaging or other materials that are "based" on another source. The references may be deliberate and striking, for example: a "spoof" of a classic television show. However, in Canada, unlike the United States, "parody" is not a defence to allegations of copyright infringement. The references may be unintentional, like George Harrison's infringement of the Chiffons' song. Often copywriters and art directors have an uneasy feeling of "déjà vu" when developing an idea. It is important to pay attention to this feeling. The concept should be reviewed by as many people as possible to ensure that a copyrighted "work" has not been unintentially infringed.

There are many subsidiary issues. Apart from a "substantial taking" of the original work, you can infringe copyright by making a "colourable imitation", *i.e.*, something which in overall appearance and feel substantially resembles the original. You can inadvertently infringe the copyright in a public domain work. The Mona Lisa was painted in the years 1503-1506 and has been in the public domain for centuries. However, a particular photograph of the Mona Lisa may belong to the Louvre and require a copyright licence. Every piece of creative material containing third party elements — including photographs, recipes and letters submitted by consumers — should be reviewed for potential copyright issues.

Copyright and trade-mark rights are the cornerstones of property protection in the advertising business. Copyright law is currently undergoing a period of upheaval. In the last ten years, there have been many attacks on the status quo: the establishment of copyright collectives such as SOCAN and CANCOPY; the application of copyright law to new media, *e.g.*, Napster software which enabled the unlawful copying over the internet of archived music; the interface between copyright and patent law with respect to software; the scope of the "fair use" exemption (which, for the record, does not apply to commercial uses such as advertising). The basic principles of copyright law, however, remain the same. They have been in place since the world's first copyright act, the Statute of Anne, was enacted in 1709, long before advertising was conceived as a profession.

E. PATENTS, INDUSTRIAL DESIGNS AND TRADE SECRETS

Patents and industrial designs have limited application to the advertising business. However, both may have implications for the broader process of marketing new products and services. They are basic and important forms of intellectual property protection.

Patents can be obtained for new and useful products, things, machines and processes. Everyone is aware of the widespread use of patents in certain industries — such as the pharmaceutical industry — to secure monopoly rights to import, sell and resell proprietary inventions. However, patent protection can be secured for something as simple as a pool-cue holder or something as non-technical as a method of swinging on a swing (this patent was obtained by a seven-year old American inventor in April 2002).

Importantly, it is now possible to obtain a patent for a "business method". Business methods could include a way of structuring a promotion or of targeting a particular group of consumers. In the U.S., companies must structure online "match and win" promotions carefully to avoid infringing a patent for this process. Many devices that are common features of the advertising business could be patentable, such as "Roll up the Rim" contest cups and rotating transit advertisements.

Before you approach a patent lawyer (which will be very expensive), consider whether your "invention" has the following attributes: it must be new (*i.e.*, not previously invented), useful and not "obvious" (*i.e.*, an obvious extension of pre-existing products, things, machines or processes). Patent protection lasts for 20 years from the date of filing. A patent confers monopoly rights which can be extremely valuable. Unlike trade-mark registrations, patents are not renewable.

1. Industrial Designs

Certain features of shape, configurations, patterns and ornamentation are protectable as industrial designs, for example, the design of a running shoe, the quilting pattern of paper towels, or the shape of a vodka bottle. There are important exceptions, however. Features which are dictated solely by a utilitarian function cannot be protected by an industrial design registration. Not every feature of an article's appearance is capable of registration. There must be something unique with a certain visual appeal before it will receive protection under the *Industrial Design Act*. Industrial designs must be registered on a country-by-country basis. In Canada, industrial designs are registered for five years and renewable for five more.

2.   Trade Secrets

Much of the critical intellectual property of a business is not protectable under trade-mark, copyright, industrial design or patent protection regimes. This unprotectable property is often the heart and soul of a business — ranging from customer lists to pricing and sales policies, product development plans, financial information, market forecasts and the secret recipes for Coca-Cola and KFC chicken. If a competitor were to obtain much of this "confidential information" (which can also be classified as "trade secrets"), the impact could be devastating. A competitor who was secretly armed with your line extension plans, for example, could beat you to market with similar products. Or equipped with a list of your most important current and prospective clients, a competitor could undermine these relationships.

The law provides certain safeguards. Key employees cannot join a competitive business and divulge their former employer's secrets without breaching a fiduciary duty they owe to their former employer. In addition, it is common for key employees to be bound by confidentiality and non-compete clauses in their employment contracts. However, it is difficult to protect against the defection of a junior employee who knows too much. The best-run businesses keep tight controls over the flow of confidential information to minimize this risk.

3.   The Bottom Line

To adapt a familiar adage, protection is nine-tenths of intellectual property law. Most of the work produced by advertising agencies and marketing departments falls into one of two categories: trade-marks or literary, artistic and/or musical "works" protected by copyright. First you have to recognize the nature of your product and second you have to take the necessary steps — whether trade-mark applications, copyright assignments or waivers of moral rights — to protect the work and police it from third party infringements. This will involve time, money and careful management but why invest time and money in the underlying product if you are not prepared to protect it?

Chapter 13

MISAPPROPRIATION OF PERSONALITY

A. OVERVIEW

Beginning in the 1980s, in an increasing drive to create compelling advertising, advertisers and their agencies uncovered a new way, on a limited budget, to cash in on the recognizability of celebrities, namely look-alikes and soundalikes, as well as similar sounding names. Not only do living celebrities have cachet, but so do dead celebrities, who may have left behind litigious heirs and estates. The characters we have grown attached to from the movies or on television and the actors who portray them have enormous marketing potential. For a time, Canadian advertisers could rely on the fact that the law regarding unauthorized use of celebrities, otherwise legally known as "misappropriation of personality", was one of many areas of advertising law that was less developed in Canada than in the United States. Today, misappropriation of personality is an important and rapidly developing area of Canadian law. The goal of this chapter is to alert you, the advertiser or marketer, to the issues, strategies, trends, and pitfalls involved in the unauthorized use of celebrity personas.

B. MISAPPROPRIATION OF PERSONALITY

1. Involving the Famous

It is a tort or a legally actionable "wrong against a person" to use a person's name, voice or likeness for the purpose of trade without first having obtained consent. "Personality" is a legal term which includes a person's name, voice, likeness and any other element(s) which easily identify a particular person — for example, Groucho Marx's moustache, glasses and cigar. The tort of misappropriation of personality has been established in Canada by several cases. The first[1] involved a large car company, which used the photograph of a well known football player in print advertising. The advertising combined a guide to players from different football teams with advertising for their cars. The advertiser did not compensate the football player for use of his photograph.

The Court established the rule that without permission and without any right, the car company had misappropriated the professional reputation of the celebrity for its own commercial ends. Unfortunately for the football player, the Court found that he had no endorsement value and let the advertiser off the hook.

Another situation[2] involved George Athans, an internationally famous water skier. A summer camp had tried unsuccessfully to obtain Athans' endorsement. Athans, who had previously exploited his achievements and personality commercially, had developed a fancy stylized "logo" or line-drawing of himself which he used for self-promotion. The camp, without his permission, used Athans' line-drawing on one of its brochures.

In this case, the Court ruled that the commercial use of a person's image without consent is an invasion of their exclusive right to market their "personality" and therefore constitutes misappropriation. However, the actions of the camp did not amount to a wrongful appropriation of Athans' personality. Waterskiing is a more esoteric sport than football and the general public would not have recognized Athans' image. In an advertising/marketing context, these cases indicate that the tort of misappropriation of personality is not committed unless the celebrity is clearly identifiable and is used to successfully "endorse" a product or business.

After these less than clear-cut cases, the legal community was anxious to see how the tort of misappropriation of personality would develop. Unfortunately, another Canadian case[3] that recognized the tort of misappropriation of personality offered little assistance. Racine, a former professional football player who had been working as a radio football announcer, succeeded in a wrongful dismissal suit against the employer radio station. Racine received $2,675 in damages for misappropriation of personality because the radio station "enjoyed an improvement in sales and popularity due to having the plaintiff as an employee". Following this reasoning, Lee Iacocca, if he had been wrongfully dismissed, could have sued Chrysler for millions of dollars on the basis of misappropriation of personality given his celebrated association with the company. There is obviously potential for abuse in the application of this tort.

---

[1] *Krouse v. Chrysler Canada Ltd.* (1973), 40 D.L.R. (3d) 15 (Ont. C.A.).

[2] *Athans v. Canadian Adventure Camps Ltd.* (1977), 17 O.R. (2d) 425 (Ont. H.C.J.).

[3] *Racine v. C.J.R.C. Radio Capitale Ltd.* (1977), 35 C.P.R. (2d) 236 (Ont. C.A.).

2.   Involving the Not-So-Famous

The tort of misappropriation of personality is not limited in Canada to famous individuals. In a 1983 Ontario case,[4] a research institute invited a group of unemployed workers to participate in a conference. The proceedings were recorded on film. The workers sought to prevent the screening of the film because it included emotional and, in one case, seditious exchanges. The participants had understood the conference to involve the usual exchange of views, but did not anticipate nor agree to an "encounter group" in which the organizers caused them to reveal their inner feelings. The emphasis in the decision appears to rest on the act of the "taking" of each participant's persona, individually and collectively, by the research institute for its own — though not necessarily commercial — gain.

3.   Under Quebec Civil Law

Unlike the common law system which governs the rest of Canada, the province of Quebec operates under the civil law system, governed by the Civil Code. The offence of misappropriation of personality also exists in this system and has been recognized in several situations. One case involved print and radio advertising, published by a Quebec amusement park, utilizing several French phrases, which the Quebec comedians, Ding et Dong had made famous. The expressions, "est effrayante" (it's scary) and "Est bonne! est bonne! est bonne!" (Great! great! great!) had been "coined" by Ding et Dong and widely used in their performances. While a sound-alike demo was produced, the radio commercial that actually aired used a female voice which merely suggested the involvement of Ding et Dong. Sadly for the two comedians, their attempt to restrain further use of the radio commercial was denied by the court. Even though relief was denied in this specific situation, the court did recognize that the tort of misappropriation of personality exists under the Quebec Civil Code.

In another situation[5] recognizing the Quebec tort, Gilbert Duclos took a photograph of a teenage girl sitting on the steps of a building on Rue St. Catherine in Montreal. The picture was taken without her knowledge. The photographer allowed it to be published, without payment, in an artistic magazine. The plaintiff was 17 at the time and brought an action for $10,000 in damages, which was high considering that the only evidence of damage adduced at trial was that she had been laughed at by friends. In the end, she was awarded $2,000 in damages.

---

[4]   *Dowell v. Mengen Institute*, [1983] O.J. No. 1090, 72 C.P.R. (2d) 238 (Ont. H.C.J.).

[5]   *Aubry v. Éditions Vice-Versa*, [1998] S.C.J. No. 30, 157 D.L.R. (4th) 577 (S.C.C.).

As a result of the decision, which was confirmed by the Supreme Court of Canada, it is clear that in Quebec the right to one's image is an element of the right to privacy and is protected under section 5 of the Quebec *Charter*. There is an infringement of a person's right to his or her image as soon as an identifiable image is published without their consent. The case revealed that it is possible for privacy rights to be infringed even if the published image does not injure a person's reputation.

C. OTHER EXAMPLES OF MISAPPROPRIATION OF PERSONALITY

There have been many other situations of alleged "misappropriation of personality" in Canada that were settled before trial. In addition, threatened actions have increased and these actions add dimension to the offence of misappropriation of personality.

In 1982, a candy bar manufacturer ran a multi-media campaign using look-alikes of famous actors. The ads, showed the lookalikes enjoying the advertiser's product with a disclaimer that said "The Celebrity Lookalike is John/Jane Doe." The advertiser inserted the disclaimer to clear up any misconception that the "real" actor was endorsing the advertiser's product. Burt Reynolds, one of the individuals whose lookalike was used, retained a Toronto lawyer to investigate the possibility of a lawsuit. Proceedings were never filed but the matter was well documented in the trade papers. The justification for the use of look-alikes in this campaign was that individuals who happen to look like famous people have just as much right to exploit their looks as the "real" celebrity.

In the late '80s, Jimmy Cagney retained Canadian counsel to bring an action in relation to a transit ad containing a still photograph of him taken from a film which was in the public domain. Mr. Cagney was alive when the photo was used but died prior to the litigation of the action; the case was reported to have been "settled" in July of 1988.

Even though this case was settled, the advertising industry may deduce the following lessons from the Cagney case:

- Even if a photograph is in the public domain, the people who appeared in the photo may still have "personality" rights independent of copyright.
- Stock photo house materials do not necessarily include the right to sell, license or use the personality rights of identifiable individuals.
- Do not assume that Hollywood South is unaware of the advertising in Hollywood North.

In the early 1990's, Chubby Checker brought a $17 million dollar action against a large fast food chain, its advertising agency, and the music producer for the use of a soundalike in a four-week Ontario television ad for twisty french fries. Although a synchronization licence was obtained for the famous song "The Twist", Checker asserted that consumers would mistakenly believe that the studio singer in the commercial was him. Again, the case was settled without comment.

In 1994, an advertising agency[6] obtained a copy of an Olympic photo of Myriam Bédard from Canadian Press (CP). Although the advertising agency told CP they did not plan to use the photo, the creatives on the account thought that permission had been obtained. The agency claimed that they made the photo "generic", that is, unidentifiable, by adding weight to Bédard's face, deleting her hair and changing her distinctive blue eyes. They also removed the Olympic rings from her shirt and the Canada symbol on her hat. The ad ran in Quebec with the headline:

"1994 — Quebec suddenly falls in love with the biathlon"

Even if Bédard had been unrecognizable in the photo, the headline made it obvious that the photo showed Bédard.

This case was settled but the moral of this story is that:

- You cannot use a person's likeness without their consent. Period.
- If the person is totally unrecognizable, it is unlikely the action will be successful. Here the doctored likeness and the context of the ad made it obvious that the photo was of Bédard.
- There is still copyright in a photo. You cannot take a photo that belongs to someone else and reproduce it, or parts of it, without consent.

1.   Misappropriation of Personality and the Privacy Acts

Five provinces have enacted privacy legislation which intersect with the tort of misappropriation of personality.[7] This legislation creates more certainty for advertisers when it comes to the use of lookalikes and film and photo clips. In Manitoba, Saskatchewan and Newfoundland, it is a violation of privacy to use the name, likeness or voice of a person for advertising or trade purposes without authorization. The legislation in British Columbia protects only the name and portrait, leaving open the possibility for advertisers to use someone's voice without permission under the statute, although this would still be prohibited at common law.

---

[6]   See the Professional Photographers of Canada, available online at <http://www.ppoc.ca/copyright/march_99.htm>.

[7]   **British Columbia:** *Privacy Act*, R.S.B.C. 1996, c. 373; **Manitoba:** *The Privacy Act*, C.C.S.M. c. P125; **Newfoundland & Labrador:** *Privacy Act*, R.S.N.L. 1990, c. P-22; *An Act Respecting the Protection of Personal Information in the Private Sector*, R.S.Q. c. P-39.1.; **Saskatchewan:** *The Privacy Act*, R.S.S. 1978, c. P-24.

In all five provinces except Manitoba, the statutory rights are extinguished upon the death of an individual; Manitoba did not legislate on this issue.

Until the federal *Personal Information Protection and Electronic Documents Act* came into force on January 1, 2001, the Quebec *Act respecting the protection of personal information in the private sector* was the most extensive privacy legislation in the country. This Act applies whatever the nature of the medium. Some important points covered by the Act are:

* Section 13: subject to the exceptions listed in Section 18, a company must have the express, purpose-related consent of a person before it may use that person's personal information or communicate it to a third party.
* Section 17: this section deals directly with personal information about Quebeckers. Companies carrying on business in Quebec and communicating information about Quebeckers to those outside Quebec must take "all reasonable steps to ensure" that the information is not used in a manner inconsistent with the purpose for which it was collected and that it is not used without consent.

Also in Quebec, Chapter III of the *Civil Code*, deals with respect of reputation and privacy. Section 36 states that using a person's name, image, likeness or voice for a purpose other than the legitimate information of the public may be considered an invasion of privacy.

Hanging on the wall of this author's office as a constant reminder of privacy rights is Brent Daniels' poster of a bodybuilder's "bulging torso" with a kitten in his arms. *Joseph v. Daniels*[8] is the first reported case under a privacy act in Canada. Notwithstanding the impressive physique of the model, the B.C. Supreme Court declared that use of Mr. Joseph's torso without his head was not in violation of the B.C. *Privacy Act* because the torso was impossible to identify as that of Mr. Joseph.

2. Misappropriation of Personality and the Deceased

At present in Canada, there is no definitive law to indicate that an action for misappropriation of personality exists in a deceased person's estate. In the U.S., many states have enacted laws which state that a right of action for "misappropriation of personality" lies with the deceased's estate and therefore, the heirs.

---

[8] *Joseph v. Daniels (Doing Business as Brent Daniels Photography)* (1986), 11 C.P.R. (3d) 544 (B.C.S.C.).

In Canada, the Glenn Gould Estate[9] sought to stop publication of a book featuring the words and photographs of Glenn Gould, the famous Canadian pianist who died in 1982. The book was based on notes, audio tape recordings and photographs taken by a journalist in 1956. Originally, the photos were taken and the interviews conducted for the purposes of an article for *Weekend Magazine*. At issue was whether the journalist was entitled, for his own exclusive benefit, to later exploit commercially the photographs he took of Gould in 1956 and to use the notes of his interviews to write the book. Such later use had never been discussed with Gould or his heirs.

The court in this case distinguished between cases where a person is represented as endorsing a product and cases in which the person is the actual subject of the work, such as a biography. This was a case where the celebrity was the subject of the work and because the public had an interest in knowing about Gould, the pianist, there was no misappropriation of personality. Gould had no rights as the subject unless there had been an express contract or implied agreement with the author that such rights existed. Since no agreement existed, neither Gould nor his estate, could complain about any further reproduction of the photos or the notes. Although, the court in this case did not need to decide whether a right of action in misappropriation descends to the heirs of a deceased's estate, the court's judgment seems to suggest that at common law in Canada, the right to an action for misappropriation of personality does in fact descend to a person's heirs.

D. MISAPPROPRIATION OF PERSONALITY AND LIABILITY UNDER THE TRADE-MARKS ACT

A potential area for liability exists under the *Trade-Marks Act*.[10] Subsections 9(1)(k) and 9(1)(l) of the Act provide as follows:

> 9(1) No person shall adopt in connection with a business, as a trade-mark or otherwise, any mark consisting of, or so nearly resembling as to be likely to be mistaken for:
>
> ...
>
> (k) any matter that may falsely suggest a connection with any living individual;
>
> (l) the portrait or signature of any individual who is living or has died within the preceding thirty years...

Neither of these subsections appears to have been used in connection with an ad using a lookalike or caricature. However, the wording of the

---

9   *Gould Estate v. Stoddart Publishing*, [1998] O.J. No. 1894, 39 O.R. (3d) 545 (Ont. C.A.).

10 R.S.C. 1985, c. T-13.

Act is sufficiently broad to create a potential action. Until such time as this matter has been litigated, the only certain way to avoid liability under the section is to utilize individuals who died more than 30 years ago (for example, Abraham Lincoln, Rudolph Valentino or Babe Ruth). However, since the tort of misappropriation of personality may well extend more than 30 years, there is a risk that using a famous celebrity who has been dead 31 years will avoid liability under the *Trade-marks Act* but not the common law. A 1980 decision found that use of the trademark "HERE'S JOHNNY" for "porta potties" falsely suggested a connection with Johnny Carson.[11] To date, however, there have apparently not been any other relevant cases under the *Trade-marks Act*.

E. MISAPPROPRIATION OF PERSONALITY IN THE UNITED STATES AND EUROPE

1. United States

California has added another twist to this area of the law. The *California Right of Publicity Statute* purports to protect the personalities of persons who lived in, or died in, the state of California in the last 70 years. The law purports to give rights to the estate of such deceased individuals to protect licensing rights for advertising purposes. While California would not have jurisdiction over Canadian advertising, film companies and the well-established "agents for the dead" may well force Canadian advertising agencies to negotiate for the personality rights of its former stars as a condition of licensing film rights. Further, while some states do not recognize descendability of the tort and the time "well dead" varies by state, the current U.S. conflict of laws principles indicate that the existence of post-mortem personality rights should be determined by the law of the domicile of the estate.

U.S. law has long recognized the "right of publicity", which is the right of a person whose identity has commercial value to control the commercial use of that identity. In the 1980's, a large New York ad agency requested that Bette Midler sing the song "Do You Want To Dance" for their client's automobile ads in an upcoming campaign. When Midler refused, the agency used Ula Hedwig, one of Midler's back-up singers, for the recording and apparently instructed her to sound as much like Midler as possible. Neither Midler's name nor her picture were used in the commercial. Nevertheless, the court held that California law recognizes an injury from an appropriation of the attributes of one's identity[12] and that a person may be as identifiable by voice as by any

---

[11] *Johnny Carson v. William A. Reynolds*, [1980] 2 F.C. 685 (T.D.).

[12] *Midler v. Ford Motor Co.*, 849 F.2d 460 (9th Cir. 1988), cert. denied, 112 S. Ct. 1513 (1992).

other indicia of identity. The tort was made out when the agency used an imitator to convey the impression that Midler was singing for them. In California and in other states with similar statutes, the right of publicity protects a distinctive voice of a professional singer who is widely known and is deliberately imitated in order to sell a product. Since the advertisers appropriated what was not theirs, they committed a tort.

In another example, Tom Waits sued a snack food manufacturer and its advertising agency for voice misappropriation following the broadcast of a radio commercial which featured a vocal performance imitating Waits' raspy singing voice.[13] Waits did not "do" commercials, and openly expressed his philosophy that musical artists should not participate in commercials because it detracts from their artistic integrity. Waits rested his claim on the *Midler* decision. The jury found that Waits had a distinctive voice that was widely known and that broadcasting the ad had violated his right of publicity. Waits had a right to control the use of his identity as embodied by his voice.

If the above cases do not strike terror into the hearts of well-meaning and not-so-well-meaning advertisers, the following will. The court, in both *Waits* and *Midler*, bypassed the traditional tort liability principle that only compensatory damages may be awarded in such cases. Tom Waits was awarded $2.6 million U.S. in compensatory and punitive damages and attorneys' fees. Punitive damages were considered in *Midler*, but denied. However, she still received $400,000 U.S. in compensation.

In the United States, even if a right of publicity action is not made out, there is another ground that plaintiffs may use to sue for wrongful personality use. Section 43(a) of the U.S. *Federal Trademark Statute*, otherwise known as the *Lanham Act*, now expressly prohibits the use of any symbol, or device which is likely to deceive consumers as to the association, sponsorship or approval of goods or services by another person. These terms include distinctive sounds and physical appearances. False endorsement was recognized in another rather famous case where a right of publicity, or a trade-mark action was not available. In this case, the ad for a chain of video stores featured a Woody Allen lookalike renting videos of Woody Allen films.[14] It was clear that the actor in the ad was only a lookalike. However, the court found that the ad created a likelihood of confusion as to Allen's voluntary participation or authorization of the advertising campaign. It is clear that a claim of "implied endorsement" may also be asserted in Canada.

---

[13] *Waits v. Frito-Lay*, 978 F.2d 1093 (9th Circ. 1992).
[14] *Allen v. National Video*, 610 F. Supp. 612 (S.D.N.Y. 1985).

2.   Europe

Canadian as well as European advertisers would be well-advised to follow the U.S. case law. In January 2006, a Spanish court awarded Tom Waits   36,000 for copyright infringement and   30,000 for violation of his moral rights for Volkswagon-Audi's adaption of one of his songs and impersonating his voice in a 2000 Audi ad in Spain. The production company, which was also named in the suit violated the DON'T ASK RULE by first asking Waits for permission and then after his refusal proceeding to do an imitation/adaptation. Waits also has a similar lawsuit pending in Germany for its use of an impersonator in an Opel ad.

F.   MISAPPROPRIATION OF PERSONALITY AND FICTIONAL CHARACTERS

Fictional characters, both human and non-human, also appeal to advertisers with the promise that their instant recognizability will provide access to vast and lucrative markets. By fictional characters, we mean non-animated characters who have entered popular culture through movies, books or other media (*e.g.*, the Indiana Jones character from the Raiders series, the Luke Skywalker character from the Star Wars series), but not animated characters such as Beavis and Butthead. Creators and owners spend large amounts of money investing in fictional characters, buying and selling ownership rights in diverse media on the assumption that their rights are secure. But are the creators and owners actually protected from misappropriation?

1.   Fictional Characters and the Trade-Marks Act

Although a creator or owner can obtain a registration for a design mark incorporating the fictional character, the *Trade-Marks Act* is not particularly well suited for the purpose of protecting the character, especially in advertising situations. Only when the character name or design is "used" as a trade-mark in relation to wares or services, rather than to ornament an article, will the Act apply. The definition of use is very specific and according to section 4 of the Act means:

* any wares which are marked with the trademark; or
* if the mark is not on the wares, it is so closely associated with them that the person buying the wares is aware of the association.

The primary purpose in applying for registration of a trade-mark for a fictional character is to implement a merchandising program. The "merchandising" rights, involve "use" of the trade-mark by licensees. The licensees will apply the trade-mark to everything from lunch boxes to plush toys. So, creators and owners must first have in place some kind of licensed merchandising arrangement before they will be able to obtain proper protection through registration of a design mark, unless the owners plan to market the trade-marked merchandise themselves.

An additional limitation to trade-mark protection for fictional characters is that use of a trade-mark for wares in advertising is not considered trade-mark "use" for the purposes of the Act because there is no use at point of sale or transfer of possession. The absurdity of this situation is illustrated by the fact that a licensee of a design mark incorporating a fictional character for one chocolate bar company may not be able to prevent a competitor from using that same fictional character in a television commercial for chocolate bars.

2.   Fictional Characters and Copyright Law

The creator/owner of a fictional character may find protection under copyright law. But, the issues in this area remain cloudy.

Copyright subsists in every original dramatic work, and the visual appearance of a character is very much a part of (most) dramatic works. Where there are visual reproductions of the actual character taken from an existing film or television series, the copyright is clearly protected. However, in many instances in the world of fictional characters, we fall into the grey area of "ideas" versus the "expression" of those ideas. Under the copyright regime, ideas themselves are not protected; copyright only protects the expression of those ideas. Therefore, where the expression or embodiment of the character is by actors on stage or in film, the physical appearance (of the character) ought to be proper subject matter for copyright. However, when stripped of the actual words, incidents, and surroundings used to create the character, as well as the actor (*i.e.*, Indiana Jones outside the Temple of Doom, without the whip and Harrison Ford), what remains is little more than an idea, an idea of substance reduced to a definite fixed form, but still, in essence, just an idea and it is not copyrightable. When a character constitutes a substantial part of the dramatic work, it may be an independently protectable matter. However, there is very little definitive law on whether copyright protection extends to the physical appearance of a character embodied in a dramatic work.

(a)   Fictional Core of Dramatic Characters

Physical appearance usually constitutes the most important element of a cartoon character. The same is not usually true for dramatic characters. Most characters outside the cartoon world do not have a particularly distinctive or original costume or appearance. The aspects of dramatic characters which distinguish them as unique are embodied in their fictional core or persona. In most cases, where dramatic characters require protection, it is to prevent the appropriation of their fictional core. Thus, for fictional characters to receive copyright protection, the law must recognize a copyrightable interest in their fictional core.

Courts in Canada and England have been slow to decide whether this aspect of the fictional character is the proper subject matter for copyright. As mentioned above, one of the primary concerns of the courts has been the distinction between "idea" and "expression" in copyright law. But even if the courts overcome this problem and find that a character is copyrightable in principle, two problems remain. One problem is to define the originality and delineation a character must have in order to qualify for protection, and the second is to define the scope of the protection afforded.

The issue of fictional core has been raised in a few situations. An early Canadian case dealt with the copyright in a fictional core and the court did not hesitate to conclude that appropriation of a character *per se* constituted copyright infringement. The court's decision would seem to have ended all doubts on the matter of copyright protection of fictional characters, at least under Canadian law. However, legal writers at the time were unable to accept the decision at its face value and their hasty editorial comments succeeded in burying the full effect of the case.

In this 1948 case,[15] the complaining party was the owner in Canada of the well known French literary works "Albums de Bécassine" in which the "Bécassine" character appeared as the central character. The offender had prepared and presented a radio show which starred the character "Bécassine" using the same "name, special expressions and distinguishing characteristics of the character in the plaintiff's works". Based on the distinctive characteristics of the "Bécassine" fictional core, including her background, personality, and relationships with other characters and the fact that the character Bécassine was the most artistically valuable part of the work, the Court found that the radio show had violated copyright in the character.

After several decades of silence, two relatively recent cases have addressed the protection of fictional core under copyright. One situation raised the question of whether the Ewok character in a script was a matter for copyright.[16] The court found that there can be no infringement of a character taken (*i.e.*, pirated) from a book or script who is indistinct, but that copyright in a distinct character may be recognized. Surprisingly, in this case, the court found that the characteristics set out in the script did not delineate the character of the Ewok sufficiently to warrant recognition as a character subject to copyright protection. So the original creator

---

[15] *Zlata v. Lever Brothers Ltd.* (1948), 9 C.P.R. 34 (Que. Sup. Ct.).

[16] *Preston v. 20th Century Fox Canada Ltd.*, [1990] F.C.J. No. 1011, 33 C.P.R. (3d) 242, 38 F.T.R. 183 (T.D.), affd. [1993] F.C.J. No. 1259 (F.C.A.).

lost his rights to the Ewok character while the party who "borrowed" this character (20th Century Fox Canada), made the Ewoks become big stars and were compensated accordingly.

In a case[17] about the character Anne Shirley from the book *Anne of Green Gables*, the court found that if the description of the character is detailed, distinctive, thorough and complete, the character itself is protected by copyright. Therefore, copyright covers not only the literary work, but may also cover characters clearly developed in the works. In this case, the literary work plus the character of Anne were protected by copyright.

G. MISAPPROPRIATION OF PERSONALITY AND PASSING OFF

Passing off is an action taken, not only to protect a trade-mark but to protect the business or goodwill that is likely to be injured by passing off one person's goods as the goods of another. Goodwill is the reputation of a business or a product that brings in customers. A creator/owner can establish goodwill and reputation in a fictional character sufficient for an action in passing-off provided the fictional character has become well known to the public by reason of the creator/owner's activities and financial investment. The essence of goodwill, whether in a product or character, is that the public recognizes the product or character as the property of the owner. Goodwill sufficient for an action in passing off has been found to exist in such characters as "James Bond" in the series of books written by Ian Fleming.

A necessary ingredient to establishing a passing-off claim with respect to a fictional character would appear to be that the public comes to associate that character with the creator/owner so that if a usurper uses a fictional character of similar characteristics, confusion will be the likely result. Absent this likelihood of confusion, the right to claim passing-off would not arise.

The likelihood of confusion may not arise merely by showing that the public would think that a licence existed between the creator/owner and the unauthorized user. It may be necessary to go further and prove that the owner's quality control of licensed products was so well known, that the public would rely on the licence as a guarantee of product quality. In essence, the public's recognition of the fictional character does not *per se* allow the creator/owner to avail themselves of any legal protection. The rights arise from commercial trade, not the character itself.

---

[17] *Anne of Green Gables v. Avonlea Traditions*, [2000] O.J. No. 740 (Ont. S.C.J.).

Another issue is that the success and widespread merchandising of a fictional character may create its own faddish genre. Once the genre is created, should the creator/owner be able to monopolize its characteristics? The answer is generally no; not everything can be included within the definition of goodwill. For example, no one has the right to establish a passing off claim to prevent other film producers from producing "western" films or "science fiction" books.

H. CONCLUSION

As with any area of the law, the application of the principles discussed above will vary with the individual facts of a particular case. However, it is safe to assume that the only sure way to avoid litigation in this area is to negotiate for the rights. The agents for the stars, dead or alive, and the characters, whether human or non-human, are eager to do business with you.

Chapter 14

COMPETITION LAW ISSUES

Contributed by William Vanveen

A. OVERVIEW

As with the other portions of this book, the purpose of this chapter is not to do away with the need to consult a lawyer, but to assist you in recognizing a potential problem and when you need to consult a lawyer. It is not that we are playing hide the ball and keeping definitive information from you which would enable you to avoid using lawyers altogether. Most aspects of competition law are heavily fact and context dependent and it is simply not possible to set out answers to the issues that may arise. The intention of this chapter is to give you an overview of the provisions of the *Competition Act*[1] and an indication of problems that might arise. It is not possible to address specific situations in advance and, therefore, you will need to get expert advice in specific instances.

The main focus of this book is on advertising law and, therefore, the advertising provisions of the *Competition Act* (the "Act") are discussed in detail throughout this book. The focus of this chapter is on the other provisions of the Act which affect marketing in Canada.

B. ADMINISTRATION AND STRUCTURE OF THE COMPETITION ACT

The *Competition Act* falls within the responsibility of Industry Canada and is administered by the Competition Bureau. The Bureau is headed by the Commissioner of Competition. The Commissioner has wide powers to investigate possible offences, as well as develop policy under the Act. The Bureau is divided into various branches assigning responsibility in reflection of the divisions of the Act itself. Accordingly, there is a branch responsible for criminal matters, another for civil matters and another for

---

[1] R.S.C. 1985, c. C-34.

mergers. In addition, there are branches for advertising and others related to policy development.

The Commissioner and her staff have wide powers to investigate criminal and civil breaches of the Act, including the use of search warrants and the ability to require the production of documents and testimony under oath to investigators.

You should never assume that misconduct contrary to the Act will go undiscovered. Competitors, customers and disgruntled former (or present) employees are fertile sources for information and complaints to the Bureau. In criminal matters, the Bureau conducts the investigation and then refers the matter to the Attorney General for possible prosecution. If a case proceeds, it is prosecuted in the usual criminal courts. Civil matters under the Act (referred to as reviewable practices) are litigated in the Competition Tribunal, which is a specialized competition court. Previously, only the Commissioner could bring a case before the Competition Tribunal, but after amendments in 2002, individuals may bring cases before the Tribunal with respect to some of the reviewable practices if they receive permission from the Tribunal. There can also be private lawsuits for civil damages brought in the usual civil courts. These claims are for breaches of the criminal provisions of the Act. Therefore, consumers, customers or competitors may well have a right to sue for damages for breaches of the Act.

All of the criminal provisions discussed below have potential penalties of fines and jail. They have different potential maximum fines which, depending upon the situation can be very high — up to millions of dollars. Prison time, though infrequently used, is a potential penalty for criminal breaches of the Act.

The civil reviewable practices are not criminal offences. They can involve orders of the Tribunal to change practices and can also be very embarrassing. There can also be administrative financial penalties in some cases. Even if you successfully defend a criminal charge or a civil case before the Tribunal, the cost and effort in dealing with the investigation and litigation proceedings are also burdensome financially, as well as in terms of distracted management effort. Therefore, great care should be taken to avoid potential transgressions.

Given the potential risks and damage to business, as well as personal exposure to liability, it is important to get appropriate legal advice if issues arise. It may be possible, with the assistance of counsel, to obtain advisory opinions from the Bureau with respect to proposed activities. The Bureau has a compliance program which involves providing various guideline publications. Also, for a fee, advisory opinions may be obtained. The advisability of obtaining such an opinion, as well as the provision of the appropriate information to pursue such an opinion, is best determined with the assistance of legal counsel. This may start to sound like advertising for legal services, but it is the practical reality.

C.   CRIMINAL MATTERS

1.   Anti-Competitive Agreements (Conspiracy)

The main conspiracy provision is in section 45 of the Act, which prohibits conspiracies, agreements or arrangements that lessen competition unduly. This is not limited to agreements related to price fixing, but also applies to other anti-competitive agreements, such as market or product allocation. It also refers to agreements preventing or limiting competition with respect to production levels or availability of facilities but, in its broadest terms, it prohibits any agreement which unduly restrains or injures competition. It is the most serious offence under the Act, carrying a maximum fine of $10 million, as well as imprisonment.

As with other criminal offences, the criminal provisions of the Act must be proved by the prosecutor beyond reasonable doubt. However, the existence of a conspiracy may be proved on circumstantial evidence without any direct evidence of communication between the parties. The prosecutor must also prove that the accused intended to enter into the conspiracy or agreement and that the agreement, if it were carried out, would prevent or lessen competition unduly. However, it is not necessary to prove that the accused intended to prevent or lessen competition unduly. The only intent necessary is to enter into the agreement. In the United States, an agreement or conspiracy restraining or injuring competition is automatically illegal, regardless of its effects. In Canada, such an agreement is only prohibited if it limits competition "unduly". This is a rather vague concept that has produced inconsistent results in the courts. Some higher courts decided that undue lessening of competition required a complete or virtual monopoly. The Act clarifies this by stating that it is not necessary that the conspiracy or agreement, if carried out, would be likely to eliminate competition in the relevant market.

Whether the agreement restricts competition "unduly" depends on several factors. Market share is an important one, but no minimum combined share of the parties to the agreement has been identified by the courts.

The Act contains specific defences to conspiracy, such as the exchange of statistical or credit information, the setting of product standards and terminology, as well as other specific exemptions, but these defences do not apply where an agreement concerning them would likely lessen competition with respect to prices, the quantity or quality of production, or if it restricted market entry or business expansion.

There is a specific exemption related to agreements which only affect the export of products from Canada. Although the export exemption will apply if the agreement reduces the volume of exports, the defence will not be available where the agreement reduces the real value of exports. The export exemption is also inapplicable if the agreement restricts persons from entering into or expanding an export business from Canada, or prevents or lessens competition unduly in the supply of services facilitating the export of products from Canada. The conspiracy offence does not apply to transactions between affiliated companies.

Pursuant to section 46, the Act prohibits any company carrying on business in Canada, wherever incorporated, from implementing directives from a foreign person to enter into a conspiracy or agreement that would violate the conspiracy provision of the Act. This is to ensure that the Canadian conspiracy provisions are not circumvented merely by the conspiracy being entered into and directed from offshore.

It is important to emphasize that conspiracies do not have to be proven by direct evidence. Indeed, there is seldom a nicely typed memorandum setting out what the conspiracy is (although, unbelievably, sometimes there is). Rather, the conspiracy is often proved by circumstantial evidence. Moreover, agreements can be inferred. It is very important to avoid inappropriate communications of confidential business information among competitors. This may give rise to an inference that an agreement has been reached or is in operation.

There is a kind of standing joke among competition lawyers about ensuring that clients don't get into hotel rooms with competitors to discuss business. As long ago as the 18th century, economist Adam Smith stated that "People of the same trade seldom meet together, even for merriment and diversion, but the conversation ends in a conspiracy against the public, or in some contrivance to raise prices." That is hardly always the case, but the risk is real and should be avoided. If you are in the presence of competitors at trade shows, social gatherings or anywhere and, if the conversation turns to customers or prices or other confidential information, end the conversation immediately and leave. Entering into cooperative arrangements with competitors or co-marketing can raise issues under this or other provisions of the Act and, therefore, advice must be sought before proceeding.

2.   Bid-rigging

Bid-rigging occurs when two or more parties agree that one or more of them will not submit a bid or, where a bid that is submitted has been arrived at by agreement between bidders. It is only necessary to prove the intention to enter into the bid-rigging agreement. There is no need to show that there would be any undue restraint on competition. The conduct is seen as inherently unacceptable.

The only defence is that the bid agreement was made known to the entity calling for the bids at or before the time that the bid was made by any party to the agreement. Courts have made it clear that the parties must directly and expressly reveal the bid agreement and they are not entitled to rely on any implied revelation. The "made known" defence was intended to allow two or more smaller parties to combine on a bid who would not otherwise be in a position to bid. It was not likely intended to allow competitors with the ability to compete to avoid doing so by merely making known their agreement. The wording of the provision may be wide enough for this purpose but it may be possible for such parties to be convicted under the conspiracy provision as an alternative. Of course, before the prosecution can succeed under the conspiracy provision it must prove undue lessening of competition, which is not necessary for bid-rigging. The bid-rigging offence also does not apply to agreements between affiliated companies. Enforcement of this provision is a priority of the Competition Bureau which views bid-rigging as particularly pernicious.

3. Price Discrimination

It is an offence for a supplier to discriminate between purchasers who are in competition with each other and who purchase like quantity and quality of articles. The offence of discriminatory pricing applies only to articles and not to the provision of services. It also differs from most other offences in the Act because it does not require proof of an anticompetitive effect. Price discrimination is prohibited regardless of impact. However, the supplier must know of the discrimination and it must amount to a practice. A one-off situation or temporary price concession for store openings and special sales or other specific purposes are allowed. Care must be taken not to repeat so often as to amount to a practice.

Under section 50 of the Act, price discrimination occurs where a seller grants a discount, rebate, allowance, price concession or other advantage to one purchaser without making the same advantage "available" to competitors of that purchaser "in respect of a sale of articles of like quality and quantity".

There are a number of specific elements for this offence which should be noted. There must be a sale of articles by a person engaged in a business. Therefore, the section does not apply to those involved on the purchasing side of the transaction. Also, because it applies to sales, it does not apply to leasing, licensing or consignment agreements or to any transaction where title to the article does not pass.

The section prohibits discounts, rebates, allowances, price concessions or other advantages being granted to one purchaser, over and above that which is available to others. The phrase "other advantage" could mean things such as better payment terms, but it is generally accepted that the phrase is restricted to things that affect the net price of the goods, as opposed to other more extended advantages such as event tickets or dinners.

Before discrimination can exist, the purchasers must be in competition with each other. Discrimination is therefore permissible between purchasers who are not competing in the same market. This refers both to geographic market, as well as product market or position in the distribution chain. Wholesalers are not in competition with retail sellers and, therefore, do not have to give the same price or advantage.

There is also no discrimination within the meaning of the Act, unless the sales to each competitor is of "like" quality and quantity. If competitors purchase different products or grade of products within the seller's line of goods, they do not have to be given the same price. Price differentiation is more common on the basis of quantity. Because purchasers of different quantities of goods can be given different prices, volume rebates or lower prices for larger quantity purchases are permissible. It is also permissible to give a price concession or larger rebate if the purchaser performs services or tasks that the seller would ordinarily have to provide, such as transportation or warehousing.

The Act requires that the same price advantage be "available" to all competing purchasers. Therefore, it is not sufficient to simply offer one customer a better price, but only provide it to another customer if they ask. To be "available", the rebate or price advantage must be made known to all competing purchasers. Thereafter, it is up to them to decide whether to take advantage of it, but they must at least know of it.

Subject to the exclusive dealing provision discussed below, it is also permissible to give a rebate or price advantage to someone who purchases all of their requirements from you. In certain circumstances, it is also permissible for franchises or cross-border corporations to aggregate their purchases to obtain a higher volume discount.

Buying groups have evolved to enable buyers to pool purchases in order to qualify for higher volume rebates. The buying group acts as a single purchaser for the purposes of the Act and receives the rebate entitled to a single purchaser of its particular volume. To qualify as a purchaser for the purposes of the Act, the buying group must be properly established according to criteria set out by the Bureau. In particular, the buying group must take legal responsibility for payment of the purchases. The goods may be ordered directly by and shipped to individual members without the orders passing through the buying group, and the individual members can pay for the orders directly, but the buying group must have ultimate legal liability, as well as the ability to cover the debts of the members. Given that the potential liability under the price discrimination section lies with the seller, a seller should take care to ensure that any buying groups it deals with are properly constituted to meet the requirements of the Act.

4.   Predatory Pricing

Not only must you be careful to charge the same price to similar competitors but, yes, you can get into trouble for charging too low a price. We normally think of the Act as protecting consumers, so it might seem odd that it would be improper to charge too low a price. However, short term gain in the form of low prices could result in long term pain for consumers if the low price results in elimination of competitors, and hence less competition and higher prices in the long run. Predatory pricing refers to pricing that stronger players use to "prey" upon weaker players, thus eliminating them from the competition. The aim of the stronger players is to recoup the losses, and more, in higher prices down the road.

There are two types of predatory pricing. In the first, the seller carries out a policy of selling products in any area of Canada at lower prices than those charged elsewhere in Canada. The second involves a policy of selling products at unreasonably low prices. In each instance, the pricing must be pursuant to a policy. The courts have refused to convict when the pricing was a temporary measure to meet aggressive competition.

Both offences also require that the pricing have the effect of substantially lessening competition or eliminating a competitor. There can be no offence of geographic predatory pricing if the seller has no competitor or no one has attempted to enter the market where the reduced price is being offered. Similarly, there will be no offence of selling at an unreasonably low price if no existing or potential competitor is affected. Even if competitors are affected by a seller's low prices, there will be no offence if those prices are justified on an economic basis rather than the elimination of all competition. For example, price reduction as a loss-minimizing measure to cover fixed costs is permissible.

For predatory pricing, it is unclear exactly what is meant by "unreasonably low" prices. It seems clear that any price above cost and which makes a profit, however small, is not unreasonably low. There are areas of debate as to what is meant by cost such as total variable cost, or total cost.

The Competition Bureau takes the view that not all pricing below cost will raise concerns. The Bureau's focus is on players with market power, who will be in a position to recoup the temporary losses once competitors have been eliminated from the market. Suffice it to say that there are numerous grey areas with respect to predatory pricing and any policy for selling below cost should be undertaken only after careful consultation.

5.   Discriminatory Promotional Allowances

A supplier may offer advertising or promotional allowances such as discounts, rebates, or price concessions only if they are offered on proportionate terms to other competing purchasers. The objective is to ensure that all competing purchasers share in a supplier's promotional budget according to their volume of purchases. Unlike price discrimination, this practice applies to both articles and services and the offence does not require a practice to be established before there can be a conviction — a single incident is sufficient.

There are other important differences between discriminatory promotional allowances and price discrimination. For price discrimination, the pricing must only be made "available" to all competing purchasers. However, promotional allowances must be "offered" on a proportional basis to all competing purchasers. Therefore, it must actually be given proportionally to all.

Another important difference is the proportionality requirement. In discriminatory pricing, a seller can use a rebate ladder, which employs different plateaus or levels of purchase volumes in order to earn a particular rebate or discount. However, plateaus or ladder type arrangements cannot be used for promotional allowances. These must be offered on a proportional sliding scale.

The section 51 definition of allowance states that it is a "discount, rebate, price concession or other advantage" that is offered for "advertising or display purposes and is collateral to a sale of products but is not applied directly to the selling price". Therefore, it refers to allowances which are granted in separate cheques or otherwise accounted for. If it is a discount that is taken off the selling price (off the invoice), it is not an allowance within the meaning of this section. Therefore, the section is relatively easy to avoid in that the rebate or discount can simply be applied to the invoice for the goods. That will avoid the obligation to provide proportional advantages to competing purchasers. However, it moves the problem from the promotional allowance section into the discriminatory pricing section. Any advantage given off the invoice to a purchaser must also be given to a competing purchaser of like quantity and quality within the requirements of the discriminatory pricing provision. It simply means that it will not have to be done on the basis of proportionality.

6.   Double Ticketing

Section 54 of the Act prohibits someone from supplying a product at a price that exceeds the lowest of two or more prices clearly expressed in respect of the product, either on the product, its wrapper or container, or on anything attached to, inserted in or accompanying the product, or on an in-store or other point-of-purchase display or advertisement. Quite simply, if you express two prices on the product or anything accompanying it at the time of sale, the lowest price governs. If a mistake is made, it is the seller who pays for the mistake, not the consumer.

This is a very minor provision which has not been considered in the courts. Presumably, this is because it is relatively straightforward and easy to spot and avoid. Conversely, we assume that purchasers can quickly spot this problem and raise it at point of purchase and that sellers will readily resolve the problem, therefore avoiding the need for intervention by officials.

7.   Multi-Level Marketing and Pyramid Sales

As discussed in Chapter 15, multi-level marketing is a relatively common and perfectly legitimate method of product distribution. However, some past abuses have led to statutory regulation. In addition to the provisions of the Act, some provinces also have specific legislation which should be consulted.

Multi-level marketing is defined in section 55 of the Act as a plan for the supply of product whereby a participant receives compensation for supplying the product to another participant who, in turn, receives compensation for supplying other participants in the plan. Such plans are permitted with some restrictions. Operators and participants in such plans are not to make representations relating to compensation to a perspective participant unless the representations include fair, reasonable and timely disclosure of the compensation actually received by typical participants or compensation likely to be received having regard to several factors. It is the obligation of the operators and participants of the plan to ensure that any representations relating to compensation contain the appropriate information.

Pyramid sales are regarded differently. Pyramid sales are defined in section 55.1 of the Act as multi-level marketing plans, whereby a participant gives consideration for the right to receive compensation by reason of recruitment into the plan of other participants who give consideration for the same right. In multi-level marketing, participants receive compensation for the supply of product. In pyramid sales, participants give consideration for the right to receive compensation for recruitment of other participants as opposed to compensation for the mere supply of product. Pyramid sales also occur where participants give consideration as a condition of participating in the plan and have to buy a specified amount of product. Pyramid sales also occur where persons supply product to participants in an amount that is commercially unreasonable (referred to as front-end loading) or where there is not a buy-back guarantee exercisable on reasonable terms. All forms of pyramid sales are completely prohibited.

There are a number of specific requirements related to multi-level marketing and pyramid sales and anyone contemplating establishing a multi-level marketing sales plan should have the plan reviewed by a knowledgeable professional.

8.   Referral Selling

Until March 1999, the Act contained a prohibition against referral sell-ing, which meant inducing a customer to purchase or lease a product and representing to the customer that they will or might receive a rebate or commission or other benefit for sales or leases of products to other per-sons whose names the customer supplied. This came to be viewed as a relatively harmless practice and therefore was removed from the Act. However, it should be noted that several provinces have referral selling provisions and some of them are broader than the provision which used to be in the Act. Therefore, before employing any marketing strategy that uses rewards for referrals, reference should be made to the various pro-vincial statutes.

9.   Price Maintenance

This is a common problem in the marketplace. Often, product suppliers do not want retailers to discount their goods and will ask resellers to maintain a certain price point. Sometimes, the supplier receives pressure from some of its distributors to discipline discounters. Whatever the reason and however it arises, the urge to engage in price maintenance is common. Suppliers often try to come up with ways to disguise price maintenance, but there is basically no legitimate way to control discount-ing by others in the distribution chain.

Section 61 of the Act prohibits a producer or supplier of a product, or a person who extends credit by way of credit cards, from directly or indirectly attempting to influence upward or to discourage the reduction of the price at which another person in Canada supplies or offers to supply or advertise a product in Canada. It is only an offence to influence prices upward or discourage reduction if it is done by use of agreement, threat, promise or any like means. Therefore, it is improper to reach an agreement with a reseller as to the price level, or to threaten some reper-cussion or promise some advantage to a reseller for keeping their prices up.

It is only improper to discourage price reduction or to influence price increase. It is not improper to seek to influence price decrease or to dis-courage price increases or to put a maximum selling price in place. How-ever, care must be taken to ensure that a maximum price or the encouragement of a price reduction does not end up in the establishment of a fixed price. Resellers must always be free to set a lower price. In fact, the basic rule of thumb should be that you do not influence or set the price once you have sold goods to others for resale. Your distribution network should be left free to set its own prices.

This does not apply as between principals and agents or affiliated cor-porations or employees of the same companies. Therefore, if your distributor is an affiliate or is a paid agent, you are free to establish the price at which they will sell. In establishing a distribution network, therefore, one legitimate means of controlling the price is to establish agency relationships. However, there are usually other business reasons for avoiding an agency relationship which take precedence over the desire to control price.

If it is improper to influence prices upward or discourage reduction, you might ask how is it that there are prices marked on some goods, or how is it that there are national advertising campaigns conducted by suppliers which state the price for the goods sold by third party resellers. You might also ask how is it that everyone uses suggested resale price lists. Done properly, none of the above need raise problems.

Suggested retail prices, whether in the form of price lists or other communications, are permissible as long as the supplier makes it clear that the reseller is under no obligation to accept the suggested price and will in no way suffer in business relations for failing to accept the suggested price. That is why it is called a suggested retail price. However, the price list or other communication must make it clear that the reseller is free to set their own price.

Advertising by the supplier which mentions a resale price will be considered an attempt at price maintenance unless the price is expressed in the advertisement to make it clear to any person that the product may be sold at a lower price. This is why in national advertising campaigns, you typically see the expression "dealer may sell for less".

These provisions related to price lists or national advertising campaigns that mention resale prices do not apply to a price that is affixed or applied to a product or its package or container. That is why it is not unusual to see packaged goods with a price affixed or printed on the packaging. Nonetheless, the retailer of those goods must still be left free to charge a lower price if they wish.

As mentioned above, one way of getting around the price maintenance provision is to have a principal/agent relationship with resellers. This is usually unacceptable for other business reasons. Another approach is to use consignment selling. In that case, title to the goods does not pass until the sale is made and, therefore, the title holder remains in control of the selling price. This method was used by the major gasoline companies who maintained title of the gasoline in the tanks at the service stations, so as to be able to set the price. There is a reviewable practice referred to as consignment selling, discussed below, which gives power to the Bureau to prevent consignment selling when used to avoid the price maintenance provision. Use of consignment selling may also arguably amount to refusal to supply.

It is important to note that the price maintenance provision applies to horizontal relationships as well as vertical. In other words, it applies as among competing suppliers and not just between suppliers and the resale distribution network. If competing suppliers entered into a price fixing scheme contrary to the conspiracy provision (discussed earlier), it would also offend the price maintenance provision. Moreover, it would be easier to prosecute under the price maintenance provision because there is no requirement of an undue lessening of competition for price maintenance. No anti-competitive effect need be proven. On the other hand, a conspiracy need not actually be put into place for an offence to occur.

If a reseller is discounting to your annoyance, you may be tempted to simply cut off supply. Others have thought of this before you and that conduct is also prohibited. It forms the second branch of the price maintenance provision which makes it an offence to refuse to supply a product or to otherwise discriminate against any person because of the low pricing policy of that person. Therefore, you cannot cut off supply to a discounter or otherwise discriminate against them by, for example, giving less favourable credit or payment terms. Suppliers regularly seek to cut off discounters and often seek to disguise the real reason for the refusal to supply. If the discounter is in arrears or is in other substantial breach of the selling conditions, it may be possible to refuse future supply without breaching this section. However, any time there is a termination of supply, great care must be taken and advice sought to ensure that it can be supported as legitimate.

It may also be acceptable to terminate supply where it is found that the discounter has been using products as loss-leaders; for bait and switch selling; has been engaging in misleading advertising; or has not been providing the level of service that purchasers might reasonably expect. These reasons may justify terminating supply, but they cannot be used to get the discounter to raise their prices. In other words, if there are legitimate concerns, you can cut them off because that still leaves pricing to operate freely in the market, but you cannot use these justifications to force a price increase which is never justified.

It is also an offence to use threats or promises to attempt to induce a supplier to refuse to supply a product to someone else as a condition of doing business with the supplier. This refers to the situation mentioned earlier where a competing reseller may complain to a supplier about the discounting being undertaken by another reseller. It is an offence for the first reseller to threaten to no longer do business with the supplier, unless the supplier refuses to supply the discounting reseller.

It all comes down to the simplest rule of thumb, which is to simply sell the product and let the market determine the prices thereafter. Any attempts to influence the prices at which other people sell are risky.

10. Reform

The latest proposed amendments to the *Competition Act* contemplate decriminalizing several of the pricing provisions mentioned above. Specifically, price discrimination, geographic price discrimination, predatory pricing and promotional allowances would become civil (reviewable) matters rather than criminal. Several other reforms to other aspects of the Act are also proposed, such as increased administrative monetary penalties and expanding their application to other provisions of the Act. As of the time of writing, it is unknown if the proposed reforms will become law.

11. Reviewable Practices

To recap, reviewable practices are matters that do not result in criminal prosecution or criminal penalties. These are matters that generally can only be raised by the Competition Bureau before the Competition Tribunal. However, with leave of the Tribunal, anyone directly affected can bring a case with respect to refusal to deal, exclusive dealing, market restriction or tied selling. It is important to note that unless and until the Competition Tribunal makes a finding of inappropriate conduct, activities which may arguably fall within these sections are not absolutely prohibited and are not necessarily wrongful. If the Tribunal concludes that the conduct is inappropriate, it may order someone to alter or cease the inappropriate behaviour and may potentially make other remedial orders.

It should be noted that although reviewable practices do not result in criminal conviction, it is a criminal offence to contravene an order of the Tribunal made in respect of one of these reviewable practices.

A qualification to the foregoing comments must be made concerning reviewable practices of misrepresentations to the public (misleading advertising) and related issues of representations as to reasonable test or publication of testimonials, as well as bait and switch selling, selling above advertised price and promotional contests. Some of these are discussed elsewhere and a couple of these matters will be discussed below. In any event, these reviewable practices are not within the exclusive jurisdiction of the Tribunal and can also be dealt with in the Federal Court or the Superior Courts of the provinces. Also, these matters can result in administrative (civil) monetary penalties in an amount up to $50,000 for individuals or up to $100,000 for corporations and these amounts can be doubled for subsequent orders. These are a type of hybrid situation between criminal matters and matters reviewable only by the Tribunal. It was an attempt to decriminalize some of these issues in less serious cases, but still providing for a monetary penalty.

12. Bait and Switch Selling

This is a recently decriminalized provision. Bait and switch selling occurs when a vendor advertises a product at a bargain price in an attempt to attract customers and then attempts to induce them to buy a different, more expensive product. Although this is the common scenario, the Act does not actually require that there be an attempt to sell a more expensive product to the customer. It is simply improper to advertise at a bargain price a product that the vendor does not supply in reasonable quantities having regard to the nature of the market, the nature and size of the person's business and the nature of the advertisement.

A bargain price is a price represented in an advertisement to be a bargain price by reference to an ordinary price or otherwise, or a price that a person exposed to the advertisement would understand to be a bargain price by reason of the usual price for the product in question. Simply put, it is improper to advertise products at bargain prices without having reasonable quantities on hand to respond to the anticipated demand created by the advertisement.

There are defences. If the vendor took reasonable steps to obtain adequate supply in a timely fashion, but was unable to obtain the needed quantity by reason of events beyond the vendor's control and that could not have reasonably been anticipated, this will provide an excuse. Similarly, if the demand surpasses the reasonable expectations of the advertiser, this can also provide a defence. Lastly, if the vendor undertook to supply the same product or an equivalent product of equal or better quality at the same bargain price within a reasonable time to all persons who requested the product and if such undertaking is fulfilled, the problem will be remedied. Hence, the ubiquitous rain check.

13. Sale Above Advertised Price

Like bait and switch selling, the prohibition against selling a product above the advertised price is another decriminalized provision. It is similar to the criminal offence of double ticketing, except that it applies to advertisements as opposed to two different prices being on the goods or packaging.

Pursuant to section 74.05, sale above advertised price refers to advertising "a product for sale or rent in a market and, during the period and in the market to which the advertisement relates", and then supplying the product at a price higher than the advertised price.

The provision does not apply in respect of an advertisement that appears in a catalogue in which it is prominently stated that the prices are subject to error, if you establish that the price advertised is an error. It also does not apply to advertisements that are immediately followed by a correcting advertisement. These are commonly seen in newspapers. There are also a couple of other more specialized defences.

Given the similarity with the double ticketing provision, it is a mystery why sale above advertised price was decriminalized, whereas double ticketing was not.

14. Refusal To Deal

Refusal to deal and all the subsequent matters to be discussed in this chapter are reviewable matters solely within the jurisdiction of the Competition Tribunal and are completely civil matters which may result in non-punitive corrective orders.

This section deals with situations where somebody is refused supply by all suppliers of a product in the market. It must be distinguished from refusal to supply related to the low pricing policy of the perspective purchaser, which is part of the criminal offence of price maintenance. Refusal to deal as a reviewable practice is different in that it is not dependent upon someone being denied supply due to a low pricing policy. It relates to refusal to supply for whatever reason. Where the required conditions are present, the Tribunal can order that a perspective purchaser be supplied with the products.

Before relief can be granted under this provision, the Tribunal must find that a person is substantially affected in his business or is precluded from carrying on business as a result of his inability to obtain adequate supplies of a product on the usual terms. The inability to obtain supply must be due to insufficient competition among suppliers in the particular market. The person must also be willing to meet the usual trade terms for the product in question and it must be in ample supply. The refusal must also result in or be likely to result in an adverse effect on competition. When these conditions are met, the Tribunal may order one or more suppliers to accept the aggrieved person as a customer on the usual trade terms.

For the purposes of this section, a product is not a separate product simply because of a trade-mark or proprietary name, unless it is so dominant in a market that a person's ability to carry on business is affected without access to that particular brand. Otherwise, access to another brand of the same product will suffice and will result in a rejection of a refusal to deal complaint.

The section does leave discretion in the Tribunal. Therefore, even if all the requirements of the section are met, if there is a good business reason to refuse to deal with someone, it may form the basis of the Tribunal rejecting the request for supply. Also, the applicant must be willing and able to meet the usual trade terms, which means terms in respect of payment, units of purchase and reasonable technical and servicing requirements. The Bureau brought a couple of high profile cases under this section, requiring Chrysler to supply proprietary parts to a parts exporter and requiring Xerox to supply parts to third party repair firms. There are likely to be few cases brought by the Bureau under this section in the future and it will be a rarely used override on the right to trade, or not trade, freely. However, the Act was recently amended to allow individuals and corporations direct access to the Competition Tribunal in situations where they allege one of their suppliers is refusing to deal. A private applicant must obtain leave from the Tribunal to bring a case. There were concerns when private access was granted that this would lead to a flood of litigation. So far, this has not been the result. As of the end of 2005, only five applications had been made to the Tribunal.

15.   Consignment Selling

We noted earlier that the criminal offence of price maintenance does not apply if the relationship between the two parties involved is one of principal and agent, as when the product is sold on consignment. Likewise, discriminatory pricing only applies to situations where there is a sale to another party, which again does not apply where there is a consignment. Section 76 of the Act addresses situations where consignment is used inappropriately for these purposes. Where the Tribunal finds that the practice of consignment selling has been introduced by a supplier of a product who normally sells the product outright for resale, and finds that the use of consignment selling was for the purpose of circumventing the price maintenance provision or the discriminatory pricing provision, the Tribunal can order the supplier to cease the practice of consignment selling of the product.

This means that the seller will have avoided criminal conviction for breach of the price maintenance or discriminatory pricing provision, but once the Tribunal orders cessation of consignment selling, that defence will be removed and the seller will also have to stop the practice of controlling the price or discriminating in the price charged to competing purchasers.

16.   Exclusive Dealing, Tied Selling and Market Restriction

Exclusive dealing occurs when a supplier requires or induces a customer to deal only or primarily in the products of the supplier, or to refrain from dealing in a class or kind of product. Market restriction involves a supplier requiring, as a condition of supplying a product, that a customer supply that product only in a defined market. Tied selling occurs when a supplier requires or induces a customer, as a condition of supplying a product, to acquire another product, or to refrain from using or distributing another product.

The Tribunal may prohibit exclusive dealing or tied selling in cases where it involves a major supplier or is widespread, and where the practice substantially lessens competition by impeding entry or expansion of businesses, products or services. A similar provision allows the Tribunal to make an appropriate order where it has found that market restriction is likely to substantially lessen competition in a product.

Such orders shall not be made in respect of exclusive dealing or market restriction engaged in only for a reasonable time, in order to facilitate entry of a new supplier or a new product into a market. Also, tied selling is not prohibited if there is a technological relationship between products, or if the practice is conducted by a lender and is reasonably necessary to better secure loans. No order may be made where the practices are engaged in between affiliated corporations.

It is commonly thought that it is absolutely wrong or prohibited to require exclusive dealing or to engage in tied selling or restricting markets. As you can see, it may only be improper if it leads to a substantial lessening of competition. Exclusive dealing is actually quite common in the marketplace and the Bureau even acknowledges that it is appropriate to give an increased discount in exchange for an exclusive dealing arrangement, as long as it does not lead to a substantial lessening of competition.

17. Abuse of Dominant Position

It is certainly not illegal or improper to become dominant in a marketplace. The question is not how big you get, but how you get there and how you maintain the position. Becoming dominant by virtue of superior service, price, quality and the like is totally appropriate and exactly what a competitive marketplace should be. On the other hand, becoming dominant or maintaining a dominant position by using anti-competitive means instead of superior price and product is a potential problem and is dealt with through this provision called abuse of dominant position.

The Act used to contain a criminal provision dealing with monopoly. It was a criminal offence to acquire or maintain a monopoly. However, given the criminal burden, this section was rarely used and prosecutions were never successful. Therefore, the provision was removed in 1985 and the abuse of dominant position was put in its place as a reviewable practice. Although it is now a civil provision, it will remain difficult for the Bureau to succeed in establishing a case.

The Tribunal must be satisfied that one or more persons substantially or completely in control of a species or class of business are engaged in a practice of anti-competitive acts. The conduct must form a practice and not merely an isolated incident and it must have the effect of preventing or lessening competition substantially in a particular market.

Section 78 of the Act contains a non-exhaustive list of anti-competitive acts for the purposes of abuse of dominant position. The concept includes, but is not limited to:

* squeezing the margin available to unintegrated customers by vertically integrated suppliers in order to impede or prevent entry or expansion in the market;

- acquisition of a customer by a supplier to ensure that the customer is not available to a competitor for the purpose of impeding or preventing competition;
- freight equalization at the plant of a competitor for the purpose of impeding competition;
- fighting brands introduced selectively on a temporary basis to discipline or eliminate competitors;
- pre-emption of scarce facilities in order to withhold them from the market;
- buying up product to prevent price erosion;
- adopting product specifications incompatible with products produced by others in order to prevent entry into, or eliminate competition from, the market;
- requiring or inducing suppliers to sell only or primarily to certain customers or to refrain from selling to competitors in order to prevent the competitor's entry into or expansion in the market; and
- selling below acquisition cost in order to discipline or eliminate competitors.

Acts carried out only in the course of exercising rights derived under the *Copyright Act, Industrial Design Act, Patent Act, Trade Marks Act* or other legislation dealing with intellectual or industrial property are deemed not to be anti-competitive. In determining whether a practice has the requisite effect on competition, the Tribunal must consider whether the practice is a result of superior competitive performance. There is a three year limitation period.

If the Tribunal finds that there has been an abuse of dominant position, it may prohibit those involved from engaging in the offending practice. Further, if the Tribunal determines that a prohibition order is insufficient to restore competition, it may also direct the participants to take such reasonable and necessary actions, including divestiture of assets or shares, to overcome the effects of the practice on the market.

18. Delivered Pricing

This provision seeks to eliminate the anti-competitive effects of basing-point pricing systems in which sellers charge a delivered price which includes transportation costs calculated from a particular point. Because the price includes transportation costs based on distance from the basing point regardless of actual distance, these pricing systems can result in a buyer paying for excess transportation (phantom freight) or in the buyer not being charged for freight (freight absorption). In effect, some buyers are forced to subsidize other buyers in order to help the seller maintain a competitive edge.

Such pricing systems are not themselves prohibited. The delivered pricing provision reviews the practice of refusing to supply a customer at any place where the supplier usually delivers to other customers. In other words, it is improper to refuse a buyer the advantage of taking delivery at a location closer to the basing point and paying his own transport costs in order to eliminate phantom freight charges. Such refusal by the seller must be a practice rather than an isolated incident.

19. Foreign Judgments and Laws

The Tribunal may issue orders restraining or prohibiting the implementation in Canada of foreign laws, judgments, or other legal processes. The Tribunal must find that such implementation would adversely affect competition in Canada, the efficiency of its trade or industry, or its foreign trade without any compensating advantages.

20. Foreign Suppliers

The Tribunal may order any person in Canada to supply another person, or to cease dealing with a foreign supplier where, by virtue of his buying power, the first person has required a foreign supplier to refuse to supply the second person.

21. Specialization Agreements

These are agreements where parties discontinue producing articles or services on the condition that the other parties to the agreement will do the same. Also included are agreements requiring the parties to buy articles or services exclusively from each other.

Parties to such an agreement may apply to the Tribunal for its approval and registration. The Tribunal must be satisfied that it will have positive efficiency gains which will more than offset any negative effects on competition, and that none of the parties has been coerced into the agreement. The Tribunal must consider whether efficiency gains will result in a significant increase in the real value of exports, or in a significant substitution of domestic articles for imported products. Further, the efficiency gain must involve more than the simple redistribution of income between or among participants.

Tribunal approval of an agreement must be for a specified period and may be conditional. Agreements may be modified through subsequent applications or can be struck out if found not to comply with any conditions of original approval.

D.   CONCLUSION

The *Competition Act* contains various other provisions not reviewed in this chapter, as they are of rarer application or less relevant to our advertising and marketing theme. In particular, there is a major portion of the Act dealing with mergers and pre-notification of acquisitions over certain size thresholds.

There has been a definite trend over the past 20 years to increased decriminalization in the *Competition Act* and increased resort to civil remedial orders. This is a positive development because the criminal law, with its standard of proof and evidentiary rules, is often too blunt an instrument to deal with the more subtle and complex economic issues involved in competition analysis. The trend to civil remedies also recognizes that there should be less restriction and interference in the marketplace. The approach is to limit only the most objectionable or anti-competitive conduct. Those provisions which remain criminal must be taken very seriously. This is especially true for the conspiracy, bid-rigging and price maintenance offences. The trend to decriminalization has taken a more ominous turn with proposed amendments, which would expand the scope and amount of administrative monetary penalties and civil damages recovery to levels where arguably greater procedural protections are needed.

The reviewable practices do not raise the same risk levels, because they do not result in criminal prosecution. Also, given that the objective of any Tribunal proceedings for reviewable practices will usually be the issuing of an order to stop the offending conduct, the proceedings can be avoided simply by stopping the conduct before the proceedings begin. However, care should still be taken to avoid running afoul of the reviewable practices provisions, because a Bureau investigation can still involve time and expense for the business and potentially result in embarrassment. Even if proceedings before the Tribunal are avoided, the Bureau is increasingly requiring consent orders to ensure that the conduct is not repeated. They like to engage in a bit of advertising themselves by publicizing their victories in national newspapers (at your expense). Also, private applicants can, in some instances, now seek leave to bring a case before the Competition Tribunal.

It should also be noted that the *Competition Act* provides for civil claims for damages for breaches of the criminal provisions. Consumers, competitors or customers can use the *Competition Act* to sue for damages if caused through breaches of the criminal provisions, such as conspiracy, bid-rigging, predatory pricing or price maintenance or discriminatory pricing.

Medium and large sized businesses should ensure that there is a compliance program in place to educate employees about *Competition Act* issues, to avoid breaches. All businesses need to be aware of the Act to avoid problems. The people at the Competition Bureau are very nice, but it is best to keep them in their shop and not at yours.

Chapter 15

CHANNELS OF MARKETING COMMUNICATIONS

Contributed by Sarah Chenoweth and John Leckie

A. OVERVIEW

The general laws applying to false and misleading advertising apply regardless of how or where a representation is made. However, advertisers need to be aware that particular marketing channels may involve unique challenges from a legal standpoint. For example, the *Competition Act* contains a special set of rules and prohibitions regarding telemarketing; and direct marketing raises unique privacy issues. Further, new and evolving channels of marketing such as ambush marketing, guerrilla marketing, internet marketing and word of mouth marketing, present new challenges to advertisers and their lawyers.

In this chapter, we will review various marketing channels, from telemarketing to ambush marketing to spamming and the legal issues particular to each.

B.   DIRECT MARKETING

Direct marketing is marketing at the individual level, allowing advertisers to select exactly *who* they market to. It may be accomplished by direct mail, direct e-mail or by other forms of direct selling.

Several legal issues affect direct marketing. One such issue is privacy — direct marketing involves the use of extensive customer lists, and marketers need to ensure that the privacy interests of their customers or prospective customers are protected. Privacy legislation, such as the federal *Personal Information Protection and Electronic Documents Act* ("PIPEDA"),[1] or its various provincial counterparts, requires this.

---

[1]   S.C. 2000, c. 5.

C. LAWS WHICH "DIRECTLY" AFFECT DIRECT MARKETING

The right mailing list is what makes a direct mail campaign. A list is a collection of customer data gathered for a very specific purpose. Due to the high cost of customer acquisition, list selection, management, profiling and analysis are all important. Almost every company has a client list. Any company which has a list is called "a list owner". Outside lists are rented from other companies. "List brokers" are companies that look for new mailing lists and make arrangements for their rental.

As stated in Chapter 16, PIPEDA is aimed at protecting personal information that is collected, used or disclosed by organizations "in the course of commercial activities". The most important PIPEDA principle is consent. Companies must have an individual's consent to collect, use or disclose that person's personal information. Personal information can only be used for the purposes for which it was collected and if a company is going to use it for another purpose, consent must be obtained again.

Since direct marketing mailing lists almost always contain PIPEDA-protected personal information, each individual on the mailing list must have given consent to be marketed to in the future. List brokers must be sure that when lists are rented out to third party businesses for marketing purposes, the individuals on the list have consented to being contacted by such third parties. A system of seeding is often used to protect against unauthorized use, theft, or even the repeated use of a mailing list which was rented for a one-time use. Seeding is the planting of predetermined names on a list, to readily identify its use. For example, if a list owner's name is John Smith, he could seed in the name Johnny Smeth. The use of his list can then be tracked and used in court as evidence of unauthorized use. Keeping careful track of your lists is very important in order to avoid violating Canadian privacy laws.

PIPEDA will not necessarily require direct marketers to cease the use of lists when the lists are potentially non-compliant because they include names collected before PIPEDA came into force. The federal Privacy Commissioner has published a fact sheet entitled *Best Practices When Dealing With Pre-PIPEDA Personal Information (Grandfathering)*. According to the Privacy Commissioner, an organization does not have to seek an established customer's express consent to use that customer's personal information in the future, as long as the organization has made a reasonable effort to specify its purposes to customers at the time of collection. If the personal information is still being used or disclosed for those original purposes and no other, then the organization may take the customer's consent to future contact for the original purposes as implied. Even if the purposes were not clearly specified at the time of collection, but were such that customers would reasonably have expected to be involved in the provision of the products or services concerned, then the organization may take the customer's consent to continued use for those purposes as implied. An organization must seek a customer's consent to any new use of the personal information.

1. The CMA Code Requirements Applicable to Direct Marketing

The *Canadian Marketing Association* (CMA) imposes media-specific marketing requirements on CMA members. The CMA has recently released an updated Code of Ethics which will come into force January 1, 2007. Regarding accuracy of representations to all media, the CMA Code of Ethics states: "photography, artwork, type size, colour, contrast, style, placement, verbal description and audio-visual portrayal must accurately and fairly describe the product or service offered. Type size, colour, contrast, style, placement or other treatment shall not be used to reduce the legibility or clarity of the offer, exceptions to the offer, or terms and conditions."

Regarding privacy and the use of personal information, the CMA Code of Ethics adopts the 10 Privacy Principles from the National Standard of Canada and five additional privacy requirements for CMA members:

(1) Business-to-business marketing is exempt from PIPEDA and from the 10 Privacy Principles above when the collection, use or disclosure of contact information is limited to name, and/or title/position, and/or business address(es), and/or business phone number(s). If any other personal information is collected, used or disclosed then the provisions of PIPEDA and and the applicable provisions of the CMA Code apply.

(2) Marketers must use CMA's Do Not Contact Service when conducting a consumer mail campaign. Marketers must also use the CMA's Do No Contact Service when conducting a consumer telephone and/or fax marketing campaign. The service must be used regardless of whether the campaign is being conducted in-house or through the use of an agency. This does not apply to B2B marketing or to current customers, who can separately request that they be included on an organization's internal do not contact list.

(3) Recognizing that a consumer can opt-out of receiving marketing communications at any time, marketers must present consumers, including current customers, an easy-to-see, easy-to-understand and easy-to-execute opportunity to decline further marketing use of their name or other information at least once every three years. There are specific CMA Code provisions regarding opt-out applicable to different media including fax opt-out and e-mail opt-out.

(4)   Marketers must provide consumers with the source of their personal information, upon request.

(5)   Marketers must only rent or transfer their lists where they have a contractual guarantee that list users will abide by the relevant privacy laws in Canada. Further, marketers should adopt a list rental and data transfer policy that limits rental of information only to organizations that agree to comply with Section J3 of the Code, the *Use of CMA Do Not Contact Service* provision.

Regarding direct mail, the CMA Code states that at the request of a consumer or business, including a current customer, marketers must promptly add names and addresses to an internal do not contact list and cease marketing to that current customer, consumer or business at that address. Names and addresses must be retained on the internal do not contact list for three years. Further, all electronic transfer of data should be password protected and encrypted. Security standards are set out in the CMA *List and Data Transfer Guidelines*.

If members are found in violation of the *Code of Ethics*, they are given an opportunity to correct their practices. If further complaints are proven, members may be expelled from the CMA.

D.   OTHER THINGS TO WATCH FOR IN DIRECT MARKETING

1.   Offers and Guarantees

Some of the most famous lead generators in direct mail campaigns are free offers and time-limited offers, including free catalogues, booklets or kits, free gifts for buying, two-step gift offers, and free samples. Contests are another successful lead generator. Other techniques involve discount offers such as cash discounts and quantity discounts. An important component in mail order marketing plans is the "money back" guarantee. It is important to remember that all these practices must comply with the misleading advertising, and misleading price advertising provisions set out in the *Competition Act*, and the *Canadian Code of Advertising Standards*, as well as various provincial laws. In addition, contests are subject to both criminal law and competition law.

2.   E-Mail Marketing

Targeted e-mail advertising is a form of direct marketing, and like print-based direct marketing, it is generally governed by the advertising rules contained in the *Competition Act*,[2] the *Canadian Code of Advertising Standards*, the various provincial consumer protection and business practice laws and Canadian privacy laws. However, e-mail marketing raises its own unique legal issues and has triggered the publication of guidelines targeted at this media-specific form of advertising.

The CMA Code of Ethics contains guidelines which require that e-mail marketers identify the purpose for which an individual's e-mail address is being requested prior to or at the time the e-mail address is collected. The e-mail address that has been collected can be used only for those purposes identified.

Marketers may not send marketing e-mails without the express consent of the recipient, except where there is an "existing business relationship" with that consumer. "Existing business relationship" means that in cases where a consumer has provided his or her e-mail address to an organization, the organization has implied consent to e-mail the consumer. Even with an existing business relationship, marketers are required to honour do-not-contact requests from consumers. E-mail addresses must be added to an internal do not contact list and retained on that list for five years.

The fact that an e-mail is a marketing message cannot be disguised. Every e-mail message must clearly identify the marketer and source of the e-mail and cannot use a false or misleading "subject" line. Marketing e-mails must provide the recipient with a simple and easy-to-use click-through means to opt-out from future contact. The body of the text must accurately reflect the advertising and marketing purpose of the e-mail message. Marketers must clearly display a privacy policy on their website. Access to the privacy policy must be provided in every location, site or page from which the marketer is collecting personal information.

3.   Spamming

Every individual in Canada who has an e-mail account has likely been bothered by spam e-mails. On May 11, 2004, the Government of Canada announced the launch of *An Anti-Spam Action Plan for Canada* and established a combined government-private sector Task Force to oversee and coordinate its implementation. The Report of the Task Force was published in May 2005, and is entitled *Stopping SPAM: Creating A Stronger, Safer Internet* ("The Task Force Report"). The Action Plan defines spam as "unsolicited commercial e-mail". The Report of the Task Force states that "spam is a direct threat to the viability of the internet as

---

[2]   R.S.C. 1985, c. C-34.

an effective means of communication".[3] It is also a vehicle for illegal activity including:

- malicious acts that cause harm to computers, networks, data and personal property through the use of viruses, worms, Trojan horses and zombie networks;
- deceptive and fraudulent business practices and fraud such as "Nigerian bank account" or "419" scams, and spoofed websites masquerading as legitimate businesses;
- phishing e-mails designed for identity theft or to steal money; and
- invasions of privacy including e-mail address harvesting.

The Task Force Report contains as an appendix a list of *Recommended Best Practices for E-Mail Marketers*. It also contains 22 recommendations for combating spam including:

- vigorous enforcement of current laws that prohibit spamming as well as amendments to existing laws and new legislation to fill in the gaps;
- stronger penalties and enforcement mechanisms to deter spamming including: strict liability offences; criminal liability offences; and a private right of action with meaningful statutory damages for affected individuals and corporations;
- defining certain e-mail practices as offences such as failing to abide by an opt-in regime for unsolicited commercial e-mails;
- making the business whose products or services are being promoted by way of spam responsible for the spamming in addition to the actual spammer;
- delegating the enforcement of anti-spamming laws to existing enforcement agencies;
- ensuring that ISPs and other network operators implement the *Recommended Best Practices* and participate in the assessment and monitoring of spam and the effect of the *Recommended Best Practices*;
- ensuring commercial e-mail marketers implement the Recommended Best Practices;
- encouraging the Federal government to actively pursue and conclude bilateral agreements on anti-spamming with foreign governments; and
- encouraging the Federal government to develop anti-spam education and awareness campaigns.

---

[3]   The Task Force Report, p. 1.

Certain Canadian laws are currently applicable to combating spam, but most have not yet been used in any spam-related cases. These laws include:

- PIPEDA, which is designed to protect personal information, in the electronic age. Unsolicited spam e-mails sent to an individual who did not consent to being contacted is likely in violation of PIPEDA. See Chapter 16 for further details on PIPEDA.
- The *Competition Act*, which prohibits false and misleading representations, applies to misleading claims made in e-mail solicitations.
- The *Criminal Code* contains provisions dealing with unauthorized access to computer systems and networks, mischief to data and general fraud provisions which could be used to combat certain spamming offences such as the use of Trojan horses.

E. DIRECT SELLING

What is a "direct (or itinerant) seller"? A direct seller sells products door-to-door, or through direct advertising asking potential purchasers to contact the vendor. The key to identifying direct sellers is that they negotiate sales contracts at places outside their normal place of business. Provincial legislation dealing with direct sellers is found either in separate direct sellers acts and regulations or in the general consumer protection laws. The legislation addresses issues that include:

(1) licensing of direct sellers;
(2) buyers' rights of cancellation;
(3) penalties for breaches of provisions; and
(4) details required to be contained within a direct sales contract.

1. Licensing of Direct Sellers

In most provinces, direct sellers have a licence or permit to carry on business. Sometimes, they have to post a security bond and have a corresponding place of business in the province in order to obtain the licence. Most licences are valid for a one year period, after which they can be renewed for a fee. The licences or permits often have conditions attached, such as restrictions on the type of goods that can be sold under the licence. It is usually a requirement that the direct seller produce their licence or identification card to the buyer when they negotiate a sale.

The provincial registrars have discretion as to whether or not to grant a licence, and may cancel a licence at any time for various reasons, including failure to comply with the conditions of the licence, or the making of false or misleading representations to would-be purchasers.

2.   Buyer's Rights of Cancellation — "Cooling-off" Periods

The buyer in a direct sales contract has the right to cancel the contract at any time during the "cooling off" period. This period in all provinces is a 10-day period following the buyer's receipt of the contract. If the buyer wants to cancel the contract, they have to give written notice to the seller. In most cases, cancellation rights may extend to one year if the seller was unlicenced or did not comply with the conditions of their licence, or if the contract did not contain the required terms. The cancellation period may also be extended if the goods were not delivered on time, typically within a 30-day period.

Once the contract has been cancelled, the seller has to refund to the buyer and return any trade-in or give the buyer its equivalent value if the trade-in cannot be recovered. This generally has to be done within 15 days of cancellation. In Quebec, this period is 10 days. The buyer is then required to return any goods purchased under the direct sales contract. In Ontario, if the buyer has paid at least two thirds of the purchase price, the seller cannot repossess the goods without a court order.

A seller may be entitled to receive compensation from the buyer for services already performed or for goods that have been used. In Newfoundland and Saskatchewan, this is restricted to contracts under $200, and the compensation cannot exceed $50. In Manitoba, Quebec, the Northwest Territories, and the Yukon, the buyer's right to cancel is lost if the buyer deliberately damages, destroys or consumes the goods or if the services have been completely performed.

It is important to review the particular legislation in detail and consider its application to any specific set of facts.

3.   Penalties for Breaches of Provisions

In most provinces, it is an offence to breach any of the direct seller's provisions. There are penalties of fines, or in some cases, imprisonment. In some provinces, there is a requirement that the licence holder forfeit their bond if convicted under the Act. Potential fines range from $100 to a maximum of $25,000 for an individual and a maximum of $100,000 for a corporation.

4.   Required Contents of Direct Sales Contracts

While there is some variation from province to province, the required contents for direct sales contracts is generally similar. A direct seller is required to give the buyer a copy of the written contract once it is negotiated and signed. The requirements for the contract generally include:

- the buyer's name and address;
- the seller's name and business address;
- the salesperson's name, if applicable;
- the date and place the contract was concluded;
- a complete description of the goods or services sold;
- a statement of the buyer's cancellation rights;
- an itemized price of the goods or services and the total amount;
- if the goods or services are to be delivered, the delivery or start date;
- if credit is extended, a statement of security given and a disclosure statement required by the legislation;
- if a trade-in is given by the buyer, a description and value of the trade-in; and
- signatures of the buyer and seller.

F.   TELEMARKETING

Deceptive telemarketing is a criminal offence under the federal *Competition Act*. There is no corresponding civil provision similar to the criminal and civil misleading advertising provisions.

Telemarketing is defined in section 52.1(1) as:

> ...the practice of using interactive telephone communications for the purpose of promoting, directly or indirectly, the supply or use of a product or for the purpose of promoting, directly or indirectly, any business interest.

The deceptive telemarketing provision prohibits telemarketers from making representations that are false or misleading in a material respect — the Crown does not need to prove that the representation was made to the public and/or that it was made deliberately.

The Competition Bureau's *Telemarketing Guidelines* indicate telemarketing only includes live voice communications between two or more persons. This excludes fax and internet communications, a customer's interaction with automated prerecorded messages; and calls to customer relations lines (*e.g.*, 1-800 numbers).

Deceptive telemarketing includes such practices as telephone solicitations made for the purpose of promoting products or other business interests that either do not exist or have been grossly exaggerated in value. An example of a typical telemarketing scam is illustrated by the 1999 case of *R v. Zouvi*.[4] The individuals charged worked for a company called

---

[4]   [1999] J.Q. No. 1564, [2000] C.C.S. No. 13069 (Que. Ct. – Crim. Div.).

American Family Publishers. Over the phone, consumers were told they had won a mystery prize. The telemarketers explained that in order to claim the prize, consumers had to purchase a promotional item. The promotional items were offered at very high prices. Consumers spent $2,000 on such items as pens worth $5 to $10, having been told that their prize would be extremely large. For example, they were told "the money you are sending us today is a drop in the ocean as compared to what you'll be receiving as a prize", and that they would "never have to worry about money again". The defendant, Mr. Zouvi, used an alias and a numbered company name to avoid identification. He was given a sentence of six months in jail to be served in the community. A prohibition order was also granted.

According to section 52.1(2)(a), telemarketers must disclose at the *beginning* of each telephone communication in a "fair and reasonable manner":

- the name of the company or person on whose behalf the communication is made;
- the type of product or business interest being promoted; and
- the reason for calling.

Telemarketers must also disclose in a "fair, reasonable and timely manner":

- the price of any product whose supply or use is being promoted;
- any material restrictions, terms or conditions that apply to the product's delivery;
- other information in relation to the product as prescribed by regulations.

No regulations have been issued.

According to the *Guidelines*, telemarketers are subject to specific requirements if they conduct a contest, lottery or game of chance. Delivery of a prize to a participant cannot be made conditional on the prior payment of any amount. The *Guidelines* indicate that an initial nominal cost of entering a contest, such as a postage stamp, will not generally be considered by the Commissioner to be a condition for the delivery of a prize. In addition, adequate and fair disclosure must be made of the number and approximate value of the prizes and of any fact that materially affects the chance of winning. These requirements are similar to the regular *Competition Act* contest disclosure requirements. The difference is that contests run by telemarketers are subject exclusively to criminal sanctions, with no option of being treated as reviewable matters.

When a corporation is accused of committing a telemarketing offence, it is sufficient proof of the offence if it was committed by an employee or agent of the corporation, unless the corporation can establish that it exercised due care to prevent the offence.

Penalties on conviction on indictment are fines in the discretion of the Court, and/or imprisonment for a term not exceeding five years. On summary conviction, the penalties are fines not to exceed $200,000 and/or imprisonment for a term not to exceed one year. In determining the sentence, certain aggravating factors are considered by the Court:

- the use of lists of persons previously deceived by telemarketers;
- characteristics of the persons targeted by the telemarketing including people who are vulnerable such as the elderly;
- the amount of proceeds realized by the telemarketing;
- previous convictions; and
- the manner in which the information is conveyed by the telemarketer including the use of abusive tactics.

Cross-border deceptive telemarketing has become an increasing problem in recent years. The Competition Bureau is now part of several cross-border initiatives developed to combat deceptive telemarketing originating in Canada, targeting U.S. citizens and *vice versa*. These initiatives include: the Toronto Strategic Partnership, which is formed by the Ontario Provincial Police, the Toronto Police Service, York Regional Police, The RCMP, Ontario's Ministry of Government Services, the U.S. Federal Trade Commission and the United States Postal Inspection Service; and the Alberta Partnership Against Cross-Border Fraud which is formed by the Alberta Government Services, Calgary Police Service, the Competition Bureau, Edmonton Police Service, RCMP, U.S. Federal Trade Commission and United States Postal Inspection Service.

In October 2004, Canada and the U.S. signed a positive comity agreement. Positive comity agreements allow Country A to ask Country B to address anticompetitive conduct in its own territory that affects Country A. The Canada/U.S. positive comity agreement has an important impact on combating cross-border deceptive telemarketing. The 2004 agreement sets out in detail the situations in which positive comity can be used. Importantly, it introduces rules for deferral or suspension of investigative activities and outlines commitments that a requested competition authority will undertake in handling a request.

1. Do Not Call Lists

On June 30, 2006, Bill C-37 amendments to the *Telecommunications Act* that will allow the Canadian Radio-Television and Telecommunications Commission (CRTC) to establish a national Do Not Call List was declared into force. The Bill C-37 amendments were initiated in part to follow in the footsteps of the U.S. Federal Trade Commission (FTC), which in 2003, amended its Telemarketing Sales Rules to include a national Do Not Call Registry. What is surprising is that the Canadian National Do Not Call List will be instituted by the CRTC and not the Competition Bureau even though the deceptive telemarketing provisions are found in the *Competition Act*.

Bill C-37 implements a legislative framework for a National Do Not Call List and the creation of investigative and enforcement powers. The CRTC has the authority to administer databases or operational systems for the establishment of the List and is permitted to delegate such powers. Exceptions from the Do Not Call List are carved out in the legislation for calls made by or on behalf of registered charities, political parties or candidates, public opinion surveys, the soliciting of newspaper subscriptions, and calls made pursuant to an "existing business relationship". "Existing business relationship" is defined as a business relationship formed by a voluntary two-way communication between caller and recipient, arising from the purchase, lease or rental of products or services so that a company may call a consumer with whom it has had a business relationship within the past 18 months, or has received an inquiry or application within the past six months. However, any "do not call" requests made by such consumers must be honoured.

Violations of the Do Not Call List are subject to hefty administrative monetary penalties including $1,500 per offending call for individuals and $15,000 per offending call for corporations. The operation of the Do Not Call List will be funded on a cost-recovery basis from telemarketers themselves. There will be a mandatory review of the legislation by a parliamentary committee after three years to ensure its effective operation.

G.   OUT-OF-HOME AND GUERRILLA ADVERTISING

Creativity, along with technology, allows for out-of-home advertising to take an almost endless variety of forms, including flags, portable or sidewalk signs, ground signs, wall signs, pole signs, billboards, bus and subway advertising, transit carriers in malls, transit shelter signs, skywriting, bathroom and stall posters, vinyl or adhesive wall, sidewalk or pole clings, loud-speaker announcements or recordings and video projection advertisements. Outdoor advertising, particularly guerrilla ads, are meant to attract attention and create buzz, but for some viewers these types of ads are simply disruptive and are considered "visual pollution", "sky trash" and "litter on a stick".

One essential difference between out-of-home and guerrilla ads is that out-of-home ads are typically "legal" ads which are posted in accordance with provincial and municipal laws and by-laws and are featured on a semi-permanent basis. Out-of-home advertisers have legitimately rented billboard or transit shelter space for publication of ads. Guerrilla ads on the other hand are typically short-lived "illegal" and aggressive campaigns whereby the advertiser takes a risk and saturates the targeted area with advertising for a short period, hopefully before the authorities catch them, require them to stop, pull the ads down or fine them. Guerrilla ads are often where creativity makes its mark; these ads usually take non-traditional forms.

Both outdoor and guerrilla ads are subject to the *Competition Act* as well as the requirements specified by provincial and municipal governments. Guerrilla ads, because of their disruptive and mischievous nature, may also raise issues under the *Criminal Code*.

1. Complying with the *Competition Act*

The *Competition Act* requires that all advertising messages be clear, easy to read and not misleading. It is not only the actual words which must be clear and accurate, but also the general look of the ad and the size of the relevant details. If, for example, a claim about a "Blow Out Sale" is made on a billboard, video projection or pole poster, but the caveat "Saturday only" is in tiny print that cannot be read from a distance or the disclaimer is only shown for a split-second, fair and adequate disclosure has not been made. Technical compliance is not enough. The limitations associated with any offer must be clearly disclosed, and if doing so is more difficult by the medium, that is the advertiser's problem, not the consumer's.

Similarly, "required disclosures" that must be made for specific ads, such as contest ads, are equally applicable to outdoor and guerrilla advertising. Disclosure should be made in a manner where people will actually see and be able to read it.

2. Advertising Outside Cities

Advertisements outside city and/or municipal boundaries must comply with provincial regulations. Advertising outside municipal boundaries often consists of billboards beside provincial highways. Provinces have regulations specific to signs or billboards posted alongside highways. In British Columbia, for example, highway advertisements are governed by section 214 of the *Motor Vehicle Act*. This section gives the Minister of Transportation and Highways discretion to approve signs in rural areas. It also gives the Minister complete discretion to have signs near highways altered, repainted or torn down. If the sign is torn down at the discretion of the Minister, the government is not required to compensate the sign's owner. Therefore, it is imperative that anyone who plans on advertising alongside a highway ensure that the ad has been pre-approved and strictly complies with provincial rules. Laws and regulations governing outdoor ads can affect the sign owner or the advertiser, or both, depending on whether the issue is related to the sign itself or the representation made on it. Sign companies should be aware of any restrictions or limitations which may affect a particular sign location.

3.   Advertising Inside Cities

All outdoor advertising within municipal boundaries is regulated by local by-laws and ordinances. Unfortunately, there are no quick references available. Different towns and municipalities impose different outdoor advertising restrictions.

Most municipal by-laws contain specific provisions regarding posting of all types of signs and bills within municipal boundaries. The definition of "sign" and "bill" in municipal by-laws is often quite broad and will catch a great many forms of guerrilla ads such as removable adhesive signs, posters and even video projections.

Many cities have established rules which specify that no person shall erect a sign or advertisement within their boundaries except in accordance with the regulations which typically mandate:

- a building permit is required for the erection of all signs and advertisements;
- permits are required for temporary signs;
- temporary signs, posters and bills can only be posted on certain designated kiosks, poster boards or display modules provided by the city;
- bills and posters can only be put up by agencies licenced to post bills;
- limited display allowances on construction hoarding, typically also regulated by the owner of the hoarding;
- no sign can be erected in a Public Right of Way;
- the people who own the land on which the sign is placed must obtain separate approval from the licensing agency;
- all signs in the city require the permission of the municipality.

Often municipal by-laws contain prohibitions regarding moveable, portable or sidewalk signs because they clutter the sidewalks, are dangerous in high winds or stormy weather, and can be a hazard to the handicapped and visually impaired.

Violations of municipal by-laws can result in hefty fines.

If approval to erect a sign or billboard is denied, it may be worth checking to see if the municipality had the authority to implement the applicable by-law. For example, in the province of British Columbia, sections 551(1) and 908(1) of the *Local Government Act*[5] permit city councils to "regulate the erection, placing, alteration, maintenance, demolition and removal of a sign, sign board, advertisement, advertising device or structure".

Other government restrictions which affect outdoor advertising may be found in statutes such as the British Columbia *Motor Vehicle Act* which regulates the placement of commercial advertising at or near a traffic control device.

4. Guerrilla Advertising and the *Criminal Code*

Guerilla marketing techniques may also result in violations of the Canadian *Criminal Code*.[6] Mischief is a criminal offence committed by anyone who wilfully:

(a) …damages property;

...

(c) obstructs, interrupts or interferes with the lawful use, enjoyment or operation of property or

(d) obstructs, interrupts or interferes with any person in the lawful use, enjoyment or operation of property.[7]

Mischief is punishable by indictment or on summary conviction with a maximum penalty on indictment of imprisonment. Everyone who commits mischief in relation to property is guilty of an indictable offence and liable to imprisonment for a term not exceeding two years or is guilty of an offence punishable on summary conviction. Mischief against religious property carries greater penalties including imprisonment for ten years.

The offence may not be made out by guerrilla advertisements on public property, as long as the property is not rendered less suited for its intended purpose. However, if the ads were to interfere with the *use* of the property, such as obstructing the view through a window, loud noises or other disturbances to those enjoying and using the property, the offence might be made out.

5. Word Of Mouth and Viral Marketing

Word of mouth and viral marketing describes various emerging techniques including e-mail marketing (discussed above), customer influence via word of mouth, paid placements, branded blogs, behavioural marketing, product placement using product influencers, branded entertainment, use of celebrities, even voice-mail blasts.

Word of mouth marketing is subject to all laws applicable to advertising including privacy laws, the *Competition Act*, the *Canadian Code of Advertising Standards*, and the various provincial and municipal laws and guidelines.

Word of mouth marketing can be strictly legitimate. Word of mouth marketers can behave with credibility and openness such that target consumers are aware of and can recognize when they are being marketed to and what the terms and conditions are applicable to any offer, product, service or campaign. For instance, a legitimate word of mouth marketing technique includes product placement using "product influencers". "Product influencers" are consumers who are members of a target market group, who are given or loaned products to use and who will "spread the word" and provide honest testimonials.

Word of mouth marketing raises legal and ethical issues when it is done by "stealth". Techniques which utilize or include falsification, masquerade, spam, infiltration or actors behaving like consumers, can be problematic.

Word of mouth marketing involves some interesting and unique legal issues and has triggered the publication of specific guidelines. The Word Of Mouth Marketing Association (WOMMA), is a U.S. based voluntary trade group formed to promote the growth of the word of mouth industry, recognizing that credibility is extremely important to the sustainability of this form of advertising. WOMMA has published a draft Code of Ethics to be adopted by all members.

The Code principles include:

(1) Consumer protection and respect is paramount: the Code recognizes that the consumer is in charge of the terms of the consumer-marketer relationship.
(2) Honesty of Relationship, Opinion and Identity: word of mouth advocates should be honest about their identity as an advocate, their relationship with a marketer, the source of any opinion and any products or incentives they are receiving.
(3) We respect the rules of the venue: word of mouth marketers should respect the rules of on-line and off-line communication venues.
(4) We manage relationships with minors responsibly: children under 13 are not included in word of mouth marketing.
(5) We promote honest downstream communications: recognizing that we cannot control and will not attempt to control what real people say or how a message will be presented after multiple generations of conversation.
(6) We protect privacy and permission: using opt-in and high standards regarding obtaining permission.

H.   SAMPLING

Sampling introduces consumers to new products and allows them to try these products without purchase. Most consumers enjoy receiving samples of new products. Sampling may include food samples in grocery stores or samples of a new product in liquor stores, or pharmaceutical companies sending out free drug samples to doctors. There are guidelines or regulations for the distribution of free products in many industries. There may also be disclosure issues, such as whether or not an advertiser is required to disclose the ingredients of a food product that is being sampled.

1.   Practical Considerations When Sampling

Advertisers should check the guidelines or regulations that apply to their industry. Some of the most regulated sectors are food, alcohol and pharmaceutical products.

2.   Pharmaceutical Industry

The federal *Food and Drugs Act*, prohibits the distribution of drug samples to anyone other than health professionals. Although food sampling is not specifically regulated by the *Food and Drugs Act*, there may be guidelines set by the particular venue in which the sampling is taking place. These guidelines may deal with issues such as food handling, disclosure of potential food allergens and the liability of food demonstrators.

Advertisers are not permitted to hand out free drugs to consumers. However, consumers are permitted to purchase certain drugs for a nominal fee such as one cent. There are also issues regarding parental consent when free samples of certain products are given to minors.

3.   Alcohol Industry

Since the advertising and sale of alcohol is heavily regulated by provincial legislation, regulatory bodies and their guidelines, there tend to be specific provisions that deal with sampling of alcohol products in liquor stores, wineries, or breweries. Generally, there are limits on the amount of alcohol that can be sampled, and samples can only be given to people who are over the legal drinking age. Sampling may be permitted only in designated areas on the premises, and pre-authorization for sampling may be required from government and regulatory authorities.

I.   MULTI-LEVEL MARKETING

1.   Multi-level Marketing Plans

Multi-level marketing is a method of distributing products or services through sales representatives called distributors. The distributors who work for multi-level marketers are independent contractors and not employees. They are compensated for the sale of goods or services. They also receive compensation, indirectly, when they convince additional distributors to join the organization. The developing network of distributors are often referred to as the "distributors downline". Commissions of multi-level marketing distributors are based on both the sales volume of the individual distributor and the distributors downline.

Multi-level marketers are governed by the federal *Competition Act*. Section 55(1) of the Act defines multi-level marketing as follows:

...a plan for the supply of a product whereby a participant in the plan receives compensation for the supply of a product to another participant in the plan who, in turn, receives compensation for the supply of the same or another product to other participants in the plan.

It is extremely important to recognize when you are doing business with a multi-level marketer, because the promotional methods of multi-level marketers are strictly regulated. Additionally, you need to be careful that you are not, in fact, involved in an illegal pyramid scheme. This is a "business" structure that is similar to the multi-level marketing structure but with slight differences which make it illegal.

Regulation in this area is principally concerned with promises about compensation made by multi-level marketing organizers when recruiting new members. Section 55(2) of the Act stipulates that such representations must reflect either the sums of money that are currently being made by distributors or the sums of money that can legitimately be made by distributors.

2.   Violations/Penalties

Under section 55(2.1), multi-level marketing organizers may be held responsible for violations of the Act perpetrated by distributors at any level downline.

Organizers of multi-level marketing structures who are charged with making false representations can defend themselves by proving that they took reasonable precautions and were diligent in trying to ensure that none of their employees, agents or representatives broke the rules by making false representations in regards to compensation.

Penalties for violation of section 55 of the Act can be severe. On conviction a court may impose sentences consisting of:

(a) a fine in the discretion of the court or a term of imprisonment not exceeding five years, or both; or

(b) on summary conviction, a fine not exceeding $200,000 or to a term of imprisonment not exceeding one year, or to both.

3.   Pyramid Schemes

Pyramid schemes are, in theory, based on the same concept as multi-level marketing plans. They constitute a method of distributing products or services through distributors, again expecting distributors to recruit additional distributors into the organization. This is where the similarities usually end.

In pyramid schemes, the product being sold is often of inferior quality and, in such schemes, the sale of products is usually secondary to the primary purpose of making money through the enlistment of new recruits.

New recruits are enticed to join pyramid schemes by promises of great financial rewards. They are expected to pay a sizeable entrance fee when they enlist. The purpose of the scheme is to make money by having successive recruits pay into the scheme. Each new recruit is expected to recruit additional members who will then pay into the scheme.

Section 55.1(1) of the Act defines a pyramid scheme as one in which:

(a) a participant in the plan gives consideration for the right to receive compensation by reason of the recruitment into the plan of another participant in the plan who gives consideration for the same right;

(b) a participant in the plan gives consideration, as a condition of participating in the plan, for a specified amount of the product, other than a specified amount of the product that is bought at the seller's cost price for the purpose only of facilitating sales;

(c) a person knowingly supplies the product to a participant in the plan in an amount that is commercially unreasonable; or

(d) a participant in the plan who is supplied with the product

    (i)   does not have a buy-back guarantee that is exercisable on reasonable commercial terms or a right to return the product in saleable condition on reasonable commercial terms, or

    (ii) is not informed of the existence of the guarantee or right and the manner in which it can be exercised.

The fundamental concern with pyramid schemes, and the reason they are illegal, is that eventually, all markets will run out of new distributors that can be enlisted. As the only form of compensation paid to the participants is the income from the recruitment of new distributors, eventually everyone loses, except those who started the plan or enlisted early.

In fact, the element of chance involved, the payment required to participate and the hope of a huge reward make pyramid schemes more like
gambling than legitimate business.

Anyone remotely associated with a pyramid scheme can be prosecuted. Section 55.1(2) of the Act provides that "no person shall establish,
operate, advertise or promote a scheme of pyramid selling". Penalties for
violation of section 55.1 of the Act can include:

(a) a fine in the discretion of the court or a term of imprisonment not exceeding
five years or both; or

(b) on summary conviction, a fine not exceeding $200,000 or a term of imprison-
ment for a term not exceeding one year, or both.

J.   REFERRAL SELLING

Referral selling is where a marketer offers a consumer a rebate, discount
or other advantage if the consumer gives the marketer names of friends
who could become new customers for the marketer or where the consumer otherwise assists the marketer in making more sales.

Referral selling used to be prohibited under the *Competition Act*, but
the provision was abolished in 1999. The reason for the repeal of the
federal prohibition was extreme lack of prosecution activity with the last
case being in 1978. In the 1960s and 1970s, referral selling was the
equivalent of the telemarketing concern today and took the form of a
commonly used tactic by door-to-door sellers. When the provision was
repealed, the Competition Bureau did not see it as a serious concern from
a modern commercial perspective. Also, of some significance was the
fact that any serious issues with referral selling were likely to fall within
the multi-level marketing or pyramid selling prohibitions of the *Competition Act*.

Several provinces have referral selling prohibitions in their consumer
protection legislation. Many of these provisions have been part of the
legislation for years but have never or almost never been the subject of a
consumer complaint and thus have never been judicially considered or
interpreted. The language in the provisions is often vague and the scope
of the application is not very clear. That being said, these provisions have
not yet been removed from the consumer protection laws (except for
Ontario in July 2005) and continue to cause concern for advertisers and
marketers since "refer-a-friend" is often a popular and effective marketing tool.

The intention of the provincial referral selling provisions is generally
to protect consumers from being coerced into signing a sales contract in
hopes of obtaining some future benefit if they refer a friend. Overall, if
the program is structured such that gaining the benefit is not directly
dependent on the consumer providing a referral, or where the referral is

provided through "no purchase" agreements, the provincial prohibitions can generally be avoided. Certain contests, containing no purchase entry mechanisms may be structured (with the help of your contest lawyer) to include "refer-a-friend" entries which avoid raising serious issues under the referral selling prohibitions.

The new Ontario *Consumer Protection Act, 2002* has repealed a previous prohibition on referral selling. Referral selling is essentially permitted, but it must be done legitimately. Referral selling is now addressed under the unfair practice provisions. It is an unfair practice to misrepresent or exaggerate the benefit that may flow to a consumer if the consumer helps a person obtain new or potential customers.

Referral selling programs raise issues of compliance with Canada's privacy laws since personal information cannot be collected, stored or disclosed without knowledge and consent of the individual. In other words, privacy laws may be violated when a consumer refers a friend by disclosing the friend's personal information to a marketer, the marketer stores the information and uses it for the purpose of contacting the referral, without consent.

K.   TESTIMONIAL ADVERTISING

Section 74.02 of the *Competition Act* prohibits the publication of a testimonial unless the advertiser can prove that the testimonial was previously published, or that prior to publication, written permission was given by the person who gave the testimonial. Testimonials must reflect the genuine, current opinion of the person or organization giving them and must be based on adequate information or experience.

The same section also requires that the advertised statements must reflect the testimonial which was actually given. In other words, not only must you get approval from someone whose testimonial you are using, you must make sure that what you claim they said is what they actually said.

In addition, the Marketing Practices Branch of the Competition Bureau has commented that testimonials must be free from ambiguity since the public may well attach greater weight to them when made by prominent figures or experts than if simply made by the advertiser. Similarly, the Branch feels that consumers identify with assessments made by other consumers and thereby place great reliance on consumer testimonials. The Branch has therefore established the following rules for proper use of testimonials:

- the person giving the testimonial must have actually used the product;

- if the testimonial conveys the impression of use of an advertiser's entire line of products, such use must have taken place;
- continued use or approval of the product by the endorser must occur if the advertisement, by its content, implies continued use;
- the third party's experience must be relevant to the views expressed;
- an impression of impartiality conveyed by the third party endorser would be misleading if, in fact, he had an undisclosed financial interest in the advertisement or was affiliated in some way with the advertiser;
- normally, the fact that a third party has been paid for endorsing a product is not objectionable since the public would expect this to have been the case; however, if in context the statements convey the impression of disinterested professional judgment, the fact that the person has been paid may create a misleading impression; and
- in the case of consumer surveys, any comments by a member of the group surveyed must truly represent the views of the whole group.

In summary, not only must the use of a testimonial be consented to and approved by the maker, but the use of it by the advertiser must not be misleading.

RULES OF THUMB

- DO have releases signed prior to publication.

- DO ensure that the release contains both the approval of the person of the testimonial's content and their consent to publication, along with their name, voice, *etc.*

- DO ensure the person providing the testimonial has actually used the product.

- DO NOT use a testimonial which you know to be untrue, even it if reflects the person's actual belief (*i.e.*, "I think this is the most effective moisturizer on the market."). It is a fundamental principle of advertising law that a third party cannot make statements that the advertiser knows to be false.

L.   ADVERTISING ON THE INTERNET

Contrary to popular belief, advertising on the internet is still advertising. As such, the basic rules, regulations and policies that apply to other more traditional media also apply to online advertising. Not surprisingly, however, the internet introduces new twists and turns that could not have been contemplated when the various pieces of legislation were enacted.

1.   Competition Bureau Guidelines

To assist the advertising community in ensuring that its online advertising conforms to legislative standards, found in the *Competition Act* and other provincial laws, on February 18, 2003, the Competition Bureau issued an *Information Bulletin on the Application of the Competition Act to Representations on the Internet*.

The highlights of the Information Bulletin are as follows:

(a)   **General Impression Test Applicable**
Just as in off-line advertising, representations must not only be literally true, but the general impression created by the representation must also be true. Similarly, the standard to determine the general impression should be the "average consumer". Finally, just as in print advertising, one cannot assume that consumers read an entire website. As such, it is up to online advertisers to ensure that all relevant information is presented in a fashion that makes it noticeable and likely to be read.

(b)   **Liability For Internet Representations**
In traditional advertising, it is possible that not only the advertisers but the advertising agencies who help create ads and get the media outlets to disseminate them can be liable for false and misleading representations.
In online media, often the web page designers, the web hosts and the service providers could potentially be found to contravene the *Competition Act*. While each situation will be considered on a case by case basis, the Bulletin states that "the Bureau focuses on the party who 'causes' the representation to be made", considering "the nature and degree of control that the person who makes a representation exercises over the content". One should also note that the "publisher's defence" set out in subsection 74.07(1) of the Act, for a person who merely prints or publishes or "otherwise disseminates a representation, including an advertisement, on behalf of another person in Canada", is available for those who accepted the representation in good faith in the ordinary course of

business and where the advertiser is in Canada and the disseminating person recorded its name and address.

(c) **How to Avoid Common Pitfalls**

• *Disclosure of Relevant Information: Disclaimers*

As in traditional advertising, disclaimers can only be used effectively to expand upon and add information to the principal representation; they cannot cure or retract a false or misleading representation:

- Disclaimers should appear on the same screen and close to the relevant representation, if possible.
- Hyperlinks to disclaimers can be used if they are obvious and clearly labelled, giving consumers a reason to click on them and are not obscured by other attention-grabbing tools.
- Audio disclaimers alone may be unacceptable since not all users have audio access.
- In some circumstances, repetition of the disclaimer may be necessary.

• *Required Disclosures*
All required disclosures must be displayed in such a manner that they are likely to be read. The Bureau does not take the position that requiring a consumer to click on a clearly labelled hyperlink is unacceptable disclosure.

• *Representation Regarding a Business*
The Bureau recommends that the businesses ensure that:

- The website in question does not create a false or misleading impression as to the physical location or identity of the business.
- The use of text, graphics, logos, marks, seals or trustmarks, accreditations or other representations do not create false impressions of affiliation, sponsorship, endorsement or popularity.
- The representations do not mislead consumers as to the type of organization making the representations or as to the purpose of the representations.
- The representations do not mislead consumers as to the relationship between the party making the representation and the supplier of the product or service.

2.   Telemarketing and Internet Advertising

The Bureau takes the position that section 52.1 of the *Competition Act* dealing with interactive telephone conversations does not apply to the internet.

3.   Jurisdictional Issues

The fact that the internet is accessible globally raises complicated jurisdictional issues. It is clear that on-line representations originating from Canada which are accessible in Canada are required to comply with Canadian law. However, is Canadian law applicable to on-line advertising which is accessible in Canada but originates from another country? Several recent cases have set out the Canadian position on the jurisdiction of Canadian courts over on-line advertising originating outside of Canada.

In 1997, the Pennsylvania District Court decided the *Zippo Manufacturing Co. v. Zippo Dot Com, Inc.*[8] case and established the "passive versus active" test. According to this test, where an individual has simply posted information on an internet website which is accessible to users in foreign jurisdictions, this is a passive website that does little more than make information available to those who are interested in it and is not grounds for the exercise of jurisdiction over the content. Canadian courts adopted a similar approach in *Braintech Inc. v. Kostiuk*,[9] In this case, a series of defamatory messages were posted on a chat site by a B.C. resident. Braintech, a B.C. based company, sued the poster in a Texas court, and was awarded approximately $400,000 in damages. When Braintech returned to B.C. to enforce the judgment, the B.C. courts used the passive versus active test, found that the postings were essentially passive in nature and ruled that the Texas court had improperly asserted jurisdiction over the case. Braintech's appeal to the Supreme Court of Canada was denied in March 2000.[10]

More recently, courts are moving towards a broader, effects-based approach when deciding whether or not to assert jurisdiction in internet cases. Under this new approach, rather than examining the specific characteristics of a website, courts focus on the actual effects that the website had in the target jurisdiction, and identify the intentions of the parties and the steps taken to either enter or avoid a particular jurisdiction. Under the effects based approach, courts should only assert jurisdiction when there is evidence that the website actively targeted an audience within the

---

[8]   952 F. Supp. 1119 (W.D. Pa. 1997).
[9]   [1999] B.C.J. No. 622 (B.C.C.A.).
[10]   (2000) 253 N.R. 395n (S.C.C.).

jurisdiction. The test is whether the targeting of a specific jurisdiction was reasonably foreseeable.

Two recent cases, one in Ontario and one in B.C., have applied the test of foreseeability. A 2005 Ontario Court of Appeal decision[11] involved a defamation lawsuit launched against the *Washington Post* by Cheickh Bangoura. Mr. Bangoura was a U.N. official posted to various countries around the world. He became a resident of Canada in 1996, receiving Canadian citizenship in 2001, and lived in Ontario ever since. Bangoura was stationed in Kenya in 1997, as a leading official in a U.N. Drug Control Program, when the *Washington Post* featured several articles accusing him of misconduct and mismanagement. Bangoura sued the *Washington Post* for defamation in the Ontario court and argued that the articles remained available on the *Washington Post* website and therefore accessible to residents in Ontario. The *Post* sought to have the case stayed, arguing that the Ontario courts should not be entitled to assert jurisdiction over the matter since there was no real and substantial connection with the province. The court denied the motion, ruling that the paper should have "reasonably foreseen that the story would follow the plaintiff wherever he resided". The case was appealed and the Ontario Court of Appeal sided with the newspaper, noting that "the connection between Ontario and Mr. Bangoura's claim is minimal at best". There was no connection with Ontario until more than three years after the publication of the articles. The court concluded that it was not reasonably foreseeable in 1997, that Mr. Bangoura would become a resident of Ontario.

The B.C. case[12] involved a defamation lawsuit against the *New York Post* launched by Brian Burke. Burke, the former General Manager of the Vancouver Canucks, complained about a column written by Larry Brooks about Burke's role during the violent on-ice incident between Todd Bertuzzi and Steve Moore. Burke sued in the B.C. court. The *Post* sought to dismiss the case, arguing that the newspaper did not maintain a physical presence in B.C. and therefore the courts could not assert jurisdiction over the case. The B.C. court denied the *Post*'s motion in favour of Burke, concluding that the *Post* knew, or ought to have known, that the column would have significant impact in B.C.

Both these decisions were made based on the foreseeability test. Canadian courts have asserted their jurisdiction over cases involving on-line content originating outside of Canada, but only in instances where impact in the Canadian jurisdiction was foreseeable. The potential for liability is real for on-line advertisers inside and outside Canadian borders. However, these cases provide some good guidance about the risks associated with internet advertising and publishing.

---

[11] *Bangoura v. Washington Post*, [2005] O.J. No. 3849 (Ont. C.A.).

[12] *Burke v. NYP Holdings Inc. (c.o.b. New York Post)*, [2005] B.C.J. No. 1993 (B.C.S.C.).

4.   Consumer Protection On-line

In addition to the Bureau policies specifically outlined for the *Competition Act*, two sets of Guidelines have also been developed to further consumer protection online.[13]

---

[13] See *Principles for Consumer Protection for Electronic Commerce — A Canadian Framework* in the Principles and Guides Section at <http://strategis.ic.gc.ca> and the Organisation for Economic Co-operation and Development's *Guidelines for Consumer Protection in the Context of Electronic Commerce* at <http://www.oecd.org/home> (found at their online bookshop).

Chapter 16

PRIVACY LAW IN CANADA

Contributed by Shelley Samel and Ariane Siegel

A.   INTRODUCTION

As a whole, Canadians are well-informed regarding the widespread use of their personal information for marketing purposes. We are also aware of the breadth of personal information that is collected about us online. With the growing sensitivity to privacy concerns, and in an attempt to ensure that our privacy laws are in line with those of the European Union, the federal government, in 2001, enacted legislation to protect personal information. The impetus for this legislation was the EU Directive on Data Protection that came into force in October 1998, permitting a ban on the transfer of personal data from the European Union to countries that do not have adequate privacy protection in place. Canada was concerned about possible trade blockages and reacted accordingly. Interestingly, the United States does not currently have comprehensive laws in place protecting personal information in the private sector (although the U.S. does have sectoral-specific laws, for example, protecting use of personal information).

This chapter will canvass the applicability of privacy laws to marketing. There are many other areas, especially relating to employment and personal health information, that are directly impacted by these laws, which are beyond the scope of this chapter.

B.   THE FEDERAL LEGISLATION

In January 2001, the *Personal Information Protection and Electronic Documents Act*[1] came into force with respect to federal businesses, works and undertakings — such as airlines, banks, telephone companies, cable television and broadcasting companies. The Act also applies to information disclosed from within one province to another province or country

---

[1]   S.C. 2000, c. 5.

for profit or gain. In January 2004, the Act was extended to apply to all organizations within Canada (except to intraprovincial commercial activities of organizations in a province where the province has enacted substantially similar legislation to the Federal Act). To date three provinces have substantially similar legislation in place. They include Quebec, Alberta and British Columbia. In addition, several provinces have specific legislation in place governing the use of personal health information.

The Act is designed to protect personal information that is *collected, used or disclosed* by organizations in the course of commercial activities. Personal information is "information about an identifiable individual, but does not include the name, title or business address or telephone number of an employee of an organization" (*i.e.*, business card information). In a recent decision, the Federal Privacy Commissioner determined that business e-mail addresses are deemed to be personal information and are not exempted from the application of the Act.[2] The Act also ensures that individuals have access to their personal information that is maintained by an organization, can correct the information and that such information is securely protected by the organization (whether the information is in a database accessible online or in a filing cabinet). Further, if the information is to be used for a purpose beyond the purpose for which it was collected, consent must be obtained for such additional purpose.

It is worth noting that the Act does not apply to individuals who collect, use or disclose personal information for personal purposes (such as a Christmas card list). It also does not apply to organizations that collect, use or disclose personal information for journalistic, artistic or literary purposes. Similarly, the Act allows organizations to use personal information without the knowledge or consent of an individual if the collection is clearly in the interest of the individual and consent cannot be obtained in a timely way (for example, a floral delivery company can collect a name and delivery address of a third party in order to deliver flowers to them) or if the information is publicly available and specified by the Regulations.

To address the concerns of marketers regarding the use of compilations of personal information such as telephone directories and professional registers, the government enacted *Regulations Specifying Publicly Available Information*.[3] These Regulations provide a further exception to the consent requirement and allow for the collection, use and disclosure of personal information without consent or knowledge of the individual, if the information is publicly available. The Regulations specify the information and classes of information that constitute publicly available information. They also provide that such information is "publicly avail-

---

[2] PIPEDA Case Summary #297.

[3] SOR/2001-7.

able" if the collection, use and disclosure relates directly to the purpose for which the information is made available. For instance, the collection, use and disclosure of personal information in a telephone directory or in a government registry, is legitimate without the consent or knowledge of the individuals in the directory. However, if this information is used for any purpose other than its primary purpose, then the use is subject to the consent requirement. If this information were to be used for the secondary purpose of creating personal profiles on individuals, including their consumption habits and lifestyles or for sending them offers for products or services, consent is required. In a recent privacy case, two real estate sales representatives complained when a broker they did not work for published their names and the number of houses they sold in a year in an advertisement in a real estate flyer. The representatives had not consented to this information being disclosed. The Assistant Commissioner considered the typical secnario that a real estate representative encounters. Specifically, members of the real estate board sign a user agreement that allows them to use the MLS system. The board's privacy policy states that information within the MLS system is considered to be personal information to the extent that it is or can be associated with an individual. As an authorized user of the MLS system, sales representatives are aware and consent that their name as well as financial particulars of the transaction are entered into the system for the purposes of selling real estate. They know that other sales representatives will see the information. They do not consent to other uses of personal information. In the Assistant Commissioner's view, there was no implied consent for listing information to be used for a comparative analysis used for advertising by other sales representatives.[4]

To better understand the scope of the Act, it is useful to review the ten principles set out in Schedule 1.

(1) **Accountability** – an organization is responsible for the personal information that it retains and an individual(s) must be designated by the organization as being accountable for the organization's compliance with the principles.

(2) **Identifying Purposes** – the purposes for which the personal information is being collected and will be used must be clearly identified at or before the time the information is collected.

(3) **Consent** – knowledge and consent of the individual is required for the collection, use and disclosure of their personal information, except where inappropriate.

---

[4] PIPEDA Case Summary #303.

(4) **Limiting Collection** – the personal information collected must be limited to that which is required for the identified purposes. The collection of information must be by fair and lawful means.

(5) **Limiting Use, Disclosure and Retention** – if the personal information is to be used for purposes other than those identified, consent is required. Organizations must only retain the personal information as long as is necessary to fulfil the purposes.

(6) **Accuracy** – the information collected must be kept as accurate, complete and current as possible for the identified purposes.

(7) **Safeguards** – protection and security is required to ensure the safe keeping of the personal information. Security measures must be appropriate to the sensitivity of the information.

(8) **Openness** – policies relating to the management of personal information should be accessible and available.

(9) **Individual Access** – an individual must be given access to their personal information maintained by an organization and be able to correct any inaccuracies.

(10) **Challenging Compliance** – the practices of an organization can be challenged.

C.   CONSENT

The essential element of the legislation is that consent is required before a company can collect, use or disclose personal information. The consent must be informed — the person providing the consent must know what uses the company will make of their information. Importantly, consent can either be express or implied, depending on the nature and sensitivity of the information.

The *Principles of the Canadian Standards Association Model Code for the Protection of Personal Information* have been included as Schedule 1 to the Act. The Schedule provides the following example: If a person has a magazine subscription there is implied consent to allow the magazine publisher to contact the person to solicit a magazine renewal. On the other hand, health-related information will almost always be considered sensitive, requiring express consent.

Also, the Act recognizes situations where consent cannot be obtained. These exceptions include "if the action clearly benefits the individual or if obtaining permission could infringe on the information's accuracy; where such data can contribute to a legal investigation or aid in an emergency where people's lives and safety could be at stake; and, if disclosure aids, in times of emergency, matters of legal investigation, or facilitates the conservation of historically important records".[5]

---

5   Department of Justice Canada, News Release, "Privacy Provisions Highlights".

D.   IDENTIFYING PURPOSES

In order to meet the "identifying purposes" element, we recommend that every company have a well-drafted privacy policy that is accessible and available to its customers. Depending on the nature of the personal information collected, it may be advisable to send the privacy policy to all customers, in order to address concerns that customers were not aware of your policies. Every single website should have a privacy policy. In fact, on every web page where personal information is collected from visitors, it makes sense to have a link to the privacy policy. For an example, see the Gowlings privacy policy at <http://www.gowlings.com/privacy.asp>.

E.   WHAT IS THE PUNISHMENT IF YOU INFRINGE?

You may be wondering what redress the Privacy Commissioner (who is charged with investigating complaints relating to the Act and attempting dispute resolution) has against an organization that violates the Act. The Privacy Commissioner has powers to investigate a complaint (after the complainant has attempted to settle the matter directly with the organization), act on her own initiative or conduct an audit. The investigation process allows the Commissioner to call witnesses, compel evidence and visit business sites. Basically, her function is that of an ombudsman who attempts to resolve disputes through mediation and persuasion. The Commissioner's recourse is to publish the complaint findings and consult and educate the organization as to how to correct any violations of the Act. If the Commissioner is unhappy with the outcome, she can appeal to the Federal Court and the Federal Court has the power to order an organization to correct its practices in order to comply with the Act and to publish its corrective action. The Federal Court may also award damages to the complainant. There is also an offence created under the Act where an organization obstructs the Commissioner in an investigation or destroys records before all recourse is exhausted. This offence carries a maximum fine of $100,000.

F.   EXPRESS VS. IMPLIED CONSENT

Since this Act came into effect, many clients have asked us to pinpoint what exactly constitutes express consent? Can the consent be in an opt-out form or does it have to be through an positive expression or action? An example of opt-out consent is: "We acknowledge the importance of protecting your personal information. At company X, we may use your personal information to inform you about some of our products that we think may be of interest to you. If you do not want to be contacted by us in the future, please check off the box below." Positive express consent would look more like this: "I would like to receive more information about your products, please feel free to send this information to me". The consent statement would include an unchecked box which requires a positive action by the customer expressing his or her response (*e.g.*, checking it off).

The CMA's new Code of Ethics, which is scheduled to come into effect on January 1, 2007, provides that where a consumer has provided his or her e-mail address to a marketer, the marketer has implied consent to e-mail that consumer.

In a series of decisions and statements, the federal Privacy Commissioner has approved of the use of opt-out consent methods in a variety of circumstances. Factors such as the nature of the personal information in question, the intended use of the personal information in question and whether and to whom disclosure is intended will determine the appropriate form of consent.

In a letter to *Southam News* dated July 17, 2001, Mr. Radwanski, the former Privacy Commissioner, stated that "the key relevant provisions of the new law are consent and the reasonable person test". He wrote that "Apart from some very limited exceptions, an organization covered under the law cannot collect, use or disclose personal information without the consent of the individual. It can only collect, use or disclose information for the purpose for which consent was given. *And even with consent, an organization may only collect, use or disclose information for purposes that a reasonable person would consider appropriate under the circumstances.*" (emphasis is added)

The former Privacy Commissioner provided further guidance in his Findings concerning an Air Canada brochure distributed to Aeroplan members entitled "All About your Privacy". The brochure explained to Aeroplan members certain circumstances under which personal information might be collected and/or disclosed to Aeroplan's partners or other third parties. However, Aeroplan members could contact Air Canada and "opt out" if they did not want their personal information shared in the manner described.

Interestingly, Mr. Radwanski wrote that certain of these circumstances were ones that Aeroplan members would reasonably expect from the Aeroplan program. In a letter to Air Canada dated July 18, 2001, he wrote: "Providing information to Aeroplan partners so that they can inform members of various promotions and exclusive products would seem to be something that a member would routinely expect to happen." However, the Privacy Commissioner took issue with the "tailoring" of information to the individual's personal or professional interests, preferences for certain products and financial status. This practice was found to be in violation of Principles 4.2.4, 4.3, 4.3.1 and 4.5 of Schedule 1 and section 5(3) of PIPEDA.

One provision of the brochure described "Exchange of Information within the Air Canada Family" but the description was extremely vague and confusing as to the nature and purpose of the exchange in question. This vague description was what Air Canada called their "forward-thinking strategy". This strategy was aimed at obtaining an equally vague consent to use and disclose personal information from Aeroplan members in an attempt to avoid obtaining further consent from them in the future. The Commissioner found that this was a violation of the knowledge and consent requirements in Principle 4.3 of Schedule 1 of the Act.

Mr. Radwanski said that the collection and dissemination of sensitive information of this sort requires "positive opt-in consent" and that "personal financial information is...particularly sensitive information". Mr. Radwanski was also puzzled by the fact that Air Canada warned members that it could take up to four months from a time the member opts-out of the use and disclosure of his or her personal information and the time when such action would be implemented. The Commissioner found that Air Canada should have had the appropriate procedures in place for the "reasonably expeditious processing of such requests".[6] The Commissioner also noted that the brochures had been sent to only 1 per cent of plan members. He remarked that the Act does not allow for token compliance and found that the attempt by Air Canada to seek consent through these brochures was "grossly inadequate".

In June 2002, the Commissioner released findings regarding a federal company that was not using appropriate security safeguards to protect information collected from participants in an online contest. Several participants received phone calls from persons falsely claiming to represent the company. Following internal and external investigations, the company could not determine how the unauthorized persons had obtained the entrants' personal information.

The Commissioner found that regardless of how the unauthorized access might have occurred, the company did not have the appropriate safeguards in place for protecting the personal information of contest participants and had therefore failed to meet its obligations under the Principles of PIPEDA. In further violation of the Principles, the Commissioner found that the company did not have adequate retention and deletion policies in place. Since release of the Commissioner's findings, the company has taken steps to bring its policies and practices into compliance with PIPEDA.

As can be discerned from the Privacy Commissioner's discussion of the Air Canada and online contest matters, it appears that if a company collects personal information for use in a contest or from individuals who request information from a company, such information — a name,

---

6   Privacy Commissioner of Canada, News Release, "Findings on Air Canada's Aeroplan Frequent Flyer Program" (March 20, 2002).

address, telephone number and/or e-mail address — will likely not be considered sensitive information (however, it may not be as clear cut if the contest is for Viagra®...). Therefore, it is likely that negative express consent is sufficient. However, we recommend including language as to what your company intends to use the information for in your privacy policy. An example of some language that we recommend is:

> When you supply Personal Information on this website, ABC Co. will use it for the express purpose for which it was collected (*e.g.*, to enter you in a contest or to send you a sample). It may also be used by ABC Co. to contact you regarding other products and services that may be of interest to you (including those we may offer jointly with other companies).
>
> ABC Co. does not share any Personal Information with any third parties, except as provided in this Privacy Policy.

We also recommend reiterating the policy in any contest rules and regulations if your company intends to use the information for purposes other than the administration of the contest. The rules can reference your privacy policy and/or provide a brief statement of the intended use of the personal information. For instance: "The personal information collected from you will be used for the purpose of administering the contest. Sponsor may also use your information to contact you regarding our products and services that may be of interest to you. Please see our privacy policy, available at www.-_____.ca for more details."

The rules seem to change where personal information is shared with unrelated third parties. In 2003, the former Commissioner released a finding in response to a complaint raised by a magazine subscriber that the organization had been selling or renting his name and address to third parties without his consent. The renting of mailing lists is one way that many Canadian magazines are able to earn some additional income in an attempt to remain competitive with their U.S.-based competition. The magazine had a notice in its masthead that subscribers' names and addresses were sometimes made available to other companies and that subscribers could have themselves removed from mailings by written request. The Commissioner noted that there was no notification as to the disclosure of personal information to third parties on the subscription card, nor was there a list of the *types* of companies to which the names were made available. The Commissioner's jurisdiction arose because the magazine rented its lists intraprovincially as well as into the United States for consideration.

The Commissioner held that since the magazine "was taking the liberty of assuming the complainant's consent to the secondary purpose [*i.e.*, opt-out consent], the organization should have also brought that purpose clearly and directly to the complainant's attention at the time he was considering his subscription".[7] The report noted:

> In sum, the Commissioner determined that the magazine, having relied wholly upon an undistinguished, sketchy, and small-printed purpose statement and opt-out opportunity not reasonably available to the complainant at the time of subscription, could in no way be deemed to have duly specified to the complainant its secondary purpose of disclosing his personal information to third parties or to have otherwise made a reasonable effort of advising him of that purpose in an understandable manner. The Commissioner found therefore that the organization was in contravention of Principles 4.2.3 and 4.3.2.

> He determined furthermore that, in neglecting to duly attend to the complainant's knowledge in accordance with his reasonable expectations, the magazine could in no meaningful sense be deemed to have obtained his consent. The Commissioner found therefore that the organization was also in contravention of Principles 4.3 and 4.5.[8]

The magazine had asserted that it was following industry practice as well as the guidelines of the CMA. The Commissioner noted that "his conclusions in a given case were never meant to be subject to industry approval". And, PIPEDA is the new industry standard. In reading the following recommendations (read: obligations) of the Commissioner, keep in mind the size of a magazine subscription card. The Commissioner recommended that the magazine include a purpose statement and a checkoff box on its subscription form and that the statement be prominently displayed in regular type size and include a description of the items to be disclosed (*i.e.*, name and address) and the organizations to which the disclosures are to be made. The Commissioner required that the magazine provide and prominently advertise a mechanism for subscribers to "conveniently, inexpensively, and promptly withdraw consent, such mechanism *to include a toll-free telephone number*". [our emphasis.] Finally, and almost unbelievably, the Commissioner required that the magazine raise these issues with the CMA and convey his expectation that all CMA members quickly adopt these procedures to set a new industry standard of compliance.

However, the Commissioner indicated that the magazine was that it could continue to use "opt-out" consent *provided* that the organizations were identified at least by type and the only information to be disclosed was the names and addresses.

This aggressive approach by the former Commissioner left many marketers fearing that unduly strict and costly interpretations of the Act would be applied going forward. However, Canada's current Privacy

---

7   PIPEDA Case Summary #167, Commissioner's Findings, April 11, 2003.
8   *Ibid.*

Commissioner and the two Assistant Privacy Commissioners have demonstrated a commitment to work with the private sector and marketers in particular to build strong relationships and avenues for resolving business concerns in a way that balances the need for important privacy protection for individuals and legitimate business interests.

The current Privacy Commissioner's team has re-affirmed a commitment towards the use of opt-out consent strategies for secondary marketing and in some cases for disclosure of non-sensitive personal information to third parties.

For example, in PIPEDA Case Summary #308, the Assistant Commissioner examined the issues of marketing inserts in account statements issued by a financial institution. An individual complained that the bank denied his request to opt-out of receiving marketing materials included in his credit card account statements (statement stuffers). These materials were advertisements for various products and services being offered by the bank in conjunction with third parties. The Assistant Privacy Commissioner noted that secondary marketing was the goal of placing such inserts (it was secondary to the reasons for which the complainant initially gave his personal information, namely to receive a credit card). The Assistant Commissioner determined that by not providing a means of withdrawing consent to secondary marketing, the bank was requiring the complainant to consent to a use of his personal information beyond that required to fulfil the purpose of servicing his credit card account. By extension, it becomes clear that opt-out consent would have been sufficient in this case.

It is important to note that organizations who have not obtained appropriate consent or who are concerned about their consent practices do not necessarily need to destroy their databases. Therefore, an organization holding an existing database may "upgrade" it to ensure that consent exists for any future use and retention of the personal information after the Act took effect in all sectors across Canada. That means you should make sure you only use personal information that you collected prior to January 1, 2004 for which you obtained the proper and necessary consents.

Another privacy concern arises from the technique identified in that famous shampoo ad — she told a friend, who told a friend and so on and so on and so on. There is a trend of using refer-a-friend (or viral marketing) promotions online. For instance, a company may ask if you would like to send an e-card to tell your friend about a new product or a great new website feature, or may run a contest whereby an entrant receives additional entries for each friend that is referred provided the friend enters the contest themselves. Notwithstanding the referral selling issues that may exist, addressed elsewhere in this book, how do you collect personal information about an individual from a third party without their consent? In our view, if the information is only held for the specific purpose for which it was collected — to send that e-card or to cross-reference whether the referred friend enters the contest — then it is probably okay. The information should be destroyed immediately after the purpose is complete unless that third party provides his or her own consent. Where a friend is being referred for a contest and the additional entries are contingent on the friend entering himself, it would be best practice to have an identifier number linked to both parties (referrer and referee) instead of actually storing the personal information of the third party for that purpose. Again, we wait to see how the Commissioner would address this issue if a complaint were to arise, but would hope that she would rely on the fact that the information is being disclosed for the benefit of the third party (much like the exemption for florists discussed above). The ramifications of acceptable standards for consent are particularly important for telemarketers. In this regard, the Canadian Radio-television and Telecommunications Commissioner (CRTC) has some jurisdiction.

Bill C-37, *An Act to amend the Telecommunications Act*,[9] was proclaimed into force on June 30, 2006 and will "provide the Commission with the authority to establish a national Do Not Call list (national DNCL) and to delegate the administration of a national DNCL and related functions to a third party. The amended Act will also empower the Commission to levy administrative monetary penalties for violations of its telemarketing rules".[10] At the time of writing, the CRTC had announced a public consultation[11] in relation to the creation and operation of a national DNCL as well as the establishment and enforcement of national DNCL rules and any other rules related to telemarketing. This important development will certainly impact marketing programs and should be followed carefully — stay tuned.

Each spring, the Federal Privacy Commissioner submits an annual report to Parliament. The report details any investigations and Commissioner's Findings, complaints, reviews, and court cases that have occurred in the preceding year under the *Privacy Act* and PIPEDA. The annual reports are posted on the Federal Privacy Commissioner's website[12] and are an excellent source of consolidated and up-to-date developments under the Acts.

---

[9] S.C. 2005, c. 50 (not yet proclaimed in force)
[10] Telecom Public Notice CRTC 2006-4.
[11] *Ibid.*
[12] Available online at <http://www.priv.com.gc.ca>.

G. COLLECTING PERSONAL INFORMATION FROM CHILDREN

What about collecting personal information from children? We wish we could provide clear guidance on this issue, but unfortunately, we are left to guess about how the Privacy Commissioner will interpret the Act with respect to children. The reason for the concern is that it is unclear whether children can provide the required informed consent. Are they capable of understanding the implications of sharing their personal information? What if they just want to enter a contest? Is parental consent needed? At law generally, a minor is not capable of entering into a binding contract. Does consent to the collection or use of personal information amount to a contract or does it require a lower threshold?

The only guidance from the Commissioner is a Principle that in certain circumstances parents/legal guardians can give consent on behalf of minors or disabled individuals.[13] The Guidelines also provide that where an individual is a minor, seriously ill or mentally incapacitated, consent *may* be obtained from a legal guardian or person having power of attorney. Despite this, there is nothing with the force of law requiring consent from a legal guardian where consent could otherwise be implied from a minor's action.

The Canadian Marketing Association's Code of Ethics and Standards of Practice includes specific provisions for marketing to children under the age of 13. These provisions require that except for contests, all marketing interactions directed to children including collection, transfer and requests for personal information require the express consent of the child's parent or guardian. Interestingly, the Code contemplates that personal information can be collected from children under 13 for the purposes of a contest, without obtaining the consent of a parent or guardian where certain limitations are placed on the use of the information. These limitations include: that minimal personal information is collected, sufficient only to determine the winners; only the winner's parent/guardian is dealt with, and the winner is not contacted; the personal information is not retained following the conclusion of the contest or sweepstakes; no use is made of the personal information other than to determine the contest or sweepstakes winners; and, the personal information is not transferred or made available to any other individual or organization.

In 2002, the Canadian Marketing Association amended its Code of Ethics and Standards of Practice to address "Special Considerations in Marketing to Teenagers". Teenagers are defined to mean those persons between the ages of 13 and the age of majority in their province or terri-

---

[13] PIPEDA, Schedule 1, s. 4.3.6.

tory of residence. It provides that marketers should not use or collect household or personal information from teenagers as a means to gain entry into the teenager's household.

The Code outlines categories of information that can be collected, used and disclosed with the corresponding types of consent required based on the teenager's age. It defines "contact information" as name, home address, e-mail address and/or home telephone number.

Where a teenager is under 16, marketers can collect and use contact information with the teenager's express consent. But the marketer cannot disclose the contact information to a third party without the express consent of a parent or legal guardian. Any collection, use or disclosure of personal information beyond contact information for a teenager under 16 requires the express consent of a parent or guardian. For teenagers 16 years and over, the Code states that the teenager's express consent is required for the collection, use and disclosure of any of their personal information.

In addition, teenagers must be provided with an easy means to withdraw consent and to end a marketing relationship. The Code obligates marketers to immediately delete all personal and contact information about a teenager if the teenager, parent or guardian withdraws or declines their consent. Marketers are relying on the CMA Code as a general guideline to help ensure compliance when collecting information from children and teenagers.

In some ways more stringent than the approach of the CMA, our neighbours to the south have introduced legislation dealing with the collection of personal information from children under the age of 13. The *Children's Online Privacy Protection Act* (COPPA) requires verifiable parental consent where information is collected from children under 13. Whether the parental consent mechanism used is sufficient to constitute verifiable parental consent will depend on the intended use of the child's personal information. Obviously, this legislation only deals with online collection, and there are several exceptions to the rule. For instance, parental/guardian consent is not required for a child under 13 to enter into a contest provided that all that is collected is the child's email address and the only contact is to notify them of the contest winners. Children's email addresses must be deleted as soon as the contest ends.

How can marketers demonstrate that the consent they have obtained is from a parent/guardian and not from a clever 12-year-old? It is almost impossible but a strong argument can be made that you, as a marketer, are taking all reasonable steps to ensure the protection of children's personal information. Marketers might consider conducting random telephone checks to verify that parents did, in fact, consent.

H.   THE PROVINCES

As indicated above, to date, only Alberta, British Columbia and Quebec have privacy legislation which is "substantially similar" to the federal Act. The federal Act, as mentioned above, applies to personal information collected in the course of commercial activity in the private sector as of January 1, 2004 if provinces do not enact substantially similar legislation. The federal government can grant exemptions to some activities and classes of information, while not to others. Therefore, a province can enact legislation regarding certain matters (such as health information) thereby being exempt in that area from the application of the federal Act, yet the federal Act could still apply to other areas of activity where there is no exemption. Ultimately, this parallel compliance infrastructure may well create some problems of enforcement and complaint handling.

The existing general privacy legislation in most provinces applies to the protection of personal information collected, used or disclosed by public bodies and most provinces have enacted legislation dealing with health information and electronic transactions (such as the use of electronic signatures). Early in 2002, Ontario released the *Draft Privacy of Personal Information Act*. Upon release, the Ministry of Consumer and Business Services in consultation with the Ministry of Health, encouraged stakeholders and members of the public to submit written comments regarding the draft bill. Based on the public comments, the government indicated that it would make substantial changes to the draft legislation. New legislation was never tabled.

Quebec has had privacy legislation regarding the private sector in force since 1994 (*An Act Respecting the Protection of Personal Information in the Private Sector*). Quebec is already exempt from the application of the federal Act. In addition, the Quebec *Charter of Human Rights and Freedoms* recognizes privacy as a human right, and the *Civil Code* (articles 35 to 41) guarantees the right to privacy.

In Alberta, the *Personal Information Protection Act* (PIPA Alberta)[14] came into force January 1, 2004. Similarly, in British Columbia, the *Personal Information Protection Act* (PIPA B.C.)[15] also came into force on the same date. Both statutes are very similar and build upon PIPEDA. In fact, to some extent, the drafters of the Alberta and B.C. privacy statutes attempted to rectify some of the deficiencies in PIPEDA. For example, both PIPA Alberta and PIPA B.C. contain some exemptions for the need to obtain consent for the disclosure of personal information in the case of a sale of a business or its business assets.

---

[14]   S.A. 2003, c. P-6.5.

[15]   S.B.C. 2003, c. 63.

I.   PRIVACY ISSUES SOUTH OF THE BORDER

1.   COPPA

The *Children's Online Privacy Protection Act* came into effect in April 2000. The general intent of the Act is to give parents control over what information is collected from their children online. Website operators who collect information from children under 13 (even if the site is targeted at a general audience) must provide parents with notice of their information practices; allow parents to review the personal information collected from their child; allow parents the opportunity to prevent further use of personal information already collected from a child or that will be collected from a child in the future; limit the collection of personal information from a child to that information that is reasonably necessary for the activity the child is pursuing on the website; and maintain reasonable procedures to protect the confidentiality, security and integrity of personal information collected.

Most importantly, COPPA requires that, with certain specific exceptions, before collecting, using or disclosing personal information from a child, the website operator must receive verifiable parental consent for such collection, use or disclosure. A sliding scale approach to acceptable verifiable parental consent was established by the Federal Trade Commission and was initially intended to apply until April 2002. The sliding scale has now been extended indefinitely.

In situations where a child's personal information is only used for internal purposes (*i.e.*, not shared with third parties or made publicly availably through chat rooms or bulletin boards), the "email plus" method of obtaining consent is sufficient. In such cases, an email can be sent to the parent containing the required notice and request consent by return email. However, some additional, confirmatory steps are required after receiving the parent's email. The FTC suggests sending another email to the parent after a reasonable time delay to confirm consent, or ask the parent in the initial email to reply with their phone number or mailing address so that consent can be confirmed by phone or postal mail. Where a child's information will be disclosed to third parties or made publicly available, the operator must use stricter measures, described by the FTC as "the most reliable methods available" to obtain parental consent. In those cases, parental consent must be recorded, subject to limited exceptions, by a verifiable means such as offline communication by telephone, fax or mail, by an e-mail accompanied by a secure electronic signature or by accepting a credit card number in connection with an online transaction.

COPPA includes certain exceptions to the requirement for parental consent, for example, where a child or parent's e-mail address is collected and used to provide notice and seek consent or where a company responds to a one-time request from a child and deletes the personal information immediately thereafter. Contest entries are thought to fall within the latter exception. A further exception, known as the *multiple-contact exception*, applies where the child's email address is collected to provide a child with a subscription to an online newsletter or notices of site updates. In this case, the operator must send a notice to the parent's email address after the first communication with the child, allowing them to opt out of the information collection and require the operator to delete the child's email address and stop contacting the child.

The FTC issued a wake up call to marketers reminding them of the importance of complying with COPPA. In October, 2001 the Federal Trade Commission (FTC) reached a settlement with Lisa Frank Inc., a company selling toys and school supplies aimed at girls, for violation of the *Children's Online Privacy Protection Act* (COPPA). The website, <http://www.lisafrank.com>, collected personal information, such as names, phone numbers, birth dates, street and e-mail addresses, from children before allowing the children to visit many of the areas of the site. Under COPPA, website operators cannot collect personal information from children under 13 without first obtaining verifiable parental consent — <http://www.lisafrank.com> did not first seek parental consent. The website further violated COPPA by failing to offer direct notice to parents about the company's data protection practices and by failing to notify parents that parental consent was required under law. Lisa Frank Inc., as a result of the settlement, had to pay $30,000 U.S. in civil fines and is required to provide a link to the FTC website's pages regarding COPPA on <http://www.lisafrank.com>.

Unless a website expressly prohibits American children from using the site, the requirements of COPPA must be met before personal information can be collected from children.

2.   Living with Your Privacy Policy

Almost everyone in marketing has heard about the "TOYSMART" fiasco, which has taught all of us some lessons about the importance of living with the privacy policies that we place on our websites.

In 1999, Toysmart began advertising, promoting and selling toys on the internet at <http://www.toysmart.com>. In September of that year, Toysmart became a licensee of TRUSTe, an organization that certifies the privacy policies of online businesses and allows the businesses to display a TRUSTe seal (see discussion below about privacy certifications).

As of September 1999, the privacy policy posted on http://www.toysmart.com stated that personal information voluntarily submitted online was never shared with a third party and was used only to personalize the customer's online experience. The Toysmart site collected detailed information online, including names, addresses, billing information, shopping preferences, family profiles, names and children's birthdays.

On May 22, 2000, Toysmart announced that it had ceased operations and was bankrupt. At the same time, it began soliciting bids for purchase of its assets — including the customer lists — to pay off some of its $18 million debt. TRUSTe notified the Federal Trade Commission (FTC) and the FTC sought injunctive relief (based on a violation of the prohibition against "unfair or deceptive acts or practices in or affecting commerce") to prevent the sale of confidential, customer information in violation of Toysmart's own privacy policy. FTC argued that Toysmart had made a representation to consumers that information would never be shared with third parties and then disclosed and offered to sell the information. FTC also argued that Toysmart's conduct would injure consumers by invading their privacy. The Chairman of the FTC said that even failing dot-coms must abide by their promise to protect the privacy rights of their customers. The case was settled with Toysmart's agreement that it would only sell its customer list as part of a package that included the entire website and only to a "qualified buyer", an entity in a related market that agreed to abide by the privacy statement.

Disney ultimately saved the day. Buena Vista Internet Group, a subsidiary of Walt Disney Co. and a 60 per cent owner of Toysmart, offered Toysmart $50,000 if Toysmart destroyed its customer list rather than sell it to a competitor. Apparently, the situation was somewhat embarrassing for Disney, which had lobbied the FTC against the passage of stricter privacy laws, insisting that the industry was capable of protecting consumer privacy without government intervention.

The law is unable to keep up with the current pace of technological change on the internet, but online business and online transactions continue to move ahead. The legal issues become particularly complicated when parties to an online transaction reside in different jurisdictions and when those jurisdictions have different, little or no legal protections in the area of privacy. Despite the lag in legal developments, internet users are still looking for a means of assurance that their privacy interests are being protected in the course of their online transactions. To address online privacy concerns, a number of organizations have developed Web Seals. Web Seals are awarded to businesses that adhere to established online privacy policies. Once awarded the Seal, the business may then post the Web Seal on their website in conjunction with their online privacy policies. Businesses must pay fees to license the use of the Web Seal and are assessed regularly to ensure compliance with the policies and procedures. The Web Seal companies provide businesses with the use of their alternative dispute resolution processes in order to settle consumer complaints and disputes. Some of the leading online privacy seals include: BBBOnLine, TRUSTe and WebTrust.

Another internet related privacy concern arises from the use of "cookies" on websites. If a company employs "cookies", it should clearly state so in its privacy policy.

J.   FUTURE DEVELOPMENTS

In recent years, Canada has reacted to the privacy concerns of its citizens and the privacy initiatives of other countries. Provincial and Federal legislation has been enacted to provide comprehensive privacy protection and privacy has become a national compliance matter for most organizations. In the future, we can expect to see more court actions and more Commissioner's Findings under the federal PIPEDA Act and under provincial privacy legislation which will lead to a growing jurisprudence, interpretation and better understanding of these laws. In addition, some privacy commissioners are taking a leadership role not only in Canada, but on the global stage, examining new and emerging privacy issues, new technologies and their implications for both government and the private sector.[16] For organizations that are structuring privacy compliance programs, it is not only legal departments that need to be involved. Participation and input is required from marketing, sales, human resources, operations and information technology personnel.

Since September 11, 2001, the public's desire for privacy has been somewhat overshadowed by its desire for safety. However, while individuals may be willing to allow certain limitations on their privacy (and maybe even carry around identification cards at all times), the expectations of privacy with respect to the use of personal information by private organizations are unlikely to change. This is especially true given new and fascinating advances in technology, such as biometrics and RFID (radio frequency identification) and greater opportunities for collecting and storing highly sensitive personal data. It is in these new emerging fields that some of the most dynamic privacy concerns will arise. The combination of improvements in software and applications that can benefit individuals and companies in research and facilitate data sharing, also pose security challenges for those who are concerned about maintaining the integrity of data and keeping it away from unintended eyes. These new applications when combined with legislative developments (such as the U.S. *Patriot Act*) have some civil libertarians crying foul over potential abuses regarding the use of personal information.

---

[16] In 2005-2006, the Privacy Commissioner's office released very practical guidelines on secure retention of personal information as well as facts and myths surrounding RFID, available on-line at <http://www.ipc.on.ca>.

Chapter 17

UNIQUELY QUEBEC ISSUES

Contributed by Andre Rivest

A. INTRODUCTION

In Chapter 1 we noted that advertising law is difficult to encapsulate because it deals with a large number of legal issues. Nowhere is this more apparent than in Quebec where a different legal environment exists and where active consumer groups proliferate. When advertising in Quebec, the most important piece of legislation is Quebec's *Consumer Protection Act* (CPA)[1] which applies to every contract for goods or services between consumers and merchants and which also regulates certain business practices. It goes without saying that anyone who does business in Quebec should be aware of this legislation. This chapter provides an overview of the CPA's most relevant provisions and of the *Charter of the French Language*,[2] the other unique piece of legislation in Quebec.

B. THE QUEBEC CONSUMER PROTECTION ACT

1. Purpose of Consumer Protection Act

The purchase of goods and services involves many legal issues. In the first place, a contractual relationship is created between the seller and the consumer. Initially, under the *Civil Code of Quebec*[3] the common law regulated this kind of relationship. However, as the power of information continued to favour merchants, and as consumers became increasingly vulnerable to complex offers, it became obvious that consumers needed more protection. Government regulators believed that under the common law regime, consumers were not sufficiently informed about products and services and were being seduced by advertising into making impul-

---

[1]   R.S.Q., c. P-40.1.
[2]   R.S.Q., c. C-11.
[3]   S.Q. 1991, c. 64.

sive decisions. The Quebec government therefore intervened and enacted the CPA to protect consumers by:

- regulating the contractual relationship between merchant and consumer; and
- regulating trade practices, including advertising, to ensure that consumers' buying decisions would not be based on frivolous and misleading information.

The *Civil Code of Quebec* has its own provisions concerning consumer consent. However, the relentless nature of advertising made the general principles in the *Code* ineffective. The CPA was enacted to address the need for increased consumer protection and represented an attempt to equalize the power between merchants, advertisers and the average consumer.

On December 22, 1978, the CPA was enacted by Quebec's National Assembly. Basically, the latest version of the CPA imposes a filter between sellers and consumers. The Act's central objectives are to compensate for the inadequacies of the *Civil Code*, address the modern realities of advertising and combat false and misleading marketing practices in the province of Quebec.

The CPA goes further than the *Civil Code* in regulating the relationship between sellers and consumers. Chapter II of the CPA deals with Business Practices and has mandatory rules with which businesses making representations to the public must comply. By regulating representations made to consumers, the CPA is involved in the pre-contractual stage of the relationship.

Article 219 of the CPA bluntly sets the tone of Chapter II:

> No merchant, manufacturer or advertiser may, by any means whatever, make false or misleading representations to a consumer.

This wording is strikingly similar to section 74.01(1) of the federal *Competition Act*. This aspect of consumer protection imposes strict requirements concerning the quality and accuracy of information contained in advertising.

Although similar to other provincial consumer protection and advertising-specific laws, the CPA's requirements are generally more stringent. The CPA also creates requirements that are particular to the Province of Quebec.

The Quebec *Consumer Protection Act* is more stringent than consumer protection legislation in other provinces both in terms of content and enforcement. The Act contains a unique prohibition on advertising to children and other provisions which limit business practices — such as credit advertising — which could be detrimental to consumers. These provisions are discussed in detail in this chapter. Equally important is the active role played by the Quebec Consumer Protection Office in enforcing the Act.

2.   To Whom and When Does the CPA Apply?

We cannot proceed without knowing to whom and in what circumstances the CPA applies. Let's look at the definitions of the key terms. A consumer is defined in section 1(e) as "a natural person, except a merchant who obtains goods or services for the purpose of his business". As for merchant, it is defined as any person doing business or extending credit in the course of business.

As for the scope of the Act, section 2 reads as follows: "This Act applies to every contract for goods or services entered into between a consumer and a merchant in the course of his business." Since this chapter is mostly concerned with Chapter II of the CPA, regarding Business Practices, it is important to note that Chapter II also applies to manufacturers and advertisers. With respect to advertisers, section 1(m) defines them as "a person who prepares, publishes or broadcasts an advertisement or who causes an advertisement to be prepared, published or broadcast".

In summary, anyone who, as a merchant, manufacturer or advertiser, advertises or sells products or services to consumers in the province of Quebec is governed by this legislation.

3.   Legislative Intervention

One way the CPA protects consumers is by imposing standards with respect to the quality of information provided to consumers by sellers, manufacturers and advertisers. By getting a fair and accurate description of the product, consumers, whether they intend to buy or not, are in a better position to make sound decisions and avoid being overwhelmed by advertising and misleading and/or overreaching information. The CPA establishes minimum requirements with respect to the quantity and quality of information provided in all representations to the public, including advertisements.

4.   Labelling

Consumers cannot easily escape information on product labels. The CPA imposes certain regulatory requirements concerning labels. These requirements complement several other statutes including the federal *Packaging and Labelling Act*, and certain provisions in the *Charter of the French Language*.

Labelling is a form of "representation" to the public, as are print or television advertisements. Therefore, it is important to keep in mind that the general principles discussed in this chapter regarding representations to consumers, apply equally to product labels as they do to any other form of advertising.

C.   DUTY TO INFORM AND TO COMPLY WITH REPRESENTATIONS MADE ABOUT PRODUCTS

1.   Duty To Inform

The CPA imposes on sellers, manufacturers and advertisers, a duty to inform consumers about product characteristics. This is only fair, since sellers and manufacturers have the most knowledge about the characteristics of their products. Conversely, consumers are faced with many options and do not have the time or means to figure out everything there is to know about the products or services they intend to buy. The duty to inform is found in Article 228 of the CPA. It requires the disclosure of any "important fact" about the product in question.

2.   Compliance

As for compliance with representations made, advertisers should keep in mind that manufacturers will be bound by any representations they make. According to Article 41, "[t]he goods or services provided must conform to the statements or advertisements regarding them made by the merchant or the manufacturer. The statements or the advertisements are binding on that merchant or that manufacturer". For instance, a vehicle manufacturer is bound by representations of the horsepower of its vehicles published in flyers it distributes through its dealership network. Therefore, any claims in advertising or labelling must accurately depict and describe a product or service.

Effectively, these Articles create a statutory warranty for consumers. If this warranty is breached, consumers can take advantage of the remedies set out in Article 272. Product claims which do not accurately describe a product (or service) can lead to many remedies including specific performance of any promise made by the merchant or cancellation of the consumer contract and exemplary damages.

There is a great deal of case law on these Articles, especially within the travel industry where consumers realize once they are standing before a resort under construction, that they did not buy the romantic getaway advertised in the glossy posters at the travel agency. Examples of similar discrepancies easily come to mind: a motorcycle whose use, contrary to the terms of the contract, is prohibited by regulations; a dog that turns out to be a different breed from the one advertised; or a couch made from cow's skin instead of calf's skin as advertised in a brochure.

The concept of "conformity" contained in Articles 40 and 41 is not legally complex. Its application depends on the specific facts, *i.e.*, what the product really is as opposed to what is advertised. Any advertiser would be well advised not to stray too far from the line between objective reality and the embellishing tendencies of advertising.

3.   Warranty Representations

According to Article 43, once a warranty is made, no matter the form, the manufacturer or the merchant will be bound by it. This provision is an example of the obligation of "conformity" set out in Articles 40 and 41. Merchants and manufacturers must stand behind their representations and claims since consumer purchase decisions are often a direct consequence of product or service representations, claims and warranties. Article 253 creates a presumption that a consumer's consent is in fact a result of warranties that are given.

D.   PROHIBITED BUSINESS PRACTICES

As discussed, Chapter II applies to all representations made by sellers, manufacturers or advertisers to consumers. In addition, its provisions take effect before a contract between the seller and consumer has been concluded. The purpose of the following provisions is to strengthen the relationship between consumers and merchants by ensuring valid consumer consent through the provision of proper information. This section examines how the legislation protects consumers from fraudulent and misleading representations.

1.   What Is A Representation?

Article 216 provides that a representation includes an affirmation, a behaviour or an omission. Article 218 further addresses the loopholes that are created from combinations of words in ads that can lead to numerous impressions and several meanings. This Article states that "to determine whether or not a representation constitutes a prohibited practice", the general impression it conveys, and the literal meaning of the terms used must be taken into account. Thus, Article 218 ensures that it is harder for deceptive marketers to trick consumers with misleading representations. The principles reflected in this Article are similar to the "general impression test" principles found under the federal *Competition Act*.

For example, if a representation gives the impression that an item will be free when, in fact, it is not, it will be prohibited (*e.g.*, an ad states that if a consumer buys a bed for $359, he will get a second one free. If, in reality, the regular price for one bed is $180, it is false to claim that the second one is free.) Another example is an ad which states that, with the purchase of a VCR, consumers will receive coupons worth $300 towards video rentals, without including important restrictions relating to the coupons. Such restrictions must always be included or the impression left by the ad will be misleading.

2.   False or Misleading Representations

As set out earlier in this chapter, Article 219 says that "no merchant, manufacturer or advertiser may, by any means whatever, make false or misleading representations to a consumer". It essentially serves as a "catch-all" provision. The articles that follow set out specific examples of false or misleading representations and there is a certain amount of overlap.

Interpretation of Article 219 has shown that "intention" is not a relevant factor; that is, it does not matter whether the representation was made in good faith or not. All representations must give an accurate impression of the goods or services in question. Moreover, every representation, whether it involves a principal or a secondary attribute of the good or service, is governed by this Article.

Examples of the application of Article 219 are endless. For example, Article 219 prohibits such things as a "business-boosting" claim by an employment agency that they have a list of employers in need of employees or a representation in a direct mail piece that the recipient has won a major prize when in fact, almost every recipient of the piece will receive a prize of very low value.

To sum up the case law and the principles established under Article 219, there is a general requirement that all claims regarding the price, quality, quantity, nature, age, attributes and value of goods or services be accurate. Any representation that has the capacity to mislead is prohibited.

3.   The Nature of the Goods

Article 220 contains the first specific prohibition regarding representations. Basically, this Article requires that advertisers and manufacturers present products and services for what they truly are. Prohibited behaviour includes attributing qualities to, or embellishing the nature of the product, in order to make it seem more attractive, resulting in the consumer getting less than expected. It is one thing to display the best features of a product and, to a certain extent, "puff it up", but it is quite another to attribute qualities to a product that it does not possess.

For example, do not try to sell a trailer by claiming it could be a second home when in reality, it is unfit for year-round use. In addition, it is

contrary to the spirit of this section of the CPA to create false expectations for hair-challenged men by representing a product as stimulating
hair-growth when it does not have this effect (not to mention the *Food &
Drugs Act* restrictions with respect to such a claim).

It is also contrary to Article 220 to claim that a heat pump will help
reduce the heating costs when evidence does not support such a claim;
or, to state that a government subsidy will cover the price of a purchased
good when this is not true.

If, through any form of representation, a disparity is created between a
consumer's expectations and reality, the advertiser may be in breach of
Article 220. Of course, the purpose of advertising is to paint a favourable
picture of the advertised goods, but the CPA limits this practice and
requires that consumers get a valid idea of what they are paying for. The
bottom-line is: the CPA restricts a no-holds barred approach to advertising. Contracts formed on the basis of unacceptable claims will be nulli-
fied and sellers, manufacturers and advertisers may incur penal liability.

4.   The Physical Description of Products

Although they are very similar, there is a difference between Article 221
and Article 220. While Article 220 prohibits the attribution of non-
existent or misleading characteristics to a product or service, Article 221
relates to the accuracy of the physical description. Article 221 states that:

No merchant, manufacturer or advertiser may, *falsely*, by any means whatever,

(a) hold out that goods or services include certain parts, components or ingredients;

(b) hold out that goods have a particular dimension, weight, size or volume;

(c) hold out that goods are of a specified standard;

(d) represent that goods are of a particular category, type, model, or year of manufacture;

(e) hold out that goods are new, reconditioned or used to a specific degree;

(f) claim that goods have particular antecedents or have been used for a particular
purpose;

(g) ascribe certain performance characteristics to goods or services.

Articles 220 and 221 are examples of the general prohibition against
misleading advertising set out in Article 219. For example, while Article
220 prevents a company from claiming that its laundry detergent provides the best colour-guard protection, Article 221 prevents the same
company from falsely claiming that the product contains particular ingredients or meets certain performance standards. Simply put, Article
221 specifically requires that advertisers and marketers do not represent
products as including something they do not, or comply with certain
standards they do not comply with.

5.   Collateral Representations

In the same spirit, Article 222 sets out further restrictions concerning how a product can be represented. Article 222 doesn't deal with the intrinsic physical characteristics of products; rather it prohibits the following: falsely leading consumers to believe that they are purchasing under certain circumstances (bankruptcy, clearance sale, *etc*.); unfairly depicting a competitive product or service or depreciating another product or service (fair and accurate comparative claims are allowed); falsely representing that a product has been handled or services have been rendered; falsely stating that a product has been made according to a certain method or standards; falsely claiming that a certain product or service is essential (*i.e.*, you need to buy x to get y); or falsely claiming that there is only a certain quantity (*i.e.*, only 50 left) available.

6.   Price Claims

Article 224 tackles another kind of possible misrepresentation: those related to price. As far as the buying behaviour of consumers is concerned, price plays a central role. Therefore, it is fundamental that price claims be truthful in order to ensure that consumer consent to buy is valid. The provisions relating to price and deceptive marketing practices in section 74 of the *Competition Act* have the same objectives.

The CPA requires that the price of products and services be placed in context. For instance, pursuant to Article 224(a), you cannot merely refer to the price of a single volume of an encyclopedia, you must indicate the price of the whole encyclopedia set, and the price of the whole set must be as prominently advertised as the price of a single unit. With respect to periodic payments, Article 224(b) allows single periodic payments to be advertised as long as the sum of these periodic payments is advertised with *greater* prominence. Finally, 224(c) states that you cannot ask for a price that is higher than the advertised price.

Article 225 adds additional restrictions concerning price claims. Article 225 prohibits any misleading or false statements relating to price. The price advertised must be the price to be paid. You cannot use invalid prices as bait and then impose a greater price. Moreover, you cannot lead a consumer to think he or she is getting a price reduction or other advantage when, in fact, he or she is not.

7.   Warranties

Article 227 requires manufacturers and sellers to make valid representations concerning the existence, scope and duration of warranties on goods. The terms and conditions of a warranty must be clearly stated. The terms and conditions of a warranty are second only to price as a selling point for goods or services. Without a solid warranty, many consumers wouldn't purchase goods or services. Under the CPA, a contract that was formed because of a misrepresentation regarding a warranty may be cancelled.

8. Disclosure of Important Factors

As previously stated, Article 228 imposes a general requirement that important facts be disclosed. It is difficult to define what is meant by the term "important facts". This term is defined on a case-by-case basis. We can nevertheless say that any information which, had it been known by the consumer at the appropriate time, and which would have influenced his or her decision to purchase, constitutes an "important fact". According to the case law, the term "important facts" is given a broad interpretation and should be read in the context of Articles 220, 221, 222, 224 and 225. The prohibited practices in these Articles give a good indication of what might be considered an "important fact". The end result is that every advertiser and marketer should ask him or herself: "What information about our product would influence the decision of a reasonable consumer who wants to make an informed purchase decision?"

9. Business Opportunities

Article 229 prohibits the making of false representations concerning the profitability of a business opportunity offered to consumers. This Article draws upon the principle highlighted in Article 220(b) which prevents making utopian profit claims to influence consumer purchase decisions. Article 229 extends the protection of the CPA beyond the definition of "consumer" in Article 1(e), to persons who obtain goods or services for the purposes of their business.

When making profitability claims regarding a good or service, the profit must be reasonable and attainable. Otherwise, such a representation will be contrary to the CPA because the consumer's decision to purchase will have been based on invalid information.

10. Unsolicited Goods

Article 230(a) of the CPA prohibits an advertiser, marketer or manufacturer from sending a consumer products he or she did not order and subsequently demanding payment for the product. This sales practice usually involves giving the consumer the option of sending the product back. In practice, however, many consumers agree to be charged for the product in order to avoid the hassle of sending it back. Article 230(b) prevents the use of false pretexts in these circumstances. For instance, an advertiser or merchant cannot justify a "sale of unsolicited goods" by falsely claiming that the sale is for an educational or charitable purpose.

11. Insufficient Quantity

Article 231 states that advertisers cannot advertise a good or service when the availability cannot meet public demand unless the advertising mentions the limited supply and the exact quantities that are available. If the advertiser fails to mention the limited supply, he or she can avoid accountability by proving he or she had reason to believe that the demand could be satisfied, or that consumers could be provided with a similar product at a similar price. This provision prevents the practice of attracting customers to one's store by advertising sale products which exist in small quantities and which sell out fast, in the hope that "trapped" consumers will purchase something else. This prohibited practice is known as "bait and switch" selling. The *Competition Act* contains a similar bait and switch prohibition. The bottom line with Article 231 is, before advertising your products, make sure you have enough to satisfy demand. If supplies are limited you must identify the available quantities.

12. Emphasis on Premiums

Article 232 prevents placing more emphasis on a premium than on the good or service associated with the premium. For example, an advertisement is in breach of this Article when the premium (free installation, free cleaning, rebates on other products, *etc.*) that accompanies the products is given greater time or space in an ad. When things are advertised as "free" or premiums are given away upon purchase, the advertising regarding the underlying product must be given at least as great an emphasis.

13. Terms and Conditions For Obtaining Gifts

Article 233 dictates that when offering any kind of rebate, gift or premium through a promotion or sweepstakes, all the terms and conditions for obtaining the gift or rebate must be included in the ad such as answering a mathematic skill-testing question. This is a complement to section 74.06 of the *Competition Act* and to the *Act respecting lotteries, publicity contests and amusement machines* since both impose greater disclosure requirements on contest advertising. Once again, transparency is paramount.

14. Distortion of Meaning, Data or Analyses

According to Article 239, if a claim is supported by an opinion, data, testimony or research, the claim must not distort the underlying substantiation. In addition, Article 239 prohibits false claims that information has a scientific basis. Consumers often rely upon the opinion of a neutral third party to evaluate the quality of goods or services. Scientific support adds credibility to a product or service. It is important that quotes and scientific claims used in advertising accurately reflect the opinions or research upon which they are based.

15. Merchant's Identity

Article 242 states that merchants must include their name and the fact that they are merchants in all advertisements. Article 243 requires that if an ad includes an address, a post office box isn't enough and the entire address must be given. These provisions ensure that consumers know they are dealing with a merchant and where that merchant is located.

16. Status of the Merchant, Manufacturer or Advertiser

Article 238 limits the representations that manufacturers, merchants or advertisers can make about themselves. Once again, truth is mandatory; merchants/manufacturers/advertisers cannot depict themselves as having characteristics or qualities they do not possess, for example, by falsely claiming to be supported or endorsed by a particular organization.

E. CREDIT ADVERTISING

Articles 244 to 247 deal with advertising in the context of credit. The CPA requires that credit advertising disclose as much information as possible regarding the financing arrangement. The CPA imposes restrictions and obligations when credit is part of the consumer-merchant contract.

1. Credit Disclosure

Article 244 requires that any claim regarding the availability of credit must be made according to the prescribed form. Section 80 of the *Regulation respecting the application of the Consumer Protection Act*[4] is adopted under the CPA and sets out the required disclosure: the identity of the credit supplier must be disclosed so that the consumer knows who

---

[4]   R.S.Q., c. P-40.1, r. 1

is party to the financing contract. Section 80 states that an ad may only mention the availability of credit in one or more of the following ways: by stating the name or corporate symbol of the credit company; by using the expression "credit offered", "credit accepted" or "credit available"; or by illustrating a credit card.

2.   Urging Consumers To Use Credit

Article 245 adds that credit cannot be advertised with pictures of the products that can be purchased on credit, nor can credit advertising "urge" consumers to purchase particular goods or services on credit. In one case, a financial institution was found to have contravened Article 245 because summer vacations were pictured in credit card advertising. This provision ensures that consumers won't be distracted from the implications of purchasing on credit. In light of the possible constitutional invalidity of this provision, there appears to have been a moratorium on the enforcement of this provision by the Quebec Consumer Protection Office during the last few years. However, it does not follow that a private plaintiff could not rely on this provision.

Article 246 deals with the credit rate that must be disclosed in credit ads. This credit rate must be calculated in accordance with the CPA and must take into account any rebate the consumer would be entitled to if he or she paid cash. The calculation of the rate must also take into consideration any rebate the merchant may be entitled to from the manufacturer on the basis of the cash sales.

3.   Terms and Conditions of Credit

Article 247 stipulates that any representation, with the exception of the interest rate, concerning credit must comply with the conditions prescribed in the Regulations. The Regulations require that if one term or condition of the credit arrangement is advertised, with the exception of the interest rate, all of the applicable terms and conditions must be disclosed in order to give consumers a complete and accurate picture of what is offered.

4.   Long-term Leases

Article 247.1 follows the same principle found in the previous sections on contracts of credit. Long-term leases are similar to instalment sales and the CPA ensures that consumers involved in long-term leases know the implications. Article 247.1 states that every ad regarding long-term leases must specify that a lease is involved and must comply with the prescribed Regulations (86.1 to 86.3). The Regulations require the disclosure of all the terms and conditions of a long-term lease, so that consumers can assess the consequences of entering into such a contractual relationship. The Regulations do not make a distinction on the basis of the medium involved; that is, all elements must be disclosed whether the advertising is made in print, on the radio, on television or on the internet.

5.   Advertising To Children Under 13

True to its main objective, namely the protection of vulnerable consumers, the CPA strictly regulates advertising to the most vulnerable group, children. Articles 248 and 249 refer to other provisions and regulations and prohibit advertising directed at children under the age of 13. However, these Articles are subject to several exceptions. For a complete overview on this issue, please see Chapter 6.

6.   Ads Involving Government Cheques

Article 250 deals with the protection of another vulnerable category — those living on welfare. It prohibits any representation that a merchant accepts or exchanges cheques remitted by the government.

F.   REMOTE-PARTY CONTRACTS

Remote-party contracts are a popular selling method. Most of the time, advertising is done at a distance, followed by the conclusion of a contract where both parties are physically present. This is not the case in remote-party contracts where the advertising, the offer and the acceptance are made while both parties remain at a distance. The definition of remote-party contracts is found in Article 20 of the CPA. Examples of this type of contract include direct-mail and telemarketing sales. Often consumers don't have enough information to give a clear and informed consent. Moreover, misrepresentations can be difficult to detect.

Anyone selling goods or services using these methods is governed by specific CPA provisions. First, Article 21 will deem the contract to have been entered into at the consumer's address thus making the contractual relationship subject to the CPA. Second, Article 22 states that the seller cannot ask for payment before it has fulfilled its obligations. For example, a merchant cannot ask for payment before delivery of a product unless they post a bond for security which is intended to cover the cost of the item. An example of an offer that would be affected by this provision is "send in 3 UPC codes plus $4.00 shipping and handling to get a free DVD". Because the consumer is required to pay shipping and handling before receiving the product, the merchant must post a bond in Quebec.

The remote-party contracts provisions of the CPA will apply to anyone selling in the Province of Quebec.

G. CONTRACTS ENTERED INTO BY ITINERANT MERCHANTS

An itinerant merchant sells products or services elsewhere than at his or her permanent address: *e.g.*, door-to-door salespeople. This is a marketing method that generates unique problems. The physical proximity between the merchant and consumer may make it hard to refuse an offer. As well, comparative shopping is impossible in a door-to-door selling situation. Having no permanent business location, the itinerant merchant may be difficult to locate if problems occur. Therefore, Articles 56 and 57 establish special rules which govern contracts of sale and service entered into by itinerant merchants.

H. DUTY TO INFORM

Article 58 lists the mandatory information that must be included in every contract between a consumer and an itinerant merchant. This Article states that the contract must be in writing and indicate: the itinerant merchant's permit number; the name, address and telephone number of each establishment of the itinerant merchant in Quebec; a description and the quantity of the goods, the duration of each service provided; the total amount the consumer must pay under the contract; the terms and conditions of payment; the frequency and dates for all deliveries of goods; and the rights granted to the consumer to cancel the contract. Failure to comply with this provision and with the Regulations it refers to, may nullify the contract.

Article 59 gives the consumer a discretionary right to cancel the contract within ten days following receipt of his or her copy of the contract. This provision is unique to itinerant merchant contracts; it gives the consumer a fast track to get out of the contractual relationship for any reason whatsoever.

I. CHARTER OF THE FRENCH LANGUAGE

The province of Quebec is a distinct society within Canada because it is French-speaking. Although many Quebeckers understand and speak English, French is the mother tongue of the vast majority of Quebec residents and the principal language of communication in the Province.

When the Parti Québecois took power in 1976, one of their first priorities was to safeguard the French language in Quebec. There are approximately eight million French-speaking Quebec residents surrounded by over 300 million English speakers in Canada and the United States. There was concern that without protection, the unique nature of Quebec society, which is founded on the French language, would be diluted over time. Hence the enactment in 1978 of the *Charter of the French Language*. The Charter makes French the sole official language of Quebec and requires all communications in Quebec, from contracts to employment situations, to signage and advertising to be solely in French or in limited circumstances, in French and another language (usually English) provided that the French portion has either equal or greater prominence.

The Charter establishes French as the language of the legislature and the courts, the civil administration, labour relations, education and commerce and business in Quebec. The Charter's provisions are enforced by the Office de la langue française which investigates non-compliant actions on its own initiative or pursuant to consumer and competitor complaints. The valuable role of the Charter and of the Office in Quebec cannot be overstated. The majority of Quebeckers value the role of the French language in their culture and the Office actively enforces the Charter.

For advertisers and marketers who sell products or services in Quebec, the Charter's critical provisions are those which make French the language of commerce and business in Quebec.

The key provisions are the following:

Section 51:

Every inscription on a product, on its container or on its wrapping, or on a document or object supplied with it, including the directions for use and warranty certificates, must be drafted in French...

The French inscription may be accompanied with a translation or translations, but no inscription in another language may be given greater prominence than that in French.

Section 58:

Public signs and posters and commercial advertising must be in French. They may also be both in French and in another language provided that French is markedly predominant.

Section 51 requires that all packaging and labelling in Quebec, including shipping containers and other materials intended for institutions and the trade, must include a French translation of equal prominence, of all non-French text. This rule applies to product inserts, brochures and other materials that accompany products sold in Quebec. The rule also applies to text on the products themselves, such as a stickers and instruments and dials on household appliances.

The "equal prominence" rule does not necessarily require that French text on packaging and labelling be in the same size type. It generally takes more words to translate an English phrase into French. Therefore, the "equal prominence" requirement is met if the French text occupies the same area as the English text provided the French text has equal billing in terms of placement on the package, colour contrast and other features of visibility.

The *Regulation concerning the language of commerce and business*[5] sets out certain exemptions to the requirements of Section 51. Two of the most important exemptions are trade-marks and "permanently engraved inscriptions". Trade-marks do not have to be translated into French provided that a French version of the trade-mark has not been registered. "Permanently engraved" inscriptions — such as the "Play" and "Eject/Stop" markings on DVD players — do not have to be translated provided that these inscriptions do not relate to safety.

Section 58 requires that public signs, posters, point-of-sale materials and commercial advertising be either in French or bilingual with the French text being "markedly predominant". "Markedly predominant" means that the French text must occupy at least two thirds of the area of posters, point-of sale and other in-store materials.

The *Regulation concerning the language of commerce and business* also sets out exemptions to Section 58. The most important of these is the exemption for non-French media. English-only advertising is legal on English television and radio stations and in English newspapers and magazines. In addition, it is legal to mail or email English-only communications to a Quebec resident if they have requested English-only materials.

The *Charter of the French Language* requires careful consideration by any manufacturer or advertiser who intends to carry on business in Quebec. There are a large number of marketing situations which may require different treatment in Quebec. For example:

*   Websites should be in French as well as English if the website operator has a place of business in Quebec and sells products or services in Quebec.
*   Billboards and other outdoor signs must be exclusively in French unless they are located on company property in which case they must be predominantly French.
*   Catalogues, brochures and similar publications may appear in two versions: one French and one non-French, provided that the French version is equally accessible.

[5] R.S.Q., c. C-11, r. 9.01.

- French television and radio advertising can feature a minimal amount of English — for example, in background music lyrics — provided the English content is not part of the ad's "message".
- Product beauty shots in print and television advertising should feature the French or a bilingual label. U.S. ads will have to be adapted to meet this requirement.
- All computer software must be available in French unless no French version of the software exists.
- Toys or games which require the use of a language other than French are legal provided a French version of the toy or game is available in Quebec.

The usual result of a breach of the Charter's bilingual labelling requirements is a letter from the Office de la langue française to participating retailers and advertisers. Merchants and manufacturers are therefore generally provided with an opportunity to voluntarily comply. Should they fail to do so, they become subject to penalties. Penalties for breach of either Section 51 or Section 58 of the Charter begin with fines ranging from $500 to $1400. Harsher penalties include: expensive changes to packaging or advertising and the public relations damage caused by a company's failure to recognize Quebec's unique character and to comply with its language laws.

J.   CONCLUSION

The provisions of the *Consumer Protection Act* impact advertisers and marketers doing business in Quebec. This Act is a detailed regulatory code which governs many types of advertising claims made in the province. Although compliance with sections of the federal *Competition Act* pertaining to misleading advertising will assist an advertiser in complying with the CPA, there are also unique rules in the CPA, which require special consideration and lead to a unique scheme in Quebec governing advertising and marketing.

Chapter 18

ADVERTISING AGENCY SERVICES AGREEMENTS

Contributed by Eric Gross

A. OVERVIEW

This is really the beginning of the process, or at least it should be. The agency and the advertiser need to set out the terms of their relationship in a clear and meaningful manner. To do so, they should, prior to commencing any projects, sign a written agreement detailing the scope of services, the compensation to be paid for those services, the rights and obligations of one party to the other, and as is increasingly becoming more important, the title to, and ownership of, the creative product.

Advertising Services Agreements are put together following a basic contract format although their form may adopt different styles. A number of years ago, the "California" style of letter agreement was popular. The classic "Whereas" version never goes out of style. It is familiar to lawyers and has been tested in the courts over many years. Lately, in line with the commoditization of many services, the "SOW" or Statement of Work", style has become popular, having been adapted from the technology sector software design and service level agreements. Some of the more important contractual provisions that the agency and advertiser will encounter in the course of negotiating their agreement are set out in this chapter using the classic "Whereas" style as the model for review.

B. THE PARTIES

Any agreement will start off with the naming of the parties. A binding contract can only be made between existing legal persons or entities. To this end, each of the agency and advertiser should ensure that the proper legal parties are named. Formal contracts begin with a naming of the parties, usually in the form of:

THIS AGREEMENT made this _____ day of _____ , 200__

BETWEEN:

ADVERTISER INC., a corporation incorporated under the laws of the Province of Ontario (hereinafter referred to as "Advertiser")

and

AGENCY LTD., a corporation incorporated under the laws of the Province of Ontario (hereinafter referred to as "Agency")

It is optional to list the business address of the parties in this naming section or substitute the business address for the jurisdiction of incorporation. The purpose of the jurisdiction reference is to identify from where a company takes its authority. This jurisdiction identifier is normally fixed throughout the life of the contracting entity allowing for the entity to be located through its incorporating jurisdiction. A business address, on the other hand, can change many times and contracting businesses would not want to amend the agreement every time such a move occurred. But conventions do change with the times and many companies have opted for the "friendlier" business address identifier, dropping the incorporating jurisdiction reference. A failure to amend the agreement because of an address change would not be fatal.

We may know where the corporate parties reside, but who is actually doing the contracting? It is not unusual in the agency world to create a dedicated division to service a particular advertiser or niche. Advertisers may also have different operating divisions. However, a non-incorporated division or a business conducted under a business style or trading name is not a legal entity and cannot effectively contract.

It is important to name the correct parties both from a legal as well as from a business relationship perspective. Legally, one always wants to know who has the duties and obligations under contract to ensure performance, and sue on those obligations if they are not met. Looking at the matter from a business vantage point, knowing who the legal entity is can avoid embarrassment in the future. A consolidation of accounts and businesses may result in conflicts which might not immediately come to light if one of the contracting parties carries on business under a trading name and purports to contract only using such trading name. It is also a requirement of various provincial laws that a contracting party must, in any contract which it intends to enforce, identify itself by its proper corporate name.

There are a few choices by which you can identify a division or trading style. Using the party identifier above as a base, a division can be identified in any of the following ways:

THIS AGREEMENT made this _____ day of _____ , 200__

BETWEEN:

ADVERTISER INC., a corporation incorporated under the laws of the Province of Ontario, **doing business as** CLIENT GUY (hereinafter referred to as "Advertiser")

and

ADGUYS **a division of** AGENCY LTD., a corporation incorporated under the laws of the Province of Ontario (hereinafter referred to as "Agency")

As a divisional business name style or trading name is not a legal entity, it is totally acceptable to dispense with the business name style or trading name in their entirety, defaulting to the original base version.

Now that we know who the parties are and where they reside, we can address that age old question/statement invariably put to all lawyers — "why so many 'whereases' and 'heretofores'? Can't you guys write in plain English?!"

Over the years, lawyers have developed their own shorthand to express certain ideas and concepts. One of these is the "Whereas" set of clauses the reader observes at the beginning of the contract. "Whereas" is a one word way of saying "the parties to this contract agree that the following represents a true set of facts and intentions on which each of them relies". Because these statements or "recitals" represent given fact, it is important to ensure they are not only accurate but represent the intentions of the parties.

Recitals usually are, and should be, limited to simple statements of fact and intention leading up to the contract and should not be used to recite terms or obligations. The reason the recitals should not be over-broad is because, as fact, they can become admissible as factual evidence in the event of a dispute. Therefore it is quite appropriate to say:

WHEREAS the Advertiser wishes to engage the services of the Agency...

but inappropriate to state:

WHEREAS the Advertiser has engaged the Agency to perform services for the next five years...

the latter expression admitting of the terms of an agreement rather than providing for their application in the body of the agreement.

However, if you still don't like the "Whereas" clauses, they can either be expressed in some other fashion or dropped altogether. Again, conventions have changed to accommodate a more casual style.

Rounding out the introduction of the agreement is the other crowd-pleaser:

> NOW THEREFORE IN WITNESS WHEREOF the parties hereto, for good and
> valuable consideration, the receipt and sufficiency of which is hereby acknowl-
> edged, agree as follows...

This phrase carries a lot of import and is structured to accommodate a
number of legal requirements for a valid and binding contract. A contract
is valid and binding at law if certain elements are met, three of which are
"an offer", "an acceptance" and the giving of "consideration". The fact
of offer and acceptance is represented by the parties recognizing their
agreement in the following pages of the contract itself and the consideration or payment is reflected in the acknowledgement of the receipt of
good and valuable consideration.

The consideration referred to in this section is of a general nature and
serves to fix the contract as a binding agreement. The actual payments to
be made for the services to be rendered in the course of the agreement
form part of this consideration, but the language is intended to fix the
contract, so that the parties can rely and sue on it without necessarily
relying on whether the actual payments for services have been earned or
if earned, paid.

In so-called "letter agreements", the formal language discussed above
is to a large extent absent. This does not make these agreements any less
of an agreement as the courts have, at least in these fundamental matters,
sought to find agreement and consideration in the actions of the parties or
as implicit in the language of less formal agreements.

C. DEFINING THE TERMS AND RULES OF INTERPRETATION

The next section of the agreement is sometimes taken up by the definitions
the parties wish to apply to the agreement. Defined terms may also appear
as they arise within the agreement. Definitions are all-important to the
reading and interpretation of the contract and it is recommended that
special care and attention be applied to their drafting. Definitions should
make sense to the people who must apply them. There is a set of boilerplate definitions which are employed by the lawyers to tie together the
legal aspects of the agreement (*e.g.*, definitions of "Persons" to include
individuals and corporations) and then there are the business/operational
terms which give substance to the contract as a business guide.

1. Term

Certainty in business is a virtue and to that end, an agreement should set
out a fixed period of time — the term of the agreement — in which it is to
be performed. Arguably, an agreement which lacks a fixed period of time
for performance becomes an agreement of indefinite duration. Such an

agreement may be unenforceable; at best, it will require mutual agreement to terminate. It is important that both sides understand the length of the term they are committing to as well as the methods for terminating the relationship. Accordingly, the term provision goes hand in hand with the termination provisions. While the term is normally placed up-front in an agreement, the termination (or "divorce") provisions are usually pushed to the end of the agreement. While this may seem to be cosmetic, it actually lends itself to the reading of the agreement. The first part of the agreement sets out what the parties are to do and how they are to do it. The termination provisions look back on what was done and what has to be done to effect a disengagement.

The term provisions usually appear straightforward and are exemplified in the following provision:

> **Term**. The term of this Agreement (the "Term") shall commence effective _____ 1, 2006 and continue until _____ 30, 2007 (the "Initial Term"), and shall be automatically renewed thereafter for successive terms of one (1) year (the "Renewal Term(s)") on the same terms and conditions as are contained herein, unless either party delivers written notice of termination as hereinafter provided.

It is the last phrase of this section which is the most relevant as it directs the reader to the provisions which provide for, in most cases with advertising services agreements, rights of early termination.

2.   Product Definition, Territory and Exclusivity

This section defines the advertiser's products or services for which the agency is to be engaged to provide the advertising services. It also defines the territory in which the services are to be performed. As with the definitions, it is important from both sides to accurately define the advertiser's products or services and the geographic range of the engagement: first, so the agency knows what resources will have to be applied in the service of its client and secondly, to define the scope of what may become the parameters of exclusivity sought by the advertiser. In some cases, the product or service is the sole measure of exclusivity (*e.g.*, "cars"). In other cases, a further definition of "category exclusivity" is set out (*e.g.*, vehicular transportation and automotive products). Defining territory is important for the obvious reason of certainty and to ensure there is no overlap between the agency and other service providers engaged by the advertiser.

> **Products.** Advertiser hereby engages the Agency to perform, throughout Canada (the "Territory"), the advertising services listed below in relation to Advertiser's [name type of products and brand] (the "Advertiser Products").

> **Competitive Products.** The Agency shall not, during the Term and any Renewal Term of this Agreement, for any reason whatsoever, without the prior written approval of Advertiser, provide, in the Territory, any services in relation to any prod-

uct or activity, directly or indirectly, competitive with the Advertiser Products or to any company, dealer group or any corporation, firm or partnership, who sells or advertises products similar to or competitive with Advertiser's Products.

3.   Services

The parties now know who they are, how long they will work together and exactly which products are covered by the engagement. Now the agency and advertiser need to define or, at least, identify the scope of the advertising services to be performed. Since the agency is not manufacturing a widget but rather providing a service at the heart of which lies an intangible creative product embodied in tangible media forms, the list can be as long or as short as the parties feel comfortable with. It is advisable, however, to be as exhaustive as possible as current agency/advertiser relationships leave less and less room for collaborative generic efforts. An example of a listing of services broken down into "core", "media", "point-of-sale/direct", "research" and "general" is set out below:

> **Services** — Agency shall provide the following advertising services in respect of the creation, production and placement of authorized Advertiser advertising for the Advertiser Products:
>
> **A.   General Advertising**
>
> (i)   the development, preparation and production of copy, layouts, and/or finished advertisements, for all types of print media including, without restriction, newspaper, magazine, all forms of outdoor advertising, billboards, transit advertising, and, subject to D below, in-store advertising;
>
> (ii)   the preparation of copy, storyboards, finished films, tapes and/or recordings for all types of broadcast media including, without restriction, television, radio, video formats of all kinds, electronic messaging, theatres and cinemas;
>
> (iii)   the purchase of artwork, engravings, film, tapes, and/or other mechanical and collateral materials;
>
> (iv)   the engagement of the services of third parties such as performing talent, models, endorsements, researchers, etc., on Advertiser's behalf with Advertiser's written approval; and
>
> (v)   talent payment administration, including processing talent payments for creative work trafficked by the Agency and acting as signatory to all Performers Unions (ACTRA, UDA, SAG, and AF of M).
>
> **B.   Media**
>
> (i)   to provide, subject to any agency of record assignments or media buying service arrangements, media planning, buying and reporting including budget control, pre-buy and post-buy recommendations, evaluation and analysis; developing and ensuring compliance with Advertiser approved buying approval documentation; providing a post-buy evaluation to communicate the actual performance versus

planned performance based on up-to-date surveys issued from time to time by syndicated media reporting services; re-evaluate and re-negotiate buys, if necessary, based on post-analysis;

(ii) subject to any agency of record assignments or media buying service arrangements, the preparation of media plans, ongoing evaluation of media performance and the provision of estimates on all media spending;

(iii) subject to any agency of record assignment or media buying service arrangements, the co-ordination and forwarding of advertising materials with proper instructions to scheduled media in accordance with Advertiser's insertion or broadcast dates; and

(iv) subject to any agency of record assignment or media buying service arrangements, the auditing and paying of all billings submitted by all media or other parties for material and services provided.

[NOTE: Media buying services have more and more been handed off to independent media buying/planning agencies specializing in those areas. While many, if not most, of the comments in this chapter would apply to media buying/planning agencies, those contracts have their own requirements and needs.]

C. Research

(i) recommending and designing research projects, at Advertiser's request, including, but not limited to, copy testing, consumer research, focus groups and related topics of a specific creative interest.

D. Point of Sale and Promotions

(i) recommend, develop and direct point of sale support as needed and approved by Advertiser; and

(ii) develop promotional extensions of advertising campaigns, the preparation and production of collateral material, merchandising aids, sales meeting material, contest administration, and other similar and comparable items.

E. Special Services

(i) the carrying out of such special assignments within the framework of this Agreement as Advertiser and Agency may agree, from time to time, in writing. Special Services will be separate to this Agreement. They will include but are not limited to:

      (a) Sales Promotion
      (b) Public Relations
      (c) Database Marketing
      (d) Interactive Marketing

4. Compensation

In exchange for the delivery of the services, the parties set out the compensation to be paid. The types and methods of compensation now available merit a chapter to themselves and are restricted only by the economic imagination. The basic commission arrangements of the past have not been completely replaced by alternative methods but fee based arrangements or fee based arrangements with bonuses for other performance incentives have gained traction in the marketplace. Bonuses, incentives and performance based fee arrangements are at their heart simply a form of compensation negotiated between the parties. The trick in incorporating them into an agreement is to articulate the specific language to achieve the parties' intentions and desires.

In order to effectively communicate incentive based compensation, advertisers and agencies include formulas, apply weightings to the results, append charts and examples, and generally take great pains to set out the metrics of measurement of performance or success. Many of these metrics include objective measurements such as sales increases measured following campaigns, cost savings and other fixed measurements, some also include objective "qualitative" measures, *e.g.*, how many consumers remembered advertiser's brand and for how long following launch — assigned weight 20% of total. However, most also include a metric for "measuring" qualitative performance of the creative based on a subjective call by the advertiser. It is important for both sides of that equation to put their minds to the meaning of this important component. In most cases, it is the advertiser who makes the subjective call, giving or taking away that important point to the total score of the combined metrics. The agency must rely on the good faith of the advertiser to a great extent, but absent a clear and unequivocal statement from the advertiser in the contract reserving to itself complete, sole and utter discretion in the decision, the courts, in the event of a dispute, would likely impose a standard on the advertiser, calling for it to make its decision fairly and reasonably.

Aside from the root compensation arrangements, there are other aspects of compensation which should be taken into account. These include discount arrangements, timing of payments and reconciliation/allocation of expenses. Samples of two provisions which deal with these incidental payment obligations are provided below:

Vendor's Discounts

All discounts in the amounts allowed to the Agency from all vendors for prompt payment, volume, frequency and other similar discounts will be passed on to Advertiser provided Advertiser has made funds available to Agency in accordance with the Payment Terms section below to secure such discount(s).

Payment Terms

The Agency will submit its accounts monthly by the _____ day of the next subsequent month. The terms of payment are based upon the principle that Advertiser's funds shall be in the Agency's hands in time for the Agency to make timely payment to the media and other suppliers and where applicable, to secure discounts.

Invoices for estimated costs of media advertising to be placed by Agency on the instruction of Advertiser will be rendered in advance of media orders being placed and funds must be in the hands of Agency before such orders will be placed. Agency shall not be responsible for any loss of discounts or failure of any advertising to run as scheduled due to the failure on the part of the Advertiser to provide Agency with funds aforesaid. Production and other non-media expenses will be billed to Advertiser within 30 days of such costs being billed to the Agency, and are payable by the _____ of the month following the billing date.

5.   "Most Favoured Nations"

A new trend trying to creep in from the manufacturing and supply arena are advertiser requests for "most favoured nations" terms. Sometimes known as "most favoured terms", "best rates", "MFN" or "MFT", these terms directly affect the compensation arrangements, and acceptance of same create additional pressures on an agency.

In effect, these provisions will require the agency to (i) affirm that the pricing quoted is the best rate given by the agency to its best customers; (ii) certify this fact yearly; (iii) adjust the fee charged to the advertiser if the provision is not met; and (iv) allow the advertiser to audit the books of the agency to confirm the agency has indeed given the advertiser the best rate.

The origin of these provisions can arguably be found in Canada's *Competition Act*. Section 50(a) of the Act states:

> Every one engaged in a business who is a party or privy to, or assists in, any sale that discriminates to his knowledge, directly or indirectly, against competitors of a purchaser of *articles* from him in that any discount, rebate, allowance, price concession or other advantage is granted to the purchaser over and above any discount, rebate, allowance, price concession or other advantage that, at the time the *articles* are sold to the purchaser, is available to the competitors in respect of a sale of *articles* of like quality and quantity, is guilty of an indictable offence and liable to imprisonment for a term not exceeding two years.

As frightening as that section sounds, the term "*article*" means tangible goods and this particular section of the *Competition Act* does not apply to services. As a result, in order to secure a similar protection for a service, a specific provision is inserted in the advertising services agreement.

The absence of coverage for services in the legislation could be explained by the fact that it is generally difficult to determine the offence objectively where services are involved. It is even more difficult with an advertising services contract tailored to an individual customer to monitor or provide MFT. How does one measure equivalency of services or the "volume" which underlies the grant of such a privilege in the manufacturing sphere? MFT clauses in the manufacturing sector are given under circumstances where hard goods are purchased and there are no qualitative differences in the product sold. The MFT in the manufacturing world is based upon the concept that competitors purchasing the same type and number of products from a specific supplier should be treated equally.

Such provisions do not have a place in the advertising industry. An agency does not necessarily provide the same services to the various purchasers of agency's services. Whether responding to an RFP or preparing the advertising and communications program for a client, in each case, the design and build-out is distinct. The time and/or effort required in one service area, or the margins in some service areas, compared to another may vary and as a result, an "apples to apples" comparison of pricing cannot be made nor is there an objective volume of sales against which to take a measure. As well, unlike hard goods being sold by a supplier to businesses who may be competitors, an agency does not normally act for (nor is it usually allowed by one client to act for) that client's competitors in respect of competing products and as a result there is no competitive equalization driving these MFT clauses. There may also be unrelated factors affecting pricing, such as special rates to gain access to new markets.

If the measurement hurdles could be overcome and the agency were to consider a MFT, the grant of MFT terms should be predicated on either an existing historical relationship where the client has demonstrated commitments and loyalty to the agency, or some type of a reciprocal commitment requiring the client's commitment that it will in fact engage the agency for the full term and/or will spend per the budget. These commitments provide the agency with some mitigation against a client who has been given MFT status terminating earlier than full term or cutting the budget for its advertising or its media at the back-end of the term after enjoying a favoured rate. A request for MFT or other best rate terms requires either the goodwill of an historical relationship to support such a concession or reciprocal client spend guarantees, long-term commitments, or failing that, "short-rated" penalties.

Further, no matter what the terms of engagement, the agency should not allow any client audit rights over the books of the company outside of the client's own accounts. An agency cannot allow one client access to the confidential business affairs of the agency's other clients and indeed, most clients will not permit their identity to be so disclosed.

D.   PRIVACY AND CONFIDENTIAL INFORMATION

Historically, an agency agreement provided for the protection of both the agency's as well as the advertiser's confidential information. This provision usually covered the trade secrets, formulas and marketing and business strategies of the advertiser.

Of note is the addition in recent years of technology related services being provided by agencies, such as database marketing and interactive marketing services. The introduction of these services has generated two very interesting spin-off issues which should now find their way into advertising services agreements — privacy and database/database engine ownership.

With respect to privacy, on March 20, 2002, the Federal Privacy Commissioner concluded that under the *Personal Information Protection and Electronic Documents Act*[1] an advertiser sending a direct mail piece "should execute appropriate agreements with all the direct-mailing houses it employs as agents to ensure that the personal information of [the advertiser's customers] is protected in accordance with the Act".[2]

This kind of finding has generated provisions in addition to the basic confidentiality provision, in some cases imposing additional obligations on the agency:

> **Confidentiality** — Advertiser will supply all information reasonably requested by the Agency as necessary for the performance of its duties and obligations hereunder. Unless otherwise specified by Advertiser, all information obtained from Advertiser shall be considered confidential information and shall be held in strict confidence by Agency and its employees, officers and agents (collectively, the "Receiving Parties") and each of the Receiving Parties agrees that it shall not disclose, provide or otherwise make available to any third party or utilize such confidential information for its own purposes and shall restrict any disclosure of such confidential information within its own personnel on a "need to know basis" both during the Term of this Agreement and after its termination. Upon the expiration or termination of this Agreement, the Receiving Parties will return to Advertiser all copies of documents or other material containing such confidential information. The Receiving Parties shall take all necessary and reasonable steps to ensure that such confidential information is not disclosed without Advertiser's prior written approval, including but not limited to securing from the Receiving Parties' employees and third parties to whom such confidential information must be disclosed, agreements to preserve the confidentiality of such confidential information.
>
> Notwithstanding the foregoing, the Receiving Parties shall have no obligation to keep confidential information which (a) is or becomes generally available to the public through no fault of the Receiving Parties, (b) is disclosed to others by Advertiser without obligation of confidentiality, (c) was known to the Receiving Parties prior to its being obtained from Advertiser by the Receiving Parties, or (d) is required to be disclosed by statute, regulation, court order or legal process.

---

[1] S.C. 2000, c. 5.

[2] Commissioner's Findings, PIPEDA Case Summary #42.

Privacy — Agency agrees to comply with applicable provisions of Advertiser's privacy and information security policies. All processes or standard form materials which Advertiser's customers encounter must have Advertiser's prior written approval. If Agency receives any privacy complaints from customers or other parties in the course of conducting work for Advertiser, it must provide Advertiser immediately with full details. Agency agrees to assist Advertiser from time to time when appropriate in responding quickly to customer requests for access or change to their personal information. Agency must have a person in its organization to deal with privacy matters and be a privacy contact for Advertiser. Advertiser has the right to visit Agency's site to audit its organization at reasonable times to ensure compliance with the terms in this section. If Agency wishes to subcontract any services, Advertiser must have prior approval over any proposed subcontractor, and Agency must ensure that the subcontractor complies with all of the above terms including providing a right for Advertiser to monitor and audit the subcontractor. Advertiser may require confidentiality agreements directly with the subcontractors as part of the approval process.

E. AGENCY AND INDEPENDENT CONTRACTOR

In most advertising services agreements, there is inserted what is known as the "independent contractor" clause. This short and apparently innocuous clause remains one of the most contentious provisions of any agreement. An example of the clause is set out below:

Independent Contractor — The Agency shall at all times conduct and represent itself as independent contractor. Notwithstanding the foregoing, the Agency is in relation to delivery of the advertising services hereunder specifically appointed to act in the capacity of agent for Advertiser for the purposes of contracting or making any commitment for the direct or indirect benefit of Advertiser provided Advertiser's approval of such contract or commitment has been first secured. The Agency shall advise Advertiser or obtain from Advertiser specific authorization before entering into any contract under which Advertiser will or might ultimately be financially liable.

Subject to the foregoing provisions of this paragraph, the Agency in performing its services hereunder for Advertiser is authorized to enter into contracts with suppliers and third parties in Advertiser's name.

The above provision was designed to provide the agency with the power and authority to act as an agent of the advertiser for essentially whatever services are contracted by the agency for the benefit of the advertiser. The caveat to the exercise of this agency authority is the need for prior client approval. An agency authority at law is the right of a third party, either related or unrelated to a particular individual or business (the agent's "principal"), to contract for and in the name of and bind the principal. Such authority is not given lightly as the third party may, unchecked, bind its principal to any number of contracts. It should be remembered that the history of advertising agencies points to the fact that "agencies" were, in their original incarnation, agents for the media selling advertising space. The advertising agency was not an agent for the advertiser. As time progressed, the services provided by the agency were services rendered to the advertiser and the agency's source of authority remained obscured and confused.

Under today's practices, absent a provision in the advertising services contract authorizing an agency to, in fact, act as the agent for advertiser, the agency is an independent contractor. As an independent contractor, not acting in an agent's capacity, an advertising agency booking time, or placing orders becomes solely liable to the supplier, even if the agency does not benefit directly from the supply.

The capacity in which the agency acts dictates the type of arrangements it can or should make. As long as the flow of orders and money remains constant and the advertiser honours its obligations and the agency remains solvent, all is well. The difficulty arises when there is a breakdown in the chain of supply and payment. There are three main events which will trigger disputes in this area. Where an agency acts solely as an independent contractor, the failure of the advertiser to pay the agency's accounts will leave the agency liable to its suppliers, notwithstanding both the supplier and the agency may have fully performed their services to the advertiser. The agency as the contracting party shoulders the entire risk. The sample provision above is intended to address this situation. Under that provision, the agency may contract with a supplier as agent with an authority to bind the advertiser for limited purposes and as a result, place responsibility with the advertiser or provide for shared responsibility.

The second scenario arises where the supplier defaults in the supply of the product or service contracted by the agency for the benefit of the advertiser. In that case, the agency remains responsible to the advertiser to perform. The failure of the "sub-contractor" puts the agency in breach of its obligations to the advertiser if the agency cannot perform, or effect the performance of the sub-contractor. This situation is not covered by the provision above *per se*. While the advertiser, as the principal of the contract in default, is entitled to sue the supplier on that contract, the advertiser would still have a cause of action against the agency. The agency's obligations to its client, the advertiser, as set out in the "Services" section of the advertising services agreement does not look to who may be contracted to perform a certain service or function, but requires the agency to either perform the services or cause the services to be performed. Accordingly, the agency does not have the luxury of pushing responsibility onto the advertiser notwithstanding the advertiser is the principal contracting party in the supply agreement.

The third circumstance where this provision has significance is in the insolvency of the agency. Where the agency has contracted as agent for the advertiser and fails to make payment to a supplier before going bankrupt, the advertiser remains responsible to the supplier for payment. This would, at first blush, appear to be a rational result. The real problem arises where the advertiser has advanced payment to the agency in anticipation of the agency's payment to the supplier, but the supplier is not paid before the agency goes bankrupt. Where the agency contracts as agent, the principal is left to pay for the services a second time as the contract is, as noted earlier, between the advertiser as principal and the supplier. The major impact is felt in the area of media purchases which can be quite significant in value.

A number of high profile bankruptcies and the resulting cases highlighted the above noted "double-payment" effect, with the result that many advertisers insist on maintaining an unequivocal independent contractor relationship with their agencies. To that end, the section provided above is often replaced with the opposite set of obligations, an example of which reads as follows:

> **Independent Contractor** — The Agency is an independent contractor and not the legal agent of Advertiser. Agency shall not conduct itself in a manner inconsistent with its status as independent contractor nor represent itself to any person as acting as Advertiser's agent. Agency must advise all third party suppliers with whom it is dealing that it is an independent contractor and not the agent of Advertiser. No employee of Agency will be deemed to be an employee of Advertiser. Each agreement entered into by Agency for or respecting the purchase of third party supplier goods or services shall be entered into by Agency in its own name and on its own behalf solely and contain a proviso stating that Agency is solely liable.

The suppliers in this triumvirate relationship may appreciate their vulnerability to one or the other of the advertiser and the agency and require the commitments of both parties to their contracts. This is especially true in the area of broadcast media where the broadcast orders specifically state that any order placed binds both the agency and the advertiser and each is responsible for payment. As the broadcast media was the crux of the disputes in the cases brought before the courts, in the face of the broadcasters' not unusual insistence that everybody is liable for payment, neither one of the two clauses above satisfy either the advertiser or the agency. In response to the reality of the situation, a middle ground of sorts can be achieved by contracts which address the possibility of supplier side demands and allow for and clarify an Agency/Advertiser jointly shared responsibility. Continuing on from the Independent Contractor clause immediately above is the following provision:

> **Selected Third Party Supplier Contracts** — Agency agrees to exercise commercially reasonable efforts to negotiate commitments or other agreements for third party suppliers of goods or services which expressly state that Agency is solely

liable and which do not impose any dual, double or similar liability upon Agency and Advertiser or otherwise expose Advertiser to financial liability to such third party supplier. However, Advertiser acknowledges that in certain cases, Agency may not be able, despite its commercially reasonable best efforts, to secure such agreement and in such circumstance Agency is authorized to bind Advertiser authorized agreement, commitment or obligation. Before entering into any agreement for a third party supplier which will or may otherwise expose Advertiser to financial liability to that supplier, Agency must:

(i) specifically advise Advertiser of the agreement and the amount of Advertiser's potential financial liability under such agreement; and

(ii) obtain Advertiser's prior written consent.

Although it can wreak havoc with prompt payment and other discounts, some advertisers will insist on making direct payment to third party suppliers who require that the advertiser be named as a party directly liable on contracts.

F. OWNERSHIP

There is no greater controversy surrounding advertising services agreements than that of ownership. Most of the controversy arises from a misunderstanding of the fundamentals of copyright law. Under first principles of copyright law in Canada, the author or creator of the literary, artistic or musical work is the copyright owner irrespective of who commissioned or paid for the work. Absent written provision in the advertising services agreement, the advertiser does not own the creative product. This has in the past come as a shock to advertisers who believe, that having paid the agency, the product is theirs to do with as they please.

For advertising purposes, there are two notable exceptions to the rule of "author equals ownership". One exception is for employees of the agency who create copyrightable works such as storyboards, TV scripts, radio commercials, graphic designs, *etc.* Under Canadian law, ownership of employee created works automatically flows up to the employer. As set out in the *Copyright Act*:

> Where the author of a work was in the employment of some other person under a contract of service or apprenticeship and the work was made in the course of his employment by that person, the person by whom the author was employed shall, in the absence of any agreement to the contrary, be the first owner of the copyright...[3]

---

[3] R.S.C. 1985, c. C-42, subs. 13(3).

It should be carefully noted that work product created by freelancers and third party suppliers to the agency are not covered by this exception. The agency, in engaging such suppliers, should clearly set out the rights of ownership.

The second exception relates to photographs which are commissioned. In that case, the agency ordering the photograph would be the owner absent a written agreement to the contrary. The *Copyright Act* states:

> Where, in the case of an engraving, photograph or portrait, the plate or other original was ordered by some other person and was made for valuable consideration, and the consideration was paid, in pursuance of that order, in the absence of any agreement to the contrary, the person by whom the plate or other original was ordered shall be the first owner of the copyright.[4]

Stock photos are not governed by the exception as they are not original orders.

Aside from the underlying rights issue, one must account for the fact that creative products are many times the aggregate of various elements owned by different parties. Notwithstanding the agency conveying ownership in its contributions to the creative product, it is necessary in any ownership provision to account for third party supplied materials.

The extensive ownership provision set out below attempts to balance the interests of the parties (with a slight weighting towards the advertiser) and provide for the aggregation of third party source material. The clause, which also addresses ownership of database material, website ownership and software/interactive tools, is based on the concept of disclosure and on the allocation of rights within that framework:

Ownership

A. All general advertising, media material, merchandising, packaging, programs, advertising concepts, plans, slogans, brand image, brand essence or campaign ideas, data, content or any creative advertising product or creative advertising material created or prepared by the Agency pursuant to or in furtherance of this Agreement, in any manner and in any medium (herein collectively referred to as "Creative Material") whether or not adopted or utilized by Advertiser shall be the sole and exclusive property of Advertiser, provided Advertiser has fully paid Agency for the costs of production, out of pocket expenses and all outstanding fees and commissions owing to the Agency under this Agreement.

B. All Creative Material shall be original, created or prepared by the Agency in accordance with this Agreement and if such Creative Material contains or is proposed to contain any material of any nature which is not original and/or any pre-existing or third party created materials in respect of which rights have been reserved by some third party (hereinafter collectively referred to as "Third Party

---

[4] Subsection 13(2).

Works"), the Agency shall specifically identify all Third Party Works to Advertiser and obtain Advertiser's written approval to the use of such Third Party Works and provide Advertiser with an opinion as to the legality of using such Third Party Works and an estimate of the availability and estimated cost of obtaining the required rights to use the Third Party Works in relation to the Creative Material which contains such Third Party Works.

C. In consideration of the payments aforesaid, the Agency hereby assigns and shall execute or cause to be executed all documents necessary to assign to Advertiser all intellectual property rights, including copyright in the Creative Material and Advertiser shall have the right to obtain and hold in its own name all intellectual property rights including copyrights and registrations therefor and similar protection which may be available in the Creative Material. The Agency shall, at Advertiser's cost, give Advertiser or its designees all assistance reasonably required to obtain ownership in and perfect such rights. The Agency shall obtain waivers of moral rights (as that term is defined in the Canada *Copyright Act*) relating to the Creative Material prepared by its employees or by third parties on behalf of the Agency and/or Advertiser pursuant to this Agreement. Subject to any restrictions or limitations on use of the Third Party Works as contained in the Creative Material, Advertiser shall have the right to prepare, independent of the Agency, derivative or modified works based upon or flowing from any of the Creative Material, and shall have the right to full ownership rights in the derivative or modified works, independent of the Agency.

D. Any agreement or licence for the Third Party Works, authorized by Advertiser and entered into by Agency on behalf of Advertiser with a third party, shall be assigned to Advertiser on request upon Advertiser's assumptions of Agency's full obligations under such agreement or licence.

E. In the course of providing the Services hereunder or ancillary to such Services, the Agency, its divisions or subsidiaries may provide database management and/or website development services. Apart from data and content provided by Advertiser or collected or created by the Agency for or on behalf of Advertiser which shall be owned by Advertiser as set out above, all systems, software, interfaces, screens, reports, specifications, tools, methodologies, techniques, applications, scripting, and utilities used or designed by the Agency, their divisions and subsidiaries in the provision of the Services hereunder or otherwise shall remain the sole and exclusive property of the Agency or its subsidiaries as the case may be. Further, any website or any portion thereof developed by or for the Agency for, or on behalf of, Advertiser shall be owned by Advertiser, and the Agency shall execute or cause to be executed all documents necessary to transfer all rights of any nature, including, intellectual property rights and ownership thereof to Advertiser.

G. INSURANCE AND INDEMNITIES

As a supplier of services, an agency is expected to provide insurance coverage relative to the manner in which it performs those services. Standard commercial liability policies will apply. Agencies also have access to Media Perils coverage, which used to be known as Advertiser's Liability Insurance. Many agreements provide for this coverage to be put in place in support of the general indemnities sought by the advertiser with respect to the services performed by the agency. A sample set of provisions is provided below (weighted towards the advertiser).

It is noteworthy that the advertiser seeks to be named as an insured under the agency's policy. This is now a normal occurrence and can usually be accommodated by the company providing the insurance coverage. It should be noted that recently, Media Perils coverage is being provided under policies of Errors & Omissions/Professional Liability coverage. As a result, some insurers will not name the advertiser as an additional insured as it creates a conflict in the coverage. In the sample below, the additional insured provisions have been left out of the obligation with respect to advertiser's liability insurance. These matters should be discussed with the agency's brokers and insurers before committing the insurance coverage to the advertiser:

Indemnification

(1) To the extent that any liability, cost or expense is not covered by the insurance policies referred to below the Agency shall indemnify, defend and hold harmless Advertiser, its directors, officers, employees, agents, its affiliates and its parent company and each of them, (collectively, the "indemnified party"), from and against any and all loss, liability, claim, cause of action, suit, damage, injury, cost, expense (including reasonable legal fees), or proceeding, including those threatened, commenced, made or brought against Advertiser by any federal, provincial or local governmental or regulatory body, arising out of or in any connection with:

    (a) any services performed by the Agency pursuant hereto and the preparation, use or presentation of any advertising material prepared or supplied by Agency under this Agreement, including, but not limited to, any causes of action and suits based upon any allegation of libel, slander, defamation, invasion of privacy, plagiarism, piracy, idea misappropriation, copyright or other proprietary infringement, infringement of a registered or otherwise known trademark or service mark, misleading advertising, the contravention of any applicable law or regulation, provided that with respect to trademark or service mark infringement, the foregoing indemnity will not be applicable in a situation in which Agency has brought to the attention of Advertiser prior to the production and dissemination of advertising materials, a potential risk of infringement;

    (b) any alleged personal injury or death to persons or property damage sustained during the rendering of services required of Agency hereunder, if such injury, death or damage occurs as a result of acts of Agency or its employees, whether said loss is sustained by Advertiser or any other person(s) or third party; and

(c) the Agency's breach of any term, condition, representation or warranty of this Agreement.

(2) Advertiser shall indemnify Agency against any liabilities and expenses (including reasonable legal fees) Agency may incur as a result of any loss, liability, claim, cause of action, suit, damage, injury, cost or expense relating to:

(a) any undertaking or obligation on the part of Advertiser under this Agreement;

(b) any product liability in respect of an Advertiser Product;

(c) any alleged personal injury or death to persons or property damage sustained during the term of this Agreement if such injury, death or damage occurs as a result of acts of Advertiser or Advertiser's employees, whether said loss is sustained by Agency or any other person(s) or third party; and

(d) false, deceptive, or misleading description, depiction or comparison of Advertiser and/or competitive products resulting directly from and to the extent that inaccurate information, material or data was supplied by or on behalf of Advertiser to Agency.

Trade-Marks, Domain Names and Copyright — The Agency shall ensure that all Advertiser advertising, creative and promotional material, including Creative Material, prepared by the Agency, as the case may be, which contains any trade-marks and/or domain names owned by Advertiser or any related company, including those listed in Schedule X attached hereto (as amended from time to time) and any copyrighted material owned by Advertiser or any related company shall be properly and accurately identified in accordance with Advertiser's intellectual property policies as they may be provided to the Agency from time to time.

Insurance — During the Term of this Agreement, the Agency shall, at its own cost and expense, maintain the following insurance in full force and effect:

(a) A commercial general liability insurance policy with a carrier and in a form acceptable to Advertiser, providing coverage for operations and for contractual liability with respect to liability assumed by the Agency hereunder, personal injury, bodily injury including death and property damage liability in an amount of at least $5,000,000, combined limit for each occurrence for personal injury, bodily injury and property damage, no aggregate and such policy shall name Advertiser as an additional insured in respect of claims against Advertiser, arising out of Agency's activities and shall provide that the insurer waives all rights of subrogation against Advertiser for any claims, liability, loss or damage;

(b) Advertiser's liability insurance for the benefit of Advertiser providing coverage with respect to liability for libel, slander, defamation, invasion of privacy, plagiarism, piracy, idea misappropriation, copyright or other proprietary infringement, infringement of a registered or otherwise known trademark or service mark or misleading advertising. The limits shall be not less than $5,000,000 per occurrence, no aggregate; and

(c) Workers' Compensation Insurance in accordance with the applicable statutory requirements covering all employees of the Agency and any sub-contractors engaged in performing the Services hereunder, including coverage for Occupational Health and Safety.

The Agency shall forward to Advertiser certificates of insurance issued by the insuring carrier(s), and the Agency shall require the insurance carrier to provide to Advertiser at least 30 days prior written notice of any cancellation, material modification or lapse of such insurance. The fulfillment of the insurance obligations hereunder shall not relieve or limit the liability or the obligations of the Agency under this Agreement.

H. TERMINATION

We conclude this chapter, ironically enough, with the termination provisions. After all the goodwill expended and efforts made to continue, the agency/advertiser relationships and contracts do come to an end. It is important to give careful thought to the disengagement of the parties as, unlike many other industries, there are many obligations to third parties which arise during the Term of the agreement and continue on post termination. Of particular note for commission based agreements is the fact that booked space or time may be used (or cancelled) post termination. The parties should discuss their expectations in those types of circumstances in advance. A sample termination provision is provided below. This sample is a reasonably balanced example of the genre:

Termination

(3) Notwithstanding anything to the contrary hereinbefore contained, either party shall have the right to terminate this Agreement at any time, at will and without cause, upon ninety (90) days prior written notice to the other.

(4) If:

    (a) a party shall default in the performance of any material obligation or breach a material provision of this Agreement and such default or breach is not cured within a period of ten (10) days after receipt of notice from the other party specifying such default or breach; or

    (b) a party becomes bankrupt or insolvent, or its business is placed in the hands of a receiver, manager, assignee, trustee or person with like comparable powers, whether by voluntary act or otherwise, or if a petition for the winding up of the business of the party is filed or if any proceedings are commenced relating to the party under any liquidation laws applicable thereto;

(which party is herein called the "Defaulting Party"),

then, in such event, the other party shall have the right to terminate this Agreement effective immediately by giving written notice to the Defaulting Party.

(5) Upon the termination of this Agreement:

    (a) The rights, duties and responsibilities of the parties shall continue during the 90 day notice period and the Agency will be paid in full in accordance with the Agreement and the attached Schedules for all authorized work in progress to the extent it is completed prior to the effective termination day, provided, however, that upon receipt of notice of termination, the Agency shall not commence work on any new advertisement without Advertiser's prior written approval. Any Agency fee or compensation payable on a periodic basis shall continue to be paid during the notice period without deduction or diminution, prorated to the effective date of termination. Advertiser may terminate all work in progress on advertisements commenced before receipt of notice of termination, upon the parties' mutual agreement to the compensation to be paid to the Agency for partially completed work.

(b) As of the effective termination date of this Agreement, and provided there are no amounts outstanding or otherwise due or owing to the Agency, the Agency shall physically transfer and/or assign to Advertiser or its authorized representative, the Creative Material, Third Party Works, all relevant data and information in Agency's possession or control regarding Advertiser's advertising, and all rights and claims which Agency may have, or may have made, against third parties then outstanding in favour of Advertiser, subject only to any rights of third parties of which the Agency has advised Advertiser.

(c) Advertiser shall, after the termination date of this Agreement, have the right to use the Creative Material and Third Party Works subject to the provisions hereof, in any proper and lawful manner, and without further payment to the Agency other than amounts chargeable which remain unpaid as of the effective termination date.

(d) Effective upon the termination of this Agreement by Advertiser or Agency, Advertiser agrees to assume, and to indemnify and hold harmless Agency from, any responsibility for all talent payments for the post-termination use or re-use of advertising materials, which payments may be required pursuant to any applicable performers' union agreement, including, without limitation, ACTRA and L'Union des Artistes; and Advertiser further agrees to so notify the applicable union in writing, copying the Agency (or to execute Agency's notification form, if so requested) forthwith upon termination of this Agreement. Agency shall provide a list of all such continuing obligations.

(e) Advertiser and the Agency agree that each, at the request of the other, shall take or cause to be taken all reasonable and expeditious action, steps and proceedings including, without limitation, the signing of such documents, agreements and other writings, which may be necessary or desirable to ensure that the provisions of this Agreement with respect to termination are carried out.

(f) The Agency shall assign and transfer to Advertiser all reservations, contracts and arrangements with advertising media or others, for advertising space, broadcasting time, or materials not yet used and all of the Agency's rights in contracts, agreements, arrangements or other transactions made with any third party for Advertiser's account effective on the date of termination. Any non-cancellable contracts made with Advertiser's authorization and still existing as at the termination date hereof, which contracts were not or could not be assigned by the Agency to Advertiser or Advertiser's designees, may be carried to completion by the Agency and shall be paid for by Advertiser.

Notwithstanding any other condition contained within this Agreement, Advertiser shall remain liable to the Agency for any and all approved advertising media purchases made by the Agency that succeed the termination of this Agreement, unless notice of cancellation of such advertising space or time has been received by the Agency in advance of termination. Such approved purchases made by the Agency and identified as non-cancellable shall in any event remain governed by the terms in this Agreement.

I.   OTHER PROVISIONS

An advertising services agreement does not actually conclude with the termination section. There are various commercial provisions which are typical to any business contract. This chapter has addressed those provisions which have particular relevance to the advertising agency business.

Chapter 19

NEGOTIATING A TALENT AGREEMENT

A. OVERVIEW

Perhaps one of the most interesting and frustrating tasks of an advertising lawyer is the negotiation of a talent agreement. Why, you may ask, would an advertising lawyer negotiate the agreement rather than the client or the producer? Experience demonstrates that one of the best ways to avoid huge gaps between the client's understanding of the deal and the final talent contract is to have the advertising lawyer negotiate and draft both the letter of intent and the contract.

Over 20 years and virtually hundreds of contracts later, we are prepared to share some of our stories (and, yes, nightmares) of lessons learned in this dynamic area.

B. TOP TEN LESSONS

1. Find the Right Agent

There are numerous ways to attempt to locate a celebrity's agent: call the record company, the studio, SAG (Screen Actors Guild), ACTRA (Association of Canadian Television and Radio Artists), your friend who reads the gossip columns, *etc.* What you should not do is call every major talent agent you know and ask if they represent that particular celebrity because, inevitably, they all do, or did or will, when it comes to Canadian commercials. We once attempted to negotiate a deal with a famous television personality who was apparently represented by ICM, William Morris and three other firms.

The fact is, some of these actors are non-exclusive in countries other than the U.S. As a result, anyone can bring the deal in. However, when the major U.S. agent finds out about your project, he or she won't be pleased and may try to "scupper" the deal. The lesson, then, is to try to deal with the primary agent or even better, the advertising agent, who is familiar with the somewhat more modest rates paid for Canadian productions.

2.   Find Out if the Talent is Available and Interested

The more famous the talent, the more likely the agent will ask you to send them a firm offer before discussing whether (a) the talent is available, (b) the talent has a conflict; or (c) how much compensation they will be seeking for the project.

This position makes your job difficult. How can the ad agency present an idea to its client with no idea as to whether the talent will be available? Conversely, how can you ask a client to approve a firm offer of $250,000 U.S. if they haven't seen a script yet?

We opt for the modified "Are you interested but I can't make a firm offer yet" deal memo. This sets out the basic points of the deal and leaves the money open for discussion. It demonstrates to the agent that you are serious about their client, but need more information to make a firm offer. If the talent is in Moscow doing a film for six months, has a product conflict or "doesn't do commercials", even in Canada, you can move on to your next prospect.

3.   Discuss Exclusivity Up Front

Invariably, the "automobiles, automotive products and services" exclusivity that you negotiate up front will be watered down to "automobiles" by the time you negotiate the final deal. It is crucial, therefore, to determine the minimum exclusivity required by the client.

Will Ford be upset if the same talent appears in an ad for Speedy Muffler? Will Molson go ballistic if the talent does a U.S. radio spot for Budweiser? Will the Milk Marketing Board find their star's endorsement of condoms distasteful? The sooner these terms can be hammered out in writing, the fewer problems you will encounter at the contract stage.

4.   Don't Forget About Withholding Tax for Non-Canadian Residents

The Canadian-U.S. tax treaty and the *Income Tax Act* provide that payments made to U.S. residents for performance in Canada are subject to a 23 per cent withholding tax for television production and a 15 per cent withholding tax for other media. Thus, the $100,000 U.S. fee you promised the agent has immediately shrunk to $77,000 U.S. in the case of television advertising or at best, $85,000 U.S. unless the performance takes place in the U.S. While the amount withheld can be claimed as a credit on their U.S. tax return, the agent will attempt to get you to "gross up" the fee to compensate for the deduction. We do not recommend this. If you gross up the fee, you will have to withhold on the gross up. Further, the talent will have effectively convinced your client to pay a substantial portion of their income taxes for them — a trick we wish we could accomplish with our partnership.

One interesting twist on the withholding tax is to have U.S. voice-over performers perform in the U.S. by voice-patch to a studio in Canada. In this way, the performance takes place in the U.S. (avoiding the withholding tax) but the production takes place in Canada (hopefully under the more favourable ACTRA/UDA rates).

5.   Canadian Immigration

Before the talent enters Canada for the shoot or production, you must make sure that they can legally work in Canada. Who must obtain a Canadian Work Permit?

Under the Canadian *Immigration and Refugee Protection Act*, most non-Canadians require work permits to enter Canada to engage in any work-related activities. However, film producers employed by foreign film or television companies, persons doing guest spots on Canadian TV and radio broadcasts and some pre-production staff will be granted "business visitor" status and will not be required to obtain Canadian work permits to enter Canada.

Canadian work permits obtained via Service Canada confirmation approvals are required for all other individuals involved in making films, TV, internet and radio broadcasts, any individual who will be in an employment relationship with the organization or business contracting for their services in Canada or any performer in a Canadian-based production or show. There is an exception for co-production agreements where actors and crew can bypass the Service Canada confirmation process and receive their work permits directly at the port of entry coming into Canada.

Be sure to submit applications to Service Canada for confirmation approvals for your talent at least one to two weeks prior to the beginning of the shoot or production to ensure that the necessary work permits can be issued in time for entry to Canada.

6.   Avoid Double Jeopardy — Have Either the Agency or the Client Enter Into the Contract — Not Both

Usually the ad agency will negotiate the talent agreement on the client's behalf. However, if the talent contract is a substantial one, the client may prefer to enter into the contract themselves to ensure contract privity, particularly if the agency/client relationship fails. The rule of privity basically means that only the parties who enter the contract directly, can sue if the contract is breached. That is why the client may prefer to enter contracts themselves. If there is a lot at stake, the client may choose to be in a position to commence, direct and maintain any litigation themselves.

Since the ad agency will not usually charge commission on the contract, and the agency/client letter of terms requires client approval on all large contracts, the agency does not usually mind having the client enter into the contract directly. In some cases, however, the producers prefer to keep the relationship between the agency and the talent to avoid bothering the client with small procedural problems. In such a case, the ad agency should enter into the agreement as principal and not as agent. This will help to avoid a catastrophe if the client pays the agency, the agency goes bankrupt and then the talent demands payment from the client directly.

7.   Creative Approval and Creative Input — Be Sure You Secure All Rights!

Every big-name performer and particularly comedians will want input into the creative process to ensure the script properly portrays his or her personality and is not detrimental to his or her image. These obligatory approval rights may well create copyright problems if the talent decides they "own" the concept or idea.

To avoid such problems, all contracts should clearly specify that the client will be the owner of all rights, including copyright and trade-marks in any work done by the performer and should specifically provide that the performer waives any and all moral rights in the work. Since the concept of moral rights is rather new to Americans, you will likely get some push back initially from the U.S. agent or attorney.

In this way, if the performer inadvertently (or deliberately) modifies the tag line in the TV ad and it becomes the new slogan for all future print advertising, no royalty payments will be required to be paid to the performer.

You should also be aware of multi-layered contract problems that can arise with professional or Olympic athletes. These athletes will already be subject to complex agreements that restrict their ability to endorse products or to grant rights to use of their team name, uniform or perhaps the fact that they won that elusive gold medal.

8.   Beware the Morality Dilemma

While a Hollywood "bad boy's" bad press and drunk driving stunts may not adversely affect his television ratings or box office performance, it may seriously affect the sale of your client's product. First, know who you are dealing with. Thoroughly research the internet, biographies and magazine articles about the talent to determine whether his or her reputation is suitable for the client's brand. Specify in the letter of intent that you will be requiring a standard morality clause, since this can be a deal-breaker. If possible, hammer out the actual morality clause up front. Beware of agents tending to limit the clause to "convictions of indictable or capital offences". These clauses would *not* have covered the Pee Wee Herman or O.J. Simpson incidents.

Ensure that the contract specifies that a pro rata portion of the performer's fee will be refunded immediately on a breach of the morality clause.

9. Union Contracts

Big name talent will undoubtedly be a member of ACTRA, the UBCP (Union of B.C. Performers), SAG, AFTRA (American Federation of Radio and Television Artists) or one or more of the other Unions. French talent will likely be a UDA (Union des artistes) member. The union is determined, for the most part, by the location of the shoot for broadcast production. If the shoot occurs in English Canada for an English commercial, ACTRA or the UBCP, if filming is in B.C., using the National Commercial Agreement, will represent the talent. French commercials or commercials shot in Canada using UDA talent are governed by UDA. Canadian commercials shot in the U.S. using SAG union talent in a union state will be under SAG's jurisdiction. (Some states are work to rule and not subject to union jurisdiction.) In addition, SAG has issued a Global Rule One encouraging its members to demand payment under the SAG agreement even if ACTRA is the appropriate jurisdiction. This "Rule" does not apply to non-English productions that are shot within ACTRA/UDA jurisdiction. In every case, the agreement should specify what reasonable portion of the fees are attributable to union services so that the appropriate Pension & Welfare amount can be paid to the union.

The contract should also set out in detail the non-union services such as print, POP, creative consulting and personal appearances and the portion of fees attributable to such services to rationalize why you will not be paying up to 14.3 per cent Pension & Welfare on the entire negotiated amount.

As mentioned throughout this book, Quebec with its predominantly French language requires special consideration.

The Union des artistes (UDA) represents performing artists such as actors, singers, dancers and other performing artists with the exception of musicians. UDA negotiates collective agreements with producers and associations of producers in different production fields for performances destined for a French-speaking audience. There is a collective agreement covering commercials. The collective agreement sets out the working conditions and the minimal fees payable to performers for television, radio and also for certain print advertising. In Quebec, the *Act respecting the professional status and conditions of engagement of performing, recording and film artists* (the "*Status of Artist Act*") provides that all performers have to be members of a union recognized under the *Status of Artist Act*. UDA is recognized under the Act and all performers hired for French commercials have to be UDA members.

In the rest of Canada, there is no such legislation. Outside Quebec, it is not compulsory for performers to be members of UDA to be hired for commercials. Nevertheless, the UDA agreement prohibits a member from performing with non-members, so the "co-performance" of members and non-members is difficult. Moreover, the collective agreement in the commercial advertising field, negotiated with the Joint Producers Association, recognizes that only UDA members will be hired. It is also expressly prohibited to air French commercials that were entirely shot outside Canada in which non-members participate.

As for commercials and advertising on multimedia and the internet, the jurisdiction of the UDA is still in dispute.

Therefore, all performers whose services are retained for French commercials must be active members of UDA, which means that they have accumulated enough experience to be accepted as an active member under the UDA statutes. The exceptions are:

(a) Younger artists, under 20 years old, are not required to be active members.
(b) In cases of a huge crowd shot for a commercial, the crowd can include non-members.

Some other exceptions can apply if the advertising agency requests a permit from UDA for the use of non-members, such as:

- a world-famous artist;
- a specialist in a field that no UDA member can replace;
- a person with very particular physical characteristics;
- a consumer testifying about his experience with the product;
- an employee of the client testifying about the quality of the products or services offered by his/her employer;
- a president, a vice-president or a director of the client testifying about the company (Christine McGee for Sleep Country);
- the official spokesperson for the client (Candice Bergen for Sprint).

There are specific conditions for each of these exceptions and they must be carefully reviewed. The basic principle of the collective agreement is that the fee paid to the performer entitles the producer to air the commercial for 13 weeks. In order to air the commercial for another 13 weeks, an additional fee must be paid to the performer. The period of 13 weeks is computed from the first air date. For shorter periods of time, a lesser fee may be payable under certain conditions.

Other Important Facts About the UDA

- The advertising agency must send to the UDA a declaration of the use of the commercial for monitoring purposes.
- The collective agreement sets out working conditions including rest periods, meals and the working conditions for child actors.
- Under the collective agreement, the producer is defined as both the client and the advertising agency and they are jointly responsible.
- UDA's jurisdiction is limited to productions destined for a French-speaking audience. The English-speaking equivalent of the UDA is ACTRA (Association of Canadian Television and Radio Artists). In cases of commercials shot simultaneously in French and English (double shoot), some sections of the UDA collective agreement provide for lower payments for the producer.
- Performers hired for dubbing (post-synchronization) French commercials created, shot and aired elsewhere are also subject to the UDA collective agreement.
- The performer must be paid for the use of images taken from a commercial and printed on posters, packages, containers, labels and other promotional material.
- All disputes concerning the hiring of a performer are resolved through arbitration. UDA provides legal services to the performer. The arbitration is final and binding on the parties.

---

10.   Jurisdiction — Make it Canadian

Do specify that the law of the contract, jurisdiction and venue of the dispute will be Ontario or the province in which you do business. This not only avoids the necessity of having the contract approved by foreign counsel, but also ensures a convenient forum for any disputes. We also find that placing the performer in the position of being a foreign plaintiff discourages spurious lawsuits. On the other hand, the talent's attorney will likely push for their home state jurisdiction.

11.   Personal Service Corporations — Be Sure the Performer is Personally Bound

The majority of performers provide their services through a personal service corporation ("PSC") for tax purposes. As such, most agents will attempt to have the contract entered into only by the corporation. In order to ensure that the talent (a) will in fact attend and give the services; (b) has agreed to the creative concepts; and (c) cannot bankrupt the PSC and attempt to back out of the deal, you should always ensure that the performer personally signs the agreement and agrees to perform the services attributable to him or her in the agreement. Sometimes this can be accomplished by a side letter from the talent personally to the agency or client which ensures that all of these points are covered.

One of our worst horror stories occurred when a big name television talent showed up to the two-day shoot, discovered he was portraying a muffler man and walked off the set refusing to come back. It turns out that his agent forged his signature and all the verbal assurances that he "loved" the script concepts was merely "blowing smoke".

TALENT NEGOTIATING CHECKLIST

Name of Talent: ☐
Name of Agent/Agency: ☐
Member of What Union(s): ☐
Client: ☐
Product: ☐
Product Exclusivity: ☐
Performance Category (Is product endorsement required?): ☐
Special Established Character or Song Required: ☐
Initial Territory (Which provinces/territories, Canada only,
    border stations): ☐
Optional Territories: ☐
Media Requirements: ☐
Optional Media (Print, sales promotion, internet, out of home,
    personal appearances, etc.): ☐
Material To Be Produced: ☐
Additional Material (Edited, changed or additional sessions): ☐
Country, Place and Length of Session: ☐
Withholding Tax (Can exemption be arranged — foreign
    residents only): ☐
Start Date of Contract (first use): ☐
Term of Initial Contract: ☐
Renewal Options for Subsequent Terms: ☐

Fee (which currency): ☐
Union Jurisdiction and Fees: ☐
Work Permits/Voice Patch Waivers Required: ☐
Travel and Accommodations: ☐
Fees for Options, Changes, Additional Territories, Renewal, etc.: ☐
Will all the material be produced at the same time?: ☐
Effect on term of contract if split production: ☐
Will talent be assisting in creation of commercial?: ☐
Waiver of Moral Rights: ☐
Script Approval: ☐

Chapter 20

CANADIANA ISSUES

A. OVERVIEW

Most Canadians, even those who grew up so close to the border that they have a slight American accent, are proud of the distinctions between Canadians and Americans. As advertising lawyers, we are often faced with the challenge of explaining to our U.S. clients or their lawyers, how something that ran so easily in the U.S. is not acceptable in Canada. The fact is, we are different. Our laws are different and despite NAFTA, you cannot assume that something that is legal in the U.S. will fly in Canada.

Over the years of attending Advertising and Promotional Law conferences in the U.S., we have compiled a list of uniquely Canadian marketing issues that you, as Canadian marketing experts, should be familiar with, particularly when dealing with U.S. clients.

B. THE MOUNTIES — DUDLEY DO-RIGHT GOES COMMERCIAL

There are few things that signify "Canadian" more readily than a Mountie. Not surprisingly, advertisers like to use Mounties, not only in hit television series, but in Canadian ads or in ads for Canadian products that are directed to Americans. The mere appearance of a Mountie seems to have the same effect on Canadians as the sound of a bagpipe has on a Scotsman.

Enter the *Royal Canadian Mounted Police Act*[1] which prohibits the use of real or costumed RCMP officers in ads without consent. The Act also prohibits use of the words "Royal Canadian Mounted Police" or "RCMP" or "Mountie" without the required consent.

Back in the 80's and early 90's, when clients wanted to use Mounties, we found the whole process of seeking permission to be consistently discouraging. The RCMP did not want to grant permission to use their

---

[1] R.S.C. 1985, c. R-10.

name or likeness in association with any particular product or service, in case it would be seen as endorsing that product or service.[2]

Needless to say, the RCMP saw the error of their ways, and perhaps in an effort to stop advertising lawyers from badgering them, licensed the rights to Disney to administer on their behalf. The Disney reign lasted about four years until the RCMP decided they could resume their licensing responsibility, without the appearance of implied endorsement or favouritism.

So, for the time being, you can obtain consent from the RCMP, for a licence fee, provided that your depiction of the Mounties is used in a manner consistent with their position and stature in our society. In other words, if your script has even the slightest suggestion that the Mounties are anything but perfect, you will likely not get consent.

C.   THE MAPLE LEAF

The next most sacred Canadian symbol is the Maple Leaf. For most people, according to Industry Canada, the mere use of the 11 point Maple Leaf is synonymous with "Made in Canada". Thus, use of the Maple Leaf on products which do not come from the Maple Tree (maple syrup) or are not made in Canada will likely be prohibited. The expression "Made in Canada" is only permitted on goods which not only "come into being" in Canada but also for which at least 51 per cent of the cost of raw materials and direct labour is incurred in Canada. Even if a product is entirely assembled in Canada using U.S. materials, if the cost of raw materials exceeds direct labour, you cannot call it "Made in Canada" but you may opt for the "Made in Canada with U.S. materials".

D.   PERILS OF FLAG WAVING

In terms of the flag and royalty, section 9 of the *Trade-marks Act*[3] prohibits the use, in connection with a business, as a trade-mark or otherwise, of the Canadian flag, the Royal Arms, the Red Cross symbol and a variety of other things associated with the Canadian and foreign governments and the Royal family.

The section does not apply, however, if the consent of Her Majesty the Queen, or whomever the section was intended to protect, is granted. So, if your ad contains a flag it better not be Canadian, British or Iranian. Yes,

---

[2]   We digress at this stage to point out that the British Royal Family has a whole department whose job it is to designate "The Royal Warrant" for products which the Royal Family officially "endorses".

[3]   R.S.C. 1985, c. T-13.

the section also protects the sign of the Red Lion and Sun used by Iran as its "Red Cross" symbol.

And the same section also to protects flags or arms or emblems of countries which have notified the Canadian Trade-Marks Office of their objection to their use — such as that bastion of capitalist sentiment, the former Soviet Union countries. Interestingly, when recently asked if the U.S. flag can be used in Canadian advertising, the U.S. Consulate advised that no permission is necessary.

In Canada, if you want to use the Canadian flag for any type of promotion or advertising, you need to seek consent from Heritage Canada. Not surprisingly, they have rules. The flag should be flowing "freely" and not defaced in any manner.[4]

E. PAPER MONEY — COUNTERFEIT ALERT

Generally speaking, the *Criminal Code*,[5] under provisions relating to counterfeiting forbids the design, printing, distribution or use of any card, notice, circular, handbill or ad that looks like a current bank note or obligation or paper money.

Perhaps while walking down the street you have been handed what appears with frightening accuracy to be half of a $50 bill. You look with interest only to find that it is an ad for $50 off the price of a used car.

In our view, this type of deceit is what Parliament was trying to prevent in section 457 of the *Criminal Code*. Those with failing vision or foreign visitors might be taken in by the authenticity of the note and give valuable consideration for it. Unfortunately, however, the section as drafted also prohibits producing a TV commercial or print ad showing real Canadian dollars (or fake Canadian dollars that closely resemble them). Pursuant to section 457, you cannot:

(1) ...make, publish, print, execute, issue, distribute or circulate, including by electronic or computer-assisted means, anything in the likeness of

    (a) a current bank-note; or
    (b) an obligation or a security of a government or bank.

The exception occurs when:

(4) ...the length or width of the likeness is less than three-fourths or greater than one-and-one-half times the length or width, as the case may be, of the bank-note and

    (a) the likeness is black-and-white only; or
    (b) the likeness of the bank-note appears on only one side of the likeness.

---

[4]   Visit the Heritage Canada website at <www.heritagecanada.org> for further details.
[5]   R.S.C. 1985, c. C-46.

Generally, all these rules make the exemption unattractive to a producer who just wanted to show "money". However, it can be done legally if you are creative and your target audience has a vivid imagination.

However, a recent policy statement issued by the Bank of Canada has added a new twist. In addition to ensuring you fit within the counterfeiting exceptions, due to the Crown copyright and trade-mark rights asserted in the bills, you are now required to also obtain a license from the Bank of Canada to use paper money in certain forms of advertising. Full details can be obtained on their website at <http://www.bankofcanada.ca/en/banknotes/legislation/repro.html>.

F.   THREE COINS IN THE FOUNTAIN

Coins create another issue. There is also Crown copyright in the designs that appear on Canadian coins.

As such, you cannot use Canadian coins in advertising without the permission of the Royal Canadian Mint. Due in no small part to advertising lawyers enlightening our clients as to these legal requirements and continuously soliciting last minute consent from the Royal Canadian Mint, they have decided to change their procedure and set up minimum times for clearance and a licence fee.[6]

G.   O CANADA

It is gratifying to know that the best things in life *are* free. "O Canada", the illustrious national anthem, was donated to Canada and is now in the public domain, which means that everyone can use it without paying a royalty fee or homage.

H.   PUFFERY AND HYPERBOLE

The most abused catch phrase when dealing with American clients on claim substantiation is "puffery". As in — "Isn't that just puffery?" or "Consumers don't really think this means anything do they?" As far as we can tell, claims of product leadership such as "America's favorite coffee" may be acceptable in the U.S., whereas in Canada, unless it is the number one seller, the claim would not be permitted. If, however, the

---

[6] For more information, contact The Royal Canadian Mint online at <http://www.mint.ca>. Note: the Mint would not previously permit the use of the Queen's head side but recently has shown some latitude in this area!

claim is so exaggerated as to be incapable of belief (*e.g.*, "Faster than a speeding bullet") in Canada, as in the U.S., the claim would not require substantiation.

Recent reports from our friends to the south suggest that American courts are starting to cut back on "puffery" defences and are approaching the Canadian school of thought.

I. WANTED PERSONALITIES — DEAD OR ALIVE. ARE THEY "WELL-DEAD"?

The law of misappropriation of personality in Canada is not as well developed as that in the U.S. The only reported case dealing with rights of personality in a deceased person is *Glenn Gould*[7] which merely suggests that rights of personality exist after death for some indeterminate period of time which we fondly refer to as "well-dead".

As a rule of thumb, we think someone should be dead at least 50 years before their persona is potentially available for use without the consent of their estate. In the U.S., some states have enacted legislation which protects these rights for up to 100 years.

J. TALENT ISSUES

The talent in a U.S.-produced spot comes under the jurisdiction of SAG (the Screen Actors Guild) and Canadian use of the spot will be governed by SAG. Canadian produced commercials are governed by ACTRA (outside Quebec) or Union of B.C. Performers in B.C. and Union des Artistes (UDA) in Quebec. Quebec's Union des artistes may pose a particular problem for double shoots. French voice-overs recorded in order to broadcast a commercial in Quebec must use UDA talent. SAG also has a Global Rule One which encourages its members to demand payment under the SAG agreement, even for Canadian productions of Canadian commercials. The jurisdictional tug of war continues.

K. QUEBEC

In addition to the obvious French language issue, the Quebec *Consumer Protection Act*[8] has some unique prohibitions that do not appear anywhere else in Canada:

---

[7] *Gould Estate v. Stoddart Publishing*, [1998] O.J. No. 1894, 39 O.R. (3d) 545 (Ont. C.A.).
[8] R.S.Q., c. P-40.1.

- You cannot advertise a "premium" (*e.g.*, a contest or bonus offer) that takes up more than one-half of the space of an ad.
- Broadcast advertising to children is prohibited in Quebec. In fact, all advertising to Quebec children is highly regulated and virtually impossible except at point of sale and in children's magazines.
- You cannot advertise a product in limited supply without specifically stating that quantities are limited and indicating how many are available in each target market.
- You cannot use a P.O. Box address in any advertising (*e.g.*, for coupon redemption or contest entries) without including a street address.

L. COMPARATIVE ADVERTISING — THE HIDDEN COPYRIGHT ISSUE

Copyright is a statutory right governed by the federal *Copyright Act*.[9] Copyright protects the songs, logos and even slogans created and used in advertisements. The *Copyright Act* prohibits the unauthorized reproduction of any copyrighted work.

The test for infringement of copyright is whether there has been substantial taking of the original work. As a basic rule of thumb, if you need to make the connection to the original work to get the point, it is likely infringement. Colourable imitation is also a basis for infringement. There is no parody defence in Canada. Similarly, there is no defence of "fair use" or "fair dealing" in most forms of advertising. What may be permitted in a journalistic piece or book or other artistic or literary work will not be permitted in advertising. Quoting the source is no defence. As such, reproducing a competitor's label, logo or box in a comparative advertisement may amount to copyright infringement, even if you are not violating any trade-mark laws. Further, taking an aisle shot of various goods in a grocery store for an advertisement may amount to copyright infringement. To avoid this, use mock-up labels.

M. PRESCRIPTION ADVERTISING — NOT IN CANADA YOU SAY?

Currently, advertising of prescription drugs to consumers is limited to name, price and quantity. As such, Canadian companies are left with "informational" type advertising campaigns that either do not name the

---

[9]   R.S.C. 1985, c. C-42.

drug or that name the drug (like Viagra) and make no mention of the condition (or lack thereof) that it treats.

N.   CANADIAN TOBACCO ADVERTISING — UP IN SMOKE

The *Tobacco Act*[10] essentially prohibits all tobacco advertising in Canada. The only exception is advertising that is clearly mailed to an adult audience or in a place where only adults are permitted.

O.   METRIC MEASUREMENT

While we are old enough to know both metric and imperial measurements, our kids don't. As a result, the young advertising lawyer may be appalled to discover that the 10 fluid ounce declaration on the North American packaging is 10 U.S. fluid ounces — different from 10 Canadian fluid ounces. To make matters worse, if you simply insert U.S. with your net quality declaration beside your ml metric declaration, the Office in Quebec may accuse you of not translating "U.S." into French.

P.   THE CANADIAN SENSE OF HUMOUR

It is possible that our most famous Canadian export is not beer or even maple syrup but Canadian comedians. Rick Moranis, Martin Short, Jim Carrey and Dr. Evil himself are all Canadians, so Americans must think we are a bundle of laughs. Interestingly, however, there are those of us who believe that the Canadian sense of humour is quite different from the U.S. and that the Canadian advertising regulators have "no sense of humour whatsoever". Be warned and consider this when exporting U.S. creative material into Canada.

Q.   WANT SOME FREE DRUGS?

In Canada, not only is "sampling" of drugs without some form of monetary consideration illegal, but we have many cosmetic-like drug products that cannot be sampled including, to name a few: antiperspirants (these are the ones that prevent you from sweating while deodorants just prevent you from smelling bad), toothpaste with fluoride (is there any without fluoride?), some mouthwashes, petroleum jelly, any lotion with

---

[10]   S.C. 1997, c. 13.

moisturizer that contains an SPF sunscreen claim and natural health products (we have a whole chapter on this!)

R. CANADIAN SWEEPSTAKES/CONTEST ANOMALIES

1. The Skill-Testing Questions

In Canada, it is considered an illegal lottery to dispose of prizes by chance alone. Some smart advertising lawyers (no doubt) found the "skill" loophole and the requirement to correctly answer a mathematical skill-testing question to win a sweepstakes or contest became "de rigueur" in Canada.

What is sufficient skill is a matter of some debate. A line of cases that concludes that shooting a turkey from 50 yards is insufficient skill but a mathematical skill-testing question *is* sufficient skill, causes most promoters to stick to mathematics.

2. The Order of Mathematics

Remember in Grade 5 when you learned the order of mathematics (in the absence of brackets) was multiplication, division, addition, and subtraction. It is surprising how many promotion houses do not remember this until they receive a complaint from a mathematics professor who claims that the correct answer to the skill question is a negative number and therefore, he is the only winner of your contest. Be sure the question either has brackets or always goes in the correct mathematical order. Also ensure that the answer is a whole number.

3. Terminology

In Canada we don't distinguish between contests and sweepstakes and the terms are used interchangeably. What the U.S. would call "contests" are usually called "skill contests" in Canada.

4. Can I Force a Purchase?

In Canada, unless it is a skill contest only, you clearly cannot force a purchase to enter a contest if the prize consists of "goods, wares or merchandise". If the prize is a service or cash and the cost to enter is *more* than the prize, you *can* force a purchase. If, for example, you had to buy a car to enter to win the cash equivalent of your car purchase less $100, the contest would be legal. However, this only works because you are not winning a *whole* car, which is clearly merchandise. If you can't fit into these limited exceptions, it is best to add a no-purchase requirement (as in the U.S.) giving equal integrity to the no-purchase entrant.

5.   Instant Win and the "Kraft" Clause

In the U.S. and in Canada, all instant win type promotions should have a "Kraft" clause which will enable the contest promoter to limit their liability if a printing or other production error occurs. The clause got its name from a famous lawsuit against Kraft U.S. where a printing error occurred in an instant win contest resulting in thousands of winning tickets being printed. In a situation like this, a "Kraft" clause would allow those holding the contest to do a random draw from all the instant win claimants and pick a certain number of names based on the number of prizes available. Without a "Kraft" clause, explicitly limiting liability, the contest promoter would conceivably be forced to award each instant winner their respective prize or face a class action. As in all cases of this type, it is debatable whether the ensuing public relations disaster truly limits the company's liability.

6.   The Régie and Quebec

All contests open to residents of Quebec are governed by a myriad of rules strictly enforced by the Régie des alcools, des courses et des jeux. For instance, contests that have a total prize pool over $100 require special consideration:

(i)   The rules must be available in French.
(ii)   You must pay a "duty" of 3 per cent of the value of prizes nationally or 10 per cent of the prize pool for Quebec or .5 per cent of the international prize pool.
(iii) If the prize pool exceeds $2,000, a security agreement (similar to New York and Florida) must be posted with the Regie (but not before the contest launch).
(iv)   Contest advertising (with specified disclosures) must be filed in Quebec.

For this reason, many contests are void in Quebec.

7.   Contests Directed at Children

Subject to the restrictions on child-directed advertising in Quebec, contests directed to children are permitted and highly successful in Canada. While there is no children's privacy regulation, most Canadian businesses advertising to children follow the COPPA guidelines. COPPA is

U.S. legislation and stands for the *Children's Online Privacy Protection Act*. Further, it is unclear whether a minor can give "informed consent" required under the new Federal privacy legislation. However, the recent Canadian Marketing Association guidelines discussed in Chapter 6 give marketers good guidance in this area and have been recognized by the Privacy Commissioner.

S. "NEW" FOR A YEAR

For those of you who are beginning to think Canadian law is always more difficult, we can use "new" or "introducing" or "improved" for a full year from product launch or relaunch as opposed to only six months in the U.S.

T. "PROPER" CANADIAN SPELLING AND PRONUNCIATION

Canadians use typical "English" (as in jolly old England) spelling, unlike "American spelling". This comes up often in labels which contain words like COLOUR and FLAVOUR and other "OUR" words. We also use different terminology. If you want a "pop" in the U.S. you ask for a "soda". In Canada, you will be handed a soda water. These subtle differences that don't get caught in the U.S. spell check can offend Canadian consumers more than you know.

All in all, while there are many common principles between Canada and U.S. law, there are enough anomalies to make it virtually impossible to transport U.S. ads into Canada in bulk. Vive la difference!

CHECKLIST OF DISTINCTLY CANADIAN ISSUES

	CANADA	UNITED STATES
Mounties/RCMP	Need consent from RCMP	N/A (except if copyright issues)
Maple Leaf	Can only be used if at least 51 per cent of raw material / production costs incurred in Canada.	N/A
Flags	Need consent from Heritage Canada to use Canadian flag in advertising.	U.S. flags can generally be used.
Paper Money	Special rules required re size to use Canadian paper money in advertising and need Bank of Canada approval.	Also special rules re use of U.S. currency but no CDN exemption for U.S. currency.
Coins	Need consent from Royal Canadian Mint	N/A
O Canada	Free to use	Americans can use it too!
Puffery / Hyperbole	Much more limited defence of puffery than U.S.	Quite a liberal interpretation.
Use of Personalities Dead or Alive	Potential tort as in U.S. but no legislated period of "well-dead".	Many states have specific legislation to extend up to 100 years after death.
Talent Issues	Three Unions. Specific Union for French Performers. Can pay P & W on less than full amount of contract.	SAG / AFTRA Must pay P & W on entire broadcast fee.
Quebec	This needs its own Chapter! See Chapter 17.	No civil law jurisdiction.

	CANADA	**UNITED STATES**
Comparative Advertising	Tricky copyright and trade-mark issues.	Special provision in *Lawham Act* for use of Comparative Brands.
RX Advertising	Not permitted for direct to consumer except for name, price and quantity.	Permitted with extensive rules and disclosures.
Tobacco Advertising	Virtually up in smoke.	Still permitted in some instances.
Metric Measurement	Required under various statutes.	Still using Imperial Measurement.
Drug Sampling	Must pay monetary consideration for all drug samples.	Apparently not required
Contests / Sweepstakes Skill Testing Question	Can't give away prizes on basis of chance alone.	Difficult rules – if no consideration can have chance alone.
Order of Mathematics	Be sure to follow proper order on mathematical skill testing question.	N/A.
Terminology	"Sweepstakes" and "contests" used interchangeably.	"Contest" only used for skill contests.
Forcing Purchase	Possible in some limited circumstances.	If skill based contest only.
The Régie in Quebec	Bonding and duty required in most circumstances.	Bonding only required in NY / Florida contests with prizes over $5,000 U.S.
Contests for Kids	CMA Guidelines	COPPA / CARU
New	Use for one year	Use for six months
Canadian Spelling	"English" spelling	"American" spelling

INDEX

Q

R

S